Corporate Taxation

Corporate Taxation

NINTH EDITION

Stephen Schwarz
Professor of Law Emeritus
University of California, Hastings College of the Law

Daniel J. Lathrope
Distinguished E. L. Wiegand Professor of Law
University of San Francisco School of Law

BLACK LETTER SERIES®

WEST
ACADEMIC
PUBLISHING

Black Letter Series is a trademark registered in the U.S. Patent and Trademark Office.

Copyright © 1991, 1994 WEST PUBLISHING CO.
© West, a Thomson business, 1997, 2003, 2005, 2008
© 2012 Thomson Reuters
© 2016 LEG, Inc. d/b/a West Academic
© 2019 LEG, Inc. d/b/a West Academic
     444 Cedar Street, Suite 700
     St. Paul, MN 55101
     1-877-888-1330

West, West Academic Publishing, and West Academic are trademarks of West Publishing Corporation, used under license.

Printed in the United States of America

ISBN: 978-1-64242-893-3

Summary of Contents

Table of Contents

Capsule Summary

I. INTRODUCTION

A. Forms of Business Organization

The most common forms for a business organization in the United States are:

1. Sole proprietorships, which are businesses owned and operated by a single individual.

2. Corporations, which are legal entities organized under state law that offer limited liability to their owners.

3. Partnerships, including general and limited partnerships, limited liability partnerships, and joint ventures. A small number of unincorporated businesses, known as publicly traded partnerships, have ownership interests that may be traded on an established securities market.

4. Limited liability companies, a popular business entity form that provides limited liability for all of its members.

B. Conceptual Taxation Models

1. Aggregate Concept

The aggregate concept treats the assets of a business as owned directly by its individual owners, who are each responsible for a proportionate share of the liabilities of the business. The business organization itself is not a taxable entity.

2. Entity Concept

The entity concept treats a business organization as a taxable entity that is separate and apart from its owners. Transactions between the owners and the entity are generally taxable events unless a specific provision of the Code provides for nonrecognition of gain or loss.

3. Hybrid Concepts

Some taxing models adopt a hybrid approach, treating an organization as an entity for some purposes and an aggregate for others.

C. Overview of Taxing Regimes Under the Code

1. Subchapter C

Subchapter C embodies an entity approach by treating most corporations as separate taxable entities and by providing rules that govern transactions between corporations and their shareholders.

2. Subchapter K

Subchapter K applies a hybrid approach to partnerships and their partners. Partnerships do not pay taxes but pass through their income and deductions to their partners. A partnership is treated as an accounting entity, however, for purposes of determining its income and filing of returns. A modified entity approach is applied in various substantive contexts.

3. Subchapter S

Subchapter S is a hybrid model governing the treatment of eligible corporations that make an "S" election. S corporations are pass-through entities that generally are not subject to tax except in limited situations where they have a prior history as a C corporation.

4. Specialized Tax Regimes

The Code includes other specialized tax regimes tailored for particular industries, such as insurance companies, banks, mutual funds, real estate investment trusts, and cooperatives.

D. Influential Policies

The taxation of corporations and their shareholders has been shaped by four broad tax policy decisions that influence taxpayer behavior. The relationship of these policies has changed as a result of tax legislation enacted over many years.

1. The Double Tax

The double tax regime of Subchapter C increases the cost of operating a business as a C corporation, especially if earnings are distributed as dividends or when the business is sold. The double tax often influences taxpayers to choose partnerships, limited liability companies, or S corporations for business and investment activities.

2. Rate Structure

For most of our tax history, the maximum individual tax rate exceeded the highest corporate rate. This rate structure made the corporation a refuge from much steeper individual rates and provided an incentive to operate as a C corporation. When the maximum individual rate is the same as or only slightly higher than the top corporate rate, as it was for many years prior to 2018, the choice of entity is not as clear. Beginning in 2018, the corporate income tax rate has been reduced to 21% as compared to a 37% maximum individual rate on ordinary income. In addition, § 199A now allows some noncorporate taxpayers a deduction of 20% of their share of certain qualified income from a business operated as a sole proprietorship, partnership, LLC, or S corporation, effectively reducing the maximum marginal rate on that income to 29.6%. Many business planning decisions are influenced by the interaction of these tax rates.

3. Preferential Rates for Capital Gains and Qualified Dividends

Whenever there is a significant capital gains rate preference, taxpayers are motivated to devise strategies to convert ordinary income into capital gains, such as "bailing out" C corporation profits at capital gains rates. The bailout strategy is much less significant, however, when dividends are taxed at the same rate as long-term capital gains, as they have been since 2003.

4. Nonrecognition of Gain or Loss

Many transactions involving corporations and their shareholders qualify for nonrecognition treatment because they are regarded as mere changes in form, which result in a continuity of investment.

E. Pervasive Judicial Doctrines

In addition to the language of the Code, the courts frequently apply various "common law" doctrines in determining the tax consequences of a transaction. The judicial doctrines have been invoked by the Service with increasing success to attack a variety of transactions known as corporate tax shelters.

1. Substance over Form

The Supreme Court has admonished that the tax consequences of a transaction should be determined by economic substance rather than form. Despite this well accepted doctrine, the Code often permits a taxpayer to assure a desired tax result by utilizing a particular form.

2. Step Transactions

Under the step transaction doctrine, separate formal steps are combined into a single integrated transaction for tax purposes. The courts disagree as to how and when the doctrine should be applied.

3. Business Purpose

Under the business purpose doctrine, a transaction may be denied certain tax benefits, such as nonrecognition of gain, if it is not motivated by a corporate business purpose apart from tax avoidance. The doctrine has been extended through regulations to patrol against abusive partnership transactions and corporate tax shelters.

4. Sham Transaction

A sham is a transaction that never actually occurred or is devoid of substance. Sham transactions are not respected for tax purposes.

5. Economic Substance

Under the judicially created economic substance doctrine, tax benefits are denied for transactions that actually occur and may comply with the literal language of the statute but do not result in a meaningful change to a taxpayer's economic position apart from a reduction in taxes.

6. Codification of the Economic Substance Doctrine

Congress has codified the economic substance doctrine and enacted a strict liability penalty on transactions found to lack economic substance.

II. CLASSIFICATION

A. Introduction

1. Impact of Classification

The operation of many Code sections varies depending upon whether the taxpayer is an individual, a partnership, a corporation or some other type of entity. Thus, the classification of an organization for tax purposes may be extremely important.

2. The Role of State Law

The classification of entities for federal tax purposes is a matter of federal law and depends on standards in the Internal Revenue Code.

3. Principal Classification Issues

Classification issues generally arise in two settings:

a.   determining whether a separate entity exists for federal tax purposes, and

b.   determining whether an entity with more than one owner should be classified as a corporation or partnership, or whether a single-owner entity should be disregarded for federal tax purposes or classified as a corporation.

B. Existence of a Separate Entity

1. In General

The regulations provide that a joint venture or other contractual arrangement may create a separate entity for federal tax purposes if the participants carry on a trade, business, financial operation, or venture and divide the profits therefrom. Courts look at a list of factors to determine the intent of the parties. A critical factor frequently is whether the parties have a joint profit motive. If an arrangement is treated as a separate entity, it generally is classified as a partnership for tax purposes.

2. Separate Entity vs. Other Relationships

The "mere co-ownership" of property which is maintained, kept in repair, and rented or leased does not create a separate entity. A separate entity exists if co-owners lease space and in addition provide services to the tenants either directly or through an agent. An expense sharing relationship does not constitute a separate entity for tax purposes.

C. Classification of Business Entities

1. Introduction

The Code defines a corporation as including "associations, joint-stock companies, and insurance companies." The interpretation of this definition has a rich and textured history.

2. The Classification Regulations

Historically, the regulations employed four corporate characteristics to classify a business organization as either an association taxable as a corporation or as a partnership. Since 1997, the regulations generally classify most unincorporated business entities as partnerships. A business entity organized under a state corporation statute is taxed as a corporation. An unincorporated business entity, such as a limited liability company or limited partnership, with two or more members is classified as a partnership. An unincorporated business entity with one owner is disregarded and thus treated as a sole proprietorship, branch, or division of the owner for federal tax purposes. Every unincorporated entity has the option of electing to be taxed as a corporation.

3. Publicly Traded Partnerships

A "publicly traded partnership" ("PTP"), as defined in § 7704(b), is generally classified as a corporation for federal tax purposes, but a PTP is classified as a partnership if 90% or more of its gross income consists of certain types of passive investment income.

4. Trusts

The fact that a business is operated in a trust will not prevent it from being classified as a business entity. The critical question in determining whether a trust will be classified as a business entity is whether a business objective is present or whether the trust was established merely to protect and conserve trust property.

D. Choice of Entity Considerations

1. Publicly Traded Businesses

Virtually all publicly traded businesses are C corporations for tax purposes.

2. Closely Held Businesses

Many closely held businesses operate as pass-through entities to: (1) avoid two levels of tax, (2) pass through start-up losses to partners or S corporation shareholders who are active in the business, and (3) enable their owners to benefit from the 20% deduction for qualified business income. Limited liability companies provide the most flexibility, while S corporations offer simplicity, a familiar governance structure, and potential employment tax savings for owners who perform services for the business. In some situations, a C corporation may be a tax efficient choice to take advantage of the 21% corporate income tax rate, especially if there is no immediate need to distribute earnings as dividends. C corporations are also widely used by start-up companies financed by venture capital firms and when the corporation qualifies to issue "small business stock" under § 1202, enabling shareholders to exclude all or part of their gain when the stock is sold.

III. THE C CORPORATION AS A TAXABLE ENTITY

A. The Corporate Income Tax

1. Introduction

A C corporation is a separate taxable entity, which computes its taxable income under general tax principles.

2. Rates

A C corporation is subject to tax under § 11 at a flat rate of 21%.

3. Determination of Taxable Income

A C corporation's "taxable income" is its gross income less allowable deductions. Most business expenses are deductible under § 162. The § 465 at-risk limitations and the § 469 passive loss limitations apply only to closely-held C corporations. Corporate shareholders may deduct 50% (and sometimes 65% or 100%) of the dividends they receive. Corporate capital gains are taxed at the same rate as ordinary income, and capital losses are only deductible to the extent of capital gains, with a three-year carryback and five-year carryforward of the excess.

4. Taxable Year

C corporations may adopt either a fiscal or calendar year. Personal service corporations must use a calendar year unless they: (a) show a business purpose for a fiscal year, or (b) make a fiscal year election under § 444 and make certain required distributions to prevent any deferral benefits to their owner-employees.

5. Accounting Method

C corporations generally must use the accrual method, with certain exceptions for farming and personal service corporations and corporations with average annual gross receipts of less than $25 million (indexed for inflation after 2018).

6. Loss Disallowance Rules

Losses from sales or exchanges of property between a shareholder and a more-than-50%-owned corporation may not be deducted.

7. Forced Matching Rules

Accrual method corporations may not deduct payments made to cash method owner-employees until the recipient includes the item in income.

8. Credits

C corporations qualify for a variety of tax credits.

B. The Corporate Alternative Minimum Tax

Prior to 2018, most C corporations were subject to the corporate alternative minimum tax ("AMT"). The corporate AMT was repealed for tax years beginning after December 31, 2017, with certain transitional rules relating to AMT credits.

C. Disregard of the Corporate Entity

1. Introduction

Most cases reject efforts by taxpayers to disregard the corporate entity for tax purposes unless the corporation is clearly shown to be a mere dummy or agent.

2. The Business Activity Test

A corporation generally is regarded as a separate taxable entity if it engages in any business activity.

3. The *National Carbide* Factors

The Supreme Court set forth six factors in the *National Carbide* case to determine if a corporate entity should be ignored as an agent. Under the most important of these factors, a corporation was not a true agent if its relations with its principal were dependent on the fact that it was owned by the principal.

4. The *Bollinger* Factors

In the more recent *Bollinger* case, the Supreme Court concluded that a corporate entity would be respected as a true agent with respect to an asset (e.g., real estate) if it had a written agency agreement, functioned as an agent with respect to the asset for all purposes and disclosed its agency status in dealings with third parties.

IV. FORMATION OF A CORPORATION

A. Introduction

Section 351 provides that certain transfers of property to a newly formed or preexisting controlled (i.e. 80% owned) corporation are not taxable events. Unrecognized gain or loss is preserved through transferred and exchanged basis rules.

B. Requirements for Nonrecognition Under § 351

No gain or loss is recognized when one or more persons transfer "property" to a corporation solely in exchange for "stock" of that corporation, and the transferors, as a group, "control" the corporation "immediately after the exchange."

1. "Property"

"Property" includes cash, inventory, intangibles and accounts receivable. Stock issued for past, present or future services rendered to the corporation is not treated as having been issued in return for property.

2. "Transfer"

The transferor must transfer all substantial rights in the property to the corporation.

3. Solely in Exchange for "Stock"

"Stock" means an ownership interest in a corporation and does not include rights, warrants or convertible debt. Certain "nonqualified" preferred stock with debt-like characteristics is treated as "other property" rather than stock for some purposes under § 351.

4. "Control"

"Control" is ownership of at least 80% of the total combined voting power of all classes of stock entitled to vote and at least 80% of each class of nonvoting stock. "Control" is determined by looking to all the transferors of property as a group.

5. "Immediately After the Exchange"

The control test is applied "immediately after the exchange." If a transferor of property disposes of stock received in an exchange pursuant to a prearranged binding agreement, the control test generally is applied after that disposition unless the disposition also qualifies for nonrecognition under § 351. A gift of stock after an incorporation exchange will not cause a transaction to fail the control requirement.

6. Special Problems

a. A service provider who receives stock for services recognizes ordinary income. The corporation may deduct the value of stock issued for services as a business expense unless the nature of the services requires the corporation to amortize or capitalize the expenditure. Timing of the income and deduction is determined under § 83. If the stock is subject to certain restrictions, the fair market value of the stock less the amount paid, if any, is taxed as ordinary income when the restrictions lapse, but the service provider may elect to be taxed on the value of the restricted stock less any amount paid when it is received.

b. If stock is received in exchange for a combination of services and property, all the stock may be counted in applying the 80% "control" test unless the property transferred is of relatively small value compared to the stock received for services. The Service does not consider property "of relatively small value" if it equals at least 10% of the value of the stock received for services.

c. Section 351 does not require shareholders to receive stock in proportion to the value of the property they transfer but, in disproportionate transfer situations, the true nature of the transaction (e.g., compensation, gift) must be determined.

d. Section 351 generally overrides all recapture of depreciation provisions. The recapture gain is preserved in the depreciable property received by the corporation.

e. The regulations provide that no gain is recognized on the transfer of an installment obligation in a § 351 transaction.

f. Transfers to an "investment company," as defined in § 351(e), do not qualify for nonrecognition.

7. Basis and Holding Period: General Rules

a. If property is transferred in a § 351 transaction solely in exchange for stock, the basis of the stock received is the same as the adjusted basis of the property transferred. If a transferor receives more than one class of stock, the aggregate exchanged basis is allocated to each class in proportion to its fair market value.

b. The transferor's holding period in stock received in exchange for capital or § 1231 assets includes the holding period of the transferred property. The holding period of stock received for other assets begins on the date of the exchange.

c. The basis of property received by a corporation in a § 351(a) exchange is the transferor's adjusted basis, and the corporation's holding period for all transferred assets includes the holding period of the transferor.

8. Limitations on Transfers of Built-in Losses

If property with a net built-in loss is transferred to a corporation in a § 351 transaction or as a contribution to capital, the transferee's aggregate adjusted basis of such property is limited to its fair market value. This limitation is applied on a transferor-by-transferor basis rather than to an aggregated group of transferors. Alternatively, the transferor and the corporation may elect to reduce the transferor's stock basis to its fair market value immediately after the transaction.

C. Treatment of Boot

1. In General

A transferor who receives property other than stock from the corporation in a transaction that otherwise qualifies under § 351 recognizes gain (but not loss) to the extent of the cash and the fair market value of any other property received. The other property is known in tax jargon as "boot."

2. Allocation of Boot

If several assets are transferred in exchange for both stock and boot, the boot is allocated among the transferred assets to determine the gain recognized on each asset. Realized gain is recognized to the extent of the boot allocable to the asset, but realized loss may not be recognized.

3. Installment Boot

A transferor who receives installment boot (e.g., a debt security of the corporation) may be able to report any recognized gain (except for depreciation recapture and certain other ordinary income) on the installment method.

4. Basis

If a transferor receives boot in a § 351 transaction, her basis in the stock received is the same as the basis of the property transferred, minus the cash and the fair market value of other boot received, plus any gain recognized on the exchange. Boot generally takes a fair market value basis. The basis of property received by the corporation is the transferor's adjusted basis plus any gain recognized by the transferor.

5. Transfer of Appreciated Boot

A corporation that transfers appreciated boot (other than its own debt obligations) in a § 351 transaction generally must recognize gain as if it had sold the property for its fair market value.

D. Assumption of Liabilities

1. In General

In a § 351 transaction, a corporation's assumption of liabilities is not treated as boot, but the liabilities are treated as money received for purposes of determining the transferor's stock basis.

2. Determination of Amount of Liabilities Assumed

A recourse liability is treated as assumed to the extent that, based on all the facts and circumstances, the transferee has agreed to and is expected to satisfy the liability, whether or not the transferor-shareholder has been relieved of it. A nonrecourse liability is treated as having been assumed by a corporate transferee when an asset is transferred subject to the liability. In some cases where more than one asset is subject to the same nonrecourse liability, the amount of a nonrecourse liability treated as assumed must be reduced.

3. Tax Avoidance Transactions

If the principal purpose of a liability assumption was tax avoidance or was not a bona fide business purpose, all liabilities assumed by the corporation are treated as boot.

4. Liabilities in Excess of Basis

If liabilities assumed by the corporation exceed the aggregate adjusted basis of all properties transferred by a particular transferor, the excess is treated as gain from the sale or exchange of property. For this purpose, debts that would be currently deductible if paid by the transferor (e.g., accounts payable) and certain contingent debts are not treated as "liabilities." Some courts have held that a taxpayer who transfers assets with liabilities in excess of basis may avoid gain recognition by transferring a promissory note with a face value equal to the excess.

5. Limit on Basis Increase Attributable to Liability Assumption

If a transferor of property in a § 351 transaction recognizes gain under § 357(b) or § 357(c), the basis of the property transferred to the corporation may not exceed the fair market value of the property. A special rule may further limit the basis increase when the transferor is not subject to U.S. tax and the liability secures more than one asset.

6. Stock Basis Reduction for Transfers of Certain Liabilities

To prevent a transaction known as a contingent liability tax shelter, § 358(h) generally requires a shareholder whose basis in stock received in a § 351 exchange exceeds its fair market value after applying the general basis rule in § 358 to reduce stock basis (but not below fair market value) by the amount of any fixed or contingent liabilities assumed as part of the exchange in cases where a basis reduction is not otherwise required.

E. Incorporation of a Going Business: Special Problems

1. Assignment of Income Doctrine

The assignment of income doctrine does not override § 351 on the transfer of accounts receivable by a cash basis taxpayer in the absence of a tax avoidance purpose. The corporation includes the receivables in income when they are collected.

2. Accounts Payable and Contingent Liabilities

Accounts payable transferred by a cash basis taxpayer in a § 351 transaction are deductible by the corporation when they are paid. Contingent liabilities transferred in a § 351 transaction for which the transferor has not received any tax benefit are either deductible by the corporation or treated as capital expenditures, as appropriate.

3. Tax Benefit Rule

The tax benefit rule requires a taxpayer deriving a tax benefit in one year (e.g., from a deduction) to recognize income in a subsequent year if an event (e.g., a refund) occurs that is inconsistent with the earlier event that provided the tax benefit. It is unlikely that the tax benefit rule overrides § 351, but the issue is not entirely settled.

4. Depreciation Methods

A corporation that acquires depreciable property in a § 351 transaction generally inherits the transferor's depreciation method and remaining recovery period.

F. Contributions to Capital

1. Contribution to Capital Defined

A contribution to capital is a transfer of cash or other property to a corporation without the receipt of stock in exchange. For contributions made after December 22, 2017, a contribution to capital does not include: (1) contributions in aid of construction or other contributions from a customer or potential customers, or (2) contributions by a governmental entity or civic group unless made by a shareholder as such.

2. Treatment of the Contributor

A shareholder does not recognize gain or loss on a contribution to capital, but the shareholder's stock basis is increased by the amount of cash and the adjusted basis of any contributed property.

3. Treatment of the Corporation

Contributions to capital are not taxable to the corporation, which takes a transferred basis in the contributed property. Special rules apply to capital contributions by nonshareholders.

4. Non Pro Rata Surrender of Stock

A controlling shareholder does not realize a deductible ordinary loss when he surrenders part of his stock for no consideration and retains voting control.

G. Collateral Issues

1. Avoidance of § 351

Taxpayers occasionally may wish to avoid § 351 to recognize a loss or step-up the basis of property. Avoidance techniques include breaking control or structuring the transaction as a taxable sale.

2. Relationship to Other Code Sections

A § 351 transaction also may qualify as a tax-free reorganization or have the effect of a dividend. When §§ 351 and 482 overlap, courts have held that § 482 takes precedence if necessary to clearly reflect income.

H. Organizational and Start-up Expenses

1. Election to Deduct and Amortize

Expenses of organizing a corporation and many start-up expenses are nondeductible capital expenditures which, at the corporation's election, may be deducted currently up to $5,000 (but the $5,000 limit is reduced by the amount of such expenses exceeding $50,000). Expenses not currently deducted may be amortized over 180 months.

2. Organizational Expenditures Defined

Examples of organizational expenses include fees for drafting the articles of incorporation and by-laws, state filing fees and other expenses of creating the entity. Costs of issuing or selling stock are not organizational expenses and thus may not be amortized.

3. Start-up Expenditures Defined

Start-up expenditures are amounts paid or incurred in connection with investigating the creation or acquisition of an active trade or business and certain expenses incurred before the business begins that could have been currently deducted if incurred by an ongoing business.

V. CAPITAL STRUCTURE

A. Introduction

1. Sources of Corporate Capital

The two sources of corporate capital are "debt" and "equity." The combination of debt and equity used to finance a corporation's operations is its "capital structure." Equity is a corporate ownership interest evidenced by shares of stock. Debt instruments represent funds borrowed by the corporation from the holder of the debt obligation. Many classification controversies involve hybrid instruments having both debt and equity characteristics.

2. Tax Differences Between Debt and Equity

The principal tax differences between debt and equity are:

a. Interest paid on corporate debt is deductible while dividends are not deductible.

b. Repayment of debt principal is tax-free to the debt holder while redemptions of stock may be a dividend to the shareholder.

c. Accumulation of earnings to repay debt principal may provide a defense against imposition of the accumulated earnings tax.

d. Equity qualifies for nonrecognition of gain on formation under § 351 while corporate debt securities constitute boot.

e. Losses on worthlessness of some types of stock (e.g., § 1244 stock) may qualify for ordinary loss treatment while losses on worthlessness of debt are usually capital losses.

f. Dividends received by corporate shareholders qualify for the § 243 dividends received deduction while interest is fully taxable.

g. Under certain conditions, noncorporate shareholders who are original issuees may exclude all or part of their gain from a sale or exchange of qualified small business stock held for more than five years.

B. Distinguishing Between Debt and Equity

1. § 385

Section 385 authorizes the Treasury to promulgate regulations to distinguish between debt and equity for tax purposes. In so doing, it may treat an interest as part debt and part equity. The factors to be taken into account are:

a. The form of the obligation;

b. Subordination to outside debt;

c. The debt/equity ratio of the corporation;

d. Convertibility into stock;

e. Proportionality—i.e., the relationship between debt and stock holdings.

The issuing corporation's classification of an interest as stock or debt is generally binding on all holders of the interest.

2. The § 385 Regulations

Although proposed regulations have been issued from time to time on various aspects of § 385, no regulations are currently effective. Debt vs. equity classification issues thus must be resolved under the case law or, in specialized situations, by narrowly tailored statutory rules.

3. Case Law

Debt vs. equity classification issues are factual questions (or mixed questions of fact and law) that are resolved by applying a list of factors, including:

a. Form of the obligation.

b. Proportionality.

c. Debt-equity ratio.

d. Intent of the parties to create a debtor-creditor relationship.

e. Subordination.

The courts usually treat reclassified debt as equity in its entirety.

4. Consequences of Reclassification

If debt is reclassified as equity, payments labeled as "interest" and repayments of "principal" are treated as constructive dividends.

5. Shareholder Guaranteed Debt

The Service may treat shareholder guaranteed debt as equivalent to a loan from the outside lender to the shareholder followed by a contribution to capital, causing "interest" payments to the lender to be treated as a constructive dividend to the shareholder.

C. Limitation on Deduction of Business Interest

For tax years beginning after December 31, 2017, § 163(j) imposes a limitation on the deduction of business interest. Relief is provided to certain small businesses and, at the taxpayer's election, to many real estate trades or businesses.

D. Character of Loss on Corporate Investment

1. In General

Because stock and debt instruments generally are capital assets, any loss on their sale or disposition is treated as a capital loss.

2. Loss on Worthlessness of Debt

A loss on a debt that is a "security" under § 165(g) is a capital loss. Losses incurred by noncorporate taxpayers on other debts are usually treated as short-term capital losses from a nonbusiness bad debt.

3. Loss on Worthlessness of Equity

Losses incurred by individual taxpayers and partnerships who are original issuees of § 1244 stock are ordinary losses, subject to various limitations. Other losses on equity investments are usually capital losses. Section 1244 stock must be issued by a "small business corporation," a status attained if the aggregate amount of money and other property received by the corporation for stock or as a capital contribution does not exceed $1 million.

E. Special Problems of Excessive Corporate Debt: Junk Bonds

Junk bonds are unsecured high-yield corporate debt obligations. Certain junk bonds known as "applicable high yield discount obligations" are subject to special tax treatment, such as deferral of any interest deduction until actual payments are made in cash or other property.

VI. NONLIQUIDATING DISTRIBUTIONS

A. Introduction

1. Distribution vs. Dividend

A "distribution" is any payment by a corporation to its shareholders with respect to their stock. "Dividends" are distributions out of the current or accumulated earnings and profits of a corporation.

2. Dividends Under Corporate Law

Dividends as defined under corporate law have no bearing on whether a distribution is a dividend for federal tax purposes.

3. Distributions and Dividends Under the Code

The three steps in determining whether a distribution is a dividend are:

a. Determine the amount of the distribution, which is the cash received plus the fair market value of any other property received reduced by any liabilities assumed by the shareholder or liabilities to which the property is subject.

b. Determine the amount of the dividend, which is that part of the distribution that is made out of "current earnings and profits" or post-1913 "accumulated earnings and profits."

c. Include the dividend in the shareholder's gross income and treat any remaining portion of the distribution first as a tax-free return of capital and then as gain from a sale or exchange of the stock.

"Qualified dividends" received by noncorporate shareholders generally are taxed at preferential long-term capital gains rates (0%, 15% or 20%). The 3.8% tax imposed by § 1411 on net investment income also applies to dividends. Qualified dividends are most dividends received from domestic corporations and certain foreign corporations that meet minimum holding period requirements.

B. Earnings and Profits ("E & P")

1. The Concept

The principal function of E & P is to measure the extent to which a distribution is made from a corporation's economic income.

2. Determination of Earnings and Profits

E & P generally are derived by starting with the corporation's taxable income for the year and making certain additions (e.g., tax-exempt interest), subtractions (e.g., federal income taxes) and adjustments (e.g., depreciation).

C. Cash Distributions

1. In General

Cash distributions are dividends to the extent they are made out of current or accumulated E & P. Current E & P are measured as of the end of the taxable year without reductions for distributions made during the year.

2. Current E & P Exceed Distributions

If current E & P exceed cash distributions made during the year, each cash distribution is a dividend.

3. Distributions Exceed Current E & P

If cash distributions exceed current E & P, a portion of each distribution is treated as coming from current E & P. The remainder of each distribution is a dividend to the extent of accumulated E & P available on the distribution date.

4. Accumulated E & P but Current Deficit

To determine available accumulated E & P, a current deficit must be ratably allocated against accumulated E & P as of the date of each distribution or, alternatively, the corporation can allocate the deficit to the time period in which it was actually incurred.

D. Property Distributions

1. Consequences to the Distributing Corporation

A corporation recognizes gain on the distribution of appreciated property as if it had sold the property for its fair market value, but it may not recognize loss on a distribution of loss property. No gain or loss is recognized on a distribution of a corporation's own obligations. Current E & P are increased by any gain recognized on the distribution. Accumulated E & P are decreased by the fair market value of appreciated property (less any liabilities assumed), by the adjusted basis of any distributed loss property, and by the principal amount of debt obligations.

2. Consequences to Shareholders

The amount of the distribution is the fair market value of the distributed property reduced by any liabilities to which the property is subject. The distributee shareholder's basis is the fair market value of the distributed property without reduction for liabilities.

E. Constructive Dividends

1. In General

Some transactions that are not formally labeled as "dividends" may be treated as constructive dividends if they provide economic benefits to shareholders.

2. Examples of Constructive Dividends

Examples of constructive dividends include unreasonable compensation, low-interest loans, bargain sales or leases, excessive payments to shareholders for purchases of corporate property, payment of a shareholder's personal expenses, and transfers between commonly controlled corporations.

F. Special Problems of Corporate Shareholders

1. The Dividends Received Deduction

Corporate shareholders generally may deduct 50% (or sometimes 65% or 100%) of dividends received from other domestic corporations.

2. Holding Period Requirements

The dividends received deduction is not available when the stock on which the dividend is paid has been held for less than 46 days.

3. Extraordinary Dividends: Basis Reduction

Corporate shareholders sometimes must reduce their stock basis by the untaxed portion of an "extraordinary dividend" or recognize gain if the untaxed portion exceeds the shareholder's stock basis. A dividend is "extraordinary" if it exceeds 5% of the shareholder's adjusted basis in preferred stock, 10% of the adjusted basis in any other stock, and in other more specialized situations.

4. Debt-Financed Portfolio Stock

The dividends received deduction is reduced to the extent that the dividend is attributable to debt-financed portfolio stock.

5. Earnings and Profits Adjustments

Although a corporation generally must make certain timing adjustments (e.g., for depreciation) in determining its E & P, those adjustments are not made in determining the tax consequences of distributions to 20% or more corporate shareholders.

6. Preacquisition Dividend Strips

A parent corporation that sells the stock of a subsidiary in a taxable transaction may be able to convert capital gain on the sale to partially deductible dividend income by causing the subsidiary to make a large distribution shortly prior to the sale. The success of the technique depends on the timing and source of the distribution.

VII. STOCK REDEMPTIONS AND PARTIAL LIQUIDATIONS

A. Introduction

1. Redemption Defined

A redemption is a repurchase of stock by its issuer.

2. Overview of Tax Consequences

The shareholder-level consequences of a redemption depend on whether the distribution resembles a dividend or a sale by the redeemed shareholders. Redemptions that do not qualify for sale or exchange treatment are treated as § 301 distributions and are dividends to the extent of E & P.

3. Tax Stakes

Individual shareholders historically preferred sale or exchange treatment because they could recover their basis in the redeemed stock and treat any gain as capital gain. When, as under current law, most dividends and long-term capital gains are taxed at the same rate, the advantage of exchange treatment for noncorporate shareholders is generally limited to recovery of stock basis. A corporation generally recognizes gain on a distribution of appreciated property in a redemption, but it may not recognize loss on a distribution of property that has declined in value.

B. Constructive Ownership of Stock

For purposes of determining stock ownership under § 302, an individual or entity is considered as owning stock owned by certain related family members and entities under the attribution rules in § 318.

C. Redemptions Treated as Exchanges

A redemption is treated as a § 301 distribution unless it meets one of the tests in § 302(b), enabling the redemption to be treated as an exchange of the redeemed stock for the cash and other property distributed by the corporation.

1. Substantially Disproportionate Redemptions

To qualify as a substantially disproportionate redemption, the redeemed shareholder must own less than 50% of the voting power of the corporation after the redemption and the shareholder's percentage of voting stock and common stock (whether or not voting) after the redemption must be less than 80% of his percentage ownership before the redemption. A redemption is not substantially disproportionate if it is made pursuant to a plan that has the purpose or effect of a series of redemptions that, taken together, are not substantially disproportionate.

2. Complete Terminations of a Shareholder's Interest

A redemption that completely terminates a shareholder's actual and constructive stock interest in the corporation is treated as an exchange. Individual shareholders or entities who completely terminate their actual stock interest may waive family attribution under § 318 if the following requirements are met:

a. Immediately after the distribution, the shareholder has no interest in the corporation other than as a creditor;

b. The shareholder does not acquire any such interest other than by bequest or inheritance within the 10-year period from the date of the distribution;

c. The shareholder agrees to notify the Service of any prohibited acquisition during the 10-year postdistribution period; and

d. No portion of the redeemed stock was acquired within the 10-year predistribution period from a § 318 related person, and no such related person who continues to own stock in the distributing corporation acquired any stock within that period from the redeemed shareholder, except that these conditions do not apply if the acquisition or disposition of stock was not principally motivated by tax avoidance.

3. Redemptions Not Essentially Equivalent to a Dividend

A redemption is not essentially equivalent to a dividend if it results in a meaningful reduction of the shareholder's proportionate interest in the corporation. A significant loss of control (e.g., from more than 50% to less than 50%) is an example of a meaningful reduction, as is virtually any reduction in control or voting rights of an isolated minority shareholder.

4. Partial Liquidations

Distributions in partial liquidation are treated as exchanges to individual but not corporate shareholders. A partial liquidation results from a genuine contraction of the corporation's business, including the termination of a trade or business that the corporation has actively conducted for the five-year period preceding the distribution. A distribution of the stock of a subsidiary or the proceeds of sale of such stock does not qualify as a partial liquidation.

D. Specific Tax Consequences of Redemptions

1. Consequences to Shareholders

Redemptions that qualify for exchange treatment are treated as if the shareholder sold the redeemed stock to an outsider. Redemptions not qualifying for exchange treatment are treated as § 301 distributions and thus are dividends to the extent of the distributing corporation's E & P and a reduction of basis or capital gain to the extent of the balance of the distribution. If a redemption is treated as a § 301 distribution, longstanding regulations permit the unutilized basis of the redeemed stock to be added to the basis of any stock retained by the redeemed shareholder or, if none, to the basis of stock held by persons or entities whose stock is attributable to that shareholder under § 318. Shareholders take a fair market value basis in any property distributed in a redemption.

2. Consequences to Distributing Corporation

The distributing corporation recognizes gain (but not loss) on a distribution of property in redemption of its stock. It increases its E & P by any gain recognized. If a redemption is treated as a § 301 distribution, E & P are reduced by the amount of money and the fair market value of the distributed property. If a redemption is treated as an exchange, E & P are reduced in an amount that may not exceed the ratable share of accumulated E & P attributable to the redeemed stock. The distributing corporation generally may not currently deduct expenses paid in connection with the redemption or reacquisition of its own stock.

E. Redemptions Through Use of Related Corporations

1. Introduction

Section 304 is designed to prevent a bailout when one or more controlling shareholders sell the stock of one corporation to another commonly controlled corporation, or when any shareholder of a parent corporation sells stock of the parent to a subsidiary. Section 304 tests these transactions for dividend equivalency by applying § 302 to determine whether the shareholder has sufficiently reduced his interest in the corporation whose stock is acquired.

2. Brother-Sister Acquisitions: § 304(a)(1)

If one or more persons in control of each of two corporations sell stock of one corporation (the "issuing corporation") to the other (the "acquiring corporation") in return for property, the property is treated as a distribution in redemption of the acquiring corporation's stock and is tested for dividend equivalence under § 302 by reference to the stock of the issuing corporation. If the constructive redemption is not treated as an exchange, it is a dividend to the extent of the E & P of the issuing and acquiring corporations.

3. Parent-Subsidiary Acquisitions: § 304(a)(2)

If a subsidiary (the "acquiring corporation") acquires stock of its parent (the "issuing corporation") from a shareholder of the parent in return for property, the property is treated as having been distributed in redemption of the parent's stock and is tested for dividend equivalency by reference to that stock. If the constructive redemption is not treated as an exchange, it is a dividend to the extent of the E & P of the issuing and acquiring corporations.

4. Relationship of § 304 to Other Code Sections

Section 304 generally overrides § 351 when the two sections overlap.

F. Redemptions to Pay Death Taxes

Even if a redemption does not qualify as an exchange under § 302, it still may qualify under § 303 if the redeemed stock was included in the decedent's gross estate for federal tax purposes and the value of the stock exceeds 35% of the gross estate less debts and expenses. Exchange treatment is available under § 303 only to the extent that the distribution does not exceed the sum of death taxes and funeral and administrative expenses. Section 303 includes a timing requirement. A corporation that distributes property in a § 303 redemption must recognize gain but may not recognize loss.

G. Redemptions and Related Transactions

1. Redemptions and Sales

If a redemption and sale are part of an integrated disposition of a shareholder's entire interest in a corporation, the redemption will qualify as a complete termination of the shareholder's interest whether it occurs before or after the sale.

2. Redemptions Pursuant to Buy-Sell Agreements

Constructive dividend issues may be raised when a continuing shareholder is personally and unconditionally obligated to purchase stock pursuant to a buy-sell agreement and that obligation is assumed by the corporation. But a mere assignment of a continuing shareholder's contractual obligation to purchase stock from a retiring shareholder does not result in a constructive dividend. Constructive dividend issues also may be raised when a corporation redeems stock in connection with a divorce. Under the regulations, a divorce-related redemption results in a constructive dividend to the nontransferor spouse and § 1041 nonrecognition to the spouse whose stock is redeemed when the redemption satisfies a primary and unconditional obligation of the nontransferor spouse or when the parties jointly elect such treatment.

3. Charitable Contribution Followed by Redemption

If a shareholder of a closely held corporation contributes stock to a charity, and the corporation later redeems the charity's stock, the transaction will not be classified as a constructive dividend to the shareholder if the charity was not legally bound to surrender the shares for redemption.

VIII. STOCK DISTRIBUTIONS AND § 306 STOCK

A. Stock Distributions

1. Introduction

A stock distribution is a distribution by a corporation of its own stock to some or all of its shareholders.

2. Nontaxable Stock Distributions

Stock distributions are generally not includible in gross income unless an exception in § 305(b) applies. The shareholder's basis in the stock held prior to a nontaxable stock distribution is allocated between the old stock and the new stock received in proportion to the relative fair market values of each on the date of the distribution. The distributing corporation recognizes no gain and it may not reduce its E & P.

3. Taxable Stock Distributions

Stock distributions are taxable in the following situations:

a. Distributions payable either in stock of the distributing corporation or in cash or other property, at the shareholder's election.

b. Distributions that result in some shareholders receiving property while others increase their proportionate interest in the earnings or assets of the corporation.

c. Distributions where some shareholders receive common stock while others receive preferred stock.

d. Distributions on preferred stock, other than an increase in a conversion ratio made to take account of a stock dividend or split.

e.   Distributions of convertible preferred stock.

f.   Other transactions (e.g., a change in conversion ratios; periodic redemption plans) that have the effect of increasing the proportionate interests of one group of shareholders while others receive cash or other property.

4.   Distributions of Stock Rights

Distributions of stock rights are generally not taxable unless they have one of the effects described in § 305(b). If rights received in a nontaxable distribution are later exercised or sold, the shareholder must allocate his stock basis in the underlying stock between the stock and the rights unless a de minimis rule applies. Taxable rights distributions are dividends to the extent of E & P.

B.   § 306 Stock

1.   The Preferred Stock Bailout

Section 306 was enacted to prevent the "preferred stock bailout," which was a device to bail out earnings at capital gains rates through a tax-free distribution and later sale of preferred stock.

2.   Definition of § 306 Stock

Section 306 stock includes:

a.   Preferred stock received as a tax-free distribution under § 305(a) unless the distributing corporation had no current or accumulated E & P.

b.   Stock which has a transferred or substituted basis determined by reference to § 306 stock (e.g., § 306 stock received by gift).

c.   Certain stock received in a tax-free corporate reorganization or division, or a § 351 exchange.

3.   Dispositions of § 306 Stock

a.   If § 306 stock is redeemed, the amount realized is taxable as a dividend to the extent of the corporation's current or accumulated E & P at the time of the redemption, and the balance of the amount realized is treated as a reduction of basis or capital gain.

b.   On a sale or other disposition of § 306 stock, the amount realized is treated as ordinary income to the extent of the dividend that would have resulted at the time of the distribution if cash rather than stock had been distributed. The remaining amount realized first reduces basis of the § 306 stock and then is capital gain. The amount treated as ordinary income is treated as a dividend for purposes of the preferential rates in § 1(h) and such other provisions as the Service may specify.

c.   Dispositions of § 306 stock that are exempt from the general rule include complete terminations of the shareholder's interest and partial liquidations, complete liquidations, dispositions that qualify for nonrecognition treatment and certain transactions that are found by the Service to not be made pursuant to a tax avoidance plan.

IX. COMPLETE LIQUIDATIONS AND TAXABLE CORPORATE ACQUISITIONS

A. Complete Liquidation Defined

A complete liquidation occurs when a corporation ceases to be a going concern and its activities are merely for the purpose of winding up its affairs, paying its debts and distributing any remaining balance to its shareholders. A complete liquidation usually is evidenced by a formal written plan, but informal plans may be found to exist if the corporation's shareholders or directors manifest an intent to liquidate.

B. Complete Liquidations Under § 331

1. Consequences to the Shareholders

    a.   Amounts distributed to a shareholder in a complete liquidation, less liabilities assumed by the shareholder, are treated as in full payment in exchange for the shareholder's stock. A shareholder thus recognizes capital gain or loss under general tax principles. Gain or loss is computed separately for separate blocks of stock with different bases or acquisition dates.

    b.   If the value of a distributed asset is in dispute, uncertain or contingent, a shareholder may be able to defer reporting gain attributable to those assets.

    c.   If a liquidating corporation makes an installment sale of its assets and distributes the installment obligations to its shareholders within 12 months after adoption of the liquidation plan, the shareholders may report their § 331(a) gain on the installment method.

    d.   The basis of property received by a shareholder on a complete liquidation is the fair market value of the property on the date of the distribution.

2. Consequences to the Distributing Corporation

    a.   Under the *General Utilities* doctrine, a corporation generally did not recognize gain or loss on a distribution of property to its shareholders. The *General Utilities* doctrine no longer applies to distributions of appreciated property by a liquidating corporation. As a result, a corporation generally recognizes gain or loss on a liquidating distribution as if it had sold the property for its fair market value.

    b.   A liquidating corporation may not recognize loss on the distribution of property to a § 267 related person (e.g., a more than 50% shareholder) if the distribution is not pro rata among the shareholders or is of "disqualified property." "Disqualified property" is any property acquired by the corporation in a § 351 transaction or as a contribution to capital during the 5-year period ending on the date of the distribution.

    c.   A liquidating corporation may not recognize certain losses on sales, exchanges or distributions of property acquired by the corporation in a § 351 transaction or as a contribution to capital as part of a plan the principal purpose of which was to recognize loss in connection with the liquidation. If there is no clear and substantial relationship between the contributed property and the conduct of the corporation's business, it is generally presumed that property acquired by the corporation after a date that is two years before the adoption of the liquidation plan, or after the adoption of that plan, was acquired as part of a plan to recognize loss. Only the loss that accrued prior to the corporation's acquisition of the property is disallowed.

d. The importance of the § 336(d) loss limitation rules has diminished since the enactment of the § 362(e)(2) loss limitation that often reduces the basis of property with a built-in loss after it is transferred to a corporation in a § 351 transaction or as a contribution to capital.

C. Liquidation of a Subsidiary

1. Introduction

Because a liquidation of an 80% or more subsidiary is viewed as a mere change in the corporate form, neither the parent shareholder nor the liquidating subsidiary recognizes gain or loss. In keeping with this policy, the subsidiary's asset bases and other tax attributes transfer to the parent.

2. Consequences to the Shareholders

a. A parent corporation ("P") does not recognize gain on the receipt of distributions in complete liquidation of a subsidiary ("S") if the following conditions are met:

1) S distributes its assets to P in complete cancellation or redemption of its stock pursuant to a complete liquidation plan.

2) P owns at least 80% of the total voting power and 80% of the total value of S's stock from the date the liquidation plan is adopted until the liquidation is complete.

3) The liquidation occurs within certain time limits.

b. The courts sometimes have allowed corporations to intentionally avoid § 332 (e.g., to recognize a loss) by violating one of these requirements.

c. If P does not meet the 80% control test, it may be able to "back in" to control by causing S to redeem stock held by its minority shareholders shortly before the liquidation plan is adopted.

d. P takes a transferred basis and a tacked holding period in the assets received from S in a § 332 liquidation. P's basis in its S stock disappears.

e. Even if a liquidation qualifies under § 332, minority shareholders of S recognize gain or loss under the general rule in § 331 and take a fair market value basis in any distributed property under § 334(a).

3. Consequences to the Liquidating Subsidiary

S does not recognize gain or loss on distributions of property to P in a § 332 liquidation. S also does not recognize gain or loss on transfers of property to satisfy preexisting debts to P. S recognizes gain but not loss on distributions of property to minority shareholders and on certain distributions to tax-exempt and foreign parents.

D.   Taxable Acquisitions of a Corporate Business

1.   Introduction

Taxable acquisitions of a corporate business may be structured as asset or stock acquisitions. The corporation whose assets or stock is acquired is often referred to as the "target," or "T," and the purchasing corporation is referred to as "P."

2.   Asset Acquisitions

T generally recognizes gain or loss on a sale of its assets, and P takes a cost basis in the assets it acquires. If T liquidates after its assets are acquired, T's shareholders recognize gain or loss under § 331(a) unless T is an 80% subsidiary of another corporation and the liquidation qualifies as tax free under § 332. If T does not liquidate, its shareholders do not recognize gain or loss, but T is likely to be classified as a personal holding company that will be subject to a penalty tax if it does not annually distribute its net income. The parties to an asset acquisition must allocate the aggregate consideration paid and received for the assets under the "residual method" prescribed by the regulations. After subtracting out cash and cash equivalents, the consideration is then allocated to government and marketable securities and then to tangible and most intangible assets to the extent of their fair market values, and any residue is allocated to goodwill and going concern value. A written agreement between the buyer and seller allocating consideration among the transferred assets is generally binding on the parties absent strong proof by one of the parties that the agreement is unenforceable.

3.   Stock Acquisitions

a.   T's shareholders recognize gain or loss on the sale of their stock to P.

b.   T generally does not recognize gain when P acquires its stock unless P purchases 80% or more of T's stock within a 12-month period and makes a § 338 election to treat the transaction as an asset acquisition. In that event, T is treated as having sold all of its assets for their fair market value to a new corporation ("new T") in a taxable transaction. Under a formula prescribed by the regulations, the sale price of T's assets generally equals P's cost for the T stock plus T's liabilities, including any liabilities resulting from the deemed sale.

c.   New T generally takes an aggregate basis in its assets that equals the price paid by P for the T stock plus T's liabilities, including any liabilities resulting from the deemed sale. That basis is then allocated among new T's assets using the residual method prescribed by the regulations.

d.   If P acquires an asset from T during a "consistency period" that generally begins one year before the stock purchase and ends one year after the purchase, and if T is a subsidiary of another corporation ("S") and T and S file a consolidated return, P generally must take a carryover basis in any T assets acquired during the consistency period.

4.   Sales and Distributions of Stock of a Subsidiary

If T is a subsidiary of another corporation ("S") and S sells 80% or more of its T stock to P, the parties may jointly elect under § 338(h)(10) to treat T as if it had sold all of its assets for fair market value to "new T" and then distributed the sales proceeds to S in a tax-free liquidation under § 332. S thus recognizes no gain on the sale of its T stock, and T's gain or loss on the deemed sale of its assets is included on the consolidated tax return filed by S and its affiliates. This election avoids two levels of corporate tax and permits S to deduct its own net operating losses against income recognized by T on the deemed asset sale. Pursuant to regulations, a similar joint election may be made under § 336(e) for distributions of stock of a subsidiary, and to combinations of sales, exchanges, and distributions, and dispositions where the buyer is not a corporation. If a transaction qualifies under both § 338(h)(10) and § 336(e), § 338(h)(10) controls.

5. Comparison of Acquisition Methods

From a tax standpoint, the preferred method for a taxable acquisition is usually a stock purchase without a § 338 election. A § 338 election may be desirable, however, where T has net operating losses or where T is a subsidiary and the parties jointly make a § 338(h)(10) election. The lower corporate income tax rate and the opportunity to expense the amount of the purchase price allocable to tangible depreciable personal property may make an actual or deemed asset acquisition more attractive in some situations.

X. ANTI-AVOIDANCE RULES

A. Introduction

Taxpayers historically have pursued strategies to reduce exposure to the corporate income tax and avoid the double tax on corporate earnings. Among the anti-avoidance provisions created by Congress to combat these strategies are the economic substance doctrine, the accumulated earnings tax, and the personal holding company tax.

B. The Economic Substance Doctrine

1. Common Law Roots

The economic substance doctrine was developed by courts to deny tax benefits to transactions that satisfy the literal requirements of the Code but are carried out primarily to reduce federal income taxes without causing any meaningful change to a taxpayer's economic position.

2. Application by Courts

The courts did not always apply the economic substance doctrine uniformly or clearly.

3. Codification

Section 7701(o) codifies the economic substance doctrine by providing that any transaction in which the doctrine is "relevant" will be treated as having economic substance only if it changes the taxpayer's economic position in a meaningful way, apart from federal income taxes, and the taxpayer has a substantial business purpose for engaging in the transaction. A penalty of 20% of the amount of any underpayment attributable to a disallowance of claimed tax benefits is imposed if a transaction is found to lack economic substance. If the taxpayer fails to disclose the relevant facts on its tax return, the penalty is increased to 40%.

C. Accumulated Earnings Tax

1. Introduction

In the distant past, when the top individual income tax rates historically were significantly higher than corporate income tax rates, C corporations were attractive vehicles to accumulate rather than distribute income. The accumulated earnings tax was enacted to combat these accumulation strategies. For many years prior to 2018, the maximum corporate tax rate was only slightly lower or the same as the top individual rate, limiting the role of the accumulated earnings tax, but the tax has assumed greater importance now that the gap between corporate and individual rates has widened again.

2. The Prohibited Tax Avoidance Purpose

The accumulated earnings tax applies to corporations formed or availed of to avoid the individual income tax by accumulating, rather than distributing, the corporation's earnings and profits. The tax is paid in addition to other taxes paid by the corporation. The existence of a prohibited tax avoidance purpose depends upon the facts and circumstances of each case.

3. Reasonable Needs of the Business

A rebuttable presumption of a tax avoidance purpose arises if a corporation accumulates its earnings and profits beyond the reasonable needs of its business. A determination of the reasonable needs of the business also depends on the circumstances of each case. The regulations provide guidance in making this determination.

4. Accumulated Taxable Income

The accumulated earnings tax is determined by applying a 20% rate to a corporation's "accumulated taxable income." Accumulated taxable income is taxable income, with adjustments to arrive at a more accurate measure of the corporation's economic performance, less a dividends paid deduction and an accumulated earnings credit.

D. Personal Holding Company Tax

1. Introduction

The personal holding company tax is designed to prevent the "incorporated pocketbooks," "incorporated talents," and "incorporated properties" tax avoidance strategies. A tax at a 20% rate is imposed on the "undistributed personal holding company income" of every personal holding company. The tax is imposed in addition to other taxes paid by the corporation.

2. Definition of a Personal Holding Company

A personal holding company is a company which meets both a stock ownership requirement and an income requirement. More than 50% in value of the corporation's stock must be owned, directly or indirectly at any time during the last half of the taxable year by five or fewer individuals. In addition, at least 60% of the corporation's "adjusted ordinary gross income" must be "personal holding company income."

3. Undistributed Personal Holding Company Income

"Undistributed personal holding company income" is equal to the corporation's taxable income adjusted so it is a more accurate measure of economic performance, less the dividends paid deduction.

XI. TAX-FREE REORGANIZATIONS

A. Introduction

1. Policy

Transactions that qualify as "reorganizations" under § 368 are wholly or partially tax free to the participating corporations and their shareholders. The rationale for nonrecognition is that a reorganization is merely a readjustment of a continuing corporate enterprise that results in a continuity of investment.

2. Types of Corporate Reorganizations

Corporate reorganizations include acquisitions, nondivisive nonacquisitive transactions (such as recapitalizations), and divisive transactions (such as spin-offs, split-offs, and split-ups).

3. Guide to Analyzing a Reorganization

A student first should determine whether a transaction qualifies as a reorganization under § 368. If so, the next step is to determine the specific tax consequences to the corporations and their shareholders under various "operative" provisions that are triggered once reorganization status is achieved. Some reorganizations may be wholly tax-free, while others (e.g., where permissible boot is used) may result in partial nonrecognition of gain.

4. Nonstatutory Requirements

a. The continuity of shareholder proprietary interest doctrine requires that the target's shareholders retain a continuing proprietary interest in the acquiring corporation. The acquiring corporation must provide consideration that represents a proprietary interest in its affairs, and that consideration must be a substantial part of the property transferred to the target's shareholders.

b. The continuity of business enterprise doctrine requires that the acquiring corporation must either continue the target's historic business or continue to use a significant portion of the target's historic business assets in a business.

c. The business purpose doctrine requires a reorganization to be motivated by a bona fide corporate business purpose apart from tax avoidance.

5. Ruling Guidelines

The Service historically issued guidelines for parties who desired an advance ruling on the tax-free status of a reorganization. Although the Service no longer issues "comfort rulings" on a transaction as a whole, it will rule on one or more issues regarding a reorganization if the issue or issues are "significant," such as an issue of law the resolution of which is not essentially free from doubt and is germane to the tax consequences of the transaction. The IRS ruling guidelines continue to offer safe harbors that sometimes are stricter than the case law.

B. Acquisitive Reorganizations

1. Type A Reorganizations (Statutory Merger or Consolidation)

a. A Type A reorganization is a merger or consolidation under local law. Mergers in which only cash is used as consideration and divisive mergers do not qualify as reorganizations.

b. A merger of a corporate-owned LLC into another corporation does not qualify, but a merger of a corporation into a single-member LLC may qualify as a Type A reorganization.

c. The most important qualification requirement is that the shareholders of the target corporation ("T") maintain continuity of proprietary interest by owning stock in the acquiring corporation ("P"). For ruling purposes, the Service historically required that at least 50% of the consideration paid by P to acquire T must consist of P stock, which need not be common or voting stock, but the regulations include an example where 40% continuity is acceptable, and several cases have approved a lower percentage.

d. If a merger agreement provides for fixed consideration, continuity of interest generally is measured by the value of the P stock at the end of the last business day before the first date that the agreement is binding (the "Signing Date Rule"). If the consideration is not fixed, the P stock is valued as of the "effective date" of the transaction (the "Closing Date Rule"). In either case, the P stock can be valued in some situations based on average trading prices over an agreed measuring period.

e. Sales and other dispositions of stock by T shareholders before or after a merger generally are not considered in applying the continuity of interest test even if they were made pursuant to a preexisting binding commitment.

f. To reinforce the policy of § 338, the continuity of interest doctrine is sometimes applied inconsistently at the corporate and shareholder levels, such as when P makes a taxable purchase of 80% but less than 100% of T stock, does not make a § 338 election, and pursuant to the same plan T merges into P and T's remaining shareholders receive P stock.

g. A transaction will not fail to qualify as a Type A reorganization if P transfers all or part of the T assets it acquires to a controlled subsidiary of P.

2. Type B Reorganizations (Stock-for-Stock Acquisition)

A Type B reorganization is P's acquisition of T's stock solely in exchange for P voting stock where P has control (i.e., 80%) of T immediately after the acquisition. No boot may be used in a Type B reorganization. Creeping acquisitions are permitted as long as P's earlier cash purchases of T stock are unrelated to the final stock-for-stock acquisition.

3. Type C Reorganizations (Stock-for-Assets Acquisition)

a. A Type C reorganization is P's acquisition of substantially all of T's assets solely in exchange for P voting stock followed by a complete liquidation of T. In applying the solely for voting stock requirement, P's assumption of T's liabilities is disregarded.

b. Under a boot relaxation rule, P's use of consideration other than voting stock is permitted provided that P acquires at least 80% of the value of all of T's assets solely for voting stock. For purposes of this rule, liabilities assumed by P are treated as cash consideration.

c. Under the regulations, P's previous acquisition of more than 20% of T's stock followed by an acquisition of T's assets solely in exchange for P voting stock (or up to 20% boot) will not by itself prevent the transaction from qualifying as a Type C reorganization.

d. A transaction that qualifies as both a Type C and Type D reorganization is treated as a Type D in determining the tax consequences to the parties.

4. Forward Triangular Mergers

A merger of T into a subsidiary of P will qualify as a tax-free forward triangular merger if:

a. S acquires substantially all of the properties of T.

b. No stock of S is used as consideration in the merger.

c. The transaction would have qualified as a Type A reorganization if T had merged directly into P. For ruling purposes, this means that the T shareholders collectively must receive at least 50% P stock in the merger.

5. Reverse Triangular Mergers

A merger of S (P's subsidiary) into T will qualify as a tax-free reverse triangular merger if:

a. After the merger, T holds substantially all of its properties and the properties of S (other than P stock and boot distributed to T shareholders).

b. In the merger, P acquires control (80%) of T in exchange for P voting stock.

6. Multi-Step Acquisitions: Special Problems

The Service sometimes treats multiple steps as a single integrated transaction in order to qualify the overall acquisition as a tax-free reorganization even if the first step, in isolation, would not qualify. In deference to the policy of § 338, however, the step transaction doctrine will not be applied when the first step is a qualified stock purchase under § 338 and the integrated transaction would not qualify as a reorganization.

7. Nondivisive Type D Reorganizations (Transfer to Controlled Corporation)

a. A nondivisive Type D reorganization is a transfer by one corporation of all or substantially all of its assets to a corporation controlled immediately after the transfer by the transferor or its shareholders provided that the stock, securities and other properties received by the transferor are distributed, along with its other properties, to its shareholders pursuant to a reorganization plan and the distribution qualifies under § 354.

b. Taxpayers once used the liquidation-reincorporation strategy to bail out corporate earnings at capital gains rates without paying a corporate-level tax. The Service often attacked this strategy by contending that the transaction was a nondivisive D reorganization in which the shareholders received a boot dividend. This controversy has abated because the technique is rarely viable under current law.

    c.   A transaction may qualify as a Type D reorganization even where the transferee corporation issues no stock or securities as consideration for the transferor's assets if the same person or persons own all the stock of both corporations in identical proportions.

    d.   The IRS has issued published rulings applying § 368(a)(1)(D) to provide flexibility and certainty with respect to certain internal restructuring transactions where no assets leave corporate solution and there is no change of control.

8. Treatment of the Parties to an Acquisitive Reorganization

    a.   If a transaction qualifies as a reorganization, the tax consequences to T's shareholders and all corporate parties to the reorganization are determined by various operative provisions.

    b.   T's shareholders generally do not recognize gain or loss on an exchange of their T stock solely for P stock, or an exchange of T securities solely for P securities. Realized gain must be recognized to the extent that the shareholder receives boot. That gain is a dividend to the extent of T's earnings and profits if the exchange has the effect of the distribution of a dividend. Dividend equivalence is tested using § 302 principles. Noncorporate shareholders usually will be indifferent to dividend classification because qualified dividends and long-term capital gains are taxed at the same rate. The basis of P stock received by T shareholders is the same as their T stock, decreased by the cash and the fair market value of any other boot received, and increased by the shareholder's recognized gain. If preferred stock received in a reorganization may facilitate a later bailout, it will be classified as § 306 stock.

    c.   The regulations provide that any boot received shall be allocated pro rata to the shares surrendered but, if the receipt of boot does not have the effect of a dividend, the terms of the agreement may specify how boot is to be allocated if the specification is economically reasonable.

    d.   T generally does not recognize gain on a transfer of its assets to P pursuant to a reorganization plan. T also does not recognize gain or loss when it distributes P's stock or debt obligations to the T shareholders or creditors, but it may recognize gain on a distribution of appreciated T assets not acquired in the reorganization or appreciated boot.

    e.   P does not recognize gain on the issuance of its stock or debt obligations in an acquisitive reorganization but generally does recognize gain on a transfer of other appreciated boot property. P takes a transferred basis in T's assets. P's basis in T stock acquired in a Type B reorganization is the same as the aggregate basis of the former T shareholders. P's basis in T stock acquired in a reverse triangular merger is generally the same as T's net basis in its assets.

9. Failed Reorganizations

An acquisition that fails to qualify under § 368 is treated as a taxable acquisition of T's assets or stock.

C. Nonacquisitive, Nondivisive Reorganizations

1. Type E Reorganizations (Recapitalizations)

Type E reorganizations are recapitalizations of a single corporation. The continuity of interest requirement does not apply to a recapitalization. Among the types of exchanges that qualify as Type E reorganizations are exchanges of stock for stock, bonds for bonds, and old bonds for new stock. An exchange of old stock for new bonds, or a combination of stock or bonds, is taxable to the extent of the boot received and may give rise to dividend treatment.

2. Type F Reorganizations (Change in Form)

Type F reorganizations are limited to a mere change in the identity, form or place of organization of a corporation. An example is when a corporation changes its state of incorporation. Because an F reorganization involves only one operating corporation, the continuity of interest and continuity of business enterprise doctrines do not apply.

3. Type G Reorganizations (Insolvency)

A Type G reorganization is a transfer by a corporation of all or part of its assets to another corporation in a bankruptcy proceeding or similar case if, pursuant to a plan, stock or securities of the transferee corporation are distributed in a transaction which qualifies under § 354, § 355, or § 356.

XII. CORPORATE DIVISIONS

A. Introduction

A corporate division is a transaction in which a single corporate enterprise is divided into two or more separate corporations that remain under the same ownership. If certain statutory and judicial requirements are met, a distribution by the parent corporation ("P") of stock in one or more subsidiaries ("S") is tax free to P and its shareholders.

1. Types of Corporate Divisions

a. A spin-off, which resembles a dividend, is a pro rata distribution of S stock by P to its shareholders.

b. A split-off, which resembles a redemption, is a distribution of S stock by P to some of its shareholders in exchange for all or part of their P stock.

c. A split-up, which resembles a complete liquidation, is a liquidating distribution by P of stock in two or more subsidiaries (S-1, S-2, etc.).

2. Type D Reorganization Preceding a Division

P may distribute the stock of an existing or newly formed subsidiary in a corporate division. If S is newly formed, P's transfer of assets to S in exchange for S stock is a tax-free Type D reorganization if the subsequent distribution of S stock to P's shareholders meets the requirements of § 355.

3. Summary of Requirements for Tax-Free Division

P's distribution of S stock qualifies as tax free under § 355 if the following statutory and judicial requirements are met:

a. P controls S immediately before the distribution; an 80% test is applied to measure control.

b. P either distributes all of S's stock or securities or distributes "control" and establishes that the retention of stock or securities is not motivated by tax avoidance.

c. Immediately after the distribution, both P and S are engaged in a trade or business that has been actively conducted for the five-year period preceding the distribution, was not acquired within the five-year period in a transaction in which gain or loss was recognized, and was not conducted by a corporation the control of which was acquired by P or any corporate distributee shareholder of P within the five-year period in a taxable transaction. In applying these rules, a corporation and all of its 80% or more subsidiaries are treated as one corporation (known as "a separate affiliated group," or "SAG").

d. The transaction is not used as a device for distributing earnings and profits of P, S or both.

e. The division is carried out for a bona fide corporate business purpose and the business or businesses existing prior to the separation are continued to be operated.

f. P's shareholders maintain continuity of proprietary interest in both P and S after the distribution.

g. The anti-avoidance rules in §§ 355(d) and 355(e) are not violated; if they are, P (but not its shareholders) may recognize gain on the distribution of S stock.

4. IRS Ruling Policy

The IRS generally will issue an advance ruling on one or more "significant" issues or issues pertaining to the business purpose requirement and device limitation if they are not inherently factual in nature. The Service also has introduced a pilot program expanding the scope of its letter rulings to include rulings on the tax consequences of a distribution of stock, or stock or securities, of a controlled corporation under § 355.

B. Active Trade or Business

1. Trade or Business

A trade or business is a specific group of activities carried on with a profit motive.

2. Active Conduct

Active conduct requires the performance of active and substantial management and operational functions either by the corporation itself or through employees, shareholders, affiliated corporations, and certain partnerships in which the corporation has an interest. A passive investment activity does not qualify.

3. Relative Size of Active Trade or Business

The IRS will not rule on the application of § 355 to transactions in which the value of the business assets relied upon by either the distributing or controlled corporation to satisfy the active trade or business requirement is less than 5% of the value of the total gross assets of such corporation. Regulations have also been proposed to address this issue.

4. Divisions of a Single Integrated Business

The active business test is met if P vertically divides an integrated business by transferring a portion of its assets and liabilities to a new corporation. The test is not necessarily violated by distributing certain distinct functions of a single business. In determining if an active trade or business has been conducted throughout the five-year predistribution period, the fact that a trade or business underwent change (e.g., expanded) is disregarded if the changes are not of such a character as to constitute acquisition of a new or different business.

5. Five-Year Business History Rule

The postdistribution active trade or business must have been actively conducted throughout the five-year period preceding the distribution and its assets or a controlling stock interest in that business may not have been acquired by P or a distributee corporation in a taxable transaction during that period. If P expands a preexisting trade or business during the five-year period, the new branches or locations are considered part of that older business.

6. Disposition of a Recently Acquired Business

P's distribution of S stock will fail the active business test if a controlling interest in P was acquired by a corporate shareholder within the five years preceding the distribution.

7. Activities Conducted by a Partnership or LLC

A corporation that owns at least a 20% interest in a partnership or LLC is treated as engaged in that firm's trade or business if the corporation or its officers performs active and substantial management services for the business. A corporation that owns at least a one-third interest in a partnership or LLC is treated as engaged in that firm's trade or business even if the corporation itself does not perform any management services.

8. Treatment of Separate Affiliated Groups

All members of a corporation's "separate affiliated group" (e.g., 80% or more controlled subsidiaries, measured by voting power and value) are treated as one corporation in determining whether the corporation is engaged in the active conduct of a trade or business. Under proposed regulations, an acquisition of stock of a corporation that becomes a subsidiary member of a separate affiliated group is treated as an acquisition of assets. This treatment may have an impact on whether the acquisition qualifies as an expansion of an existing trade or business and in several other contexts.

C. Device Limitation

1. Introduction

The purpose of the device limitation is to prevent bailouts of corporate earnings at capital gains rates. The importance of the limitation is diminished whenever there is no significant capital gains rate preference. The determination of whether a transaction was used principally as a device is often factual and turns on the presence of certain device and nondevice factors specified in the regulations.

2. Device Factors

The presence of any of the following factors is evidence of a device:

a. A pro rata distribution of S stock (i.e., a spin-off).

b. A sale or exchange of P or S stock after the distribution. A subsequent sale that was prearranged is substantial evidence of a device, while other sales are only evidence.

c. The nature and use of certain assets, such as where either P or S holds excessive liquid assets not related to its business, or where the business of P or S principally services the business of the other corporation and could be sold without adversely affecting the business it serves.

3. Nondevice Factors

The presence of any of the following factors is evidence of a nondevice:

a. A corporate business purpose. The stronger the evidence of device, the stronger the corporate business purpose must be to outweigh the device factors.

b. The fact that P is publicly traded and widely held.

c. The fact that the S stock is distributed to a domestic corporate shareholder which would be entitled to claim a dividends received deduction in the absence of § 355.

4. Presumptive Nondevice Transactions

The following types of distributions "ordinarily" are not treated as a device:

a. A distribution in which P and S have neither accumulated nor current E & P.

b. The fact that, absent § 355, the distribution would qualify as an exchange redemption under § 302 or a redemption to pay death taxes under § 303.

D. Distribution of Control Requirement

P must distribute either all the S stock or securities or an amount of S stock constituting "control" (80%) and satisfy the Service that the retention of S stock or securities is not motivated by tax avoidance.

E. Business Purpose

The business purpose test requires the distribution to be motivated by a bona fide corporate business purpose. A shareholder purpose will not suffice. The test is not met if P's goals could have been achieved without having to distribute the stock of S. The business purpose for a transaction is used as evidence in determining whether the transaction was used principally as a device for the distribution of E & P. The IRS has provided numerous examples of valid and invalid corporate business purposes.

F. Continuity of Interest

After P's distribution of S stock, one or more of P's historic predistribution shareholders must maintain, in the aggregate, continuity of interest in both P and S. For this purpose, the Service uses a 50% (by value) benchmark in testing for continuity.

G. Distributions Involving Significant Cash and Investment Assets

Section 355(g) was enacted to curb certain transactions known as cash-rich split-offs. It provides that a distribution does not qualify under § 355 if either the distributing or controlled corporation is a disqualified investment corporation ("DIC") immediately after the transaction and any person holds a 50% or greater interest in such corporation immediately after and did not hold such an interest immediately before the transaction. A corporation is a DIC if the fair market value of its cash and other liquid assets is two-thirds or more of the value of all its assets. Section 355(g) does not apply to some transactions with similar characteristics. The IRS has issued proposed regulations under which many of these transactions will violate the device limitation or the active trade or business requirement.

H. Real Estate Investment Trusts

A transaction does not qualify under § 355 if either the distributing or controlled corporation is a real estate investment trust.

I. Tax Treatment of the Parties to a Corporate Division

1. Shareholders and Security Holders

a. P's shareholders and security holders generally do not recognize gain on their receipt of S stock unless they receive boot in the distribution. Boot includes cash, nonsecurity debt of P, P securities to the extent their principal amount exceeds the principal amount of any P securities surrendered, and any stock of S acquired by P or a P subsidiary in a taxable transaction within the five-year period preceding the distribution ("hot stock") unless S became a member of P's "separate affiliated group" upon the acquisition.

b. In a spin-off, the receipt of boot is treated as a § 301 distribution and is a dividend to the extent of P's E & P. In a split-off or split-up, a shareholder recognizes gain to the extent of the boot received. If the receipt of boot has the effect of a dividend, the shareholder's recognized gain is a dividend to the extent of P's E & P. In no event may loss be recognized.

c. If no boot is received, a P shareholder allocates her old basis in the P stock between the P and S stock (or S-1 and S-2 stock in a split-up) in proportion to their relative fair market values. If boot is received, the aggregate basis of the P and S stock (or S-1 and S-2 stock in a split-up) equals the basis of the old P stock, less the cash and the fair market value of any boot received, plus any gain recognized on the distribution. That amount is then allocated between the distributed and retained stock in proportion to their relative fair market values. Boot property takes a fair market value basis.

2. The Distributing Corporation

Whether or not the distribution is preceded by a reorganization, P generally does not recognize gain on the distribution of S stock or securities to the P shareholders. P recognizes gain on any distribution of appreciated boot. In no event may P recognize loss. In some situations, P may recognize gain on a distribution of S stock when the distribution is treated as a disguised sale under the "anti-avoidance" rules in §§ 355(d) and 355(e).

J.   Corporate Division Combined with Tax-Free Reorganization

1.   Background

Corporate divisions historically have been used to facilitate an acquisition of one of several corporate businesses in a tax efficient manner. The tax consequences often depended on the form used by the parties.

2.   Historical Opportunities and Pitfalls

Prior to the enactment of § 355(e), P's spin-off of a trade or business with a five-year history followed by the acquisition of P's assets or stock in a Type A or Type B reorganization qualified as tax-free under § 355. If a spin-off of unwanted assets was followed by an attempted Type C reorganization, however, neither transaction qualified as tax-free. If P retained unwanted assets and spun off a wanted business by distributing the stock of a newly formed subsidiary which was then acquired in an attempted reorganization, neither the spin-off nor the acquisitive reorganization qualified as tax-free unless P was a public company, S was not a newly formed subsidiary, and no negotiations with respect to the acquisition took place prior to the spin-off.

3.   Corporate-Level Gain Recognition: § 355(e)

A distributing corporation (but not the distributee shareholders) must recognize gain in an otherwise qualified § 355 transaction if, as part of a "plan," one or more persons acquires a 50% or greater interest in either the distributing or controlled corporations within two years before or after the distribution. The gain is determined by treating the distributing corporation as if it had sold the stock of the distributed controlled subsidiary for its fair market value on the date of the distribution. The existence of a "plan" is determined by all the facts and circumstances. Although a plan is presumed if the acquisition occurs two years before or after the distributions, the regulations provide numerous safe harbors and other factors that may be invoked by the taxpayer to rebut the presumption and avoid gain recognition under § 355(e).

XIII.   CARRYOVERS OF CORPORATE TAX ATTRIBUTES

A.   Introduction

The Code includes a comprehensive set of rules governing the carryover of corporate tax attributes, such as earnings and profits and net operating losses, on reorganizations and other major corporate transactions.

B.   Operation of § 381

1.   In General

In an acquisition of a target corporation's assets in a § 332 liquidation or certain reorganizations, the acquiring corporation succeeds to and takes into account certain tax attributes of the target corporation. Only one corporation may be the "acquiring corporation" with respect to the tax attributes governed by § 381.

2.   § 381 Limitations on Carryovers

Certain limitations on the carryover of the target corporation's tax attributes may be imposed when the target has an E & P deficit or NOLs.

3.   Carryovers in Divisive Reorganizations

The carryover rules of § 381 do not apply to divisive reorganizations. Unless otherwise provided, the tax attributes of the distributing corporation in a divisive reorganization are not altered by the transaction. The E & P of the distributing corporation, however, may have to be allocated or reduced as a result of a divisive reorganization.

C.   Limitations on Carryovers of Corporate Tax Attributes

1.   Introduction

The principal limitations on the general § 381 carryover rules are contained in § 382. The purpose of § 382 is to prevent abusive "trafficking" of corporations with net operating losses.

2.   Limitation on Net Operating Loss Carryforwards: § 382

a.   Section 382 limits the use of a corporation's NOL carryforwards if there is a substantial change in ownership of the loss corporation. An ownership change occurs if the percentage of stock of a loss corporation owned by one or more "5-percent shareholders" increases by more than 50% over the lowest percentage of stock owned by such shareholders during the "testing period". An ownership change may result from an "owner shift involving a 5-percent shareholder", an "equity structure shift", or a combination of the two. Modified § 318 attribution rules are applied to determine stock ownership.

b.   If an ownership change has occurred, all NOLs are disallowed if the new loss corporation does not continue the business enterprise of the old loss corporation at all times during the two-year period following the date of the ownership change. If the business is continued, a loss corporation's NOLs are limited to an amount equal to the value of the old loss corporation multiplied by the long-term tax-exempt rate.

c.   Special rules exist when a loss corporation has a "net unrealized built-in gain". The § 382 limitation is increased by any recognized built-in gains during the five-year period following the ownership change. This rule applies only if the corporation's net unrealized built-in gain exceeds either 15% of the fair market value of its assets (less cash and certain cash equivalents) or $10 million.

d.   If a loss corporation has a "net unrealized built-in loss", its recognized built-in losses during the five-year period following the ownership change are subject to the § 382 limitations as if they were a NOL carryover. This rule applies only if the corporation's net unrealized built-in loss exceeds either 15% of the fair market value of its assets (less cash and certain cash equivalents) or $10 million.

3.   Special Limitations on Other Tax Attributes: § 383

Section 383 applies § 382 limitation principles with respect to carryovers of the general business credit, foreign tax credit, and capital losses of a loss corporation after an ownership change.

4. **Limitation on Use of Preacquisition Losses to Offset Built-in Gains: § 384**

Section 384 prevents a loss corporation from using its preacquisition NOLs to offset built-in gains of an acquired corporation during the five-year period following the acquisition. Section 384 applies if a corporation acquires either control (generally 80% ownership) of another corporation or the assets of another corporation in a Type A, C, or D reorganization and either corporation has a net unrealized built-in gain.

5. **Acquisitions Made to Evade or Avoid Income Tax: § 269**

Under § 269, the Service may disallow a deduction, credit, or other allowance following certain corporate acquisitions if the principal purpose of the acquisition was the evasion or avoidance of income tax.

6. **Consolidated Return Rules**

All the statutory limitations on carryovers of tax attributes apply to corporations filing a consolidated tax return. In addition, the consolidated return regulations contain special rules which apply to a "separate return limitation year" situation.

XIV.   AFFILIATED CORPORATIONS

A. Introduction

The theory that each corporation is a separate taxpayer is limited in certain situations when corporations are "affiliated."

B. Restrictions on Multiple Tax Benefits

1. In General

In limited situations, taxpayers have an incentive to multiply the number of corporations used to operate a business to take advantage of certain tax benefits.

2. § 1561

Section 1561 prevents "component members of a controlled group" from obtaining more than one accumulated earnings tax credit.

3. Other Restrictions

Other Code sections contain specific limitations on multiple tax benefits for affiliated corporations. Under § 269, for example, the Service may disallow a tax benefit of a person or persons who acquire "control" (at least 50% of total vote or value) of a corporation and the principal purpose of the acquisition is avoidance of income tax by securing a tax benefit which would be otherwise unavailable.

C. Transactions Involving Related Corporations and Other Taxpayers

The Code has a number of provisions designed to prevent tax avoidance in transactions between controlled and commonly owned corporations. Under § 482, the Service may apportion or allocate tax items between or among enterprises which are owned or controlled by the same interests in order to prevent evasion of taxes or to clearly reflect income.

D. Consolidated Returns

Commonly controlled corporations meeting certain requirements (an "affiliated group of corporations") may elect to compute and pay tax on their consolidated taxable income. Because the members of the group are treated as a single taxpayer, special rules are applied to intercompany distributions and intercompany transactions.

XV. S CORPORATIONS

A. Introduction

A Subchapter S election allows a "small business corporation" to avoid almost all corporate-level taxes. The shareholders of an S corporation are taxed directly on corporate-level profits, thereby avoiding the corporate double tax.

B. Eligibility for S Corporation Status

The special tax provisions of Subchapter S are available only to "small business corporations" making an election under § 1362(a). "Small business corporations" must meet all of the following requirements:

1. Ineligible Corporations and Subsidiaries

Ineligible corporations, as defined by § 1361(b)(2), do not qualify as small business corporations. The category includes certain types of banks and insurance companies. A corporation is not "ineligible" if it has a subsidiary.

2. 100-Shareholder Limit

A small business corporation may not have more than 100 shareholders. Spouses and their estates are considered one shareholder for purposes of the 100-shareholder limit. Members of a "family" (including spouses) also are treated as one shareholder. A family generally is defined to include up to six generations with a common ancestor plus spouses and former spouses.

3. Restrictions on Types of Shareholders

Small business corporations may not have shareholders who are not individuals except for certain estates and trusts. Nonresident aliens are not eligible shareholders.

4. One-Class-of-Stock Requirement

A small business corporation may not have more than one class of stock. Differences in rights to profits or assets on liquidation create a second class of stock. Differences in voting rights are disregarded when determining whether a corporation has more than one class of stock. Except in abuse cases, buy-sell and redemption agreements, and stock transfer restrictions also are disregarded. Debt that complies with a "straight debt safe harbor" rule will not be considered a second class of stock.

C. Election, Revocation and Termination of Subchapter S Status

1. Electing S Corporation Status

The shareholders of a small business corporation must make a unanimous election to be an S corporation. Elections made up to the 15th day of the third month of the taxable year are effective for that taxable year and all succeeding years until terminated.

2.   **Revocation and Termination of S Corporation Status**

An S corporation election may be revoked with the consent of more than 50% of the shares of stock of the corporation. An election is terminated if the corporation ceases to meet the definition of a small business corporation. An election also may be terminated if an S corporation has accumulated E & P (e.g., from when it was a C corporation) and more than 25% of its gross receipts was derived from certain types of passive investment income over a three-year period. Revocations and terminations generally will preclude the corporation from reelecting S corporation status for five years. If a corporation inadvertently terminates its S status, the Treasury has the option to disregard the termination and allow the corporation to continue as an S corporation.

D.   Tax Treatment of S Corporation Shareholders

1.   Introduction

In general, an S corporation is not a taxable entity. Its income, loss, deductions, and credits are passed through to its shareholders.

2.   Corporate Level Determination of Tax Results

a.   An S corporation calculates its gross income and taxable income to determine the tax results to be passed through to its shareholders and it may select its own accounting method subject to certain limitations. The taxable year of the S corporation can be either a calendar year or a fiscal year for which it establishes a business purpose. Legislative history, revenue rulings, and revenue procedures have established criteria by which the business purpose standard is evaluated.

b.   An S corporation computes its taxable income in the same manner as an individual except that certain deductions unique to individuals are not allowed. Items of income, deductions, losses, and credits which could affect the tax liability of the shareholder if treated separately, such as capital and § 1231 gains and losses, investment interest expense, charitable contributions, and foreign taxes, must be separately reported by the S corporation. Tax elections are made by the S corporation and not its shareholders.

3.   Tax Consequences to Shareholders

a.   Shareholders of an S corporation must account for their pro rata share (on a per share, per day basis) of the corporation's separately stated items and nonseparately computed income or loss in the taxable year in which the S corporation's taxable year ends.

b.   A shareholder's share of an S corporation's losses and deductions is limited to the shareholder's adjusted basis in the stock of the corporation and the bona fide indebtedness of the corporation to the shareholder. Losses and deductions disallowed under this rule may be carried forward and used when the shareholders obtain additional stock or debt basis.

c.   S corporation shareholders may not include either their share of the corporation's indebtedness or corporate debt they have guaranteed in their stock or debt basis. If a shareholder is required to make a payment on corporate indebtedness as a result of a guarantee or similar arrangement, the shareholder may increase basis by the amount of the payment.

d. Losses which pass through to the shareholder also may be limited by the § 465 at-risk limitations, the § 469 passive loss limitations, and the § 461(*l*) limitation on excess business losses of noncorporate shareholders.

e. The shareholder's share of the S corporation's income and losses which are passed through to the shareholder will increase and decrease, respectively, the shareholder's basis in the S corporation stock.

f. In the case of an S corporation, the § 199A deduction for qualified business income is determined at the shareholder level. The S corporation provides the shareholders with the relevant information needed to compute the deduction on the shareholder's return. Reasonable compensation paid by an S corporation to a shareholder-employee for services or recharacterized as such is not qualified business income.

g. The regulations apply a partial look-through rule to characterize gain or loss on the sale of S corporation stock. In general, gain or loss on the sale of stock held for more than one year is long-term capital gain. If an S corporation owns appreciated collectibles, some of the shareholder's gain may be treated as collectibles gain taxable at a maximum rate of 28%.

E. Distributions to Shareholders

Since S corporation shareholders are taxed directly on their share of the corporation's taxable income, subsequent distributions of this income by the corporation are generally not taxed to the shareholder.

1. S Corporations Without E & P

If an S corporation has no E & P, a distribution is tax free to the extent of the shareholder's basis in the corporation's stock. Any excess of the distribution over the stockholder's adjusted basis is treated as a gain from the sale or exchange of the stock. The shareholder's adjusted basis is reduced by the amount of any distribution that is not included in the shareholder's taxable income.

2. S Corporations with E & P

If an S corporation has E & P, distributions are first treated as recovery of stock basis and then as stock gain to the extent of corporation's accumulated adjustments account ("AAA"). Any remaining distribution is first treated as a dividend to the extent of the corporation's accumulated E & P and then as recovery of stock basis or gain.

3. Distributions of Property

An S corporation recognizes gain on the distribution of appreciated property. The gain passes through and is taxed to the shareholders in the same manner as other income.

The amount of the property distribution to the shareholder is the fair market value of the property. The shareholder takes a fair market value basis in the property received. The shareholder reduces her adjusted basis in the corporation's stock by the fair market value of the distributed property.

4. Ordering of Basis Adjustments

An S corporation shareholder's stock basis is first increased by her pro rata share of income and gain items for the year before making downward adjustments for distributions. Adjustments for distributions are made before any basis reductions for losses.

5. Distributions Following Termination of S Corporation Status

Shareholders receiving distributions during a "post-termination transition period" (at least one year after the last day of the corporation's last taxable year as an S corporation) can be applied against the shareholder's stock basis to the extent of the AAA.

F. Taxation of the S Corporation

S corporations generally are relieved of paying all corporate-level taxes except for the taxes in § 1374 and § 1375.

1. § 1374 Tax on Built-in Gains

Section 1374 applies to S corporations which were once C corporations. Gain in appreciated assets held by the corporation at the time of its S election may be taxed at the highest corporate income tax rate (21%) if the S corporation sells the asset at a gain within five years of making an S election. The amount of built-in gain that may be taxed under this provision is limited to the total net gain inherent in all of the corporation's assets at the time of the election.

2. § 1375 Tax on Excessive Passive Investment Income

An S corporation with E & P from Subchapter C operations is subject to tax (at 21%) on its "excess net passive income" if more than 25% of its gross receipts consist of "passive investment income."

G. Coordination of Subchapter S with Subchapter C and Other Tax Provisions

1. Subchapter C

S corporations can engage in the wide range of corporate-shareholder transactions available to C corporations. The provisions of Subchapter C generally apply to an S corporation and its shareholders unless such treatment would be inconsistent with Subchapter S.

2. Other Tax Provisions

Tax principles applicable to individuals generally apply to S corporations.

3. Employment Taxes

Wages paid to owner-employees of S corporations are subject to federal employment taxes, but neither the distributive share of an S corporation's net business income nor distributions to owner-employees are considered self-employment income if reasonable compensation is paid for their services. Attempts to avoid employment taxes by paying no or unreasonably low salaries to owner-employees who render significant services generally have not been successful because the courts have reclassified S corporation distributions as "wages" subject to employment tax.

4. **Net Investment Income Tax**

S corporations pass through items subject to the net investment income tax ("NIIT") to their shareholders. Gain from the sale of S corporation stock by shareholders not active in the business is generally subject to the NIIT. Net business income passing through to shareholders who are active in the business and gain on the sale of their stock attributable to assets used in the business are generally not subject to the NIIT.

Perspective

■ ANALYSIS

A. The Subject in General
B. Preparing for Examinations
C. Other Sources
D. Acknowledgments

A. THE SUBJECT IN GENERAL

This outline has been written for students enrolled in basic courses in Corporate Tax or a course on Business Enterprise Taxation. It also may be useful for some of the topics covered in more advanced business tax courses.

Whatever the format, corporate tax is regarded as among the most challenging subjects in the law school curriculum. This reputation is well deserved. Quite apart from the intricacies of the Internal Revenue Code, the underlying transactions are complex and often unfamiliar even to students with some business or accounting background. The goal of this outline is to make the rules more accessible to students by presenting them in a structured and intelligible format that includes definitions, examples, cross references and practice questions. Although the outline is generally organized to follow the life cycle of a corporation from formation to termination (the so-called "cradle to grave" approach), it should be easily adapted to whatever organization your instructor uses. We reiterate what your instructor no doubt has already preached at the first class—a study aid is no substitute for a careful reading of the primary materials assigned in your course. This outline is intended to support but not replace your armed combat with the Code and regulations.

Students quickly will become aware that corporate tax courses devote very little time to the determination of the entity's taxable income. Those concepts should have been mastered in the basic income tax class. For students who may have suffered some memory loss, we recommend generally reviewing the concepts of gross income, deductions, timing and characterization, focusing particularly on the issues raised by the *Crane* and *Tufts* cases, the basic workings of a nonrecognition provision (such as § 1031), and some fundamental timing rules (such as installment sale reporting under § 453).

The vast majority of time in corporate tax is devoted to studying transactions between corporations and their shareholders and taxable and nontaxable dispositions of a corporate business. The study of S corporations also revolves, to a large degree, around transactions between the entity and its owners. Your study of all these topics will be enhanced by an understanding of "the big picture"—the basic models for taxing a business enterprise and the way in which those models influence taxpayer behavior. For some additional perspective, we recommend a careful reading of Chapter I of this outline.

B. PREPARING FOR EXAMINATIONS

As in any law school course, preparing for an examination requires a student to connect with the instructor's wave length. Some tax teachers emphasize statutory construction and problem solving. Their exams are likely to parallel the coverage during the semester but may require you to understand the relationships of concepts covered at different points in the course.

If your instructor uses the problem method, it is likely that the exam will ask you to analyze the tax consequences of hypothetical fact situations. Other instructors may spend more time on cases, tax policy, and less quantifiable issues, and their essay questions may reflect this approach. Many of these instructors, however, still require students to analyze discrete fact patterns on the exam—in both short answer and essay questions—if only because it is easier to grade a more "objective" exam. In short, it is a safe bet that virtually all corporate tax exams will be rather specific and require a mastery of many statutory details along with the broad concepts and tax policy issues.

As with any law school exam, it is essential that you do not write a mini-treatise on the law in general but relate the applicable rules to the facts presented in the question. Even in tax, there may not be a right answer for the essay questions. Where the law is uncertain, it is best to discuss the possibilities and reach a reasoned conclusion (perhaps one that is consistent with what the instructor may have described in class as "the better view.")

C. OTHER SOURCES

So much additional reading is available on corporate tax that students need to protect themselves against "information overload." Among the leading professional treatises in the area are *Federal Income Taxation of Corporations and Shareholders* by Bittker and Eustice; *Mergers, Acquisitions and Buyouts* by Ginsburg, Levin and Rocap; and *Federal Income Taxation of S Corporations* by Eustice, Kuntz and Bogdanski. Although these are all superb texts, keep in mind that they are not written principally for law students and they often prove to be overwhelming in their level of sophistication and detail. It may be best to confine your reading to the assigned materials and a study aid (such as this outline) specifically designed for students.

D. ACKNOWLEDGMENTS

We remain forever grateful for the hard work and thoughtful advice of the three student research assistants at Hastings College of the Law who worked on the first edition, Ray Kawasaki, Terri Murray and Mitch Salamon, and to Bruce McGovern and Marc Yassinger for their help on later editions, and to Bev Lathrope for her continuing support.

Chapter I

Introduction

■ **ANALYSIS**

A. Forms of Business Organizations
    1. Sole Proprietorship
    2. Corporation
    3. Partnership
    4. Limited Liability Company
B. Conceptual Taxation Models
    1. Aggregate Concept
    2. Entity Concept
    3. Hybrid Concepts
C. Overview of Taxing Regimes Under the Code
    1. Subchapter C
    2. Subchapter K
    3. Subchapter S
    4. Specialized Tax Regimes
    5. Demography
D. Influential Policies
    1. The Double Tax
    2. Tax Rates on Ordinary Income
    3. Preferential Rates for Capital Gains and Qualified Dividends
    4. Nonrecognition of Gain or Loss
E. Pervasive Judicial Doctrines
    1. Substance over Form
    2. Step Transactions
    3. Business Purpose
    4. Sham Transaction
    5. Economic Substance
    6. Codification of the Economic Substance Doctrine

A. Forms of Business Organizations

The permissible forms for business enterprises in the United States are governed principally by the laws of the various states. The most common forms in which a business may be conducted are sole proprietorships, corporations, partnerships and limited liability companies.

1. Sole Proprietorship

A sole proprietorship is owned and operated by a single individual. Sole proprietors take into account the income and expenses of their businesses on their individual tax returns (Form 1040), filing a Schedule C (sole proprietorships generally), Schedule E (rental real estate and royalties), or Schedule F (farms), and Schedule SE (self-employment tax).

2. Corporation

A corporation is a fictitious legal entity that is the most commonly used form for operating a large, publicly held business. The corporate form is also used by closely held businesses where the owners wish to insulate themselves from personal liability for debts of the enterprise.

3. Partnership

A partnership is a business owned by two or more persons as co-owners.

a. General Partnership

In a general partnership, the partners have unlimited liability and generally are bound by the acts of the other partners. General partners ordinarily are personally liable for partnership debts.

b. Limited Partnership

A limited partnership has a general partner (which may be a corporation or limited liability company). The general partner manages the business, while limited partners ordinarily have no role in day-to-day management. The general partner has unlimited liability, but the limited partners are not personally liable for partnership debts except to the extent of their capital contributions.

c. Limited Liability Partnership

Many states authorize limited liability partnerships (LLPs). A partner of an LLP is protected, in varying degrees depending on state law, from vicarious liability for acts of the other partners. Some states authorize limited liability limited partnerships, which extend personal immunity from liability to the general partners.

d. Publicly Traded Partnership

A publicly traded partnership ("PTP") has ownership interests that are traded on an established or secondary securities market. PTPs generally are taxed as C corporations, with a major exception for PTPs having 90% or more of their gross income from certain broadly defined types of investment income. See II.C.3., at page 60, *infra*.

e. Joint Venture

A joint venture is a term used to describe an arrangement between two or more parties to share the profits of a particular project. Many tax and nontax rules applicable to partnerships also apply to joint ventures, which typically are organized as partnerships or LLCs under state law but also may be governed by a contract between the parties.

4. Limited Liability Company

The limited liability company ("LLC") is a form of noncorporate entity that is permitted under the laws of every state. All of an LLC's owners, known as "members," have limited liability for the entity's debts and claims. LLCs also may have "managers," who are analogous to general partners. The organizing document of an LLC is known as an "operating agreement." All 50 states and the District of Columbia permit single-member LLCs. For income tax purposes, LLCs with more than one member are treated as partnerships and single-member LLCs are treated as disregarded entities unless the LLC elects corporate status. See II.C.2.b. & c., at pages 58–59, *infra*.

B. Conceptual Taxation Models

The appropriate tax treatment of a business enterprise initially depends on a policy decision as to the nature of the organization. The two principal views are the "aggregate" and "entity" concepts.

1. Aggregate Concept

Under the aggregate concept, a business organization is viewed as an aggregation of its owners, each of whom holds a direct undivided interest in the assets and operations of the enterprise. The organization itself is not treated as a separate taxable entity under this theory. Rather, each of the owners takes into account his or her respective share of income and expenses. Contributions to or distributions from the entity generally are ignored for tax purposes, and sales of an owner's interest are treated as sales of undivided interests in each of the organization's assets.

2. Entity Concept

Under the entity concept, a business organization is viewed as an entity that is separate and distinct from its owners. As such, the entity is subject to tax on its taxable income, and transactions between the owners and the entity are taxable events unless a specific provision of the Internal Revenue Code provides for nonrecognition of gain or loss. This is sometimes referred to as "a double tax regime."

3. Hybrid Concepts

S corporations (and partnerships) are taxed using a hybrid taxing model that treats an organization as a separate entity for some purposes (e.g., determination of income, filing of tax returns) and as an aggregate for other purposes (e.g., by passing through income and expenses to the owners).

C. Overview of Taxing Regimes Under the Code

The Internal Revenue Code ("the Code") has adopted three principal taxing models for business organizations. These three "regimes" are found in Subchapters C, S and K.

1. Subchapter C

All corporations other than "S" corporations (see I.C.3. at page 50, *infra*) are "C" corporations. § 1361(a)(2). Subchapter C (§§ 301–385) adopts an entity concept by treating C corporations as separate taxpaying entities. The taxable income of a C corporation is subject to tax at a flat rate of 21%. § 11(b). Subchapter C governs the following categories of transactions between corporations and their shareholders:

a.   Nonliquidating distributions of cash, property or stock (§§ 301–317).

b.   Complete liquidations (§§ 331–346).

c.   Corporate organizations (including formations) and reorganizations (e.g., mergers, recapitalizations, insolvencies), and carryover of tax attributes following a corporate acquisition (§§ 351–384).

d.   Classification of corporate interests as stock or debt (§ 385).

The taxation of C corporations is covered in Chapters III–XIV.

2. Subchapter K

Under Subchapter K (§§ 701–761), partnerships and limited liability companies are not treated as separate taxpaying entities. Partnership income and deductions pass through to the individual partners and are taxed at the partner level. A partnership, however, is treated as an accounting entity for purposes of determining its income, and it must file an informational tax return showing how all the partnership's tax items have been allocated among the partners. A partnership and its partners also are taxed under an entity or modified-entity approach in several substantive contexts, such as formation and termination, transactions between partners and partnerships, and sales of partnership interests.

The taxation of partnerships is covered in Schwarz, Lathrope & Hellwig, Black Letter on Partnership Taxation (West 2019).

3. Subchapter S

Subchapter S (§§ 1361–1379) is a hybrid model that governs the tax treatment of "S corporations" and their shareholders. It was enacted to minimize the influence of taxes on the choice of form for smaller, closely held businesses. Like partnerships, S corporations are treated as pass-through entities that generally are not subject to tax. S corporation status is limited to eligible corporations that make an election. In general, S corporations can have only one class of stock and no more than 100 shareholders, all of whom must be individual U.S. citizens or residents, or certain qualified trusts and tax-exempt organizations.

S corporations are covered in Chapter XV.

4. Specialized Tax Regimes

The Code also includes taxing regimes tailored for particular industries. Examples include Subchapter F (tax-exempt organizations and cooperatives), Subchapter H (banks), Subchapter L (insurance companies), and Subchapter M (mutual funds and real estate investment trusts). Because these specialized regimes are rarely covered in law school corporate tax courses, they are not discussed in this Black Letter.

5.   Demography

In 2017, the latest year for which IRS data is available, there were 2.05 million C corporations, 4.8 million S corporations, and 4.05 million partnerships and limited liability companies. Approximately 68% of partnership returns were filed by LLCs.

D. Influential Policies

Our system of taxing corporations has been influenced by at least four broad tax policy decisions. The relationship of these policies impacts taxpayer behavior, both as to the choice of form in which to conduct a business and the tax saving opportunities within each form. Tax legislation enacted over the past several decades, culminating with the enactment of the Tax Cuts and Jobs Act in 2017, has radically altered some of these policies and contributed to instability in the system. As a result, some cases and Code sections that traditionally were studied in corporate tax courses (and are still included in some casebooks) are obsolete or less significant, but they could become important again with future changes in the law. The following discussion is a greatly simplified overview of the most influential policies and their past and present impact on taxation of business organizations.

1.   The Double Tax

Earnings of C corporations are taxed once at the corporate level when earned and again when distributed as dividends to shareholders. In the Tax Reform Act of 1986, Congress significantly strengthened the double tax by providing that a C corporation generally recognizes gain on all distributions of appreciated property to its shareholders. Under a prior rule known as "the *General Utilities* doctrine," such distributions often were nontaxable events. Partnerships and S corporations, as pass-through entities, are generally not subject to an entity-level tax on either operating income or asset appreciation. The 1986 Act strengthened the double tax and also narrowed the gap between the top corporate and individual rates on ordinary income, thereby increasing the relative costs of operating as a C corporation. In that rate environment there was an incentive for taxpayers to use partnerships, S corporations or limited liability companies to conduct many closely held business and investment activities.

2.   Tax Rates on Ordinary Income

a.   Relationship Between the Corporate and Individual Rates

For most of our early tax history, the maximum individual tax rate on ordinary income was much higher than the top corporate rate. Despite the double tax, this rate differential motivated taxpayers to operate profitable businesses as C corporations. The typical strategy was to distribute profits to owner-employees in the form of tax-deductible compensation or interest and accumulate what was left in the corporation. Accumulated profits would compound at a lower rate of tax and often were later withdrawn at highly preferential capital gains rates when the business was sold, or tax-free after an owner died. Congress enacted several anti-avoidance provisions, such as the accumulated earnings and personal holding company taxes, to curtail these strategies.

For a brief time between 1987 and 1992, the maximum corporate rate (then 34%) exceeded the highest marginal individual rate. The pendulum shifted back slightly in 1993, when individual rates were increased to 39.6% and then changed again in 2003, when the top individual rate on ordinary income dropped to 35% (the same as the maximum corporate income tax rate). In 2013, the highest individual rate on ordinary income rose back to 39.6% and a new 3.8% tax on net investment income for high-income taxpayers became effective. Beginning in 2018, the Tax Cuts and Jobs Act reduced the corporate income tax rate to 21% and the top marginal individual rate on ordinary income to 37%. The interrelationship of corporate and individual rates may influence the choice of legal form for a business or investment entity. See II.D. at page 60, *infra.*

b.   Deduction for 20% of Qualified Business Income

Beginning in 2018, taxpayer behavior also is influenced by the deduction provided by § 199A (through 2025) to individuals, trusts, and estates for up to 20% of their share of qualified business income from domestic businesses operated as a sole proprietorship, partnership, LLC or S corporation. See XV.D.3.e., at page 309, *infra.* If the § 199A deduction is fully available, its effect is to reduce the maximum tax rate on qualified business income from 37% to 29.6%. The deduction is subject to complex limitations and phase-out rules. It was intended to provide partial tax relief to the owners of pass-through entities, which do not benefit from the reduction of the corporate income tax rate to 21%.

3.   Preferential Rates for Capital Gains and Qualified Dividends

Historically, the policy decision to tax long-term capital gains at substantially lower rates than ordinary income motivated C corporations and their shareholders to structure transactions designed to "bail out" earnings at preferential capital gains rates instead of paying dividends taxable at the higher ordinary income rates. Many of the Code sections in Subchapter C were enacted to curtail these conversion devices.

After a brief period during which there was little or no capital gains preference, Congress shifted back to the historical policy by providing a significant rate reduction for long-term capital gains of individual taxpayers. In addition, it reduced the rate on most dividends received by noncorporate shareholders. Since 2003, these "qualified dividends" have been taxed at the same preferential rate as long-term capital gains. As long as dividends and long-term capital gains are taxed at the same rate, the bailout strategies described above are much less significant, and the major tax advantage of a bailout is the ability of noncorporate shareholders to recover the basis in any stock that is treated as sold or exchanged.

4.   Nonrecognition of Gain or Loss

The nonrecognition concept has always played an important role in the taxation of corporations and partnerships. In general, all realized gains or losses must be recognized unless the Code provides otherwise. § 1001(c). Transactions typically qualify for "nonrecognition" treatment if they are mere changes in form which result in a continuity of investment. To ensure that realized gain or loss is only deferred, a nonrecognition provision is coupled with transferred and exchanged basis rules that preserve the gain or loss for recognition at a later time. Many corporate and partnership transactions, ranging from simple formations to complex liquidation and acquisitions, will qualify for nonrecognition treatment.

E.   Pervasive Judicial Doctrines

Corporate tax issues usually can be resolved by a careful application of the statute and regulations to the transaction in question. To protect the integrity of the system, however, the courts have gone beyond the statutory language and formulated "common law" doctrines that may alter the tax treatment of a transaction that literally complies with the Code but is incompatible with its purpose. The Service has successfully invoked these judicial doctrines in attacking transactions known as corporate tax shelters. Despite years of litigation, the judicial doctrines are imprecise and often are applied interchangeably. The purpose of this summary is to introduce some of the most familiar terminology.

1. Substance over Form

In one of the earliest articulations of the "substance over form" doctrine, the Supreme Court stated that "[t]he incidence of taxation depends upon the substance of a transaction. . . . To permit the true nature of a transaction to be disguised by mere formalisms, which exist solely to alter tax liabilities, would seriously impair the effective administration of the tax policies of Congress." *Comm'r v. Court Holding Co.*, 324 U.S. 331, 65 S.Ct. 707 (1945). It is difficult to generalize as to when and how the doctrine is applied. Some illustrative controversies that are discussed later in this outline include:

a. Is a corporate instrument labelled as "debt" in reality "equity?" See V.B., at page 99, *infra*.

b. Is a payment to a shareholder-employee really "compensation" or is it a disguised dividend? See VI.E., at page 120, *infra*.

c. Is a distribution a dividend or part of the purchase price for the business? See VI.F.6., at page 123, *infra*.

d. Was a sale of assets made by the corporation or its shareholders? See IX.B.2.a.2., at page 173, *infra*.

Despite the substance over form doctrine, the parties to a transaction often can dictate a tax result by utilizing a particular form. This will become particularly apparent in the area of taxable and tax-free corporate acquisitions. See IX.D, at pages 180–190, *infra* and XI.B., at pages 210–236, *infra*.

2. Step Transactions

The substance of a transaction is often determined by application of the step transaction doctrine, under which the separate "steps" of formally distinct transactions are combined into a single integrated transaction for tax purposes. The courts disagree on when and how to apply the step transaction doctrine. Three principal formulations have emerged.

a. The Binding Commitment Test

A series of transactions is combined if, when the first step was taken, there was a binding commitment to undertake the later steps. This is the narrowest formulation of the doctrine and usually is the most favorable to taxpayers, who often can demonstrate that the parties were not legally obligated to engage in the later steps.

b. The End Result Test

Separate steps are combined if it is determined that they were prearranged components of a single transaction in which the parties intended from the outset to reach a particular end result. This is the broadest and least precise articulation of the doctrine because it requires a determination of the "intent" of the parties.

c. The Interdependence Test

This is a variation of the end result test which looks to whether the separate steps are so interdependent that the legal relations created by one transaction would have been fruitless without completion of the later steps. The court must determine whether the steps had independent legal significance or were merely part of the larger transaction.

Courts have resisted applying the step transaction doctrine when the Service does not simply combine steps but invents new ones that never took place in order to reach a particular result adverse to the taxpayer. See, e.g., *Esmark, Inc. v. Comm'r,* 90 T.C. 171 (1988). In addition, the Service has shown a greater willingness in recent years to "turn off" the step transaction doctrine where it otherwise might apply in deference to statutory policies that require the form of a transaction to be respected.

3. Business Purpose

The business purpose doctrine is sometimes applied to deny tax benefits (e.g., nonrecognition of gain on a corporate acquisition) when a transaction lacks a corporate business purpose. The doctrine is most frequently applied in connection with tax-free corporate divisions. See XII.E. at pages 256–258, *infra.*

4. Sham Transaction

A "sham" transaction will not be respected for tax purposes. This is often another way of saying that the transaction is devoid of economic substance because no reasonable possibility of profit exists, or was not motivated by a bona fide business purpose other than obtaining tax benefits. See, e.g., *Rice's Toyota World v. Comm'r,* 752 F.2d 89 (4th Cir.1985). The term "sham" may include a transaction that never in fact occurred and, in that context, it connotes fraudulent conduct.

5. Economic Substance

Under the common law economic substance doctrine, tax benefits are denied for transactions that actually occur but do not result in a meaningful change in a taxpayer's economic position apart from a reduction in federal income taxes. The courts disagree over the precise formulation of this doctrine. Some apply a conjunctive test requiring a taxpayer to establish the presence of both economic substance and a business purpose. Others apply a disjunctive test under which either a business purpose or economic substance is sufficient. A third approach regards economic substance and business purpose as simply "more precise factors to consider." The courts have disagreed about the type of nontax economic benefit a taxpayer must establish for a transaction to have economic substance. Some deny tax benefits because a transaction lacks profit potential; others focus on the degree of economic risk or require an objective inquiry of whether a "reasonable possibility of profit" exists apart from tax benefits.

6. Codification of the Economic Substance Doctrine

Congress has codified the economic substance doctrine and enacted a strict liability penalty for transactions lacking economic substance. §§ 7701(*o*); 6662(a), (b)(6) & (i). For further discussion, see X.B., at page 194, *infra.*

Chapter II

Classification

■ **ANALYSIS**

A. Introduction

1. Impact of Classification

The classification of a business relationship may have profound tax consequences. Entities classified as "corporations" are subject to the double tax regime of Subchapter C while income realized by a "partnership," which for tax purposes includes limited liability companies, is taxed directly to the partners under the pass-through taxing scheme of Subchapter K. If a business arrangement is classified as a "partnership," a partnership tax return (Form 1065) must be filed and tax elections generally must be made at the partnership level. §§ 703(b), 6031. The timing and character of the income realized by the owners also may be affected if a business activity is classified as a partnership. §§ 702(b), 706(a).

The operation of many Code sections also varies depending on whether the taxpayer is an individual, a partnership, a corporation or some other type of entity. For example, under § 179 a taxpayer may elect to currently deduct a certain amount of the cost of "§ 179 property" each year. In the case of a partnership, the dollar limit is applied at both the partnership and partner levels. § 179(d)(8). Thus, if two individuals enter into a business relationship which is not classified as a partnership, each taxpayer will be eligible to expense up to the § 179 cost limit, but if the activity is classified as a partnership the benefits of § 179 will be restricted to one limit for the partnership.

The stakes in the classification area have changed in response to provisions in the Internal Revenue Code and planning strategies that, at different times, have offered incentives to classify entities as partnerships or corporations. See II.C.1. at page 57, *infra*.

2. The Role of State Law

The classification of entities for federal tax purposes is a matter of federal law and depends on standards in the Internal Revenue Code. Reg. § 301.7701–1(a)(1). Thus, the classification or label placed on an organization under state law will not control its classification under the Code.

3. Principal Classification Issues

Tax classification issues generally arise in two settings. In the first, the issue is whether an unincorporated business relationship is an entity separate from its owners, or rather is some other form of arrangement, such as co-ownership of property, employer-employee, principal-agent, debtor-creditor, etc. On this end of the spectrum, the question is whether the business relationship among the parties is such that a separate entity is recognized for tax purposes. If a separate entity is recognized, it generally will be classified as a partnership for federal tax purposes.

In the other setting, the question is whether or not an entity should be classified as a corporation or partnership for federal tax purposes. On this end of the spectrum, the issue generally narrows to whether an entity formed under state law as a limited partnership, limited liability company or trust will be classified as a corporation under the Code.

B. Existence of a Separate Entity

1. In General

The regulations provide that a joint venture or other contractual arrangement may create a separate entity for federal tax purposes if the participants carry on a trade, business, financial operation, or venture and divide the profits therefrom. Reg. § 301.7701–1(a)(2). If a separate entity is created, its classification for federal tax purposes will be determined under the regulations. Generally, the separate entity will be classified as a partnership. See II.C.2.b. at page 58, *infra.* The determination of whether an organization is an entity separate from its owners for federal tax purposes is a matter of federal law and does not depend on whether the organization is recognized as an entity under local law. Reg. § 301.7701–1(a).

2. Separate Entity vs. Other Relationships

"Mere co-ownership" of property which is maintained, kept in repair, and rented or leased, and expense sharing arrangements do not constitute separate entities for federal tax purposes. Reg. § 301.7701–1(a)(2).

Example (1): If two individuals jointly purchase a parcel of real property to hold as an investment, no separate entity is formed. But if they purchase the parcel to subdivide and develop the parcel with the intention of selling lots, a separate entity does exist because they are actively carrying on a trade or business and dividing a joint profit. Unless the separate entity elects to be taxed as a corporation, it will be classified as a partnership for tax purposes.

Example (2): If Doctor A and Doctor B agree to share office and support expenses but each will retain her own clients, a separate entity is not created because there is no joint profit being produced. If the doctors agree to combine practices and divide profits from their joint activity, a separate entity does exist.

C. Classification of Business Entities

1. Introduction and History

The Code defines a corporation as including "associations, joint-stock companies, and insurance companies". § 7701(a)(3). Thus, certain unincorporated entities— "associations"—potentially are treated as corporations for federal tax purposes, as are corporations routinely organized under state law.

"Associations" historically were defined in terms of their corporate characteristics. In *Morrissey v. Comm'r,* 296 U.S. 344, 56 S.Ct. 289 (1935), the Supreme Court upheld the Service's classification of a business trust as an association taxable as a corporation. The Court identified four characteristics common to corporations which the IRS later incorporated in regulations: (1) continuity of life, (2) centralization of management, (3) limited liability of investors, and (4) free transferability of interests.

At one time, the regulations based on the *Morrissey* resemblance test had an anti-association bias. They were adopted when professionals (doctors, lawyers, accountants, etc.) were prohibited by state law from incorporating but wished to achieve corporate status in order to obtain tax benefits from qualified retirement plans and other employee fringe benefits. Although incorporation was no longer necessary to obtain most of these benefits, the regulations continued to reflect a bias against achieving corporate status.

Beginning in the 1960s, investors in tax shelters sought partnership rather than corporate status. Limited partnerships became the preferred vehicle because they permitted losses to pass through to investors and provided protection for the limited partners against personal liability for debts of the enterprise. The Service argued that limited partnerships should be classified as associations despite its regulations, which had a bias in favor of partnership status. These efforts were unsuccessful. See *Larson v. Comm'r*, 66 T.C. 159 (1976). The restrictions on tax shelter investments that were enacted in the Tax Reform Act of 1986 reduced but did not eliminate the importance of the association versus limited partnership classification issue.

After 1986, many corporate classification battles were motivated by attempts to avoid the double tax imposed on profits of C corporations. The Treasury eventually concluded that state law developments, such as the popularity of limited liability companies, had largely blurred the classic distinctions between corporations and unincorporated entities. In response, new regulations were proposed to make classification for tax purposes essentially elective for unincorporated entities. Those "check the box" regulations were finalized and became effective in 1997, greatly simplifying the law. Under the regulations, new unincorporated entities generally are automatically classified as partnerships unless they elect to be taxed as C corporations. These regulations have been upheld as a valid exercise of the IRS' authority. *Littriello v. United States*, 484 F.3d 372 (6th Cir.2007), *cert. denied*, 552 U.S. 1186, 128 S.Ct. 1290 (2008).

2. The "Check-the-Box" Classification Regulations

a. Introduction

Under the current regulations, if a separate entity is not a trust, it is a "business entity." Reg. § 301.7701–2(a). See II.C.4 at page 60, *infra*, regarding classification of trusts. Certain business entities are automatically classified as corporations for federal tax purposes. These include a business entity organized under a federal or state statute if the statute describes or refers to the entity as "incorporated or as a corporation, body corporate, or body politic." Reg. § 301.7701–2(b)(1). Thus, corporations routinely organized under state corporation statutes are automatically considered corporations for federal tax purposes. A business entity that is taxable as a corporation under some other provision of the Code, such as a publicly traded partnership, also is classified as a corporation for federal tax purposes. Reg. § 301.7701–2(b)(7).

b. Entities with Two or More Members

A business entity with two or more members that is not automatically classified as a corporation is classified as a partnership for federal tax purposes, unless an election is made for the entity to be classified as a corporation. Reg. §§ 301.7701– 2(c)(1), –3(a), –3(b)(1)(i). Consequently, an unincorporated entity, such as a limited liability company or limited partnership, with two or more members will automatically be classified as a partnership unless such an election is made.

c. Business Entities with One Owner

A business entity with only one owner that is not automatically classified as a corporation is disregarded for federal tax purposes, unless an election is made to classify the entity as a corporation. Thus, if such an election is not made for the entity, it will be treated like a sole proprietorship, branch, or division of the owner (a "disregarded entity"). Reg. §§ 301.7701–2(a), –2(c)(2), –3(a), –3(b)(1)(ii).

d. Series LLCs

In some states, an LLC may create one or more "series" within itself ("series LLC"). Each series can be organized as a separate LLC, with its own managers, members, assets, business purpose, debts, etc. Debts of a particular series are enforceable only against that series and a series is not liable for the debts of the LLC generally. One advantage of a series LLC is that it is one entity for state law purposes and costs may be reduced because each series does not have to separately comply with state law. For classification purposes, proposed regulations provide that a series generally is considered to be an entity formed under local law. Prop. Reg. § 301.7701–1(a)(5)(i). As a result, the general classification regulations, including the check-the-box rules, apply to determine whether each series is an entity separate from its owners and its ultimate classification for federal tax purposes.

Example: Properties LLC is a series LLC, with two series each of which owns rental real estate. Series 1 has two owners, and Series 2 has one owner. Under the default check-the-box rules, Series 1 is taxed as a partnership and Series 2 is a disregarded entity, but either series could elect to be taxed as a corporation.

e. Entity Owned as Community Property

An entity that is solely owned by a married couple as community property may be treated by the owners as either a disregarded entity or a partnership unless it elects to be taxed as a corporation. Rev. Proc. 2002–69, 2002–2 C.B. 831.

f. Foreign Entities

The regulations list certain entities formed under foreign laws that will be automatically classified as a corporation (e.g., an Aktiengesellschaft formed in Germany). Reg. § 301.7701–2(b)(8). Unless a contrary election is made, a foreign entity that is not a corporation is classified as (1) a partnership if it has two or more members and at least one member does not have limited liability, (2) a corporation if all members have limited liability, or (3) disregarded as an entity if it has a single owner that does not have limited liability. Reg. § 301.7701–3(b)(2)(i).

g. Election

An entity which wishes to change its classification under the regulations must file an election. The election may be effective up to 75 days before or twelve months after it is filed. Reg. § 301.7701–3(c)(1)(iii). An election must be signed by (1) each member of the entity, including prior members affected by a retroactive election, or (2) an officer, manager, or member authorized to make the election. Reg. § 301.7701–3(c)(2). If an entity makes a classification election, it may not make another election to change its classification for 60 months unless the Service permits the change and 50% of the entity's ownership interests are owned by persons who did not own any interests when the first election was made. Reg. § 301.7701–3(c)(1)(iv).

h. Pre-1997 Entities

In the absence of an election, an entity in existence before 1997 generally retains the same classification that it had under the prior association regulations. An exception is made for an entity with a single owner that claimed to be a partnership. Such an entity will be disregarded as an entity separate from its owner. Reg. § 301.7701–3(b)(3)(i).

3. Publicly Traded Partnerships

"Publicly traded partnerships" are generally classified as corporations. § 7704(a). A "publicly traded partnership" is a partnership whose interests are traded on an established securities market or are readily tradable on a secondary market (or the substantial equivalent thereof). § 7704(b). Section 7704(c) provides an exception for publicly traded partnerships in which 90% or more of the gross income consists of various types of passive investment income.

4. Trusts

The regulations distinguish between "ordinary trusts"—arrangements created by will or inter vivos declaration under which trustees take title to property in order to protect and conserve it for beneficiaries—and "business trusts." Business trusts are formed to carry on a profit-making business rather than for the protection and conservation of property. Reg. § 301.7701–4(a), (b). The fact that a business is cast in trust form will not prevent it from being classified as a business entity. Reg. § 301.7701–4(b). The critical question in determining whether a trust will be classified as a business entity is whether a business objective is present or the trust was established merely to protect and conserve trust property. If a trust is a business entity, it will be classified as a partnership if it has two or more owners or members, unless an election is made for it to be classified as a corporation.

D. Choice of Entity Considerations

1. Publicly Traded Businesses

Publicly traded businesses, whether or not they are incorporated, almost always are taxed as C corporations, except for publicly traded partnerships that qualify for the passive investment income exception (see II.C.3., supra) or in other very specialized situations (e.g., certain real estate investment trusts).

2. Closely Held Businesses

a. In General

A closely held business must choose whether to be taxed as a C corporation or a pass-through entity, such as an S corporation, partnership, or limited liability company. When, as was the case for many years prior to 2018, the highest marginal individual income tax rate is the same as or only slightly higher than the top corporate rate, there is a greater incentive to operate as a pass-through entity to avoid two levels of taxation. The decision is more complex now that the

21% corporate income tax rate is significantly lower than the 37% top individual rate and some owners of pass-through entities may deduct 20% of their share of the entity's qualified business income. Choice of entity decisions also are heavily influenced by the type of business, the owners' desire either to withdraw earnings or reinvest them in the business, the composition of and relationships among the investors, and the exit strategy (e.g., whether and when an initial public offering or sale is contemplated), compensation and fringe benefit considerations, compliance costs, and state and local taxes.

b. C Corporations

The principal disadvantage of a C corporation is the double tax on earnings distributed to shareholders as dividends and, if the corporation holds highly appreciated assets (e.g., real estate), the additional tax cost when the business is sold and liquidated. Historically, C corporations were often used by: (1) closely held businesses able to take advantage of the then lower corporate income tax rates by limiting their taxable income to $75,000 or less; and (2) companies intending to reinvest their earnings for the reasonable needs of the business rather than paying dividends. A C corporation was attractive in those situations because of: (1) the ability to minimize any corporate-level tax or defer the shareholder-level tax for a considerable time, or (2) completely avoid the shareholder-level tax upon the shareholder's deaths. Beginning in 2018, with the reduction of the corporate income tax rate to 21%, some closely held businesses may find it more advantageous to operate as C corporations notwithstanding the double tax, especially if there is no immediate need to withdraw earnings or dividends. Start-up ventures seeking venture capital financing often are formed as C corporations because many institutional investors are more comfortable with the corporate form. Unlike S corporations, C corporations are permitted to have different types of ownership interests (e.g., common stock and convertible preferred stock or debt) and may be able to issue qualified small business stock, enabling individual shareholders to exclude some or all of the capital gain on the sale of their stock. See § 1202. C corporations also can be acquired in a tax-free reorganization or more easily sell equity in an initial public offering.

c. S Corporations

An S Corporation's income is only subject to one level of tax, its losses pass through to its shareholders (subject to various limitations), and S corporations have a simpler and more familiar governance structure than LLCs or partnerships. They can have traditional stock option plans; participate in tax-free corporate reorganizations; and more easily convert to C corporation status in anticipation of an initial public offering. S corporation shareholders who are active in the business also may enjoy employment tax advantages as compared to partners and LLC members. S corporations are less flexible, however, because of strict eligibility restrictions (e.g., no more than 100 shareholders; only one class of stock; inability to make special allocations; no shareholder basis credit for entity debt). In some situations, S corporation shareholders may be eligible to deduct 20% of their pro rata share of the corporation's qualified business income under § 199A.

d. Limited Liability Companies

Limited liability companies avoid entity level tax and, unlike partnerships, provide limited liability to all their owners. LLCs are more flexible than S corporations because they may issue different classes of ownership interests and enjoy other tax benefits of the Subchapter K tax regime (e.g., special allocations, tax-free distributions of appreciated property, and inclusion of entity-level debt in the basis of LLC members' ownership interests). LLCs may pass through losses, which generally may be deducted by owners who are active in the business, and some or all of the individual owners of an LLC may benefit from the 20% deduction for qualified business income under § 199A. Losses are less beneficial, however, to passive investors because of the barriers imposed by the § 469 passive loss limitations, and many large institutional investors, such as pension funds and wealthy charities, do not derive any tax benefit from their allocable share of losses.

e. Limited Partnerships

Limited partnerships enjoy most of the same tax benefits as LLCs but general partners do not have limited liability under state law (although a general partner organized as a corporation or LLC can limit its liability exposure). In the early days of LLCs, some advisors continued to recommend limited partnerships because partnership agreements and governing law were more familiar to them and their clients, but LLCs gradually became more widely used based on the ability of all their owners to enjoy limited liability.

f. Converting from Corporation to Pass-Through Entity

For business ventures already operating as a C corporation, an S corporation election may be a good alternative for moving to a single-tax regime without immediate recognition of gain at either the corporate or shareholder level. Subchapter S, however, has rules that prevent the easy avoidance of the double tax on built-in gains attributable to the period when the business operated as a C corporation. See XV.F.1. at page 315, *infra*. Converting a C corporation to a partnership or LLC requires a complete liquidation, which is a taxable transaction to the corporation and its shareholders.

g. State Tax Considerations

The choice among a limited partnership, LLC or S corporation may be influenced by state and local tax considerations, including whether the entity's resident state provides pass-through tax treatment. Other considerations are whether the state imposes an entity-level tax; the tax treatment of nonresident owners; and overall complexity, such as the need for investors to file nonresident returns in many different states.

E. Review Questions

1. X and Y agree to build an irrigation system to drain surface water from their properties. Is X and Y's activity a "separate entity" for federal tax purposes?

2. If A and B form a limited liability company or limited partnership to conduct their business venture, how will the entity be classified for federal tax purposes? What if A alone forms a limited liability company to operate a business?

Chapter III

The C Corporation as a Taxable Entity

■ ANALYSIS

A. The Corporate Income Tax

1. Introduction

A C corporation is a separate taxable entity. It selects its own taxable year and accounting methods, computes its taxable income under general tax principles, files a corporate income tax return (Form 1120) and pays tax at the rates specified in § 11.

2. Rates

Beginning in 2018, C corporations are taxed at a flat 21% rate. § 11(b). Under prior law, C corporations, except for certain "personal service corporations," were subject to a four-step graduated rate structure which peaked at 35% for taxable income over $10 million. The lower graduated rates were phased out for taxable income over $100,000.

3. Determination of Taxable Income

The taxable income of a C corporation is its gross income minus allowable deductions. § 63(a). Corporations are not required to determine adjusted gross income and are not entitled to any "standard deduction." Income and deductions are determined under general tax principles, with the exceptions and special problems discussed below.

a. Deductions: In General

Corporations are not entitled to certain personal deductions allowed to individuals, such as the medical expense deduction. Virtually all of a corporation's routine expenses are deductible either as business expenses under § 162, losses under § 165 or depreciation under § 168. Some other deduction rules applicable to corporations are:

1) Business losses, including casualty losses, are deductible without limitation. § 165(a).

2) All bad debts are fully deductible as business bad debts. § 166(a).

3) Charitable contributions generally must be paid within the taxable year, and a corporation's charitable deduction is limited to 10% of taxable income (determined before the dividends received deduction or the net operating loss deduction). § 170(b)(2). A corporation on the accrual method of accounting may deduct a contribution authorized by its board of directors during the taxable year if the contribution is made by the 15th day of the third month after the close of the prior year. § 170(a)(2).

4) The § 465 at-risk limitations apply only to "closely-held C corporations" as defined in § 542(a)(2)—i.e., corporations where five or fewer individuals own directly or indirectly (through attribution rules) more than 50% of the stock (by value) at any time during the last half of the taxable year. § 465(a)(1)(B).

5) The § 469 passive loss limitations apply only to "closely-held C corporations" (see definition above) and personal service corporations. § 469(a)(2). A closely-held C corporation (other than a personal service corporation) may deduct passive losses against net active business income but not against portfolio income (such as dividends, interest and capital gains). § 469(e)(2).

6) Annual compensation in excess of $1 million paid by a publicly held corporation to its chief executive officer, principal financial officer, and its three other most highly compensated employees is not deductible. § 162(m).

b. The Dividends Received Deduction

Corporate shareholders may deduct 50% of dividends received from other domestic corporations. § 243(a)(1). This deduction reduces the effective corporate tax rate on dividends from 21% to 10.5% (21% x the 50% includible portion). A corporate shareholder may deduct 65% of dividends received if it owns 20% or more of the stock (by vote and value) of the payor corporation. § 243(c). Dividends paid by one corporation to another member of its "affiliated group" (see VI.F.1., at page 122, *infra*) qualify for a 100% dividends received deduction. § 243(a)(3), (b).

c. Deduction for Domestic Production Activities

Prior to 2018, corporations and other U.S. taxpayers engaged in domestic production activities could deduct 9% of the lesser of their "qualified production activities income" or taxable income without regard to the deduction. § 199(a)(1). § 199(a). This deduction was repealed by the Tax Cuts and Jobs Act, effective for tax years beginning after December 31, 2017.

d. Capital Gains and Losses

Corporate capital gains are taxed at the same 21% rate as ordinary income. Corporations may deduct capital losses only to the extent of capital gains. Any excess may be carried back for three years and carried forward for five years. §§ 1211(a); 1212(a). Corporate shareholders are not eligible for the § 1202 exclusion for capital gains from certain small business stock. § 1202(a).

4. Taxable Year

a. In General

Subject to a few limitations discussed below, C corporations generally may adopt either a calendar year or a fiscal year. § 441.

b. Personal Service Corporations

"Personal service corporations" must use a calendar year unless they can show a business purpose for using a fiscal year. § 441(i)(1). A "personal service corporation" is a corporation whose principal activity is the performance of services that are substantially performed by "employee-owners" who collectively own more than 10% (by value) of the corporation's stock. §§ 269A(b)(1); 441(i)(2).

c. Fiscal Year Election for Personal Service Corporations

A personal service corporation that otherwise would be required to use a calendar year may elect under § 444 to adopt a fiscal year having a "deferral period" of not more than three months (i.e., a fiscal year ending September 30, October 31 or November 30) provided the corporation makes certain minimum distributions (e.g., of compensation) to employee-owners during the portion of the employee's fiscal year that ends on December 31. § 280H. If these minimum distributions are not made, some deductions must be deferred. Id.

d. S Corporations

See XV.D.2.b., at page 300, *infra*.

5. Accounting Method

C corporations generally must use the accrual method of accounting. § 448(a). The cash method is available, however, to C corporations whose average annual gross receipts for a three-year measuring period do not exceed $25 million, indexed for inflation for tax years beginning after December 31, 2018. § 448(b), (c).

6. Loss Disallowance Rules

Losses from sales or exchanges of property between a shareholder and a more-than-50%-owned corporation may not be deducted. § 267(a)(1), (b)(2). Ownership for this purpose is determined after application of attribution rules in § 267(c).

7. Forced Matching Rules

An accrual method corporation may not deduct payments (e.g., compensation, interest or rent) made to a cash method owner-employee until the recipient includes the amount in income. § 267(a)(2). For this purpose, an "owner-employee" is a person who owns directly or indirectly 50% or more of the payor corporation except that, in the case of personal service corporations, the forced matching rules apply to payments to any owner-employee, regardless of percentage ownership. Id.

8. Credits

Corporations qualify for a variety of tax credits, including the foreign tax credit, the rehabilitation and energy credit, the work opportunity credit, the employer credit for paid family and medical leave, and the credit for research and development expenditures. §§ 27; 41; 45S; 46–48; 51.

B. The Corporate Alternative Minimum Tax

For many years, C corporations generally were subject to the corporate alternative minimum tax ("AMT"), which generally was payable to the extent that it exceeded a corporation's regular tax liability. § 55(a). Certain "small" corporations were exempt from the corporate AMT. The corporate AMT was repealed for tax years beginning after December 31, 2017, with transitional rules for corporations with AMT credits under prior law.

C. Disregard of the Corporate Entity

1. Introduction

Taxpayers sometimes argue that an entity formed as a corporation under state law should not be taxed as a corporation. Such corporations may be formed for the sole purpose of obtaining loans at rates that would violate state usury laws if the loan had been made to an individual. The taxpayer may wish to avoid the separate corporate income tax and attribute income or losses of the entity to the shareholders or some other taxpayer. Most cases reject attempts by taxpayers to disregard the corporate entity unless the corporation is clearly shown to be a mere dummy or agent.

2. The Business Activity Test

A corporation generally will be recognized as a taxable entity distinct from its shareholders if it engages in any business activity even if it has only one shareholder who exercises total control over its affairs. *Moline Properties v. Comm'r*, 319 U.S. 436, 63 S.Ct. 1132 (1943).

3. The *National Carbide* Factors

In *National Carbide Corp. v. Comm'r*, 336 U.S. 422, 69 S.Ct. 726 (1949), the Supreme Court enunciated six factors to be considered in deciding whether a corporate entity could be ignored because it was merely an agent:

a.   Whether the corporation operates in the name and for the account of the principal.

b.   Whether the corporation binds the principal by its actions.

c.   Whether the corporation transmits money received to the principal.

d.   Whether receipt of income is attributable to the services of employees of the principal and to assets belonging to the principal.

e.   If the corporation is a true agent, whether its relations with its principal are dependent upon the fact that it is owned by the principal.

f.   Whether the corporation's business purpose is the carrying on of the normal duties of an agent.

The corporations involved in *National Carbide* were held not to be agents because they represented to outsiders that they manufactured and sold products and they had substantial assets and many employees. Subsequent cases often relied on the fifth *National Carbide* factor in holding that a corporation which is not compensated and is owned by one or more of its principals was not a true agent. See, e.g., *Frink v. Comm'r*, 798 F.2d 106 (4th Cir.1986), vac'd, 485 U.S. 973, 108 S.Ct. 1264 (1988).

4. The *Bollinger* Factors

In *Comm'r v. Bollinger,* 485 U.S. 340, 108 S.Ct. 1173 (1988), the Supreme Court placed less importance on the *National Carbide* factors in holding that a corporation which held record title to real property as an agent for its shareholders was not the true owner of the property for tax purposes. The Court rejected the Service's contention that *National Carbide* required a corporation to have an arm's-length relationship with its shareholders before it could be recognized as their agent for tax purposes. It concluded that an agency relationship could be found if:

a.   The relationship with respect to a particular asset (e.g., real estate) is set forth in a written agreement at the time the asset is acquired.

b.   The corporation functions as an agent with respect to the asset for all purposes.

c.   The corporation's agency status is disclosed in all dealings with third parties relating to the asset.

D. Review Question

X Corp., an accrual basis taxpayer, had the following results for 2019, its first year of business:

Gross Income from Operations	$230,000
Operating Expenses	$ 85,000
Long-Term Capital Loss	$ 40,000
§ 1231 Gain—Sale of Land	$ 30,000
Bad Debt	$ 10,000
Dividend from 100% Subsidiary	$ 20,000
Dividend from IBM Corp.	$ 5,000
Depreciation	$ 45,000
Municipal Bond Interest	$ 37,500

Determine X Corp.'s:

(a) Taxable income for the year.

(b) Regular tax liability.

Chapter IV

Formation of a Corporation

■ ANALYSIS

A. Introduction

Without a nonrecognition provision, a taxpayer who transfers property to a newly formed corporation in exchange for stock would recognize gain or loss measured by the difference between the fair market value of the stock received and the taxpayer's adjusted basis in the transferred property. § 1001(a), (c). In theory, a corporation also might realize and recognize gain on the issuance of its stock in exchange for property. At the shareholder level, § 351 overrides these general tax principles by providing that shareholders do not recognize gain or loss on certain transfers of property to a controlled (i.e., 80% owned) corporation. Section 351 applies to transfers to newly formed C and S corporations (including the creation of corporate subsidiaries) and transfers of property to preexisting corporations by their controlling shareholders. At the corporate level, § 1032(a) provides that a corporation does not recognize gain or loss when it receives money or property in exchange for its stock. The rationale is that these transactions are mere changes in the form of the shareholders' investment and are thus inappropriate taxable events. Like other nonrecognition provisions, § 351 is accompanied by rules that preserve any unrecognized gain or loss in the shareholder's stock basis (§ 358) and in the corporation's basis in the transferred property (§ 362). These basis rules, however, include some limitations to prevent the duplication of losses (§ 362(e)).

B. Requirements for Nonrecognition Under § 351

The requirements for complete nonrecognition of gain or loss under § 351(a) are: (1) one or more persons (including individuals, corporations, partnerships and other entities) must transfer "property" to a corporation; (2) the property must be transferred solely in exchange for "stock" of the transferee corporation; and (3) the transferors, as a group, must be in "control" (as defined in § 368(c)) of the corporation "immediately after the exchange." For convenience, the transferee corporation will be referred to as "Newco" throughout this chapter.

1. "Property"

"Property" includes cash, inventory, accounts receivable, patents and other intangibles such as goodwill and industrial know-how. Stock issued for past, present or future services rendered to Newco will not be treated as having been issued in return for property. § 351(d)(1); Reg. § 1.351–1(a)(1)(i). The performance of services may result in the creation of an intangible right (e.g., a contract to develop real estate) that qualifies as § 351 property. See IV.B.6.a., at pages 75–76, *infra,* for special problems involving the receipt of stock for services.

2. "Transfer"

All substantial rights in the property must be transferred to Newco. A limited license of property (e.g., a nonexclusive license to use technology) does not satisfy the "transfer" requirement, and any Newco stock received for the license is considered royalty income. One court has held that the "transfer" requirement is met if stock is issued for a perpetual nonexclusive license. *E.I. Du Pont de Nemours & Co. v. United States,* 471 F.2d 1211 (Ct.Cl.1973).

3. Solely in Exchange for "Stock"

a. In General

"Stock" represents an equity ownership interest in a corporation; it does not include stock rights, warrants, or convertible debt securities. Reg. § 1.351–1(a)(1). Any corporate interest received by a transferor of property from Newco that is not "stock" is treated as "other property"—"boot" in tax jargon. For the treatment of boot under § 351, see IV.C., at pages 80–83, *infra*.

b. Nonqualified Preferred Stock

"Nonqualified preferred stock" is treated as "other property" (i.e., boot) rather than stock for purposes of § 351. § 351(g)(1). "Nonqualified preferred stock" is preferred stock (i.e., stock that is limited and preferred as to dividends and does not participate in corporate growth to any significant extent) with any of the following debt-like characteristics:

(1) The shareholder has the right to require the issuing corporation or a "related person" (e.g., certain family members or controlled entities) to redeem or purchase the stock;

(2) The corporate issuer (or a related affiliate) is required to redeem or purchase the stock;

(3) The issuer (or a related affiliate) has the right to redeem or purchase the stock and, as of the issue date, it is more likely than not that such right will be exercised; or

(4) The stock's dividend rate is variable—e.g., set by reference to market interest rates, commodity prices or similar indices.

§ 351(g)(2)(A). The first three of the above characteristics apply only if the right or obligation to redeem or purchase may be exercised within the 20-year period beginning on the issue date of the stock and such right or obligation is not subject to a contingency which, as of the issue date, makes remote the likelihood of the redemption or purchase. § 351(g)(2)(B). Stock is not treated as participating in corporate growth to any significant extent unless there is a "real and meaningful likelihood" that the shareholder will actually participate in the corporation's earnings and growth. § 351(g)(3)(A). If there is not a real and meaningful likelihood that dividends beyond any limitation or preference will actually be paid, the *possibility* of such payments is disregarded in determining whether stock is limited and preferred as to dividends. Id.

Although nonqualified preferred stock is treated as boot for gain recognition purposes, the legislative history of § 351(g) states that it is still treated as stock for purposes of the § 351(a) control test until regulations are issued that provide otherwise (as of early 2019, none had been issued). H.R.Rep. No. 105–220, 105th Cong., 2d Sess. 561 (1997).

4. "Control"

To be in "control" of Newco, the transferors of property collectively must own at least 80% of the total combined voting power of all classes of stock entitled to vote and at least 80% of each class of nonvoting stock. § 368(c). Some transferors may receive voting stock while others receive nonvoting stock as long as all the transferors of property, as a group, own at least 80% of each class of stock immediately after the exchange. Simultaneous exchanges are not required where the rights of the parties have been "previously defined" and the agreement proceeds with an "expedition consistent with orderly procedure." Reg. § 1.351–1(a)(1).

Example (1): Upon the formation of Newco, A, B and C each transfer appreciated property. A receives 50 shares of voting common stock, B receives 50 shares of nonvoting common stock and C receives 50 shares of nonvoting preferred stock that is not nonqualified preferred stock. The control test is satisfied because the property transferors, as a group, own at least 80% of each class of Newco stock.

Example (2): Same facts as Example (1), except that C receives her nonvoting preferred stock solely in exchange for services rendered to Newco. C is not a transferor of property and may not be counted in testing for control. Because transferors of property do not own 80% or more of *each* class of nonvoting stock, the transaction does not qualify under § 351(a). A and B must recognize gain or loss on their property transfers. C recognizes ordinary income on her receipt of stock for services.

5. "Immediately After the Exchange"

The transferors of property must have control of Newco "immediately after the exchange." When a member of the transferor control group disposes of stock shortly after an incorporation exchange, an issue arises as to whether the control test should be applied before or after the disposition. Resolution of this issue is often imprecise because it requires application of the judicially created step transaction doctrine (see I.E.2., at page 53, *supra*).

a. Binding Agreements to Dispose of Stock: In General

If in a taxable transaction a shareholder disposes of stock received in exchange for property pursuant to a prearranged binding agreement entered into prior to an incorporation exchange, the control test is applied after the stock disposition. A disposition of more than 20% of voting power or more than 20% of any class of nonvoting stock will cause a loss of control because the person ultimately acquiring the stock was not a transferor of property to Newco.

Example: On the formation of Newco, A transfers land with a basis of $10,000 and a value of $60,000, in exchange for 60 shares (60%) of Newco common stock, and B transfers equipment with a basis and value of $40,000, in exchange for 40 shares (40%). Two months later, pursuant to a prearranged binding agreement, B transfers all her Newco stock to C for $40,000 cash. The control test is applied after the transfer to C. Since C was not a transferor of property to Newco, her ownership of Newco stock will not be counted in testing for control. A only owns 60% of Newco stock immediately after the exchange and thus the 80% control test is not satisfied. A must recognize $50,000 gain on the transfer of the land. See *Intermountain Lumber Co. v. Comm'r*, 65 T.C. 1025 (1976); Rev. Rul. 79–70, 1979–1 C.B. 144. If B's disposition had not been pursuant to a preexisting binding commitment, a loss of § 351 control normally would not result unless the original transfers to Newco and the subsequent disposition of Newco stock were mutually interdependent—i.e., the legal relations created by the first step would have been fruitless without completion of all the steps. See *American Bantam Car Co. v. Comm'r,* 11 T.C. 397 (1948), aff'd per curiam, 177 F.2d 513 (3d Cir.1949), cert. denied, 339 U.S. 920, 70 S.Ct. 622 (1950).

b. Binding Agreement to Dispose of Stock in Nontaxable Transaction

A transfer of assets to a newly formed corporation ("Newco") in exchange for all of its stock satisfies the "control immediately after the exchange" requirement even though, pursuant to a prearranged binding commitment, the transferor ("A") loses control by immediately transferring the Newco stock to Oldco, another corporation already engaged in the same line of business, in exchange for Oldco stock simultaneously with the transfer of assets to Oldco by its sole shareholder ("B") in exchange for additional shares of Oldco stock. The Service ruled that A's transfer to Newco satisfies the control requirement on these facts because the two transactions, viewed independently, each qualify for § 351 nonrecognition. The rationale is that treating a qualifying transfer of property in exchange for stock followed by a prearranged *nontaxable* disposition of the stock is not inconsistent with the policy of § 351. Rev. Rul. 2003–51, 2003–1 C.B. 938.

Example: A and B (unrelated to A) are each engaged in the same line of business. A's business is worth $40 and B's business, conducted through a wholly owned corporation, Oldco, is worth $30. A and B desire to consolidate their businesses in a new corporation with a holding company structure. To that end, A transfers his business assets to Newco, a newly formed corporation, in exchange for all of Newco's stock, and then A immediately contributes the Newco stock to Oldco in exchange for Oldco stock. B simultaneously contributes $30 cash to Oldco in exchange for additional Oldco stock. Oldco then transfers its original assets and the $30 of cash (total value of $60) to Newco. After that final transaction, A and B own 40% and 60%, respectively, of Oldco, which owns 100% of the stock of Newco, and Newco holds all the operating assets of the consolidated businesses. Even though A loses control of Newco as a result of these prearranged transactions, the Service will not apply the step transaction doctrine, and A's initial transfer of assets to Newco qualifies for nonrecognition under § 351.

c. Voluntary Donative Dispositions of Stock

A voluntary disposition of stock—e.g., a gift—after an otherwise qualified § 351 transfer will not cause the transaction to fail the control requirement. See *Wilgard Realty Co. v. Comm'r,* 127 F.2d 514 (2d Cir.1942), cert. denied, 317 U.S. 655, 63 S.Ct. 52 (1942). The result is likely the same even if Newco issues the stock directly to the transferor's donee. *D'Angelo Associates, Inc. v. Comm'r,* 70 T.C. 121 (1978).

Example: On the formation of Newco, A and B each transfer appreciated property in exchange for 50 shares of Newco common stock. Two days later, B gives 25 shares to his daughter, C. The transfers qualify for nonrecognition under § 351(a) because control is determined immediately after the incorporation transfers and before the gift to C.

d. Corporate Transferors

In determining "control," the fact that a corporate transferor distributes part or all of the Newco stock that it receives to its shareholders is not taken into account. § 351(c).

6. Special Problems

a. Stock for Services

1) Taxation of the Service Provider

Stock issued for services is not considered as issued in return for property. § 351(d)(1); Reg. § 1.351–1(a)(1)(i). A service provider recognizes ordinary income under § 61 on the value of any stock received from Newco for past, present or future services. The timing of the income is determined under § 83. If the stock is subject to a substantial risk of forfeiture or is not transferable, the service provider is taxed on the fair market value of the stock at the time the restrictions lapse less the amount (if any) paid for the stock. § 83(a). The service provider, however, may elect under § 83(b) to be taxed on the fair market value of the stock at the time of transfer less any amount paid. In that event, no additional income is recognized when the restrictions lapse, and no loss (except for any amount paid) is allowed if the stock is forfeited. Reg. § 1.83–2(a)(1). In either case, the service provider's basis for the stock is the amount paid plus any amount included in income. Reg. § 1.83–4(b)(1).

> ***Example:*** On the formation of Newco in Year 1, Executive receives 200 shares of Newco stock (value—$50,000) in exchange for $1,000 cash and future services. The stock is subject to a substantial risk of forfeiture and will not vest until Year 5. Assume that the stock will be worth $200,000 in Year 5. Under § 83(a), Executive has no income in Year 1 and $199,000 ordinary income (the value of the stock less the $1,000 paid by Executive in Year 1) in Year 5, and his basis in the stock is $200,000. If Executive makes the § 83(b) election, he has $49,000 ordinary income in Year 1, his basis in the stock is $50,000, and he has no additional income when the restrictions lapse in Year 5. If Executive sells the stock in Year 5 after having made an election under § 83(b), he recognizes $150,000 long-term capital gain. If he forfeits the stock in Year 3, Executive may only deduct the amount he paid ($1,000) as a long-term capital loss.

2) Deduction to Corporation

If a corporation issues stock for services rendered to the corporation, it may deduct as a § 162(a) business expense the amount of ordinary income that is taxable to the service provider at the time that income is recognized unless the nature of the services requires the corporation to deduct or amortize (e.g., organizational services) or capitalize (e.g., services related to the construction or acquisition of an asset) the expense. § 83(h); Reg. § 1.83–6.

3)   Service Provider Not a Transferor of Property

A shareholder who receives stock solely for services is not considered a transferor of property. If more than 20% of any class of stock is issued to a service provider, the entire transaction fails to qualify under § 351 because transferors of property do not have control immediately after the exchange. As a result, even shareholders who receive solely stock in exchange for appreciated property must recognize gain and shareholders who receive stock for property with a built-in loss may recognize that loss.

4)   Stock Received for Services and Property

A person who receives stock in exchange for both property and services recognizes ordinary income to the extent of the stock received for services but generally is still considered as a transferor of property and may count all the stock received for purposes of the 80% control requirement—unless the value of the property transferred is of relatively small value relative to the stock received for services and the primary purpose of the property transfer is to qualify the exchanges of other transferors for nonrecognition. Reg. § 1.351–1(a)(1)(ii). Under the Service's ruling guidelines, property is not considered to be "of relatively small value" if it equals at least 10% of the value of stock received for services. Rev. Proc. 77–37, 1977–2 C.B. 568.

Example (1):   On the formation of Newco, A receives 70 shares of Newco common stock (value—$70,000) in exchange for land (value—$70,000; basis—$20,000), and B receives 30 shares (value—$30,000) in exchange for $1,000 cash and services. The stock received by B for cash is of relatively small value compared to the stock received for services, and thus B is not a transferor of property. The only transferor of property is A, who is not in "control." The transaction does not qualify under § 351.

Example (2):   Same facts as Example (1), except B receives 5 shares (value—$5,000) in exchange for $5,000 cash and 25 shares (value—$25,000) in exchange for services. Because the cash transferred ($5,000) exceeds 10% of the value of the stock received for services (10% × $25,000, or $2,500), the cash is not considered to be of relatively small value. B is thus treated as a transferor of property, and all 30 shares received by B are counted in testing for control. The transaction qualifies under § 351(a), but B still recognizes ordinary income on the stock received for services.

b.   Disproportionate Transfers

Section 351 does not require shareholders to receive Newco stock in proportion to the value of the property they transfer. In disproportionate transfer situations, the shareholders are first treated as having received stock in proportion to the value of the transferred property and then as having retransferred the stock among themselves. The tax consequences of the entire transaction are determined in accordance with its "true nature"—e.g., as a gift, payment of compensation or satisfaction of a debt. Reg. § 1.351–1(b)(1), (b)(2) Example (1).

Example: On the formation of Newco, A transfers appreciated property worth $6,000 in exchange for 40 shares of stock and B transfers appreciated property worth $4,000 in exchange for 60 shares. The transaction qualifies under § 351. A and B are first treated as having received 60 and 40 shares, respectively, and then A is treated as having transferred 20 shares to B. If A and B are related, it is likely that A will be treated as having made a gift to B. If B had rendered past services to A, the transfer of 20 shares may be treated as the payment of compensation from A to B; B is taxed on the value of the 20 shares received as compensation and takes a fair market value basis for those shares, and A realizes gain on the transfer of the 20 shares to satisfy his obligation to B.

c. Recapture Provisions

Section 351(a) overrides the recapture of depreciation provisions. See, e.g., § 1245(b)(3). The potential recapture gain is preserved in Newco's basis in the asset. A transferor who receives boot (i.e., property other than stock in the controlled corporation) must recapture depreciation to the extent of any recognized gain. See IV.C.1., at page 80, *infra.*

d. Installment Obligations

Section 453B(a) generally requires a taxpayer to recognize gain on any disposition of an installment obligation. If an installment obligation (e.g., a note received by a taxpayer on an installment sale of property) is transferred to the controlled corporation in a § 351(a) transaction, however, no gain is recognized. Reg. § 1.453–9(c)(2); Prop. Reg. § 1.453B–1(c).

e. Investment Companies

Transfers to an "investment company" do not qualify for nonrecognition. § 351(e). The purpose of this rule is to prevent unrelated taxpayers from achieving tax-free diversification by transferring appreciated portfolio securities in exchange for stock of a newly formed pooled investment vehicle. For details on this exception, see Reg. § 1.351–1(c).

7. Basis and Holding Period: General Rules

a. Shareholder's Basis in Newco Stock

If property is transferred in a § 351 transaction solely in exchange for Newco stock, the transferor's basis in the stock received will equal his basis in the transferred property immediately prior to the exchange. § 358(a)(1). (This is known in tax jargon as an "exchanged" or "substituted" basis.) If a transferor receives more than one class of Newco stock, the aggregate basis determined under § 358(a)(1) is allocated among all classes of stock received in proportion to the fair market values of each class. § 358(b); Reg. § 1.358–2(a)(2).

b.   Shareholder's Holding Period in Newco Stock

A transferor's holding period for Newco stock received in a § 351 transaction in exchange for a capital or § 1231 asset includes the holding period of transferred property. § 1223(1). (This is known as "tacking.") The holding period of stock received in exchange for an ordinary income asset (or for services rendered) begins on the date of the exchange. If stock is received for a combination of capital and ordinary income assets, each share of Newco stock takes a split holding period allocated in proportion to the fair market values of the transferred assets. Rev. Rul. 85–164, 1985–2 C.B. 117.

c.   Corporation's Basis and Holding Period in Transferred Assets

In general, Newco's basis in the assets transferred in a § 351 transaction is the same as the transferor's basis. § 362(a). (This is known as a "transferred" or "carryover" basis.) Newco's holding period for the transferred property includes the transferor's holding period, without regard to whether the property was a capital or § 1231 asset in the transferor's hands. § 1223(2).

Example (1):   On the formation of Newco, A transfers land (a § 1231 asset) held long-term with a basis of $10,000 and a value of $60,000, and inventory with a basis of $30,000 and a value of $40,000, in exchange for 100 shares of Newco common stock with a value of $100,000. The transaction qualifies under § 351(a). A's basis in the Newco stock is $40,000, which is the sum of A's bases in the land and inventory. § 358(a). Because A received the Newco stock in exchange for a § 1231 asset and an ordinary income asset, each share takes a split holding period: 60% includes A's holding period in the land and 40% commences as of the date of the exchange. § 1223(1). If A were to sell all the stock on the next day for $100,000, A would recognize $36,000 long-term capital gain and $24,000 short-term capital gain. Newco takes a $10,000 basis in the land and a $30,000 basis in the inventory under § 362(a) and a tacked holding period in each asset under § 1223(2).

Example (2):   Assume the same facts as in Example (1), except A receives 80 shares of Newco common stock and 20 shares of Newco preferred stock. A's aggregate basis in both classes of stock is $40,000, which is allocated in proportion to the fair market value of each class: $32,000 (80%) to the common and $8,000 (20%) to the preferred. Each share of common and preferred stock has a split holding period, 60% tacked from the land and 40% commencing on the date of the exchange.

8.   Limitations on Transfer of Built-in Losses

a.   In General

If property with a "net built-in loss" is transferred in a § 351 transaction or as a contribution to capital, the transferee corporation's aggregate adjusted basis of such transferred property is limited to its fair market value immediately after the transfer. § 362(e)(2)(A). The limitation is applied on a transferor-by-transferor basis rather than to an aggregated group of transferors. Reg. § 1.362–4(b). The policy for this rule is to prevent the duplication of economic losses for tax purposes when property with a built-in loss is transferred to a corporation in a § 351 transaction.

b. Net Built-in Loss

Transferred property has a "net built-in loss" when its aggregate adjusted basis exceeds the fair market value of the property immediately after the transfer. Reg. § 1.362–4(g)(3). Any gain recognized by a transferor that increases the transferee corporation's basis in the transferred property is taken into account in determining whether that property has a net built-in loss. Reg. § 1.362–4(h) Example 6.

c. Multiple Properties Transferred

If multiple properties are transferred in the same transaction, some with built-in gains and others with built-in losses, t § 362(e)(2) basis limitation only applies when there is a *net* built-in loss. § 362(e)(2)(A)(ii). If there is a net built-in loss and more than one property with a built-in loss is transferred, the aggregate basis reduction is allocated among those properties in proportion to the relative amount of built-in loss in each property. § 362(e)(2)(B); Reg. § 1.362–4(g)(5).

d. Election to Reduce Basis

As an alternative to reducing the corporation's basis in the transferred assets, the transferor and transferee may jointly elect to reduce the transferor's basis in the stock received in the exchange to its fair market value. § 362(e)(2)(C). The stock basis reduction is the amount of asset basis reduction that would have been required under § 362(e)(2) if the election had not been made. Reg. § 1.362–4(d)(2).

e. Importation of Built-in Loss

Section 362(e)(1) is a narrower loss limitation rule that applies in the case of an "importation" of a built-in loss, which generally occurs on a transfer of loss property where the transferee is subject to U.S. tax but the transferor (e.g., a foreign corporation) is not. In such cases, the transferee's basis in each property acquired is limited to its fair market value immediately after the transaction. Section 362(e)(1) is primarily relevant in cross-border transactions and does not apply to § 351 transactions where the transferee and transferor are both subject to U.S. tax.

Example: On the formation of Newco, A transfers land (a capital asset) held long-term with a basis of $180,000 and a value of $100,000 in exchange for 100 shares of Newco common stock with a value of $100,000. The transaction qualifies under § 351(a), and A may not recognize the $80,000 loss on the land. A's basis in the Newco stock is $180,000 (the same as A's basis in the land), and A's holding period in the stock includes the time that A held the land. §§ 358(a); 1223(1). Newco's basis in the land is limited to its $100,000 fair market value. § 362(e)(2). Alternatively, A and Newco may elect to limit A's basis in the Newco stock to $100,000 and, if so, Newco may take a transferred basis of $180,000 in the land. § 362(e)(2)(C).

C. Treatment of Boot

1. In General

If a transferor receives property other than stock—e.g., cash, corporate debt securities, nonqualified preferred stock, or other property (collectively known as "boot")—in a § 351 transaction, § 351(b) provides that the transferor's realized gain is recognized to the extent of the cash and the fair market value of any other boot received. Even if a transferor receives boot, however, no loss may be recognized. § 351(b)(2). The character of any gain recognized is determined by reference to the character of the transferred asset to which the gain is attributable, taking into account the depreciation recapture provisions (e.g. § 1245) and other applicable characterization rules (e.g. § 1239). As explained below (see IV.C.4., at page 82, *infra*), gain triggered by the receipt of boot results in increases to the shareholder's basis in the stock received and the corporation's basis in the transferred property.

Example (1):   On the formation of Newco, A transfers $50,000 cash in exchange for 50 shares of Newco stock, and B transfers investment land with a basis of $10,000 and a fair market value of $50,000 in exchange for 40 shares of stock and $10,000 cash. The cash received by B is boot. B's realized gain on the land is $40,000, of which $10,000 must be recognized as capital gain under § 351(b).

Example (2):   Assume the same facts as Example (1), except B receives 5 shares of Newco stock and $45,000 cash. Although B receives $45,000 of boot, B's recognized gain is limited to the $40,000 gain realized on the land.

2. Allocation of Boot

When several assets are transferred in exchange for a combination of stock and boot, the boot is allocated among the transferred assets in proportion to their relative fair market values. Realized gain on a transferred asset is recognized to the extent of the boot allocable to that asset, but no realized losses may be recognized under § 351(b). Rev. Rul. 68–55, 1968–1 C.B. 140. Thus, boot allocated to a loss asset will not cause recognition of loss.

Example (1):   On the formation of Newco, A transfers $50,000 cash in exchange for $50,000 of stock, and B transfers a capital asset with a basis of $5,000 and a value of $30,000, and equipment with a basis of $5,000 and a value of $20,000 (and $10,000 of potential § 1245 recapture), in exchange for $40,000 of stock and $10,000 cash. As to B, the $10,000 of cash boot is allocated between the capital asset and the equipment in proportion to the relative fair market values of those assets—i.e., $6,000 (60%) to the capital asset and $4,000 (40%) to the equipment. B recognizes $6,000 of capital gain on the capital asset and $4,000 of ordinary income on the equipment.

Example (2):   Assume the same facts as in Example (1), except that B's basis in the $30,000 capital asset is $40,000 rather than $5,000. The $10,000 cash boot is still allocated $6,000 to the capital asset and $4,000 to the equipment. B recognizes $4,000 of ordinary income on the equipment but may not recognize any of the realized loss on the capital asset.

3. Installment Boot

A transferor who receives boot in the form of a Newco debt instrument may be allowed to defer recognition of any § 351(b) gain under § 453. Application of the installment sale rules to a § 351 transaction requires bifurcating the exchange into two parts: a § 351(a) nonrecognition exchange to the extent of the stock ("permitted property") received by the transferor and a taxable installment sale to the extent of the boot received. The basis of the transferred property is first allocated to the nonrecognition exchange, and any remaining basis (known as "excess basis") is allocated to the installment sale. Cf. § 453(f)(6); Prop. Reg. § 1.453–1(f)(1), (3)(ii). Recapture gain and gain attributable to dispositions of dealer property do not qualify for deferral. § 453(b)(2), (i), (*l*).

Example (1): A, the sole shareholder of Newco, transfers Gainacre (value—$100,000; basis—$10,000) in exchange for 80 shares of Newco stock (value—$80,000), $5,000 cash and a $15,000 Newco note providing for market rate interest and a single principal payment in five years. A recognizes $20,000 gain under § 351(b); the timing of that gain is determined under § 453. Under the regulations, A is treated as having exchanged $80,000 of Gainacre for Newco stock; A's entire $10,000 basis in Gainacre is allocated to this nonrecognition transaction. The remaining $20,000 of Gainacre (with a zero basis) is treated as having been exchanged for $5,000 cash and the $15,000 note in a § 453 installment sale. For § 453 purposes, the "selling price," "total contract price" and "gross profit" are all $20,000, and the gross profit fraction is 100%. (The fraction always will be 100% if the boot received is less than the realized gain.) Payments in the year of sale are limited to the $5,000 cash. A recognizes $5,000 gain in year one and the remaining $15,000 gain when the note is paid in year five.

Example (2): Assume the same facts as in Example (1), except that A's basis in Gainacre is $90,000 rather than $10,000. A's realized gain is $10,000. Although A receives $20,000 of boot, his recognized gain is limited to $10,000. A is treated as having exchanged $80,000 of Gainacre in exchange for Newco stock; $80,000 of his $90,000 basis in Gainacre is allocated to this nonrecognition transaction. The remaining $10,000—A's "excess basis" in Gainacre is allocated to the installment sale. For § 453 purposes, the selling price and total contract price are $20,000, the gross profit is $10,000, and the gross profit percentage is 50%. A recognizes $2,500 gain in year one ($5,000 cash × 50%) and $7,500 gain (15,000 × 50%) when the $15,000 note is paid in year five.

Example (3): Assume the same facts as in Example (1), except Gainacre is depreciable equipment and the entire realized gain would be recaptured as ordinary income under § 1245. None of the recognized gain may be deferred under § 453.

4. Basis

a. Shareholder's Basis

1) A transferor who receives Newco stock and boot in a § 351 transaction determines his basis in the Newco stock according to the following formula: (1) transferor's basis in property transferred, minus (2) amount of cash and fair market value of boot (Newco debt and other nonstock property) received, plus (3) gain recognized by transferor. § 358(a)(1). If the transferor receives more than one class of Newco stock, the aggregate basis determined above is allocated among the various classes in proportion to the fair market value of each class. § 358(b); Reg. § 1.358–2(a)(2).

2) The increase for gain recognized by the transferor is made at the time of transfer even though the gain may be deferred under the § 453 installment method. Prop. Reg. § 1.453–1(f)(3)(ii).

3) In general, the basis of boot received by a transferor is its fair market value. § 358(a)(2). If a transferor who receives installment debt boot (e.g., a corporate note) reports the gain recognized under the installment method, the basis of the debt obligation is its face value less the amount of income that will be taxable to the transferor if the obligation is satisfied in full. § 453B(b).

b. Corporation's Basis

1) If the transferor recognizes gain because of the receipt of boot, the corporation's basis in the property received is generally the transferor's basis plus any gain recognized. § 362(a). If the transferred property had a "net built-in loss," however, the corporation's basis may be limited to fair market value under § 362(e). See IV.B.8, at page 78, *supra*.

2) If the transferor defers any gain recognized under the § 453 installment method, the corporation may increase its basis under § 362(a) only when that gain is recognized. Prop. Reg. § 1.453–1(f)(3)(ii).

3) If a transferor recognizes gain when several assets are transferred in exchange for a combination of Newco stock and boot, no published authority indicates how the § 362(a) basis increase for gain recognized is to be allocated among the assets. Based on the Service's approach to boot allocation (see IV.C.2., at page 80, *supra*), it is logical for the corporation's basis in each asset to be the same as the transferor's basis increased by any gain recognized that is attributable to that asset.

Example: On the formation of Newco, A transfers Gainacre, with a value of $100,000 and a basis of $10,000, in exchange for Newco stock with a value of $80,000, $5,000 cash and a $15,000 Newco five-year note. A recognizes $20,000 gain, $15,000 of which may be deferred until year five. A's basis in the Newco stock is: $10,000 (basis of Gainacre), less $20,000 (value of boot received), plus $20,000 (gain recognized and to be recognized by A), or $10,000. Since the stock is worth $80,000, this preserves $70,000 of gain that went unrecognized on the transfer of Gainacre. Newco's initial basis in Gainacre is: $10,000 (A's basis), plus $5,000 (gain recognized by A in year one), or $15,000. Newco's basis increases to $30,000 when Newco pays off the $15,000 note to A. If Newco sells Gainacre for $100,000 before the note is paid off, it will recognize $85,000 gain, but it may deduct $15,000 as a capital loss when the note is paid off in year five. Prop. Reg. § 1.453–1(f)(3)(iii) Example (1).

4) For a special limitation on any basis increase under § 362(a) attributable to Newco's assumption of a liability, see IV.D.5., at page 87, *infra*.

5. Transfer of Appreciated Boot

If a corporation transfers stock and appreciated boot property (other than its own debt obligations) to a shareholder in a transaction that otherwise qualifies under § 351 but is not a tax-free reorganization under § 368, the corporation must recognize gain as if it had distributed the property in a transaction governed by § 311(b). § 351(f). This is an unlikely result on an incorporation but could occur on a § 351 transfer by a controlling shareholder to an existing corporation. See VI.D.1.b., at page 118, *infra*.

Example: A, the sole shareholder of X Corp., transfers to X property with a fair market value of $20,000 in exchange for $15,000 of X stock and other property (boot) with a fair market value of $5,000 and an adjusted basis to X of $1,000. Even though the transaction generally qualifies under § 351, X must recognize $4,000 gain.

D. Assumption of Liabilities

1. In General

If, as part of the consideration in an otherwise qualified § 351 exchange, Newco assumes a liability of the transferor shareholder, the assumption generally is not treated as boot received by the transferor. § 357(a). To preserve any gain that otherwise would have been recognized, the liability is treated as boot for purposes of determining the transferor's basis in the Newco stock. § 358(d). These rules are subject to two exceptions, described at IV.D.3., at page 84, *infra,* and IV.D.4., at page 84, *infra*.

Example: On the formation of Newco, A transfers land with a basis of $20,000, a value of $60,000, and subject to a $10,000 liability, in exchange for Newco common stock worth $50,000. A recognizes no gain on the transfer because relief of the $10,000 liability is not treated as boot. A's basis in the Newco stock is: $20,000 (basis of property transferred), minus $10,000 (liability is treated as boot for basis purposes), or $10,000. This basis preserves A's $40,000 gain on the land in the Newco stock.

2. Determination of Amount of Liabilities Assumed

The determination of the amount of liabilities assumed by Newco for purposes of § 357 (and certain other provisions of the Code discussed later) depends on whether the liability is "recourse" (the transferor has personal liability on the debt) or "nonrecourse" (the liability is limited to the value of the property securing the debt).

a. Recourse Liability

A recourse liability is treated as having been assumed to the extent that, based on all the facts and circumstances, the transferee (Newco) has agreed and is expected to satisfy the liability, whether or not the transferor-shareholder has been relieved of it. § 357(d)(1)(A). Where more than one person agrees to satisfy a liability, only one of them would be "expected" to satisfy it.

b. Nonrecourse Liability

In general, a nonrecourse liability is treated as having been assumed when an asset is transferred to Newco subject to the liability. § 357(d)(1)(B). But in situations where more than one asset secures a nonrecourse liability, the amount of the liability treated as assumed must be reduced by the lesser of:

1) The amount of such liability that an owner of other assets not transferred to Newco and also subject to the liability has agreed with Newco to and is expected to satisfy; or

2) The fair market value of the other assets to which the liability is subject.

§ 357(d)(2). The purpose of this somewhat mysterious rule is to foreclose an abusive result by preventing the liability from being counted more than once in making upward basis adjustments under § 362. For the corresponding basis rules, see IV.D.5., at page 87, *infra*.

3. Tax Avoidance Transactions

The assumption of a liability is treated as boot if the taxpayer's principal purpose in transferring the liability was the avoidance of federal income taxes or was not a bona fide corporate business purpose. § 357(b). If this exception applies, *all* the relieved liabilities, not just the abusive debts, are treated as boot. Reg. § 1.357–1(c). The taxpayer has the burden of proving the absence of an improper purpose by "the clear preponderance of the evidence." § 357(b)(2). Encumbering property for personal reasons shortly before a § 351 transfer or causing Newco to assume a transferor's personal debts are examples of improper or tax avoidance purposes.

Example: On the formation of Newco, A transfers land with a basis of $20,000, a value of $60,000 and subject to a $10,000 liability, in exchange for Newco stock worth $50,000. A encumbered the land shortly before the transfer in order to raise funds to pay personal expenses. It is likely that the transfer of the land subject to the liability was not motivated by a bona fide business purpose, and thus the $10,000 debt relief is treated as boot. A recognizes $10,000 gain under § 351(b); A's basis in the Newco stock is: $20,000 (basis of land), less $10,000 (debt relief), plus $10,000 (gain recognized), or $20,000.

4. Liabilities in Excess of Basis

a. In General

If the sum of the liabilities assumed by Newco in a § 351 transaction exceed the aggregate adjusted basis of the properties transferred by a particular transferor, the excess is treated as gain from the sale or exchange of property. § 357(c)(1). This rule is applied separately to each transferor of property. The likely purpose of the rule is to prevent a transferor from having a negative basis in the Newco stock. If § 357(b) and § 357(c) both apply to a transfer, § 357(b) takes precedence. § 357(c)(2)(A).

Example: On the formation of Newco, A transfers land with a basis of $30,000, a value of $100,000 and subject to a $55,000 liability, in exchange for Newco stock worth $45,000. If § 357(a) applied, without more, A would recognize no gain, but A's basis in the Newco stock would be: $30,000 (basis of land), less $55,000 (debt relief), or negative $25,000. Under § 357(c), however, A must recognize $25,000 gain (the excess of the $55,000 liability over A's $30,000 basis in the land). A's basis in the Newco stock is: $30,000 (basis of land), less $55,000 (debt relief), plus $25,000 (gain recognized), or zero. The transferor's basis in the Newco stock always is zero if § 357(c) applies.

b. Transferor Remains Liable to Creditor

The courts have held that a transferor may not avoid § 357(c) gain by remaining personally liable for debts encumbering property transferred to Newco in a § 351 transaction, either directly or as a guarantor. *Owen v. Comm'r,* 881 F.2d 832 (9th Cir.1989), cert. denied, 493 U.S. 1070, 110 S.Ct. 1113 (1990); *Seggerman Farms, Inc. v. Comm'r,* 308 F.3d 803 (7th Cir.2002). In *Seggerman Farms, supra,* the court indicated in dicta that a transferor's remaining personally liable and providing a personal guarantee for a transferred recourse debt was not equivalent to being "expected" to satisfy that debt and thus could not prevent the transferee corporation from having "assumed" the debt under § 357(d)(1)(A).

c. Avoiding § 357(c) by Transfer of Note

1) The *Lessinger* Case

The Second Circuit held in *Lessinger v. Comm'r,* 872 F.2d 519 (2d Cir.1989), that a taxpayer who transfers his own enforceable note to a controlled corporation in a § 351 transaction may avoid recognizing gain under § 357(c). The court concluded that since the corporation took the note with a basis equal to its face value, the taxpayer should not be required to recognize any § 357(c) gain. This rationale is not supported by the statute.

2) The *Peracchi* Case

Applying somewhat different reasoning, the Ninth Circuit reached a similar result in *Peracchi v. Comm'r,* 143 F.3d 487 (9th Cir.1998). The court concluded that the taxpayer had a basis equal to face value in his own note transferred to a wholly owned corporation because the note was a corporate asset subject to the claims of creditors in the event of a bankruptcy. It thus represented a real and substantial increase in the taxpayer's corporate investment. This reasoning is limited to notes that have economic substance and have a fair market value roughly equal to face value. The court observed that contributing a promissory note did not differ economically from other transactions that would avoid § 357(c) gain, such as borrowing from an outside lender and contributing the cash to the corporation.

3) Synthesis of § 357(c) Cases

Lessinger and *Peracchi* enable the transferor to avoid recognizing § 357(c) gain. The Service and several other courts have held, however, that a taxpayer has a zero basis in his own note for § 357(c) purposes. See, e.g., *Alderman v. Comm'r*, 55 T.C. 662 (1971). The law remains unsettled.

Example: On the formation of Newco, A transfers land subject to a $20,000 mortgage and having a basis of $10,000 and a value of $50,000, in exchange for Newco stock worth $30,000. Under *Lessinger* and *Peracchi*, A could avoid what otherwise would be $10,000 of § 357(c) gain by transferring his own personal note for $10,000. Other courts have held that A has no basis in his note and must recognize $10,000 of gain.

d.　Character of § 357(c) Gain

According to the regulations, the character of any § 357(c) gain is determined by allocating the gain among the transferred assets in proportion to their respective fair market values. Reg. § 1.357–2(a). Under this sometimes anomalous approach, § 357(c) gain may be characterized by reference to an asset that has no built-in gain.

Example: On the formation of Newco, A transfers inventory with a basis and value of $10,000 and a capital asset subject to a $25,000 liability with a basis of $5,000 and a value of $30,000. A recognizes $10,000 of gain under § 357(c) (excess of $25,000 liability over $15,000 aggregate basis of two assets transferred). Of the gross asset value of $40,000 transferred by A, 25% is attributable to the inventory and 75% is attributable to the capital asset. Under the regulations, $2,500 (25%) of the gain is ordinary income and $7,500 (75%) is capital gain even though A had no built-in realized gain on the inventory.

e.　Excluded Liabilities

Liabilities assumed by Newco that have not yet been taken into account by the transferor for tax purposes (either by the transferor's taking a current § 162 deduction or increasing the basis of property) are not treated as "liabilities" for purposes of determining gain recognized under § 357(c)(1) or basis under § 358. §§ 357(c)(3); 358(d)(2). Examples of such excluded liabilities are cash basis accounts payable and some contingent liabilities.

Example (1): On the formation of Newco, A, a cash method taxpayer, transfers $50,000 cash and $200,000 accounts receivable (with a zero basis) in exchange for $150,000 of Newco stock and Newco's assumption of $100,000 of A's accounts payable which would have been deductible under § 162(a) if paid by A. Under § 357(c)(1), without more, A would recognize $50,000 gain (the excess of the $100,000 accounts payable over the $50,000 cash transferred by A). Under § 357(c)(3), however, the accounts payable are not treated as "liabilities." A thus recognizes no gain. A's basis in the Newco stock is $50,000 (cash transferred); it is not reduced by the accounts payable assumed by Newco.

Example (2): On the formation of Newco in Year 1, B, an accrual basis taxpayer, transfers contaminated land with associated contingent environmental liabilities in exchange for all of Newco's stock. B neither deducted nor capitalized any amount with respect to the liabilities. The liabilities assumed by Newco in the exchange are not "liabilities" for purposes of § 357(c)(1) and § 358(d) because they were never deducted by B and they did not create or increase the basis of any property prior to the transfer. Rev. Rul. 95–74, 1995–2 C.B. 36.

5. Limit on Basis Increase Attributable to Liability Assumption

a. In General

When gain is recognized by a transferor as a result of the assumption by Newco of a liability (e.g., when § 357(b) or § 357(c) applies), in no event may the basis of the property transferred to Newco be increased above the fair market value of the property. § 362(d)(1).

b. Recognized Gain on Liability Assumption Not Taxable

A special rule applies when: (1) a transferor of property recognizes gain as a result of the assumption of a nonrecourse liability by Newco, (2) that liability also is secured by assets not transferred to Newco, and (3) no person is taxable on the recognized gain (e.g., because the transferor is a foreign person not subject to U.S. tax). Under this special rule, for purposes of § 362 basis adjustments, the transferor's gain recognized as a result of the assumption is determined as if the liability assumed by Newco equaled Newco's ratable portion of the liability as determined on the basis of the relative fair market values of all assets subject to the liability. § 362(d)(2).

6. Stock Basis Reduction for Transfers of Certain Liabilities

a. Background

As discussed above (see IV.D.4.e., at page 86, *supra*), liabilities that the taxpayer could currently deduct upon payment or contingent liabilities not yet taken into account (i.e., deducted or capitalized) by the transferor for tax purposes are not treated as "liabilities" for purposes of § 357(c)(1) and do not require a reduction in the basis of the transferor's stock under § 358(d). Some corporations exploited these rules by transferring property to a controlled corporation in exchange for both stock and the transferee corporation's assumption of contingent liabilities. After taking the position that no stock basis reduction was required with respect to these assumed liabilities, the transferor would then sell the stock and deduct the capital loss against gains from other business activities. The effects of this transaction were to duplicate and accelerate a deduction for a contingent loss. See, e.g., *Black & Decker Corp. v. United States*, 436 F.3d 431 (4th Cir.2006) and *Coltec Industries, Inc. v. United States*, 454 F.3d 1340 (Fed. Cir.2006), where the courts disallowed the losses claimed by the taxpayers under the economic substance doctrine even though they were authorized by the literal language of the stature.

b. Basis Step-down Rule

To prevent the abuse described above, § 358(h) requires that if, after application of the general § 358 stock basis rules to a § 351 transaction, the transferor's stock basis exceeds the fair market value of the stock, the basis must be reduced (but not below fair market value) by the amount of any liability assumed by another person as part of the exchange if a basis reduction under § 358(d) is not otherwise required with respect to the assumption—e.g., because the liability is excluded under § 357(c)(3) or is a contingent liability. § 358(h)(1). For this purpose, a "liability" includes any fixed or contingent obligation to make payment without regard to whether the obligation is otherwise taken into account for tax purposes. § 358(h)(3).

c. Exceptions

Under § 358(h)(2), the basis stepdown rule in § 358(h)(1) does not apply where:

1)   The trade or business with which the liability is associated is transferred to the person assuming the liability as part of the exchange; or

2)   Substantially all of the assets with which the liability is associated are transferred to the person assuming the liability as part of the exchange.

Example: X Corp. contributes $3 million cash to Newco, a newly formed subsidiary, in exchange for all of Newco's stock and Newco's assumption of $2 million in contingent employee healthcare claims from a separate business that X Corp. conducts. Without regard to § 358(h), X Corp.'s basis in the Newco stock is $3 million under § 358(a). X Corp. intends to sell the stock for its fair market value of $1 million, hoping to recognize a $2 million capital loss. Under § 358(h), however, X Corp. must reduce its basis in the Newco stock to $1 million and will not recognize any loss on the sale.

E. Incorporation of a Going Business: Special Problems

1. Assignment of Income Doctrine

In general, the assignment of income doctrine does not apply to a transfer to Newco of accounts receivable by a cash basis taxpayer unless the taxpayer has a tax avoidance purpose. *Hempt Brothers, Inc. v. United States,* 490 F.2d 1172 (3d Cir.1974), cert. denied, 419 U.S. 826, 95 S.Ct. 44 (1974); Rev. Rul. 80–198, 1980–2 C.B. 113.

Example: On the formation of Newco, A transfers the assets of her cash method sole proprietorship, including zero basis accounts receivable, in exchange for Newco stock. Although A "earned" the income, she is not taxed on the transfer; Newco takes over A's zero basis and recognizes income when it collects the receivables. If A is an accrual basis taxpayer, she has a basis in the receivables equal to the amount already included in income; Newco takes that same basis and recognizes no additional income when it collects the receivables.

2. Accounts Payable and Contingent Liabilities

Accounts payable transferred to Newco by a cash basis taxpayer or contingent liabilities for which the transferor has not received any tax benefit are not treated as "liabilities" for purposes of § 357(c)(1) (see IV.D.4.e., at page 86, *supra*). Although some older cases (e.g., *Holdcroft Transp. Co. v. Comm'r*, 153 F.2d 323 (8th Cir.1946)) treated Newco's assumption of these obligations as a nondeductible capital expenditure, the Service now permits Newco to deduct the payables when they are paid if they would have been currently deductible by the transferor or to treat them as capital expenditures as appropriate under Newco's method of accounting. See Rev. Rul. 80–198, 1980–2 C.B. 113; Rev. Rul. 95–74, 1995–2 C.B. 36.

3. Tax Benefit Rule

The tax benefit rule requires a taxpayer who derives a tax benefit (e.g., from a deduction) in one year to recognize income in a subsequent year on the occurrence of an event that is inconsistent with the earlier deduction. An example would be taking a deduction and receiving a refund of all or part of the amount previously deducted in a subsequent year. It is unsettled whether the tax benefit rule overrides § 351. In *Nash v. United States*, 398 U.S. 1, 90 S.Ct. 1550 (1970), the Supreme Court held that the tax benefit rule did not require an accrual basis taxpayer to recognize income on the transfer of accounts receivable in a § 351 transaction when the taxpayer had previously deducted some of the receivables as uncollectible by creating a bad debt reserve. The Court held that there was no "recovery" because the taxpayer received Newco stock equal to the value of the receivables less the previously deducted bad debt reserve. The specific result in *Nash* is no longer important because accrual method taxpayers generally may not deduct bad debt reserves. As a policy matter, § 351 should override the tax benefit rule in situations where the tax benefit can be preserved and later "recaptured" through a transferred basis. Cf. § 1245(b)(3).

4. Depreciation Methods

If Newco acquires depreciable property in a § 351(a) exchange, it continues to use the transferor's depreciation method and remaining recovery period. § 168(i)(7). If the transferor recognizes § 351(b) gain allocable to a depreciable asset, Newco's § 362(a) basis increase for gain recognized may be depreciated under § 168 as if it were a separate newly acquired asset. Prop. Reg. § 1.168–5(b)(7).

F. Contributions to Capital

1. Contribution to Capital Defined

a. In General

When a shareholder transfers property to a corporation but does not receive stock or other consideration in exchange, the transaction is a contribution to capital and is not governed by § 351. If, however, a *sole* shareholder transfers property or all shareholders transfer property in the same proportion as their holdings, the issuance of new stock has no economic significance. Several cases have held that § 351 applies to these latter types of transfers because the issuance of stock would be "a meaningless gesture." See, e.g., *Lessinger v. Comm'r*, 85 T.C. 824 (1985), aff'd, 872 F.2d 519 (2d Cir.1989).

b. Exceptions

For contributions made after December 22, 2017, the term "contribution to capital" does not include: (1) any contribution in aid of construction or any other contribution from a customer or potential customer, and (2) any contribution by a governmental entity or civic group (other than a contribution made by a shareholder as such). These types of contributions are included in a corporation's gross income.

The purpose of these exceptions is to eliminate a federal tax subsidy for financial incentives that some corporations were receiving from public utilities and customers to locate operations within a particular municipality or general location.

2. Treatment of the Contributor

A shareholder does not recognize gain or loss on a contribution of property to capital. The shareholder may increase his basis in the corporation's stock by the amount of cash and the adjusted basis of any contributed property. Reg. § 1.118–1.

3. Treatment of the Corporation

Contributions to capital are not taxable to the transferee corporation. § 118(a); Reg. § 1.118–1. The corporation's basis in property received as a nontaxable contribution to capital by a shareholder is the same as the transferor's basis. § 362(a)(2). The corporation's basis in property (other than cash) contributed by a nonshareholder is zero. § 362(c)(1). If cash is contributed to capital by a nonshareholder and not within the exceptions described above, the corporation must reduce its basis in any property acquired within 12 months of the contribution by the amount of the contributed cash, and the excess of the contribution over the reduction of basis of newly acquired property must be applied to reduce the basis of any other property held by the corporation. § 362(c)(2).

4. Non Pro Rata Surrender of Stock

A majority shareholder of a financially distressed corporation may surrender stock on a non pro rata basis in order to improve the company's credit rating. After many years of controversy, the Supreme Court has held that a controlling shareholder does not realize a deductible ordinary loss when he surrenders part of his stock without receiving cash or property in return and continues to retain voting control over the corporation after the surrender. *Comm'r v. Fink*, 483 U.S. 89, 107 S.Ct. 2729 (1987). Analogizing this transaction to a shareholder's voluntary forgiveness of a debt owed to him by the corporation, the Court held that a stock surrender is a contribution to capital. The shareholder must reallocate his basis in the surrendered shares to the shares that he retains.

G. Collateral Issues

1. Avoidance of § 351

a. Incentive to Avoid Qualification

Although § 351 is not elective, taxpayers sometimes may wish to avoid qualification in order to accelerate recognition of a loss or to recognize gain on an asset and step-up its basis for depreciation in the hands of the corporation.

b. Avoidance Techniques

Techniques to avoid § 351 include failing the "immediately after the exchange" requirement by a prearranged disposition of stock, or structuring a transfer as a taxable "sale" rather than a tax-free § 351 transfer. These issues raise factual questions that are not susceptible to precise generalization.

Example: A owns undeveloped land with a basis of $50,000 and a value of $200,000. A intends to subdivide the land and sell homes at an anticipated aggregate sale price of $500,000. If A develops the land, he would recognize $450,000 ordinary income. A might wish to transfer the land to a controlled corporation in order to recognize $150,000 of predevelopment capital gain that is taxable at preferential individual capital gains rates, step-up the basis of the land to $200,000 and limit the anticipated ordinary income to $300,000. A may attempt to avoid § 351 by transferring the land to Newco in exchange for a small amount of stock and Newco debt. Some cases (e.g., *Burr Oaks Corp. v. Comm'r*, 365 F.2d 24 (7th Cir.1966), cert. denied, 385 U.S. 1007, 87 S.Ct. 713 (1967)) would reclassify the debt as stock and hold that A recognizes no gain under § 351, while others (e.g., *Bradshaw v. United States*, 683 F.2d 365 (Ct.Cl.1982)) would respect the taxpayer's form and treat the transaction as a taxable sale.

2. Relationship to Other Code Sections

a. Reorganization Provisions

A § 351 exchange may be part of a larger transaction known as a tax-free reorganization. For an example of the overlap between § 351 and a Type D reorganization, see XII.A.2., at page 246, *infra*.

b. Dividend Provisions

An existing corporation may engage in a § 351 transaction that, in part, has the effect of the distribution of a taxable dividend. Reg. § 1.351–2(d). See Chapter VI, *infra*.

Example: A, the sole shareholder of X Corp. transfers property with a value of $20,000 in exchange for $20,000 of X stock and $2,000 cash. The $2,000 excess value may be classified as a taxable dividend.

c. § 482

Section 482 permits the Service to reallocate income between two or more commonly controlled trades or businesses if necessary to prevent tax evasion or clearly reflect the income of the taxpayers. See XIV.C.2., at page 286, *infra*. In situations where §§ 351 and 482 overlap, the courts have held that § 482 takes precedence and permits the Service to reallocate income or expenses from the transferee corporation back to a transferor of property if the purpose of the transfer was to avoid taxes. See, e.g., *Foster v. Comm'r*, 756 F.2d 1430 (9th Cir.1985); Reg. § 1.482–1(d)(5).

H. Organizational and Start-up Expenses

1. Election to Deduct and Amortize

Expenses of forming a corporation and certain expenditures incurred before the corporation begins business operations are nondeductible capital expenditures. A corporation may elect to take a current deduction in the taxable year in which it begins business for up to $5,000 of organizational expenditures. The $5,000 maximum current deduction is reduced, however, by the amount by which such organizational expenditures exceed $50,000. Organizational expenditures that are not currently deductible may be amortized over the 180-month period (15 years) beginning with the month in which the corporation begins business. § 248(a). A similar rule applies to start-up expenditures with respect to an active trade or business. § 195(b).

2. Organizational Expenditures Defined

"Organizational expenditures" are defined by § 248(b) as expenditures which are: (1) incident to the creation of the corporation, (2) chargeable to capital account, and (3) of a character which, if expended to create a corporation having a limited life, would be amortizable over that life. Examples include legal fees for drafting the articles of incorporation and bylaws, state filing fees and necessary accounting services. Reg. § 1.248–1(b)(2). Costs of issuing or selling stock are not organizational expenses and must be capitalized. Reg. § 1.248–1(b)(3)(i). Expenses related to the transfer of particular assets also are not amortizable, but the corporation may add these expenses to its basis in the asset.

3. Start-up Expenditures Defined

"Start-up expenditures" are amounts paid or incurred in connection with investigating the creation or acquisition of an active trade or business or with the creation of an active trade or business, and certain expenses incurred before the business begins (such as for advertising and training employees) that would have been currently deductible as trade or business expenses if they had not been paid or incurred before the business begins. § 195(c)(1).

I. Review Questions

1. A and B incorporate a house painting business ("Newco"). A transfers a van (value—$11,000, basis—$15,000, subject to outstanding debt—$8,000) in exchange for 3,000 shares of Newco common stock. B transfers $7,000 cash in exchange for 7,000 shares of Newco common stock.

   (a) Does the incorporation qualify for nonrecognition under § 351(a)?

   (b) Determine A and B's bases and holding periods in their respective shares of Newco common stock, and Newco's basis and holding period in the van.

   (c) If B gives her shares to her favorite nephew shortly after the incorporation, will the transaction still qualify for nonrecognition under § 351?

   (d) Assume that A's adjusted basis in the van was only $7,000, and A had taken $8,000 of depreciation on the van as a sole proprietor. What result to A on the incorporation?

   (e) How might A have avoided any gain recognized in (d), above?

2.   Shelterer forms a new corporation ("Newco") and transfers land (value—$100,000, basis—$140,000) in exchange for 1,000 shares of Newco common stock with a value of $100,000. Under § 351(a), Shelterer may not recognize his $40,000 built-in loss upon the transfer of the land to Newco. What is Shelterer's basis in the Newco stock and Newco's basis in the land?

3.   A and B form a development company ("Newco"). A transfers land (value—$50,000, basis—$30,000) in exchange for 45,000 shares of Newco common stock (value—$45,000) and $5,000 cash. In consideration of B's past and future promotional and management services, Newco issues to B 5,000 shares of Newco common stock (value—$5,000) on the condition that if B resigns his position with Newco within two years he must return 2,500 shares to Newco.

   (a)   Does the transaction qualify for nonrecognition under § 351?

   (b)   Determine A's recognized gain and A's basis in the Newco stock.

   (c)   Determine the tax consequences of the transaction to B in the year of transfer, assuming first that § 83(a) applies and then that B made the § 83(b) election.

   (d)   If B makes the § 83(b) election and then leaves Newco at the beginning of year 2, how much loss, if any, may B recognize on the forfeiture of his 2,500 shares?

4.   On an incorporation of Newco that qualifies under § 351, A transfers Gainacre (value—$40,000, basis—$8,000) and Lossacre (value—$10,000, basis—$15,000) in exchange for 4,000 shares of Newco stock (value—$40,000) and $10,000 of cash.

   (a)   How much gain, if any, must A recognize?

   (b)   Determine A's basis in the Newco stock and Newco's basis in Gainacre and Lossacre.

5.   On an incorporation of Newco that qualifies under § 351, A transfers Gainacre (value—$50,000, basis—$5,000) in exchange for 3,000 shares of Newco common stock (value—$30,000), $5,000 cash and a $15,000 Newco note to be paid in five equal annual installments (with market rate interest) beginning in the year after the incorporation.

   (a)   Determine the tax consequences (gain recognized, basis in Newco stock) to A in the year of the incorporation and as payments are received on the Newco note.

   (b)   Determine Newco's basis in Gainacre.

Chapter V
Capital Structure

■ ANALYSIS

A. Introduction

1. Sources of Corporate Capital

The sources of corporate capital fall into two broad categories: "debt" and "equity." The combination of debt and equity used by a corporation to finance its operations is known as the corporation's "capital structure."

a. Equity Capital

Equity capital is contributed to a corporation in exchange for an ownership interest evidenced by shares of stock.

1) Preferred Stock

Preferred shareholders have limited financial rights that are preferred over the rights of common shareholders. Conventional preferred stock has fixed dividend and liquidation preferences. Other types of preferred stock have more of the characteristics of debt, such as a variable dividend rate (e.g., based on an index) or a mandatory redemption feature. Preferred stock can be voting or nonvoting. It often is subject to repurchase ("redemption") at a stated price at the option of the corporation. A corporation may have several different classes of preferred stock.

Example: Newco issues $8 nonvoting preferred stock with a liquidation preference of $100 per share. A holder of the stock is entitled to a dividend of $8 per share before Newco may pay dividends to common shareholders, and to a distribution of $100 per share (after payment of all corporate debts) if Newco should liquidate.

2) Common Stock

Common stock is the most basic form of corporate ownership. Common shareholders are not entitled to receive dividends or assets on liquidation until the rights of creditors and preferred shareholders have been satisfied. Common stock represents "residual" ownership because the interests of common shareholders are not fixed or limited, enabling them to benefit from the growth of a corporation's earnings and assets. At least one class of common stock must have voting rights. Most states also permit a corporation to issue nonvoting common stock or different classes of common stock with variations as to voting power, dividends and liquidation rights.

3) Convertible Stock

Stock is "convertible" if it can be converted from one class into another— e.g., preferred stock may be convertible into common at a ratio or price stated at the time of issuance.

Example: Newco issues a class of convertible preferred stock with a value and liquidation preference of $100 per share. The preferred is convertible into common stock at a rate of 2 shares of common for each share of convertible preferred. A preferred shareholder would not be economically motivated to convert until the value of the common equals or exceeds $50 per share.

b. Debt Capital

Corporate debt securities include bonds, debentures, notes and more complex variations. Debt also may be in the form of advances to the corporation that are not evidenced by a formal instrument. Debt usually is evidenced by a written unconditional obligation of the corporation to pay a specified amount on demand or on a certain date. Debt differs from preferred stock in that interest on debt is an unconditional obligation of the corporation while dividends on preferred stock, even if fixed in amount, are discretionary with the board and normally may not be paid unless the corporation has sufficient earnings. Holders of debt also have priority over preferred shareholders on liquidation.

1) Bonds and Debentures

Bonds and debentures are usually evidenced by a written unconditional obligation to pay a specific amount at a future date. They may be registered in the name of the holder or in "bearer" form with interest coupons attached. "Registered" means that the debt instrument is made payable to a specific payee whose name is registered with the corporation. Interest and principal at maturity on bearer debt are payable to whomever has physical possession of the coupons and the certificate. Bonds are secured debts; debentures are unsecured.

2) Notes

Notes are negotiable written instruments evidencing an unconditional promise to pay. Notes may be secured or unsecured. Notes usually have a shorter term than bonds or debentures.

3) Convertible Debt

Some debt may be convertible into equity—e.g., a debenture may be convertible into common stock at a ratio stated at the time the debt is issued.

c. Hybrid Instruments

Many tax classification controversies involve hybrid instruments (including convertible debt) which have characteristics common to both debt and equity. The investment community has exploited the lack of clear guidance in this area by designing financial products that seek "best of both worlds" treatment—i.e., debt for tax purposes and equity for regulatory, financial rating, and accounting purposes. For many years, the Service has threatened to reclassify debt instruments with long maturities or provisions permitting repayment of principal with corporate stock. See, e.g., IRS Notice 94–47, 1994–1 C.B. 357; IRS Notice 94–48, 1994–1 C.B. 357. Despite these warnings, hybrid securities continue to be designed and marketed by large financial institutions.

2. Tax Differences Between Debt and Equity

a. Tax Advantages of Debt

In the case of C corporations, the federal tax laws historically created a bias in favor of debt. These tax advantages are influential when a corporation is formed and later when additional capital is needed. In reviewing the advantages listed below, keep in mind that the shareholders and principal creditors of a closely held corporation may be the same persons.

1) Interest Deduction

The principal tax advantage of debt is avoidance of the "double tax" on corporate profits. A corporation may deduct interest paid on its debt, subject to the limitations on deduction of business interest under § 163(j), but it may not deduct dividends.

2) Repayment of Principal

The repayment of principal on corporate debt is a tax-free return of capital to the lender. If the amount repaid exceeds the lender's basis in the debt, the excess generally is treated as a capital gain. See § 1271. By contrast, when a corporation redeems (i.e., buys back) its stock from a shareholder, the entire amount received may be a dividend if the redeemed shareholder or related persons continue to own stock. See Chapter VII, *infra*.

3) Defense Against Accumulated Earnings Tax

The existence of debt may permit a corporation to accumulate earnings to retire the debt and thus provide a defense against imposition of the accumulated earnings tax. A comparable accumulation to redeem stock normally is not regarded as reasonable for purposes of the accumulated earnings tax. See X.C.3.g, at page 199, *infra*.

b. Tax Advantages of Equity

The tax advantages of equity are limited to special transactions and situations.

1) § 351 Nonrecognition

A transfer of property to a controlled corporation qualifies for complete nonrecognition under § 351(a) only if it is solely in exchange for stock. Debt securities received in a § 351 transaction are boot which may result in the recognition of gain under § 351(b). See IV.C., at page 80, *supra*.

2) Character of Loss on Worthlessness

If a shareholder loans money to a corporation and is not repaid, the loss usually is a capital loss. See V.D.2., at pages 106–107, *infra*. If stock becomes worthless, the loss also is generally a capital loss, except that § 1244 provides limited ordinary loss treatment on the sale or worthlessness of stock issued by certain small, closely held corporations. See V.D.3., at page 107, *infra*.

3) Corporate Shareholders

Equity may be preferable to debt for corporate shareholders because interest income is fully taxable but dividends qualify for the 50% (or sometimes 65% or 100%) dividends received deduction. § 243. See VI.F.1., at page 122, *infra*.

4) Qualified Small Business Stock

Noncorporate shareholders may exclude from gross income 100% of the gain from a sale or exchange of "qualified small business stock" issued after September 27, 2010. The exclusion is available for both the regular and alternative minimum tax. Reduced exclusion percentages (50% or 75%) are allowed for dispositions of stock issued between August 11, 1993 and September 27, 2010, but 7% of the amount excluded is treated as an alternative minimum tax preference item. §§ 1202(a); 57(a)(7). The exclusion is generally available for the greater of: (1) up to $10 million of recognized gain per qualifying corporation for the taxable year (less eligible gains for earlier years), or (2) ten times the original basis of the stock disposed of during the taxable year. § 1202(b)(1). Generally, a "qualified small business" must be a domestic C corporation with aggregate gross assets through and immediately after the issuance of the stock of not more than $50 million if at least 80% of the corporation's assets are used in the active conduct of one or more qualified trades or businesses. § 1202(c)(2), (d), (e)(1). A qualified trade or business does not include providing services in various professions (e.g., health, law, engineering, architecture, and brokerage), banking, insurance, financing, farming, extraction of natural resources, and operation of hotels, motels, and restaurants. § 1202(e)(3). To qualify for the exclusion, the shareholder generally must be an original issuee who has held the stock for more than five years prior to the disposition. § 1202(b), (c).

c. **Changing Stakes and Other Factors**

The tax bias in favor of debt financing is reduced when, as under current law, dividends received by noncorporate shareholders are taxed at preferential capital gains rates. See VI.A.3.e., at page 113, *infra*. The tax advantage for corporate debt has been further eroded by the limitations on the deduction of business interest in § 163(j) and the lower corporate income tax rate. In some situations, however, the use of debt by a C corporation still may result in overall tax savings, such as where a high percentage of the corporation's stock is owned by institutional investors, such as pension funds and charitable endowments, which do not pay taxes on their investment income.

B. Distinguishing Between Debt and Equity

The Service may seek to reclassify nominal debt instruments as equity for tax purposes. These controversies typically involve closely held corporations that are capitalized with an excessive amount of shareholder debt.

1. **§ 385**

    a. **Delegation to Treasury**

    Section 385(a) authorizes the Treasury to promulgate regulations "as may be necessary or appropriate" to determine for all tax purposes whether an interest in a corporation is to be treated as stock or debt. Section 385 also permits the regulations to characterize an instrument "as part stock and in part indebtedness." § 385(a).

    b. **§ 385 Factors**

    Section 385(b) lists five factors that may be taken into account under the regulations in determining whether an interest in a corporation is debt or equity:

    (1) Form—i.e., whether the instrument pays a fixed rate of interest and is evidenced by a written unconditional promise to pay a sum certain on demand or on a specific date in return for an adequate consideration.

    (2) Subordination—i.e., whether the debt under scrutiny is subordinated to or has preference over any other indebtedness of the corporation.

    (3) The debt/equity ratio of the corporation. Section 385 is silent as to how the ratio is computed or when it is excessive, but see V.B.2., at page 101, *infra,* for the approach of the courts.

    (4) Convertibility—i.e., whether the interest is convertible into stock.

    (5) Proportionality—i.e., the relationship between the holdings of stock in the corporation and holdings of the debt under scrutiny.

    c. **Obligation of Consistency**

    The issuing corporation's classification of an interest as stock or debt at the time of issuance is binding on the issuer and all holders of the interest, but not the Service. This obligation of consistency does not apply to holders who disclose on their tax returns that they are treating the interest in a manner inconsistent with the issuing corporation's characterization. § 385(c).

2. **The § 385 Regulations**

    a. **The 1980 Proposed Regulations**

    In 1980, eleven years after § 385 was enacted, the Treasury promulgated proposed regulations, which were amended several times before being withdrawn. Even though § 385 is approaching its 50th birthday, it is unlikely any new regulations will be issued in the immediate future, or perhaps ever. In the meantime, Congress encouraged the Treasury to increase the number of published revenue rulings on debt vs. equity questions, but very few such rulings have been issued in response to this directive. Until more guidance from the Service is forthcoming, most debt vs. equity questions must be resolved by applying the case law.

    b. **The 2016 Proposed Regulations**

    In 2016, the Service issued a new set of proposed regulations affecting the tax classification of indebtedness between related parties. These regulations were intended to curb certain abusive transactions used by multinational corporations to shift income outside the United States. Major elements included strict documentation requirements, bright line tests, and authority for the Service to treat certain instruments as part debt and part equity. Implementation of the regulations has been delayed while they are reevaluated in light of the significant changes made by the Tax Cuts and Jobs Act to the U.S. international tax regime.

3. Case Law

Most courts treat debt vs. equity classification issues as factual questions (or mixed questions of fact and law) to be resolved by applying a list of factors. The numerous decisions are impossible to synthesize. Some courts list as many as 16 separate factors to consider but emphasize that no single factor is conclusive. The ultimate question is often framed as whether the investment, analyzed in terms of its economic reality, constitutes risk capital or a strict debtor-creditor relationship, viewing the transaction as if it were with an outside lender. See, e.g., *Scriptomatic, Inc. v. United States*, 555 F.2d 364 (3d Cir.1977). Another classic formulation defines debt as "an unqualified obligation to pay a sum certain at a reasonably close fixed maturity date along with a fixed percentage in interest payable regardless of the debtor's income or lack thereof" and adds that while "some variation from this formula is not fatal" to debt classification, "too great a variation will . . . preclude such treatment." *Gilbert v. Comm'r*, 248 F.2d 399, 402–403 (2d Cir.1957). The principal factors are summarized below.

a. Form of the Obligation

To be classified as debt, an instrument should have the formal indicia of a debt obligation—e.g., an unconditional promise to pay, a specific term, and a fixed rate of interest payable in all events. Hybrid instruments that have voting rights or make interest payments contingent on earnings are likely to be treated as equity, as are obligations with excessively high interest rates relative to market rates. The absence of a fixed maturity date is relevant but not controlling, and the courts have been willing to classify demand loans as debt. See *Indmar Products Co., Inc. v. Comm'r*, 444 F.3d 771 (6th Cir.2006).

b. Proportionality

Debt held by shareholders in the same proportion as their stock is subject to special scrutiny. The rationale is that if debt is held in the same proportion as stock, the shareholders have no economic incentive to act like creditors by setting or enforcing the terms of the purported debt.

Example: A, B and C are equal shareholders of Newco. They each contribute $10,000 cash in exchange for 100 shares of common stock and each loan Newco $50,000 in exchange for a 5-year Newco note. The nominal debt may be reclassified as equity.

c. Debt/Equity Ratio

The ratio between a corporation's debt and its equity capital is known as the "debt/equity ratio." A corporation with a high debt/equity ratio is often said to be "thinly capitalized," making it more likely that the Service will reclassify the debt as equity on the theory that the purported debt is really at risk in the venture because no rational creditor would loan money to a thinly capitalized corporation. The cases are not consistent as to how the debt/equity ratio is computed or when a ratio is excessive.

1) Debt

In computing the ratio, "debt" includes all loans from shareholders. The ratio of shareholder debt to equity is sometimes called the "inside debt/equity ratio." Some courts also include other long-term liabilities but exclude short-term accounts payable. The ratio of all long-term liabilities to equity is sometimes called the "outside debt/equity ratio."

2) Equity

"Equity" is the shareholders' ownership interest in the corporation—i.e., the difference between the corporation's assets and liabilities. Courts disagree as to whether to reflect assets at their adjusted basis for tax purposes or current fair market value. The proposed § 385 regulations provided that assets were to be reflected at their adjusted basis, but current value may be a more accurate measure in some situations. The cases also conflict over whether intangible assets, such as goodwill, should be taken into account in determining equity.

3) When Is Debt/Equity Ratio Excessive?

Generalizations are perilous here, but an inside debt/equity ratio of 3:1 or lower is normally not excessive. Whether or not a ratio is excessive may depend on norms for the particular business in which the corporation is engaged. The withdrawn § 385 regulations included two safe harbors: a corporation's debt was not "excessive" if its outside debt/equity ratio did not exceed 10:1 and its inside debt/equity ratio did not exceed 3:1. See Prop. Reg. § 1.385–6(g)(3) (withdrawn in 1983).

d. Intent

Some cases turn on whether the parties "intended" to create a debtor-creditor relationship. Intent may be measured by objective criteria such as a lender's reasonable expectation, evaluated in light of the financial condition of the corporation and its ability to pay principal and interest. Often the inquiry is whether an outside lender would have loaned money to the corporation under the same terms. See, e.g., *Fin Hay Realty Co. v. United States*, 398 F.2d 694 (3d Cir.1968), which frames the ultimate question as whether the investment, analyzed in terms of its economic reality, is risk capital or represents a strict debtor-creditor relationship. Adherence to certain formalities (such as treatment of the interest on the corporate books, and payment of interest and principal when due) may be relevant in determining intent. One appeals court has framed the "intent" question in terms of whether the transaction was "in substance" a loan or whether it was "a mere sham or subterfuge set up solely or principally for tax-avoidance purposes." *J.S. Biritz Construction Co. v. Comm'r*, 387 F.2d 451 (8th Cir.1967).

e. Subordination

Subordination of shareholder debt to claims of outside lenders and trade creditors is sometimes regarded as evidence that the shareholder debt should be reclassified as equity. But because many lenders typically require shareholder loans to be subordinated, this factor alone is not controlling.

f. Source of Repayments

An expectation of repayment solely from corporate earnings is not indicative of bona fide debt regardless of its reasonableness because it implies that an advance is really an equity contribution. To be classified as debt, the source of repayment generally is viewed as coming from four possible sources: (1) liquidation of assets, (2) corporate profits, (3) cash flow, and (4) refinancing with another lender. *Roth Steel Tube Co. v. Comm'r*, 800 F.2d 625, 631 (6th Cir.1986).

g. All or Nothing Approach

The case law rarely, if ever, treats a single instrument as part debt and part equity. If debt is reclassified, it usually is treated as equity in its entirety. Section 385(a), however, authorizes the Treasury to issue regulations treating an instrument as part debt and part equity.

4. Consequences of Reclassification

If debt is reclassified as equity, payments labeled as "interest" are recharacterized as constructive dividends to the extent of the corporation's earnings and profits. Repayment of the principal of reclassified debt is treated as if stock were redeemed by the corporation and may result in a dividend to the shareholder rather than a tax-free return of capital. See VII.C., at page 131, *infra*.

5. Shareholder Guaranteed Debt

Instead of making direct loans, shareholders may guarantee repayment of corporate loans from outside lenders. The Service sometimes argues that, in substance, shareholder guaranteed debt is equivalent to a loan from the outside lender to the shareholders followed by a contribution to capital. Under this reclassification, an "interest" payment from the corporation to the lender is treated as a constructive dividend to the shareholders followed by a transfer of the same amount by the shareholders to the lender as interest. See *Casco Bank & Trust Co. v. United States*, 544 F.2d 528 (1st Cir.1976), cert. denied, 430 U.S. 907, 97 S.Ct. 1176 (1977); *Plantation Patterns, Inc. v. Commissioner*, 462 F.2d 712 (5th Cir.1972), cert. denied, 409 U.S. 1076, 93 S.Ct. 683 (1972).

Example: On the formation of Newco, A, B and C each transfer $20,000 cash in exchange for 100 shares of Newco common stock. Newco also borrows $600,000 from Bank at market rate interest, and Bank requires A, B and C to personally guarantee the loan. Newco pays $30,000 to Bank at the end of year one and deducts that amount as "interest." Because Newco may be thinly capitalized (it has a debt/equity ratio of 10:1) and the bank debt is guaranteed by the shareholders in proportion to their stock holdings, the Service may treat the transaction as if the shareholders borrowed $600,000 from Bank and contributed that amount to Newco's capital. In that event, Newco's $30,000 "interest" payment will be treated as a nondeductible dividend. A, B and C each realize $10,000 dividend income and, logically, they each should be treated as paying $10,000 interest to Bank, which should be deductible as investment interest subject to the limitations in § 163(d).

C. Limitation on Deduction of Business Interest

1. In General

For tax years beginning after December 31, 2017, § 163(j) limits the deduction for interest paid or accrued on indebtedness properly allocable to a trade or business. The limitation applies to all business taxpayers, not just corporations, and is applied after any other limitations, such as those requiring deferral or capitalization of interest expense in certain situations. Special rules, not directly relevant to C corporations, apply to pass-through entities. § 163(j)(4).

2. Business Interest

"Business interest" is any interest paid or accrued on indebtedness properly allocable to a trade or business. § 163(j)(5). It does not include investment interest, which is subject to a separate set of limitations under § 163(d). The Service has taken the position that all interest income and interest expense of a C corporation will be allocable to its trade or business activities for purposes of § 163(j). Prop. Reg. § 1.163(j)–4(b)(1).

3. Amount of Limitation

For any taxable year, the deduction for business interest is limited to the sum of: (1) the taxpayer's business interest income (i.e., interest income allocable to a trade or business); (2) 30% of its "adjusted taxable income;" and (3) the taxpayer's "floor financing interest" (a specialized category for retail car dealers). § 163(j)(1). Business interest disallowed under § 163(j) may be carried forward and treated as business interest in succeeding taxable years. § 163(j)(2).

4. Adjusted Taxable Income

a. Tax Years Through 2021

For tax years through 2021, "adjusted taxable income" ("ATI") is the taxpayer's taxable income without regard to: (1) tax items not properly allocable to a trade or business; (2) business interest expense or business interest income; (3) any allowed net operating loss deduction; (4) the 20% deduction provided to noncorporate taxpayers by § 199A for qualified business income from pass-through entities; and (5) deductions for depreciation, amortization, or depletion (including any amounts expensed under §§ 168(k) or 179). § 163(j)(8). ATI also is computed with such other adjustments as provided by the Treasury in regulations.

b. Tax Years Beginning After 2021

Beginning in 2022, ATI is determined without adding back depreciation and amortization. § 163(j)(8)(A)(v). In most cases, the impact of this change is to further limit the deduction for business interest because a major component of the ATI formula will be 30% of a lower number.

5. Relief Provisions

a. Small Businesses

The limitation does not apply to business taxpayers with average annual gross receipts not exceeding $25 million for the three-year period ending with the prior taxable year. § 163(j)(3), incorporating the gross receipts test of § 448(c).

b. Real Property Trade or Business

At the taxpayer's election, the limitation does not apply to a real property trade or business, which is broadly defined to include real estate development, redevelopment, construction, reconstruction, acquisition, conversion, rental, operation, management, leasing, brokerage, and operation or management of a lodging facility. § 163(j)(7)(A)(ii), (B), incorporating the definition of "real property trade or business" in § 469(c)(7)(C). Taxpayers who make this election must use the alternative depreciation system under § 168(g), which requires straight line cost recovery over 30 years for residential rental property (instead of 27.5 years) and 40 years for commercial property (instead of 39 years). §§ 163(j)(10)(A); 168(g)(1)(F).

c. Specialized Exceptions

At the taxpayer's election, a farming business (with some exceptions) and certain agricultural and horticultural cooperatives are not subject to the interest deduction limitation. § 163(j)(7)(A)(iii), (C). Certain regulated public utilities also are exempted. § 163(j)(7)(A)(iv).

6. Proposed Regulations

The IRS has issued extensive proposed regulations interpreting various aspects of the limitation on business interest. REG–106089 (Nov. 26, 2018), 2019–05 I.R.B. 431. The proposed regulations: (1) define "business interest" expansively; (2) explain how the business interest limitation interacts with other provisions of the Code, including deduction limitations; (3) clarify the statutory definition of adjusted taxable income and provide the other adjustments authorized by § 163(j)(8)(B); (4) address specialized situations, such as the treatment of partnerships and S corporations and application of the limitation to affiliated groups of domestic corporations, foreign corporations, and other foreign persons with income effectively connected to a U.S. trade or business; and (5) much more. The proposed regulations also make it clear that the business interest limitation rules of § 163(j) have no effect on a corporation's earnings and profits. Prop. Reg. § 1.163(j)–4(c)(1).

7. Implications for Capital Structure

The economic implications of the business interest limitation vary depending on the nature of the business and the corporation's capital structure. The limitation will negatively impact industries that customarily rely more on debt or most highly leveraged companies. Overall, the limitation on deducting business interest, coupled with the lower corporate income tax rate, may increase the cost of issuing corporate debt.

D. Character of Loss on Corporate Investment

1. In General

Stock and debt instruments (unless held by a dealer) are almost always capital assets, and thus any loss on their sale or exchange is treated as a capital loss. Special problems may arise when stock or debt becomes worthless.

2. Loss on Worthlessness of Debt

The tax treatment of a worthless corporate debt investment depends on whether the instrument is a "security," as defined in § 165(g)(2) and, if not, whether the debt is a business or nonbusiness bad debt.

a. Debt Evidenced by Security

If a "security" which is a capital asset becomes worthless during the taxable year, the holder's resulting loss is treated as a loss from the sale or exchange of a capital asset as of the last day of the taxable year. § 165(g)(1). For this purpose, the term "security" includes bonds, debentures, notes or other corporate debt instruments with interest coupons or in registered form. A loss by a corporation on the worthlessness of securities in an "affiliated corporation" is an ordinary loss. A corporation is "affiliated" if the corporate holder owns at least 80% of its voting power and value and more than 90% of its gross receipts are from sources other than passive investment income. § 165(g)(3).

Example: In year one, A loans Newco, Inc. $50,000 and receives a Newco bond with a face amount of $50,000. Two years later, Newco is unable to repay the principal of the bond, which is a capital asset in A's hands. The bond is a § 165(g)(2) "security," and A recognizes a $50,000 long-term capital loss as of the last day of the year in which the bond becomes worthless.

b. Debt Not Evidenced by Security

Losses on corporate debts that are not evidenced by a security are characterized by the bad debt provisions in § 166. Losses from wholly or partially worthless business bad debts are ordinary. § 166(a). Losses of noncorporate lenders from a wholly worthless nonbusiness bad debt are treated as a short-term capital loss. § 166(d). Losses from partially worthless nonbusiness bad debts are not deductible.

1) Business vs. Nonbusiness Bad Debt

A nonbusiness bad debt is a debt other than (1) a debt created or acquired in connection with the taxpayer's trade or business or (2) a debt the loss from the worthlessness of which is incurred in the taxpayer's trade or business. § 166(d)(2).

2) Shareholder-Employees

If a shareholder also is an employee loans money to a closely held corporation, any resulting loss usually is treated as a nonbusiness bad debt on the theory that the loan was made in the taxpayer's capacity as an investor. To be deductible as a business bad debt, a taxpayer must show that his dominant motivation for making the loan was related to his trade or business. *United States v. Generes,* 405 U.S. 93, 92 S.Ct. 827 (1972).

> ***Example:*** A is the president and majority shareholder of X, Inc. A's salary is $90,000 per year and her stock is worth $500,000. To assist X in meeting working capital requirements, A advanced $150,000 in open account loans. X subsequently went bankrupt and was unable to pay back the $150,000 to A. If, as is likely, the dominant motivation for A's loan was to protect her investment in X rather than her job as president, her loss is from a nonbusiness bad debt and is treated as a short-term capital loss.

3. Loss on Worthlessness of Equity

a. In General

A loss incurred by a noncorporate shareholder on the sale of stock is treated as a capital loss if, as is likely, the stock is a capital asset. Because stock is a "security," as defined by § 165(g)(2), a loss on the worthlessness of stock held as a capital asset is treated as a capital loss on the last day of the taxable year in which the loss is incurred. § 165(g)(1).

b. § 1244 Stock

A loss incurred by an individual shareholder on the sale or worthlessness of "§ 1244 stock" is deductible as an ordinary loss, subject to various requirements and limitations described below.

1) Qualifying Shareholders

Only individual taxpayers and partnerships who were original issuees of § 1244 stock are eligible for ordinary loss treatment. § 1244(a). Trusts, estates and corporate shareholders do not qualify. Partners qualify only if they were partners when the partnership acquired the stock. Reg. § 1.1244(a)–1(b)(2).

2) Qualifying Stock

Section 1244 applies to common or preferred stock that has been issued by a domestic corporation for money or property. § 1244(c)(1). Stock issued for services does not qualify. Reg. § 1.1244(c)–1(d).

3) Small Business Corporation Status

An issuer of § 1244 stock must be a "small business corporation" when the stock is issued. That status is attained if the aggregate amount of money and other property received by the corporation for stock, as a capital contribution and as paid-in surplus does not exceed $1 million. § 1244(c)(3). For this purpose, property is valued at its adjusted basis, less encumbering liabilities, at the time it is contributed. § 1244(c)(3)(B). The $1 million cap applies to amounts received for the shares seeking to qualify as § 1244 stock and all previously issued stock. If the $1 million cap is exceeded in the same taxable year, the corporation may designate which shares are to be treated as § 1244 stock. Reg. § 1.1244(c)–2(b).

Example: On the formation of Newco, A contributes $100,000 cash and B contributes land with a value of $100,000 and an adjusted basis of $50,000, each in exchange for 100 shares of Newco common stock. In the following taxable year, C contributes $1,000,000 cash in exchange for 1,000 shares of Newco common stock. The aggregate amount of money and property received by Newco when it issues stock to A and B is $150,000 (valuing the land at its adjusted basis), and all 200 shares qualify as § 1244 stock. After Newco issues the 1,000 shares to C, the aggregate amount of money and property received is $1,150,000. Because the $1 million threshold is exceeded, only 850 ($850,000) of the 1,000 shares qualifies as § 1244 stock. If the shares had all been issued in the same taxable year, Newco could designate the shares to be treated as § 1244 stock.

4) Gross Receipts Test When Loss Sustained

Even if stock qualified under § 1244 when it was issued, ordinary loss treatment is denied unless the corporation derived more than 50% of its aggregate gross receipts from sources other than certain passive income items (e.g., dividends, interest, royalties, rents, and gains from the sale or exchange of stock or securities) for the five taxable years ending before the year in which the loss was sustained (or the period of the corporation's existence, if shorter). § 1244(c)(1)(C).

5) Limit on Amount of Ordinary Loss

The maximum amount that a taxpayer may treat as an ordinary loss under § 1244 for any one taxable year may not exceed $50,000 ($100,000 on a joint return). § 1244(b). In the case of a partnership, the loss ceiling is determined separately as to each partner. Reg. § 1.1244(b)–1(a).

6) Reduction of Ordinary Loss

In computing any § 1244 ordinary loss, a taxpayer who has a transferred basis in § 1244 stock received in exchange for "loss property" (i.e., property with a basis in excess of its value) must reduce his stock basis by the built-in loss in the contributed property. § 1244(d)(1)(A). Any ordinary loss disallowed under this provision is treated as a capital loss. The purpose of this rule is to prevent a taxpayer from converting the character of a loss from capital to ordinary.

Example: In a transaction that qualifies under § 351(a), A transfers a capital asset with a value of $10,000 and a basis of $15,000 in exchange for 100 shares of Newco stock. A takes a $15,000 transferred basis in the stock, which qualifies as § 1244 stock. Five years later, the stock becomes worthless, and A recognizes a $15,000 loss. A's § 1244 ordinary loss is limited to $10,000; the remaining $5,000 is a long-term capital loss.

E. Special Problems of Excessive Corporate Debt

1. Background

Debt/equity classification issues historically were confined to closely held corporations with excessive shareholder debt. During the 1980s, however, a wave of corporate takeovers and restructurings was fueled by an increased use of debt financing. As an initial response, Congress enacted several narrow provisions aimed at curbing perceived abuses of debt financing by public companies. Several of these statutory restrictions, relating to "earnings stripping" through the payment of interest to a tax-indifferent foreign affiliate, and disallowance of certain net operating loss carrybacks, have since been repealed and replaced by broader provisions, such as the limitation on deduction of business interest in § 163(j) and the elimination of net operating loss carrybacks. One remaining anti-abuse provision addressing "junk bonds" is summarized below.

2. Junk Bonds

a. "Junk Bond" Defined

A "junk bond" is an unsecured high-yield corporate debt obligation that a bond rating service would classify as below investment grade because of its high risk. Junk bonds often are issued in debt-financed corporate acquisitions, such as leveraged buyouts. Although some junk bonds pay interest currently, many are issued as "zero coupon" obligations with an issue price that is significantly lower than the stated redemption price at maturity. A variation, known as a "pay in kind" bond, pays interest in the form of additional debt securities or preferred stock rather than cash. Issuers of junk bonds often deducted interest as it accrued even if actual payment was deferred for many years.

b. Applicable High Yield Discount Obligations

1) Definition

An "applicable high yield discount obligation" is an instrument with (a) more than a five-year maturity, (b) a yield to maturity that is five percentage points or more than the applicable federal rate in effect under § 1274(d) for the month in which the obligation is issued, and (c) "significant" original issue discount, as defined by § 163(i)(2). § 163(i)(1).

2) Tax Treatment

A corporation that issues an applicable high yield discount obligation must defer any interest deduction until it makes actual payments in cash or property other than its own stock or debt. § 163(i)(3). If an instrument with significant original issue discount, as defined, has a yield that is more than six percentage points over an indexed cap, a portion of the interest deduction is disallowed. § 163(e)(5)(C).

F. Review Questions

1. Identify four important factors that the courts utilize in determining whether to reclassify "debt" as "equity."

2. X Corp. has the following balance sheet:

Assets	Adj. Basis	F. Mkt. Value
Cash	$ 100,000	$ 100,000
Inventory	20,000	100,000
Land	380,000	600,000
Goodwill	0	200,000
Total	$ 500,000	$1,000,000

Liabilities and Capital	Adj. Basis	F. Mkt. Value
Bank Loan	$ 100,000	$ 100,000
Shareholder Loans	300,000	300,000
Capital Stock	100,000	600,000
Total	$ 500,000	$1,000,000

What is X Corp's debt/equity ratio? If the shareholder loans are pro rata, what is the risk of those loans being reclassified as capital contributions?

3. A is the sole shareholder and principal employee of X Corp. A's adjusted basis in her X stock is $50,000. A also has loaned $100,000 to X Corp.; the debt is evidenced by an X Corp. promissory note that is not in registered form. X goes bankrupt and A's stock and note are both worthless. What is the character of A's losses?

Chapter VI

Nonliquidating Distributions

■ ANALYSIS

A. Introduction

1. Distribution vs. Dividend

For purposes of Subchapter C, a "distribution" is any kind of payment by a corporation to its shareholders with respect to their stock. A "dividend" is a distribution out of the current or accumulated "earnings and profits" of a corporation. Payments to shareholders that are unrelated to their ownership of stock (e.g., salary, interest, rent, etc.) are neither distributions nor dividends. "Nonliquidating" (sometimes called "operating") distributions are made by an ongoing corporation. "Liquidating" distributions are made by a corporation that is dissolving under state law. This chapter covers nonliquidating distributions of cash or property other than stock of the distributing corporation. Later chapters examine distributions by a corporation to buy back (redeem) its own stock (see Chapter VII, *infra*), distributions of stock (see Chapter VIII, *infra*) and distributions in partial or complete liquidation of a corporation (see Chapters VII and IX, *infra*).

2. Dividends Under Corporate Law

The term "dividend" under corporate law ordinarily is used in state statutes restricting the power of corporations to make distributions that invade or reduce their permanent capital. These rules have no bearing on whether a distribution is a dividend for federal tax purposes.

3. Distributions and Dividends Under the Code

a. Statutory Roadmap

The order of analysis in evaluating the tax consequences of a nonliquidating distribution is to determine: (1) the amount of the distribution under § 301(b), (2) how much of that amount is a "dividend" as defined in § 316, (3) the specific tax treatment of these amounts as provided in § 301(c), and (4) whether the dividend is "qualified" and thus entitled to be taxed at long-term capital gains rates under § 1(h). The impact of the net investment income tax under § 1411 also must be taken into account.

b. Amount of the Distribution

The amount of a distribution is the amount of cash received by the shareholder plus the fair market value (determined as of the date of the distribution) of any other property received, reduced by any liabilities assumed by the shareholder in connection with the distribution or liabilities to which the property is subject before and after the distribution. § 301(b).

c. Amount of the Dividend

A distribution is a dividend to the extent it is made out of the "earnings and profits" (see VI.B., at page 115, *infra*) for the taxable year in which the distribution is made ("current E & P"), or, if current E & P are insufficient, out of earnings and profits accumulated by the corporation since February 28, 1913 ("accumulated E & P"). § 316(a).

d. Tax Treatment of Distributions

1) In General

A dividend is includible in the gross income of the distributee shareholder. §§ 61(a)(7); 301(c)(1). The portion of a distribution that is not a dividend (because it exceeds both current and accumulated E & P) is first treated as a tax-free return of capital that reduces the shareholder's basis in the stock. § 301(c)(2). Any amount in excess of basis is treated as a gain from a sale or exchange of stock—generally capital gain if the shareholder holds the stock as a capital asset. § 301(c)(3). For additional rules applicable to corporate shareholders, see VI.F., at page 122, *infra*.

Example: X Corp. has $5,000 of current E & P and no accumulated E & P. X distributes $12,000 cash to A, its sole shareholder, who has an $8,000 basis in her X stock (held long-term). Of the $12,000 distribution, $5,000 is taxable as a dividend, and the remaining $7,000 reduces A's stock basis to $1,000. If A's basis had only been $6,000, she would reduce her basis to zero and the remaining $1,000 of the distribution would be long-term capital gain.

2) Multiple Blocks of Stock: Proposed Regulations

In 2009, the IRS issued proposed regulations providing that, if a shareholder holds multiple blocks of stock acquired at different times for different prices and receives a § 301 distribution all or part of which is a return of capital, the distribution would be allocated pro rata on a share-by-share basis to each share of stock within the class of stock upon which the distribution was made. Those regulations were withdrawn in 2019 when the IRS concluded that the regulatory project of which they were a part required significant modifications before being finalized. In so doing, the IRS indicated its view that that the results of a § 301 distribution should be based on the consideration received by a shareholder in respect of each share of stock notwithstanding designations otherwise. REG–143686–07 (Mar. 28, 2019). It seems likely that any future proposed regulations will adopt a similar approach.

e. Qualified Dividends

1) Preferential Tax Rate

"Qualified dividends" received by noncorporate shareholders are taxed at preferential long-term capital gains rates: 0% (for lower income taxpayers); 15%; and 20% (for taxpayers with certain high levels of taxable income). These rate reductions are accomplished by including qualified dividend income in a taxpayer's "net capital gain." § 1(h)(11)(A). These rates apply for both the regular and alternative minimum tax. Qualified dividend income is still ordinary income for other purposes—e.g., it may not be offset by capital losses except to the extent allowed (usually $3,000) under § 1211(b).

2)   "Qualified Dividend" Defined

Qualified dividends are all dividends received during the taxable year from domestic corporations and foreign corporations that meet certain criteria. § 1(h)(11)(B). Some income that is called a "dividend" but is really interest, such as "dividends" paid on money market funds or fixed income mutual funds, does not qualify for the reduced rates.

3)   Minimum Holding Period Rule

An otherwise qualified dividend is not eligible for the reduced rate if the shareholder does not hold the stock for more than 60 days during the 121-day period beginning 60 days before the ex-dividend date. § 1(h)(11)(B)(iii), cross-referencing to § 246(c)(1). The ex-dividend date is the first date on which the stock can be sold without the buyer being entitled to the dividend. The required holding period is extended for certain preferred stock. The purpose of the holding period rule is to prevent short-term traders from acquiring stock a few days before the ex-dividend date, paying tax on the dividend at preferential rates, and then selling the stock soon thereafter, realizing a short-term capital loss that may be deducted against short-term capital gain.

4)   Extraordinary Dividends

If a taxpayer receives an "extraordinary dividend" that qualifies for the reduced rates, any loss on a subsequent sale of the stock with respect to which the extraordinary dividend was paid must be treated as a long-term capital loss to the extent of the dividend, even if the taxpayer's holding period was short-term. § 1(h)(11)(D)(ii). A dividend is "extraordinary" if it exceeds 10% of the basis of the common stock with respect to which the dividend was paid (5% for preferred stock). § 1059(c)(1), (2). For this purpose, all dividends received in any 85-day period are aggregated. § 1059(c)(3)(A). If aggregate dividends paid with respect to stock in any one year exceed 20% of the shareholder's adjusted basis for the stock, all those dividends are treated as extraordinary. § 1059(c)(3)(B). Shareholders may elect an alternative test using fair market value instead of basis. § 1059(c)(4).

f.   **Impact of Net Investment Income Tax**

Nonqualified and qualified dividends received by an individual, estate, or trust are subject to the 3.8% tax on net investment income imposed by § 1411. That tax generally applies to the lesser of the taxpayer's net investment income or adjusted gross income (with some specialized modifications) over a threshold amount ($200,000 for unmarried taxpayers and $250,000 for married taxpayers filing a joint return). When it applies, the net investment income tax results in tax rates on qualified dividends of 18.8% or 23.8% (the sum of the 15% or 20% income tax rates and 3.8%).

B. Earnings and Profits ("E & P")

1. The Concept

The principal function of earnings and profits is to measure the extent to which a distribution is made from a corporation's economic income. "Taxable income" is an inaccurate measure for this purpose because it excludes many economic receipts and outlays. "Retained earnings," an accounting concept, also is inadequate because it can be eliminated on a corporation's financial statement without any actual economic outlay (e.g., by an accounting transfer to paid-in capital resulting from a stock dividend).

2. Determination of Earnings and Profits

The term "earnings and profits" is not defined in the Code or the regulations, but § 312 describes the effect of various transactions on E & P. E & P generally are determined by starting with taxable income and making certain additions, subtractions, and adjustments, as described below. Remember that E & P represent a tax accounting concept, not a particular corporate bank account or fund.

a. Add Back Items Excluded from Taxable Income

Certain items that are excluded from taxable income are added back to taxable income in determining E & P. Examples include tax-exempt municipal bond interest, life insurance proceeds and federal tax refunds. Reg. § 1.312–6(b). Examples of excludable items that are not added back are contributions to capital and realized gains that are not recognized for tax purposes. § 312(f)(1).

b. Add Back Certain Tax-Deductible Items

Tax-deductible items that do not represent actual economic outlays are added back to taxable income for E & P purposes. A common example is the § 243 dividends received deduction. Because net operating losses and capital losses are taken into account for E & P purposes in the year incurred, any carryover amounts deducted in computing taxable income must be added back.

c. Subtract Nondeductible Items

Some nondeductible items represent actual outlays that must be subtracted from taxable income in computing E & P. Examples include federal income taxes, expenses related to tax-exempt income, losses between related taxpayers and charitable contributions in excess of the percentage limitations. Excess corporate capital losses and net operating losses, although not currently deductible, reduce E & P in the year incurred.

d. Add Back or Subtract Timing Adjustments

To ensure that E & P represent a corporation's true economic gain or loss, various adjustments are required to override rules that permit a corporation to defer income artificially or accelerate deductions in computing taxable income. Some examples include:

1) Depreciation

For E & P purposes, a corporation must depreciate tangible property under the alternative depreciation system in § 168(g) rather than the accelerated cost recovery system (ACRS). § 312(k)(3). (This rule is stated as an "exception" in the Code; the "general rule" in § 312(k)(1) applies to intangible property and older tangible assets not depreciated under § 168 and rarely applies.) Machinery and equipment that would be "5-year property" under ACRS generally must be depreciated on the straight line method over a seven-year recovery period using a half-year convention. Additional first year depreciation, known as "bonus depreciation under § 168(k), is not allowable in computing in E & P. Reg. § 1.168(k)–2(f)(7). Real estate generally must be depreciated over a forty-year recovery period. See § 168(g)(2).

2) Gain or Loss on Sale of Depreciable Asset

As a result of the E & P depreciation adjustments described above, an asset's E & P adjusted basis will differ from its taxable income adjusted basis. An appropriate E & P adjustment to taxable gain or loss is required when the asset is sold.

3) § 179 Deduction

A corporation that elects to expense the cost of depreciable property under § 179 must amortize that expense ratably over five years in determining E & P. § 312(k)(3)(B).

4) Installment Sale Reporting

Realized gains that are deferred under the installment sale method of accounting must be included in E & P in the year of sale. § 312(n)(5).

5) Inventory Accounting

Profits on the sale of inventory that have been reported under the last-in-first-out (LIFO) method must be reported for E & P purposes under the first-in-first-out (FIFO) method. § 312(h)(4).

e. Accounting for Earnings and Profits

A corporation determines its E & P under the same accounting method (e.g., cash or accrual) that it uses to compute taxable income. Reg. § 1.312–6(a).

C. Cash Distributions

1. In General

Cash distributions are dividends to the extent they are made out of current or accumulated E & P. The source of a cash distribution is determined by first looking to current E & P, as of the end of the taxable year without reduction by distributions made during the year, and then (if necessary) looking to the most recently accumulated E & P. § 316(a); Reg. § 1.316–2(a).

2. Current E & P Exceed Distributions

If current E & P exceed cash distributions made during the taxable year, then each distribution is a taxable dividend out of current E & P. Any remaining current E & P are added to the accumulated E & P account. Reg. § 1.316–2(b).

Example: At the beginning of the taxable (calendar) year, X Corp. has $10,000 of accumulated E & P. X has $30,000 of current E & P, all realized during the last six months of the year. On July 1, X distributes $20,000 to its shareholders. The entire distribution is a dividend out of current E & P. X's accumulated E & P at the end of the year are $20,000 ($10,000 current E & P remaining after reduction for the distribution plus $10,000 accumulated E & P from prior years). The entire distribution is a dividend even if X has an accumulated E & P deficit at the beginning of the year.

3. Distributions Exceed Current E & P

If cash distributions exceed current E & P, the portion of each distribution that is treated as coming from current E & P is determined by the following formula in Reg. § 1.316–2(b):

$$\text{Amount of Each Distribution} \times \frac{\text{Current E \& P}}{\text{Total Current Distributions}}$$

The remainder of each distribution is a dividend to the extent of the accumulated E & P available on the date of the distribution. In this situation, "accumulated" means E & P accumulated through the end of the taxable year preceding the distribution, less any distributions made earlier in the current year out of accumulated E & P.

Example: At the beginning of the taxable (calendar) year, X Corp. has $5,000 of accumulated E & P. X has $12,000 of current E & P and distributes $20,000 cash to A, its sole shareholder—$10,000 on April 1 and 10,000 on October 1. Applying the formula in Reg. § 1.316–2(b), 60% of each $10,000 distribution, or $6,000, is treated as a dividend paid out of current E & P. X has $5,000 of accumulated E & P available as of the April 1 distribution; thus, the $4,000 balance of that distribution is a dividend, leaving $1,000 accumulated earnings and profits available as of October 1. Of the $4,000 balance of the October 1 distribution, $1,000 is a dividend and $3,000 is a reduction of A's basis in the X stock. The separate tax treatment of the April and October distributions would be more important if A sold X stock on a date between the two distributions.

4. Accumulated E & P but Current Deficit

If a corporation has accumulated E & P at the beginning of the year and a current deficit, the tax treatment of a distribution depends on the accumulated E & P available at the date of distribution. For this purpose, accumulated E & P as of the beginning of the current year are reduced by that portion of the current deficit allocable to the period prior to the distribution. Unless the corporation can trace the deficit to a particular time of the year, it must be prorated on a daily basis to the date of distribution. Reg. § 1.316–2(b); Rev. Rul. 74–164, 1974–1 C.B. 74 (but the Ruling does not consider the possibility of tracing the deficit).

Example: At the beginning of the taxable (calendar) year, X Corp. has $12,000 of accumulated E & P. X has a $10,000 current deficit and makes cash distributions of $20,000 to A, its sole shareholder—$10,000 on April 1 and $10,000 on October 1. A has a $40,000 basis in his X stock. If X is unable to show when the deficit was incurred, it must prorate the deficit over the year ($2,500 per calendar quarter) in determining the accumulated E & P available at the date of the distributions. On April 1, accumulated E & P are $9,500 ($12,000 less $2,500 current deficit prorated to March 31). Of the $10,000 April 1 distribution, $9,500 is a dividend and $500 is a reduction of basis. No further accumulated E & P are available at the time of the October 1 distribution, and thus the entire $10,000 is a reduction of A's basis. X's accumulated E & P deficit as of the beginning of year two is $7,500. See Rev. Rul. 74–164, *supra.* If X were able to show that it incurred its $10,000 deficit in the first quarter of the year and broke even for the remaining nine months, the deficit would eliminate $10,000 of accumulated E & P as of the April 1 distribution, and only $2,000 of the distribution would be a dividend.

D. Property Distributions

1. Consequences to the Distributing Corporation

a. Background

In *General Utilities & Operating Co. v. Helvering,* 296 U.S. 200, 56 S.Ct. 185 (1935), the Supreme Court held that a corporation did not recognize gain on a distribution of appreciated property to a shareholder even though the shareholder took a fair market value basis in the distributed asset. This rule—known as "the *General Utilities* doctrine"—is codified in § 311(a). Congress gradually concluded, however, that the *General Utilities* doctrine was inconsistent with the double tax regime of Subchapter C. Although § 311(a) remains in the Code as a "general rule," it now applies only to nonliquidating distributions of "loss" property. Section 311(b) applies to nonliquidating distributions of appreciated property. Liquidating distributions are governed by § 336, which is discussed in Chapter IX, *infra.*

b. Appreciated Property

1) General Rule

A corporation recognizes gain on a nonliquidating distribution of appreciated property (other than its own debt obligations) in an amount equal to the difference between the fair market value of the property and its adjusted basis. § 311(b)(1).

Example: X Corp. distributes Gainacre ($30,000 value, $10,000 adjusted basis) to its sole shareholder, A. X recognizes $20,000 gain on the distribution. As discussed below (see VI.D.1.e., at page 119, *infra*), the distribution also increases X's current E & P by $20,000.

2) Treatment of Liabilities

If distributed property is subject to a liability or if a shareholder assumes a liability of the distributing corporation in connection with the distribution, the fair market value of the distributed property is treated as not less than the amount of liability. §§ 311(b)(2); 336(b).

c. Loss Property

A corporation may not recognize loss on the distribution of property with an adjusted basis that exceeds its fair market value. § 311(a).

Example: X Corp. distributes Lossacre ($10,000 value, $30,000 adjusted basis) to its sole shareholder, A. X may not recognize its $20,000 loss. X should have sold Lossacre, recognized the $20,000 loss (which would have reduced current E & P by $20,000) and distributed the $10,000 cash proceeds to A.

d. Distribution of Corporation's Own Debt Obligations

The general gain recognition rule in § 311(b) does not apply to distributions of a corporation's own debt obligations. As a result, § 311(a) applies, and no gain or loss is recognized by the distributing corporation.

e. Effect of Distributions on Earnings and Profits

1) In General

Current E & P are determined as of the end of the taxable year without regard to distributions made during the year. Consequently, although a distribution may be a dividend "out of" current E & P, it does not reduce current E & P. Technically speaking, to determine accumulated E & P at the beginning of the following year, accumulated E & P as of the beginning of the year are increased by current E & P of the prior year and then reduced by the amount of the distribution. A distribution may not, however, create a deficit in accumulated E & P. § 312(a).

2) Appreciated Property

On a distribution of appreciated property, the distributing corporation first increases its *current* E & P by the gain recognized under § 311(b). § 312(b)(1). (The Code does not distinguish between the effect of a distribution on current and accumulated E & P but the rules outlined here are generally accepted.) *Accumulated* E & P are reduced by the fair market value of the distributed property. § 312(a)(3), (b). If a shareholder assumes liabilities encumbering the distributed property or takes the property subject to liabilities, the decrease in E & P resulting from the distribution is reduced by the amount of the liabilities. § 312(c); Reg. § 1.312–3. (In other words, liability relief *increases* E & P.) This treatment is equivalent to the result if the corporation had first sold the appreciated property and then distributed the net cash proceeds.

Example: Before any distributions, X Corp. has $35,000 of accumulated E & P and no current E & P. X distributes Gainacre ($50,000 value, $30,000 adjusted basis) to its sole shareholder, A, who takes the property subject to a $10,000 mortgage. X recognizes $20,000 gain under § 311(b), and the distribution generates $20,000 of current E & P. The amount of the distribution is $40,000, all of which is a dividend—$20,000 out of current E & P and $20,000 out of accumulated E & P. Accumulated E & P at the beginning of the next year are $15,000, calculated: $35,000 (balance at beginning of year 1), plus $20,000 (current E & P), minus $50,000 (value of distributed Gainacre), plus $10,000 (mortgage relief). The result would be the same if X had sold Gainacre for $50,000 and distributed the $40,000 net proceeds to A.

3) Loss Property

Current E & P are unaffected by a distribution of loss property, and the corporation reduces accumulated E & P by the adjusted basis of the distributed property. § 312(a)(3).

4) Corporation's Own Obligations

A corporation that distributes its own debt obligations reduces accumulated E & P by the principal amount of those obligations. If a corporation distributes a debt obligation with a fair market value that is less than its face amount (because, for example, the obligations have a stated interest rate that is below prevailing market rates), it reduces accumulated E & P by the "issue price" of the obligations (determined under the original issue discount rules) at the time of the distribution.

2. Consequences to Shareholders

The amount of a property distribution is the fair market value of the distributed property on the date of the distribution reduced by any liabilities to which the property is subject. § 301(b). The portion of the distribution that is a dividend is determined under the same rules applicable to cash distributions. See VI.C., at page 116, *supra*. The shareholder's basis in the distributed property is its fair market value on the date of the distribution without any reduction for liabilities. § 301(d).

E. Constructive Dividends

1. In General

A corporation may attempt to avoid the double tax by providing economic benefits to its shareholders (or close relatives of shareholders) in transactions that are not formally labeled as dividends. The Service may reclassify these transactions as "constructive dividends" for tax purposes. Whether or not a payment or economic benefit is a constructive dividend is usually a factual question. Some illustrative controversies are described below. Note that in all cases, a constructive distribution is not a dividend under § 316 unless the corporation has sufficient E & P. As long as dividends are taxed at preferential capital gains rates, taxpayers may prefer to have a distribution classified as a constructive dividend rather than a more heavily taxed alternative, such as compensation.

2. Examples of Constructive Dividends

a. Unreasonable Compensation

A payment of unreasonable compensation (see § 162(a)(1)) to shareholder-employees or their relatives is income to the shareholder in all events (unless it is an excludable fringe benefit), but the corporation may not deduct excessive compensation that is reclassified as a dividend. Although the failure of a closely held corporation to pay dividends is a significant factor in determining whether compensation paid to shareholder-employees is reasonable, compensation will not automatically be reclassified as a dividend solely because the corporation has not paid more than an insubstantial portion of its earnings as dividends. Rev. Rul. 79–8, 1979–1 C.B. 92.

b. Low Interest Loans

Section 7872 treats the "foregone" interest on a genuine corporate-shareholder demand loan as a dividend to the shareholder followed by a retransfer of the same amount as interest back to the corporation.

c. Loans Without Expectation of Repayment

If a corporation loans money to a shareholder without any expectation of repayment, the constructive dividend is the entire amount loaned, not just the foregone interest.

d. Payments on Debt Reclassified as Equity

Interest or principal payments by a corporation on purported shareholder debt that is reclassified as equity (see V.B.3., at page 101, *supra*) are treated as constructive dividends.

e. Bargain Sales or Leases to Shareholders

On a bargain sale, the dividend is the difference between the amount paid by the shareholder and the value of the property or, in the case of a lease, the spread between rent paid, if any, and fair market rent. See Reg. § 1.301–1(j).

f. Excessive Payments to Shareholders for Purchase or Rental of Property

This is the flip side of a bargain sale or lease. The dividend is the excessive purchase price or rent paid by the corporation to the shareholder.

g. Personal Benefits to Shareholder

Corporate payments of expenses (e.g., for meals, travel and entertainment) that provide only an incidental benefit to the business and are primarily for the personal benefit of a shareholder or his family may be classified as constructive dividends. See, e.g., *Nicholls, North, Buse Co. v. Comm'r*, 56 T.C. 1225 (1971) (75% personal use of corporate yacht was constructive dividend to extent of 75% of yacht's fair rental value); *Ireland v. United States*, 621 F.2d 731 (5th Cir.1980) (personal use of corporate aircraft; value determined by comparable charter air flights).

h. Transfers Between Commonly Controlled Corporations

Transfers of funds or the use of property from one corporation to another corporation controlled by the same shareholders may be treated as a dividend from the payor corporation to the controlling shareholders followed by a capital contribution to the payee corporation.

F. Special Problems of Corporate Shareholders

1. The Dividends Received Deduction

To alleviate multiple taxation at the corporate level, corporate shareholders generally may deduct 50% of dividends received from other domestic corporations. § 243(a)(1). This deduction results in an effective corporate tax rate of 10.5% on dividends received (21% corporate rate × 50% includible portion of dividend = 10.5%). The deduction is increased to 65% for certain corporations that own 20% or more of the distributing corporation's stock, or to 100% if the shareholder and distributing corporations are members of the same electing "affiliated group" (see XIV.D.2., at page 288, *infra*). § 243(a)(3), (b)(1)(A), (c).

2. Holding Period Requirements

The lower effective corporate rate on dividends may motivate a corporate shareholder to convert capital gain (taxed at 21%) into partially excludable dividend income by acquiring stock shortly before a dividend is paid, collecting the dividend, and then realizing a short-term capital loss on sale of the stock for its lower post-dividend value. Section 246(c) blocks this technique by disallowing the dividends received deduction on any share of stock which is held by the taxpayer for 45 days or less during the 91-day period beginning on the date which is 45 days before the date on which the taxpayer becomes entitled to receive the dividend (the "ex-dividend date"). § 246A(c)(1)(A). For certain preferred stock, the required holding period is 90 days. § 246(c)(2). A shareholder's holding period is tolled whenever it diminishes its risk of loss in any one of several manners specified in § 246(c)(4).

3. Extraordinary Dividends: Basis Reduction

To prevent an opportunity for tax arbitrage, a corporate shareholder that receives an "extraordinary dividend" must reduce its basis in the underlying stock (but not below zero) by the "nontaxed portion" of the dividend (i.e., the amount not includible in gross income after the dividends received deduction) if the shareholder has not held the stock for more than two years before the earliest of the date at which the distributing corporation declares, announces or agrees to pay the dividend. § 1059(a)(1), (b), (d)(5). The required basis reduction occurs at the beginning of the ex-dividend date of the extraordinary dividend to which the reduction relates. § 1059(d)(1). If the nontaxed portion of an extraordinary dividend exceeds the shareholder's adjusted basis in the stock, the excess is treated as gain from the sale or exchange of property in the taxable year in which the extraordinary dividend is received. § 1059(a)(2). A dividend is "extraordinary" if it exceeds 5% of the shareholder's adjusted basis in preferred stock or 10% of its adjusted basis in the case of any other stock. § 1059(c)(1), (2). These rules do not apply to dividends that qualify for the 100% dividends received deduction and in certain other specialized situations. § 1059(e)(2), (3). For special rules applicable to distributions in partial liquidations and non pro rata redemptions, see § 1059(e)(1) and VII.D.1.e., at page 140, *infra*.

4. Debt-Financed Portfolio Stock

To prevent another type of arbitrage opportunity, the dividends received deduction is reduced to the extent that the dividend is attributable to debt-financed portfolio stock. § 246A. "Portfolio stock" is all stock held by a corporation unless the corporate shareholder owns either 50% of the total voting power and value, or at least 20% of the total voting power and value and five or fewer shareholders own at least 50% of the voting power and value (excluding preferred stock) of the distributing corporation. § 246A(c)(2). Portfolio stock is "debt-financed" if it is encumbered by any indebtedness directly attributable to the investment in the stock (e.g., all or part of the stock was acquired with borrowed funds). § 246A(d)(3)(A).

5. Earnings and Profits Adjustments

Section 312(n) requires certain adjustments to E & P to more accurately reflect economic gain and loss. See VI.B.2.d., at page 115, *supra*. For example, if a corporation reports gain on the installment method in computing taxable income, E & P must be computed as if the corporation did not use the installment method, resulting in an increase to E & P in the year of sale and decreases in later years. § 312(n)(5). For purposes of determining the taxable income of (and the adjusted basis in any stock held by) a corporate shareholder that owns (directly or indirectly through attribution rules) at least 20% of the voting power or value of another corporation's stock, § 301(e) provides that the § 312(n) adjustments shall not be made to the E & P of the distributing corporation. This rule has the effect of reducing the distributing corporation's E & P—but only for purposes of determining the tax consequences of distributions to 20% corporate shareholders.

6. Preacquisition Dividend Strips

A parent corporation that is about to sell the stock of a subsidiary in a taxable transaction may attempt to convert capital gain on the sale to dividend income by causing the subsidiary to make a large distribution shortly prior to the acquisition. Under the case law, the success of this technique depends primarily on the timing of the distribution and the source of the distributed money or property.

Example: X, Inc. owns all the stock of T, Inc., which has a value of $1,000,000. X's basis in the T stock is $200,000. T has ample E & P. P, Inc. wishes to purchase the T, Inc. stock. If X sells its T stock to P for $1,000,000 cash, X realizes $800,000 of gain taxable at 21%. If X causes T to distribute $800,000 to X and the entire amount is a dividend, X may deduct 100% under § 243(a), and it realizes no further gain on the sale of the T stock for $200,000. If, after negotiations began for the sale of T, the distribution were paid in the form of a T promissory note that was later paid off with funds supplied by P, it likely will be reclassified as a payment of the purchase price. But if T distributed its own excess liquid assets, the dividend likely will not be reclassified even if the buyer infuses T with liquid assets shortly after the purchase. Compare *Waterman Steamship Corp. v. Comm'r,* 430 F.2d 1185 (5th Cir.1970), with *TSN Liquidating Corp. v. United States,* 624 F.2d 1328 (5th Cir.1980) and *Litton Industries, Inc. v. Comm'r,* 89 T.C. 1086 (1987).

Caveat: This strategy may not be viable if X and T file a consolidated return or if the distribution to X is an "extraordinary dividend" under § 1059.

G. Review Questions

1. The concept of "earnings and profits" is identical to "taxable income." True or False?

2. Able Corp. properly elected to expense the cost of depreciable property under § 179. Must Able make any adjustment with respect to this item for E & P purposes? What if Able Corp. deducts 100% of the cost of the property under § 168(k)?

3. What is the principal function of E & P? Are E & P relevant when a corporation makes no distributions during the taxable year?

4. Baxter Corp. distributes $10,000 cash to its shareholders on July 1 of the current year. At the close of the year, Baxter has $10,000 of current E & P, but it had only $2,000 of current E & P on July 1. Baxter has no accumulated E & P. What are the tax consequences of the distribution?

5. Calder Corp. distributed to its sole shareholder, A, property with a fair market value of $50,000 and an adjusted basis of $40,000. Does Calder recognize gain on the distribution? What is the effect of the distribution on current and accumulated earnings and profits? What is the amount of the distribution to A and A's basis in the distributed property?

6. Would the result in question 5, above, be different if the adjusted basis of the distributed property were $60,000?

7. Name five different situations in which a shareholder may be deemed to have received a constructive dividend.

Chapter VII

Stock Redemptions and Partial Liquidations

■ ANALYSIS

A. Introduction

1. Redemption Defined

A redemption is a repurchase of a corporate security by its issuer. This chapter is concerned with redemptions of stock. For tax purposes, a redemption is defined as an acquisition by a corporation of its stock from a shareholder in exchange for cash, debt securities or other property, whether or not the acquired stock is cancelled, retired or held as treasury stock. § 317(a). Some redemptions are known as "partial liquidations" for tax purposes. See VII.C.4., at page 137, *infra*.

2. Overview of Tax Consequences

a. Consequences to Distributee Shareholder

The shareholder-level tax consequences of a redemption depend on whether the distribution more resembles a dividend or a sale. If a corporation distributes money or property in exchange for its own stock and the distributee shareholder's equity interest in the corporation is essentially unchanged, the distribution resembles a dividend and should be taxed as such. If a redemption significantly reduces a shareholder's equity interest, however, it is more akin to a sale or exchange of stock. Consistent with these policies, a redemption is taxed as a distribution under § 301 (i.e., a dividend to the extent of E & P) unless it qualifies for "exchange" treatment under one of five tests in § 302(b). Three of these tests (§ 302(b)(1)–(3)) measure whether the redemption significantly reduces the shareholder's interest in the corporation. The fourth test (§ 302(b)(4)) looks to whether the redemption results in a meaningful contraction of the corporation's business activities. The fifth test (§ 302(b)(5)) provides that redemptions by a mutual fund or real estate investment trust generally are treated as an exchange.

b. Consequences to Distributing Corporation

As in the case of nonliquidating distributions, the distributing corporation recognizes gain on a distribution of appreciated property in redemption, but it may not recognize loss on a distribution of property that has declined in value. § 311(a), (b). For the details and the effect of a redemption on earnings and profits, see VII.D.2., at page 140, *infra*.

3. Tax Stakes

Noncorporate shareholders historically preferred a redemption to be treated as an exchange rather than a dividend. Exchange treatment results in immediate recovery of the shareholder's basis in the redeemed stock, and recognition of capital gain or loss in the usual case where the redeemed stock is a capital asset. Corporate shareholders usually prefer dividend treatment if the distribution qualifies for the § 243 dividends received deduction (and assuming it is not an "extraordinary dividend" under § 1059) or if the consolidated return rules apply. The tax stakes have become less significant for noncorporate shareholders now that dividends and long-term capital gains are taxed at the same preferential rates. Some remaining advantages of exchange treatment are recovery of basis and the ability to offset capital losses against capital gains (but not against qualified dividends).

B. Constructive Ownership of Stock

1. In General

In determining stock ownership for purposes of § 302, an individual or entity is treated as owning stock owned by certain related family members, corporations, partnerships, estates and trusts under the attribution rules in § 318. § 302(e)(1). The rules arbitrarily assume that these related individuals and entities have a unity of economic interest. Section 318 is most directly relevant to redemptions, but it also may apply to other transactions described elsewhere in this outline.

2. Family Attribution

An individual is treated as owning stock owned by her spouse, children (including legally adopted children), grandchildren and parents, but not her siblings or in-laws. Grandchildren are not considered to own stock owned by their grandparents. § 318(a)(1). Stock constructively owned by one family member may not be reattributed to another family member—e.g., no attribution is permitted from parent to child and then to child's spouse. § 318(a)(5)(B).

Example: X Corp.'s 100 outstanding shares are owned by Husband (10), his Wife (20), their Child (20), Wife's Father (30) and Wife's Sister (20). The actual and constructive ownership of X Corp.'s shares is:

Shareholder	Actual	Constructive
Husband	10%	40%
Wife	20%	60%
Child	20%	30%
Wife's Father	30%	60%
Wife's Sister	20%	30%

Husband constructively owns shares from Wife and Child but not from Wife's Father or Sister. Wife owns shares from her Husband, Child and Father, but not from her Sister. Child owns her parents' shares, but no shares from her grandfather or aunt. Father owns shares from his children and grandchild, but not from Wife's Husband. Sister is deemed to own only her Father's shares.

3. Entity to Beneficiary (or Owner) Attribution

a. From Partnerships or Estates

Stock owned by or for a partnership or estate is considered as owned by the partners or beneficiaries with present interests (e.g., life estates) in proportion to their beneficial interests. § 318(a)(2)(A). A person ceases to be a beneficiary of an estate when he receives all property to which he is entitled (e.g., a specific bequest) and the possibility that the person must return the property to satisfy claims is remote. Reg. § 1.318–3(a).

Example (1):   A, B and C are equal partners in the ABC general partnership. The partnership owns 120 shares of X Corp. stock. A, B and C each are considered to own 40 shares of X.

Example (2):   D dies, leaving a $50,000 specific bequest to E, and his residuary estate to F. E is no longer a beneficiary for attribution purposes after she receives her bequest, but F remains a beneficiary until the estate is closed.

b. From Trusts

Stock owned by a trust (other than a qualified employee retirement plan) is considered as owned by its beneficiaries in proportion to their actuarial interests in the trust, however small or remote. § 318(a)(2)(B)(i). Stock owned by a grantor trust is considered as owned by the person who is taxable on the income of the trust. § 318(a)(2)(B)(ii).

Example: Trust owns 100 shares of X Corp. A is the income beneficiary of Trust and B is the remainderperson. A's and B's actuarial interests are 60% and 40%, respectively, and thus they are considered to own 60 and 40 shares of X Corp., respectively.

c. From Corporations

Stock owned by a corporation is considered as owned proportionately (by reference to value) by a shareholder who owns, actually or constructively, 50 percent or more in value of the corporation's stock. § 318(a)(2)(C).

Example: A owns 60% (by value) of the stock of X Corp. X Corp. owns 100 shares of Y Corp. A is considered to own 60 shares of Y Corp. If A owned only 40% of X, A would not be considered as owning any shares of Y through X. If A owned 40% of X Corp. actually and another 20% constructively (e.g. from a family member), A would be a 50% or more shareholder and thus would constructively own 60 shares of Y through X.

4. Beneficiary (or Owner) to Entity Attribution

a. To Partnerships or Estates

All stock owned actually or constructively by partners or beneficiaries of an estate is considered as owned by the partnership or estate. § 318(a)(3)(A).

Example: A, B and C are equal partners of the ABC general partnership. A owns 60 shares of X Corp. actually and is considered as owning 40 shares from his Wife, W. ABC is considered to own 100 shares of X Corp. from A, as well as any shares owned actually and constructively by B and C.

b. To Trusts

All stock owned by a trust beneficiary is attributed to the trust unless the beneficiary's interest is both remote and contingent. A beneficiary's contingent interest is remote if its actuarial value is 5% or less of the value of the trust property, assuming the trustee will exercise maximum discretion in favor of the beneficiary. § 318(a)(3)(B)(i). Grantor trusts are considered as owning stock owned by the grantor or other person taxable on the trust's income. § 318(a)(3)(B)(ii).

Example: A is the income beneficiary of Trust. A owns 100 shares of X Corp., all of which are considered owned by Trust. If A had only a contingent remainder interest in Trust that was worth 5% or less than the value of the trust property, none of A's shares would be attributed to Trust.

c. To Corporations

All stock owned by a shareholder who actually and constructively owns 50% or more of a corporation's stock is attributed to the corporation. § 318(a)(3)(C).

Example: A owns 60% (by value) of X Corp. stock. A owns 100 shares of Y Corp. X Corp. is considered to own 100 shares of Y Corp. from A. If A owned less than 50% of X, however, none of A's shares in Y would be attributed to X.

5. Option Attribution

A person holding an option to acquire stock is considered as owning that stock. § 318(a)(4). If stock may be considered as owned by an individual under either family attribution or option attribution, the option attribution rules take precedence. § 318(a)(5)(E). This may permit reattribution of the optioned stock to another family member despite the no double family attribution rule.

Example: Husband has an option to acquire 100 shares of X Corp. stock owned by Child. Husband is considered to own Child's 100 shares under the option attribution rules. As a result, these shares may be reattributed to Husband's parents, grandparents and other children. If Husband did not hold the option, he still would be considered as owning Child's shares under the family attribution rules, but the shares could not be reattributed to another family member.

6. Other Operating Rules

a. Reattribution

With exceptions noted below, stock constructively owned by a person under § 318 is considered as actually owned for purposes of reattributing that stock to another person. § 318(a)(5)(A).

Example: A and B (who are unrelated) each own 50 of the 100 outstanding shares of X Corp. X Corp. owns 100 shares of Y Corp. A is a 50% partner in the AC Partnership. B is the sole beneficiary of Trust. A and B each is considered as owning 50 shares of Y through X. A's shares of Y are reattributed to the AC Partnership, and B's shares of Y are reattributed to Trust. In addition, the Partnership and Trust each is deemed to own 50 shares of X directly from A and B, respectively.

b. No Double Family Attribution

As noted earlier (see VII.B.2., at page 128, *supra*), stock constructively owned under the family attribution rules in § 318(a)(1) may not be reattributed to another family member. § 318(a)(5)(B).

c. No "Sidewise" Attribution

Stock owned by a beneficiary, partner or shareholder that is attributed to an entity may not be reattributed from the entity to another beneficiary, partner or shareholder. § 318(a)(5)(C).

Example: A and B, who are unrelated, are equal partners in the AB general partnership. A owns 100 shares of X Corp. stock. The partnership is considered to own A's 100 shares of X Corp. under § 318(a)(3)(A), but those shares may not be reattributed to B from the partnership under § 318(a)(2)(A).

d. S Corporation Treated as Partnership

For purposes of § 318, an S corporation is treated as a partnership, and shareholders of an S corporation are treated like partners. § 318(a)(5)(E). This rule applies for purposes of attributing stock to and from the S corporation, but not for determining constructive ownership of stock in the S corporation.

Example: A, B and C (unrelated) are equal shareholders in S Corp., which owns 120 shares of X Corp. A's wife, W, owns 100 shares of Y Corp. (X and Y are C corporations.) A, B and C each is deemed to own 40 shares of X from S Corp. because S Corp. is treated as a partnership for this purpose. If S were not treated as a partnership, none of S's shares of X would be attributed to its shareholders because neither A, B nor C is a 50% or more shareholder of S. A is deemed to own W's 100 shares of Y, and all these shares are reattributed to S.

C. Redemptions Treated as Exchanges

A redemption that is described in § 302(b)(1)–(4) is treated as an exchange of the redeemed stock for the cash or other property distributed by the corporation. § 302(a). Otherwise, it is treated as a distribution to which § 301 applies. § 302(d).

1. Substantially Disproportionate Redemptions

a. Requirements

A distribution in redemption is treated as an exchange if it is "substantially disproportionate" with respect to the shareholder. § 302(b)(2). A distribution is "substantially disproportionate" if it meets three mechanical requirements:

1) Immediately after the redemption, the shareholder must own less than 50% of the total combined voting power of all classes of stock entitled to vote.

2) The percentage of voting stock owned by the shareholder immediately after the redemption must be less than 80% of the percentage of voting stock owned by that shareholder immediately before the redemption.

3) The percentage of common stock (whether or not voting) owned by the shareholder immediately after the redemption must be less than 80% of the percentage of common stock owned immediately before the redemption. If there is more than one class of common stock outstanding, this test is applied in the aggregate by reference to fair market value. Rev. Rul. 87–88, 1987–2 C.B. 81.

The § 318 attribution rules fully apply in determining ownership.

> ***Example:*** A owns 60 out of the 100 outstanding shares (60%) of X Corp. X redeems 20 of A's shares so that, after the redemption, A owns 40 out of the 80 X Corp. shares (50%) still outstanding. The redemption is not substantially disproportionate because A does not own less than 50% of X's voting power and A's percentage ownership after the redemption is not less than 80% of her ownership before. If X redeemed 25 of A's shares, A would own 35 out of the 75 X shares still outstanding after the redemption. The redemption would be substantially disproportionate because A owns less than 50% of X's voting power, and her percentage ownership after the redemption (46.7%) is less than 80% of her ownership before—i.e., 46.7% is less than 48% (80% × 60%).

b. Series of Redemptions

A redemption is not substantially disproportionate if it is made pursuant to a plan which has the purpose or effect of a series of redemptions that, taken together, result in distributions that are not substantially disproportionate. § 302(b)(2)(D). Whether or not such a plan exists is determined from all the facts and circumstances. Reg. § 1.302–3(a). The Service has ruled that a plan exists if a series of redemptions are "causally related" even if they are not part of a joint plan or arrangement. Rev. Rul. 85–14, 1985–1 C.B. 92.

> ***Example:*** A and B each own 50 out of the 100 outstanding shares of X Corp. On January 1 of the current year, X redeems 20 shares from A. Six months later, X redeems 20 shares from B. In isolation, A's redemption would be substantially disproportionate because her interest drops from 50% ($^{50}/_{100}$) to 37.5% ($^{30}/_{80}$). Taken together, the two redemptions result in pro rata distributions because before and after the series of distributions, each shareholder owns 50% of X.

c. "Piggyback" Redemptions

Redemptions of nonvoting stock are not within § 302(b)(2) because the shareholder does not reduce voting power. If a corporation redeems sufficient voting stock from a shareholder to meet § 302(b)(2), however, a redemption of nonvoting preferred stock which is not § 306 stock (see VIII.B.2., at page 163, *infra*) in the same transaction also qualifies as an exchange. Reg. § 1.302–3(a).

2. Complete Terminations of a Shareholder's Interest

a. In General

A redemption that completely terminates a shareholder's actual and constructive stock interest in the corporation is treated as an exchange under § 302(b)(3). If the corporation distributes its debt obligations in exchange for the redeemed stock and the shareholder may recover the stock if the corporation defaults, the Service may contend that the shareholder has not terminated her equity interest.

b. Waiver of Family Attribution

A redemption that completely terminates a shareholder's *actual* interest in a corporation will be treated as an exchange even if the shareholder (called the "distributee" in § 302(c)) constructively owns stock of a family member under § 318(a)(1), provided the following requirements for waiver of family attribution in § 302(c)(2) are met.

1) All Interests Terminated

The distributee must have no interest in the corporation as a shareholder, officer, director or employee immediately after the distribution. § 302(c)(2)(A)(i). In *Lynch v. Comm'r,* 801 F.2d 1176 (9th Cir.1986), the court held that a taxpayer who performs post-redemption services for the corporation as an independent contractor retains a prohibited interest. The Tax Court has been more lenient, looking to the degree of managerial control or financial stake retained by the taxpayer. See, e.g., *Estate of Lennard v. Comm'r,* 61 T.C. 554 (1974). The retention or acquisition of an interest as a creditor is permitted. A person is considered to be a creditor only if her rights are not greater or broader in scope than necessary for enforcement of the claim. Reg. § 1.302–4(d). In determining whether a redeemed shareholder has retained a prohibited post-redemption financial interest, the Tax Court has rejected the Service's position that multiple retained interests are determinative and instead holds that each interest should be analyzed independently. *Hurst v. Comm'r,* 124 T.C. 16 (2005).

2) Ten-Year-Look-Forward Rule

The distributee may not acquire any of the forbidden interests (other than stock acquired by bequest or inheritance) during the 10-year period beginning on the date of the distribution in redemption. § 302(c)(2)(A)(ii). A distributee who remains a creditor of the corporation after a redemption is not considered as acquiring a prohibited interest by acquiring corporate assets to enforce her rights as a creditor, but an acquisition of stock is prohibited. Reg. § 1.302–4(e).

3) Procedural Requirement

The distributee must attach a statement to her income tax return for the year of the redemption reciting that she has not acquired any prohibited interest since the distribution and agreeing to notify the Service of any such acquisition within 30 days after it occurs during the 10-year-look-forward period and to extend the statute of limitations for assessing and collecting a tax with respect to the distribution to one year after the notice. § 302(c)(2)(A)(iii). The Service may grant extensions for filing the agreement if the taxpayer shows "reasonable cause" for a late filing. Reg. § 1.302–4(a)(2).

4) Ten-Year-Look-Back Rule

This rule has two tests and a liberal exception. First, the distributee must not have acquired any portion of the redeemed stock within the 10-year period preceding the distribution from a person whose stock is attributable to the distributee under the family attribution rules in § 318(a)(1). Second, at the time of the distribution no person may own stock which is attributable to the distributee under the family attribution rules if that related family member acquired *any* stock in the corporation from the distributee within the 10-year-look-back period. Neither rule applies, however, if the acquisition or disposition by the distributee during the 10-year-look-back period was not principally motivated by a tax avoidance purpose. § 302(c)(2)(B). A gift of stock is not principally motivated by tax avoidance merely because the donee is in a lower income tax bracket. Reg. § 1.302–4(g).

> ***Example:***   Parent and Child each own 50 of the 100 outstanding shares of X Corp. Parent, who wishes to retire and shift control of X to Child, makes a gift of 20 shares to Child and X Corp. redeems Parent's other 30 shares, leaving Child as the sole shareholder. Parent retains no other interest in X Corp. Tax avoidance was not one of the principal purposes of the transfer to Child, and the 10-year-look-back rule will not prevent the redemption from qualifying for waiver of family attribution under § 302(c). See Rev. Rul. 77–293, 1977–2 C.B. 91.

c. Waiver of Family Attribution by Entities

Section 302(c)(2)(C) permits an entity to waive the family attribution rules. A waiver may be useful when a redemption terminates an entity's actual stock ownership but the entity still owns stock that is attributed from one family member to another "related person" and is then reattributed to the entity. This rule applies only to waive *family* attribution under § 318(a)(1); it does not waive direct beneficiary (or owner) to entity attribution under § 318(a)(3).

1) Entity Defined

For this purpose, an entity means a partnership, estate, trust or corporation. § 302(c)(2)(C)(ii)(I).

2) Related Person Defined

A "related person" is any person to whom ownership of stock in the corporation is (at the time of the distribution) attributable under the family attribution rules if the stock is further attributable to the entity. § 302(c)(2)(C)(ii)(II).

> ***Example (1):***   A and Estate each own 50 of the 100 outstanding shares of X Corp. The sole beneficiary of Estate is A's son, S. A's shares are attributed to S under § 318(a)(1) and are further attributable from S to Estate under § 318(a)(3). S is a "related person." If S actually owned 50 shares, he would not be a related person.

3) Conditions for Entity Waiver

An entity may waive family attribution if the entity and each "related person" meet the usual requirements for a waiver under § 302(c) (i.e., the

10-year-look-back and forward rules and the notice requirement described above), and each related person agrees to be jointly and severally liable for any tax deficiency that may result if an interest is acquired in the 10-year-look-forward period. § 302(c)(2)(C)(i).

Example (2): Assume in Example (1) that X Corp. redeems Estate's 50 shares. Estate has terminated its actual ownership in X but continues to own 50 shares from A through beneficiary S. Assuming no 10-year-look-back rule problems, Estate can waive family attribution and break the chain from A to S if Estate and S jointly agree not to acquire a prohibited interest for 10 years and agree to notify the Service if an interest is so acquired. S also must agree to be jointly and severally liable for any tax deficiency resulting from such an acquisition. If S actually owned 50 shares of X, S's shares would be directly attributed to Estate, and the entity waiver rules would not allow Estate to terminate its interest under § 302(b)(3).

3. Redemptions Not Essentially Equivalent to a Dividend

a. The Meaningful Reduction Standard

If a redemption does not satisfy one of the specific § 302 safe harbors, it still is treated as an exchange under § 302(b)(1) if it is not "essentially equivalent to a dividend." The Supreme Court held in *United States v. Davis,* 397 U.S. 301, 90 S.Ct. 1041 (1970), reh. denied, 397 U.S. 1071, 90 S.Ct. 1495 (1970), that a redemption is not essentially equivalent to a dividend if it results in a "meaningful" reduction of the shareholder's proportionate interest in the corporation. Id. at 312, 90 S.Ct. at 1048. Dividend equivalence "depends upon the facts and circumstances of each case." Reg. § 1.302–2(b). The § 318 attribution rules fully apply, and a business purpose or lack of tax avoidance motive is irrelevant.

Example: On its formation in Year 1, X Corp. issues 25 shares of common stock each to Father, Mother and their two children. In Year 3, for a valid business purpose, Father contributes $25,000 to X Corp. in exchange for 100 shares of nonvoting preferred stock. In Year 5, X distributes $25,000 to Father in redemption of all his preferred stock. Under the attribution rules, Father is considered to be a 100% shareholder before and after the redemption. The redemption of the preferred stock is essentially equivalent to a dividend.

b. Examples of Meaningful Reductions

Although the *Davis* case limits the applicability of § 302(b)(1), the Service has identified several situations that do not qualify under the specific § 302(b) tests but still are not essentially equivalent to a dividend. In determining whether a reduction is "meaningful," the Service considers the three most significant shareholder rights: (1) voting, (2) participation in current earnings and corporate growth, and (3) sharing in net assets on liquidation. Rev. Rul. 81–289, 1981–2 C.B. 82. If the redeemed shareholder has a voting interest, a reduction in voting power is a key factor, together with the potential to participate in a control group with other shareholders. Rev. Rul. 85–106, 1985–2 C.B. 116.

1) Partial Redemption of Nonvoting Preferred Stock

If a corporation redeems one-half of the nonvoting preferred stock of a shareholder who owns no other class of stock, the distribution ordinarily is not essentially equivalent to a dividend. Reg. § 1.302–2(a), third sentence.

2) Significant Loss of Control

A reduction of voting rights from 57% to 50% (with corresponding reductions in rights to earnings and net assets on liquidation) has been ruled to be "meaningful" where the remaining shares are held by one unrelated shareholder. Rev. Rul. 75–502, 1975–2 C.B. 111.

3) Loss of Control in Concert with Others

A reduction of common stock ownership from 27% to 22% is meaningful where the remaining shares are owned by three unrelated shareholders because the redeemed shareholder lost the power to control the corporation in concert with one other shareholder. Rev. Rul. 76–364, 1976–2 C.B. 91.

4) Reduction of Ownership by Isolated Minority Shareholder

A reduction of common stock ownership by a minority shareholder from 30% to 24.3% is meaningful. Rev. Rul. 75–512, 1975–2 C.B. 112. Even a very minimal reduction of a shareholder's interest is meaningful if the shareholder exercises no control—e.g., a de minimis reduction resulting from a tender offer by a publicly traded corporation. Rev. Rul. 76–385, 1976–2 C.B. 92. But a pro rata redemption of stock by a public company is not a meaningful reduction even if the redeemed shareholder has a small minority interest. Rev. Rul. 81–289, 1981–2 C.B. 82.

5) Family Discord

One court has held that evidence of family discord may negate the presumption of the family attribution rules for purposes of § 302(b)(1). *Haft Trust v. Comm'r,* 510 F.2d 43 (1st Cir.1975). The Service and other courts disagree, but the Tax Court concedes that family discord may be a relevant "fact and circumstance" under § 302(b)(1) *after* the family attribution rules have been applied. See, e.g., *David Metzger Trust v. Comm'r,* 693 F.2d 459 (5th Cir.1982), cert. denied, 463 U.S. 1207, 103 S.Ct. 3537 (1983); *Cerone v. Comm'r,* 87 T.C. 1 (1986).

Example: X Corp. has 100 shares of stock outstanding, 50 of which are owned by Mother and the other 50 by her Daughter. Mother and Daughter have been estranged for many years. X Corp. redeems 10 shares from Mother. If the attribution rules apply, the redemption is essentially equivalent to a dividend because Mother is a 100% shareholder before and after the distribution. The courts disagree over whether only Mother's actual ownership of shares should be considered because of the hostile relationship with Daughter.

4. Partial Liquidations

a. The Concept

A partial liquidation occurs when a corporation significantly contracts its business and makes a related distribution (of assets or their sale or insurance proceeds) to its shareholders in redemption of all or part of their stock. Congress concluded that when a distribution in redemption results from such a "corporate contraction," the transaction is more like a sale than a dividend. Section 302(b)(4) reflects this policy by providing exchange treatment for distributions in redemption of stock held by noncorporate shareholders if the transaction is a "partial liquidation" (as defined in § 302(e)) of the distributing corporation. Unlike the three other tests for exchange treatment, which look to the effect of a redemption on the distributee shareholder, qualification under § 302(b)(4) turns on the nature of the assets distributed and the corporation's reason for making the distribution.

b. Only Noncorporate Shareholders Qualify

Only noncorporate shareholders qualify for partial liquidation treatment. § 302(b)(4). S corporations in their capacities as shareholders of other corporations are treated as individuals for this purpose and thus also should qualify. Stock held by a partnership, estate or trust is treated as if held proportionately by its partners or beneficiaries. § 302(e)(5).

c. Partial Liquidation Defined

A distribution is treated as in partial liquidation if: (1) it is not essentially equivalent to a dividend, (2) the distribution is pursuant to a "plan" (a simple corporate resolution will suffice), and (3) the distribution occurs within the taxable year in which the plan is adopted or the succeeding taxable year. § 302(e)(1).

d. Not Essentially Equivalent to a Dividend

Whether a distribution is not essentially equivalent to a dividend is determined at the corporate rather than shareholder level. The requirement is met by satisfying the amorphous "corporate contraction" doctrine (a product of case law), or a more precise "termination of business" safe harbor in § 302(e)(2).

e. Corporate Contraction Doctrine

Under the case law, a distribution in partial liquidation is not essentially equivalent to a dividend if it results from a contraction of the corporation's business. Examples include:

1) Involuntary Events

After a fire damages a manufacturer's factory, the company distributes the insurance proceeds and contracts its business operations. *Imler v. Comm'r*, 11 T.C. 836 (1948); Reg. § 1.346–1(a).

2)   Change in Nature of Business

A corporation distributes working capital that is no longer needed because of a change in the scale of its operations.

3)   Reserve for Expansion

A corporation no longer needs funds that had been accumulated for expansion. Some older cases hold this is a legitimate contraction, but the Service has ruled to the contrary. See Rev. Rul. 78–55, 1978–1 C.B. 88; Reg. § 1.346–1(a).

The corporate contraction standard is amorphous and cannot be relied upon with any assurance for planning purposes.

f.   Termination of Business Safe Harbor

A distribution will not be essentially equivalent to a dividend if: (1) it is attributable to the termination of a "qualified trade or business," and (2) immediately after the distribution, the corporation continues to be engaged in the conduct of another qualified trade or business. § 302(e)(2).

1)   Qualified Trade or Business

A qualified trade or business is any trade or business that was actively conducted throughout the five-year period ending on the date of the distribution and was not acquired (by the distributing corporation) in a taxable transaction during that five-year period. § 302(e)(3). Raw land held for investment or a securities portfolio is not an active trade or business. See Reg. § 1.355–3(b)(2)(iv), which applies to the similar active trade or business requirement under § 355. See XII.B., at page 247, *infra*.

2)   Distribution of Assets or Proceeds of Sale

The terminated business must be operated directly by the distributing corporation. The distribution must be of the assets of that business, or the proceeds of sale of those assets. The distribution of the stock of a subsidiary, or the proceeds of sale of such stock, will not qualify as a partial liquidation. Rev. Rul. 79–184, 1979–1 C.B. 143. A distribution of stock, however, may qualify as a tax-free corporate division. See § 355 and Chapter XII, *infra*.

3)   Pro Rata Redemptions

Qualification as a partial liquidation under the termination of business safe harbor is determined without regard to whether the redemption is pro rata to the shareholders. § 302(e)(4).

g.   No Surrender of Stock Required

Although a partial liquidation is a redemption in form, the Service has ruled that an actual surrender of shares is not required if it would be a "meaningless gesture," such as on a pro rata distribution. In that case, each shareholder is deemed to have surrendered shares with a value equal to the amount of the distribution, and an appropriate portion of the shareholder's stock basis is allocated to the shares deemed surrendered. See Rev. Rul. 90–13, 1990–1 C.B. 65.

Example: A, B and C each own 100 shares of X Corp. with a basis of $15,000 and a value of $100,000. X Corp. distributes $40,000 cash pro rata to each shareholder in a transaction that qualifies as a partial liquidation, but the shareholders do not surrender any stock. Each shareholder is deemed to have surrendered 40 shares of X Corp. stock with a basis of $6,000 (40% of $15,000) in exchange for the $40,000 distribution, and each recognizes a $34,000 long-term capital gain.

D. Specific Tax Consequences of Redemptions

1. Consequences to Shareholders

a. Redemption Treated as Exchange

If a redemption is treated as an exchange, the distributee shareholder computes gain or loss as if the redeemed stock had been sold to an outsider. In the case of losses, however, § 267(a)(1) disallows a deduction if the redeemed shareholder owns (directly or indirectly) more than 50% of the corporation's stock. A shareholder who holds more than one block of stock with different bases may designate the shares to be redeemed.

Example: A owns 100 shares of X Corp. stock held long-term with an adjusted basis of $50,000. X Corp. distributes $90,000 to A in a redemption of 60 shares that qualifies as substantially disproportionate under § 302(b)(2). A allocates $30,000 (60% of her overall basis) to the redeemed stock and recognizes a $60,000 long-term capital gain on the redemption. If A's basis in the 100 shares had been $200,000, A would allocate $120,000 to the redeemed stock and recognize a $30,000 long-term capital loss.

b. Redemption Treated as § 301 Distribution

If a redemption is not treated as an exchange, it is subject to the general distribution rules in § 301. § 302(d). See VI.C., at pages 116–118, *supra.* The distribution is a dividend to the extent of the distributing corporation's E & P, and the balance is a reduction of basis or capital gain. § 301(c). If a distribution in redemption is a dividend, the shareholder may not offset her basis in the redeemed stock. In that event, the basis does not disappear but is added to the basis of any remaining shares held by the distributee or, if no shares are retained, to the basis of shares held by a § 318 related shareholder. Reg. § 1.302–2(c).

Example (1):   A, the sole shareholder of X Corp., owns 100 shares with a basis of $50,000. X, which has ample E & P, distributes $80,000 in redemption of 40 shares. The distribution is a dividend. The basis of the redeemed shares ($20,000) is added to the basis of the shares retained by A.

Example (2):   Same facts as in Example (1), except A owned 40 shares with a basis of $20,000; his son, S, owned the other 60 shares with a basis of $30,000; and X redeemed A's shares in a transaction that does not qualify for waiver of family attribution. The entire distribution is a dividend, and A's $20,000 basis would be reassigned to S, who then would hold his 60 shares with a basis of $50,000. Reg. § 1.302–2(c) Example (2).

c. Proposed Regulations

In 2009, the IRS issued proposed regulations that would have changed some of the straightforward rules described above. The regulations were primarily aimed at abusive basis shifting transactions—e.g., between related foreign and U.S. taxpayers—but would have applied to all redemptions treated as § 301 distributions. The proposed regulations were withdrawn in 2019 when the IRS concluded they required significant modifications before they became final. The IRS continues to study these issues and new proposed regulations may be issued in the future.

d. Basis of Distributed Property

If a shareholder receives property (other than cash) in a redemption treated as a § 301 distribution, the shareholder's basis is the fair market value of the property on the date of the distribution. § 301(d). The result should be the same in the case of a redemption treated as an exchange, although the only applicable authority is the general "cost basis" rule of § 1012. "Cost" for this purpose is the fair market value of the redeemed stock, which ordinarily will be the same as the value of the distributed property.

e. Corporate Shareholders

If a redemption is treated as an exchange, the tax consequences to a corporate shareholder are the same as described above. If a redemption is treated as a dividend, the dividend generally qualifies for the § 243 dividends received deduction, except that a dividend resulting from a redemption that is part of a partial liquidation, or is not pro rata to all shareholders, is treated as an "extraordinary dividend" under § 1059 without regard to the corporate shareholder's holding period in the stock. § 1059(e)(1). A corporation receiving an "extraordinary dividend" must reduce its basis in the stock of the distributing corporation by the portion of the dividend that was not taxed because of the dividends received deduction. If the nontaxed portion of the extraordinary dividend exceeds the corporate shareholder's stock basis, the excess is treated as gain from the sale or exchange of stock for the taxable year in which the extraordinary dividend is received. § 1059(a). See VI.F.3., at page 122, *supra*.

2. Consequences to Distributing Corporation

a. Recognition of Gain or Loss

The distributing corporation recognizes gain on a distribution of appreciated property in redemption of its stock, but it may not recognize loss on a distribution of property that has declined in value. § 311(a), (b). The rules are the same whether or not the redemption is treated as an exchange to the shareholders.

b. Effect on Earnings and Profits

1) Distribution of Appreciated Property

The distributing corporation increases its current earnings and profits by the gain recognized on a distribution of appreciated property. § 312(b). If the basis of the property for E & P purposes is different from its basis for taxable income purposes, the increase is the E & P gain, not the taxable gain.

2) Redemption Treated as § 301 Distribution

If a redemption is treated as a § 301 distribution, the effect on E & P is the same as on any other ordinary distribution. Accumulated E & P are reduced by the amount of money, the fair market value of any appreciated property distributed, the E & P adjusted basis of any loss property distributed, and the principal amount of debt obligations. § 312(a), (b).

3) Redemption Treated as Exchange

If a redemption is treated as an exchange, accumulated E & P are reduced in an amount that may not exceed the ratable share of accumulated E & P attributable to the redeemed stock. § 312(n)(7). For this purpose, "accumulated" E & P includes any current E & P available at the time of the redemption, which are determined after current E & P are first applied to characterize as dividends any § 301 distributions made during the year. Rev. Rul. 74–338, 1974–2 C.B. 101. In no event may the E & P reduction exceed the amount of the distribution. If the corporation has only one class of stock outstanding, the E & P attributable to the redeemed stock are determined by multiplying accumulated E & P by the ratio of redeemed shares over total outstanding shares. More complex computations are required if a corporation has more than one class of stock outstanding.

> *Example:* X Corp. has 1,000 shares of common stock outstanding (its only class), owned equally by A and B. X has $160,000 of accumulated E & P and no current E & P. In a redemption treated as an exchange, X distributes $100,000 in redemption of A's 500 shares. Since the redeemed stock is 50% of the total number of shares outstanding, X may reduce E & P by $160,000 × 50%, or $80,000. If X had accumulated E & P of $240,000, the reduction would be limited to $100,000 (the amount of the distribution).

c. Stock Reacquisition Expenses

A corporation generally may not currently deduct any expenses paid in connection with the reacquisition (including redemption) of its own stock. Rather, such expenses are nondeductible, nonamortizable capital expenditure. § 162(k)(1). This deduction disallowance rule does not apply to the allocable costs of borrowing to finance a stock redemption. Those costs may be amortized over the term of the indebtedness. § 162(k)(2)(ii). The policy for this exception is that the borrowing transaction is separate from the redemption. Other corporate payments made contemporaneously with a reacquisition (e.g., payments to employees to discharge a contractual obligation under an employment agreement) are not subject to the disallowance rule in § 162(k).

E. Redemptions Through Use of Related Corporations

1. Introduction

a. Policy

Section 304 prevents a shareholder from selling stock of one corporation to another related corporation in order to withdraw ("bail out") earnings while treating the transaction as a sale rather than a dividend. Section 304 applies when one or more controlling shareholders sell stock of one corporation to another controlled corporation (a "brother-sister acquisition"), or when any shareholder of a parent corporation sells stock of the parent to a subsidiary (a "parent-subsidiary acquisition"). Section 304 tests these transactions for dividend equivalency by applying § 302 to determine whether the shareholder has sufficiently reduced his interest in the corporation whose stock has been transferred. As with actual redemptions, the distinction between dividend and exchange treatment is less significant for noncorporate shareholders as long as dividends and capital gains are taxed at the same preferential rate. As in the past, corporate shareholders typically will prefer dividend treatment because of the dividends received deduction.

Example: A owns all the stock of both X Corp. and Y Corp., each of which have ample E & P. If either corporation were to redeem shares held by A, the distribution would be a dividend. If A sells all or part of her X stock to Y, the effect of the transaction is the same as a dividend because A has withdrawn funds from Y without reducing her 100% control of both corporations. The same would be true if A owned all the stock of X Corp. which in turn owned all the stock of Y Corp., and A sold all or part of her X stock to Y for cash. Section 304 treats these transactions as constructive redemptions and tests them for dividend equivalency under § 302.

b. § 304 Glossary

Familiarity with several statutory terms of art is essential to an understanding of § 304.

1) Property

Section 304 applies only to acquisitions of stock in return for "property." For this purpose, "property" includes money, securities and other property but not stock in the corporation making the acquisition. § 317(a). See *Bhada v. Comm'r,* 89 T.C. 959 (1987), *aff'd sub nom., Caamano v. Comm'r,* 879 F.2d 156 (5th Cir.1989).

2) Acquiring Corporation

The "acquiring corporation" is the corporation that acquires stock from a shareholder of another related corporation in return for property. In a parent-subsidiary acquisition, the acquiring corporation always is the subsidiary.

3) **Issuing Corporation**

The "issuing corporation" is the corporation whose stock has been transferred. In a parent-subsidiary acquisition, the issuing corporation is always the parent.

4) **Control**

For purposes of § 304, "control" means the ownership of stock possessing at least 50% of the total combined voting power of all classes of stock entitled to vote, *or* at least 50% of the total value of shares of all classes of stock. § 304(c)(1). This is not the same as the 80% "control" test in § 368(c) that is used for certain other corporate-shareholder transactions, such as corporate formations and reorganizations. In determining control, the attribution rules in § 318 apply except that stock may be attributed between a corporation and a 5% or more (instead of 50% or more) shareholder. § 304(c)(3). In the case of a corporation with more than one class of stock, the value prong of the "control" test is applied to the aggregate value of all classes of stock, not class-by-class. Rev. Rul. 89–57, 1989–1 C.B. 90. Thus, a shareholder who owns 50% or more of the value of all the corporation's stock has "control" even if she owns less than 50% of a particular class. If a person or persons are in "control" of one corporation which in turn owns at least 50% of either the total combined voting power or stock value of a second corporation, then that person or persons are treated as in "control" of the second corporation. § 304(c)(1).

c. Mode of Analysis

In analyzing § 304 issues, the following four-step process may be helpful:

1) Determine if § 304 applies—i.e., is the sale either a "brother-sister" or "parent-subsidiary" acquisition. If so, the transaction is treated as a constructive redemption.

2) If § 304 applies, determine whether the constructive redemption qualifies for exchange treatment under § 302(b) by comparing the shareholder's actual and constructive ownership in the issuing corporation's stock before and after the transaction. In so doing, remember that all or part of the transferred stock is still outstanding and may be attributed back from the acquiring corporation to the shareholder.

3) If the constructive redemption is treated as a § 301 distribution, determine the amount and source of any dividend by looking first to the E & P of the acquiring corporation and then to the E & P of the issuing corporation. § 304(b)(2).

4) Finally, determine the collateral consequences of the transaction—e.g., effect on basis and earnings and profits.

d. Regulations

The § 304 regulations predate various statutory amendments. Proposed regulations were issued in 2009 as part of a comprehensive regulatory project to provide guidance regarding the recovery of stock basis on § 301 distributions and transactions treated by § 304 and other Code sections as distributions to which

§ 301 applies. The regulations were withdrawn in 2019 to permit the IRS to study various specific issues, including § 304.

2. Brother-Sister Acquisitions: § 304(a)(1)

a. The Constructive Redemption

If one or more persons are in "control" of each of two corporations and sell stock of one corporation (the "issuing corporation") to the other (the "acquiring corporation") in return for property, the property is treated for purposes of §§ 302 and 303 as a distribution in redemption of the stock of the acquiring corporation. § 304(a)(1). Note that § 304(a)(1) applies when two or more unrelated shareholders who in the aggregate control each of two corporations sell stock of one corporation to the other in related transactions even if no single shareholder has control. § 304(a)(1)(B). The constructive redemption is then tested for dividend equivalence under § 302 by reference to the stock of the issuing corporation. § 304(b)(1).

b. Tax Consequences

1) § 301 Distribution

If the constructive redemption is treated as a § 301 distribution, the amount and source of any dividend is determined first by reference to the E & P of the acquiring corporation and then, if necessary, to the E & P of the issuing corporation. § 304(b)(2). The transferor is treated as having transferred the stock of the issuing corporation to the acquiring corporation in exchange for acquiring corporation stock in a transaction to which § 351(a) applies. Then, the acquiring corporation is treated as if it had redeemed the stock that it was treated as issuing in the hypothetical § 351 exchange. § 304(a)(1). The acquiring corporation takes a transferred basis from the shareholder in the acquired stock under § 362(a). Under § 358, the shareholder's basis in the acquiring corporation stock deemed issued in the hypothetical § 351 exchange is equal to the basis of the issuing corporation stock that the shareholder was treated as having transferred in that exchange. Under the now withdrawn proposed § 304 regulations, the shareholder's basis in the acquiring corporation stock held or deemed held by that shareholder is decreased as a result of the distribution if part of the distribution is treated as a reduction of basis under § 301(c)(2), such as when there are insufficient E & P to characterize the entire distribution as a dividend. Prop. Reg. § 1.304–2(a)(4) (withdrawn).

2) Exchange

If the transaction is treated as an exchange, the shareholder recognizes gain or loss measured by the difference between the amount realized and the adjusted basis in the transferred stock. (Allowance of losses may be limited by § 267). Under the withdrawn proposed regulations, the shareholder's basis in the stock of the acquiring corporation remains unchanged after the exchange, and the acquiring corporation takes a § 1012 cost basis in the issuing corporation's stock. Prop. Reg. § 1.304–2(a)(5) (withdrawn). It is likely that regulations issued in the future will reach the same result. Any E & P reduction is limited by § 312(n)(7) to an amount not in excess of the redeemed stock's ratable share of accumulated E & P (see VII.D.2.b.3., at page 141, *supra*), but it is unclear which corporation's E & P will be affected. A reasonable answer is that the required E & P reduction should be made first to the acquiring corporation's E & P and then, if necessary, to the issuing corporation's E & P.

Example (1): A and B (unrelated) each own 100 of the 200 outstanding shares of X Corp. and Y Corp., respectively. X has $70,000 of E & P, and Y has $40,000 of E & P. A sells 30 shares of X Corp. stock (having an adjusted basis to A of $10,000) to Y for $100,000. X is the "issuing corporation" and Y is the "acquiring corporation." Because A is in control of both corporations (he owns at least 50% of each) and sells X stock to Y in exchange for cash, § 304(a)(1) applies.

The transaction is treated as a constructive redemption of Y stock which is tested for dividend equivalence by reference to A's stock holdings in X. Before the sale, A owns 50% (100 shares) of X. After the sale, A owns 42.5% of X (70 shares actually and 15 shares constructively from Y Corp.). Since A's percentage ownership of X stock after the sale is not less than 80% of his percentage ownership before the sale, the redemption does not qualify as substantially disproportionate under § 302(b)(2).

If (as is likely) § 302(b)(1) does not apply, the entire $100,000 received by A is a dividend—$40,000 from Y's E & P and $60,000 from X's E & P. A is treated as having transferred 30 shares of X Corp. to Y Corp. in exchange for Y Corp. stock of equivalent value in a tax-free § 351 transaction, and then Y Corp. is treated as if it redeemed the Y Corp. shares that it issued in that hypothetical transaction. Y Corp. takes a $10,000 basis under § 362 in the 30 shares of X Corp. stock transferred by A to X Corp. A may add $10,000 (the basis of his 30 shares of X stock) to the basis of his Y stock. If § 302(b)(1) applies, the transaction is treated as a sale. A recognizes $90,000 long-term capital gain ($100,000 minus $10,000) and Y takes a $100,000 cost basis in the 30 shares of X stock, and A's basis in the Y stock does not change as a result of the sale.

Example (2): Same as Example (1), except A owns only 40% of the stock of X Corp. and Y Corp., and B owns 60%. If only A transfers X stock to Y, § 304 does not apply because the X stock has not been acquired from a person or persons in "control" of both corporations.

Example (3): Same as Example (2), except A is B's father. Applying the § 318 attribution rules, A is in control of both X and Y, and § 304(a)(1) applies.

3. Parent-Subsidiary Acquisitions: § 304(a)(2)

a. The Constructive Redemption

If a subsidiary (the "acquiring corporation") acquires stock of its parent (the "issuing corporation") from a shareholder of the parent in return for property, the property is treated as a distribution in redemption of the issuing corporation's (i.e. parent's) stock. § 304(a)(2). The constructive redemption is tested for dividend equivalency by reference to the stock of the parent. § 304(b)(1). For this purpose, the parent-subsidiary relationship is determined by the 50% control test in § 304(c). Reg. § 1.304–3(a). See VII.E.1.b.4., at page 143, *supra.*

b. Tax Consequences

1) § 301 Distribution

If the constructive redemption is treated as a § 301 distribution, the amount and source of the dividend is determined first by reference to the E & P of the acquiring corporation and then, if necessary, by the E & P of the issuing corporation. § 304(b)(2). The shareholder's basis in the transferred parent stock is added to the basis of his remaining parent stock. Reg. § 1.304–3(a). The subsidiary takes a cost basis in the stock of the parent that it acquires in the transaction. See *Broadview Lumber Co. v. United States,* 561 F.2d 698 (7th Cir.1977). Logically, the acquiring (subsidiary) corporation's E & P are reduced to the extent they are the source of the dividend and then the issuing (parent) corporation's E & P are reduced to the extent they were the source.

2) Sale

If the constructive redemption is treated as a sale or exchange, the selling shareholder recognizes gain or loss under normal tax principles, and the subsidiary takes a cost basis in the parent stock that it acquires. The impact on E & P under § 312(n)(7) is unsettled, leaving taxpayers the leeway to use any reasonable approach.

Example: A owns 60 of the 100 outstanding shares of X Corp., which owns 80 of the 100 outstanding shares of Y Corp. and thus "controls" Y. A sells 20 shares of X (basis—$20,000) to Y in exchange for $80,000. The transaction is treated by § 304(a)(2) as a distribution in redemption of X Corp. stock. Before the sale, A owns 60% (60 out of 100 shares) of X. After the sale, A owns 40 shares actually and 6.4 shares constructively (80% of the 20 shares of X owned by Y, or 16 shares, are attributed to X, and 40% of those 16 shares, or 6.4 shares, are reattributed to A), for a total of 46.4%. A's ownership of X is reduced from 60% to 46.4%, qualifying the redemption for substantially disproportionate exchange treatment under § 302(b)(2). A thus recognizes $60,000 LTCG and Y takes an $80,000 cost basis in the Y stock.

c. Overlap Situations

If a transaction is both a brother-sister and a parent-subsidiary acquisition, the parent-subsidiary rules in § 304(a)(2) take precedence. § 304(a)(1). But because the attribution rules transform virtually all actual brother-sister relationships into parent-subsidiary, an actual brother-sister acquisition is subject to § 304(a)(1) even if it also may be a constructive parent-subsidiary acquisition. Reg. § 1.304–2(c) Example (1).

4. Relationship of § 304 to Other Code Sections

a. Coordination with § 351

In overlap situations, § 304(b)(3)(A) provides that § 351 will not apply to any "property" received in a § 304(a) distribution, except that § 304 will not apply to any debt incurred or assumed in connection with the acquisition of the transferred stock. § 304(b)(3)(B). Keep in mind that stock of the acquiring corporation is not "property" (§ 317(a)), and thus a transaction may be bifurcated into a § 351 nonrecognition exchange and a § 304 distribution.

> *Example (1):* A owns 80 out of the 100 outstanding shares of X Corp., and Y Corp., respectively. Both corporations have ample E & P. The remaining stock is owned by unrelated shareholders. A sells 20 shares of X (basis—$4,000; value—$20,000) to Y in exchange for 15 newly issued shares of Y (value—$15,000) and $5,000 cash. The transfer qualifies under § 351, which applies to the exchange of X stock for Y stock (§ 304 does not apply because the Y stock is not "property"), but § 304 applies to the exchange of X stock for $5,000 cash.

> *Example (2):* Same as Example (1), except A transfers 20 shares of X to Y in exchange for 15 shares of Y, and Y takes the stock subject to a $5,000 liability incurred by A when he acquired the X stock. A recognizes no gain on the transaction under §§ 351 and 357; § 304 does not apply to Y's assumption of the $5,000 liability.

b. Relationship to Partial Liquidation Rules

If a § 304 transaction also qualifies as a partial liquidation under § 302(b)(4), it may qualify for exchange treatment. In testing the transaction, the courts have looked to the contraction in the acquiring corporation's business. See *Blaschka v. United States*, 393 F.2d 983 (Ct.Cl.1968).

F. Redemptions to Pay Death Taxes

1. Policy

Section 303 treats certain redemptions as exchanges even if the transaction would not have qualified for exchange treatment under § 302. The redeemed stock must have been included in the gross estate of a decedent for federal estate tax purposes. The policy of § 303 is to facilitate redemptions of closely held stock by estates (or, in some cases, beneficiaries) who may need to raise funds to pay death taxes and other estate administration expenses. Since the stock ordinarily has a date-of-death basis under § 1014, a redemption qualifying under § 303 usually results in recognition of little or no gain or loss.

2. Requirements and Limitations

a. Stock Included in Decedent's Gross Estate

The redeemed stock must have been included in the decedent's gross estate for federal estate tax purposes (§ 303(a)), or the stock must take its basis from stock that was included in the decedent's gross estate and the "old stock" must have qualified for § 303(a) exchange treatment (§ 303(c)).

b. Relationship of Stock to Decedent's Estate

1) 35% Rule

The value of the distributing corporation's stock that is included in the decedent's gross estate must exceed 35% of the value of the gross estate less debts, claims and administrative expenses allowable as deductions under §§ 2053 and 2054. § 303(b)(2)(A).

2) Two or More Corporations Aggregation Rule

The stock of two or more corporations may be aggregated for purposes of the 35% rule if 20% or more in value of each corporation's total outstanding stock is included in the decedent's gross estate. For purposes of the 20% requirement, stock held by the decedent's surviving spouse as community property, or held with the decedent in joint tenancy, tenancy-by-the-entirety or tenancy-in-common is treated as if it were included in determining the value of the decedent's gross estate. § 303(b)(2)(B).

> ***Example:*** D died with a gross estate less deductible debts and expenses of $16,000,000. Included in D's gross estate were 1,000 shares of X Corp. (value—$4,800,000) held by D as separate property and constituting 25% of X's outstanding stock, and 500 shares of Y Corp. (value—$1,600,000), constituting 12% of Y's outstanding stock, and representing D's 50% interest in 1,000 shares held by D and his surviving spouse, S, as tenants-in-common. Since the value of the X and Y stock included in D's gross estate constitute 20% or more in value of the total outstanding stock of those corporations (treating S's interest in the Y Corp. stock as having been included in determining the value of D's gross estate for this purpose), the X and Y stock are treated as stock of a single corporation, with a value of $6,400,000, allowing D's estate to satisfy the 35% test.

c. Dollar Limitations

Section 303 exchange treatment is available only to the extent that the distribution does not exceed the sum of: (1) death taxes imposed because of the decedent's death, and (2) funeral and administrative expenses allowed as estate tax deductions under § 2053.

d. Timing of Redemption

A § 303 redemption generally must occur within 90 days after the expiration of the statute of limitations for assessment of federal estate taxes (usually three years). The period is extended if a petition for redetermination of an estate tax deficiency is filed in the Tax Court or if the estate is eligible and elects to pay estate taxes in installments under § 6166. § 303(b)(1). Additional limitations are imposed for distributions made more than four years after the decedent's death. § 303(b)(4).

e. Shareholder Must Bear Burden of Estate Tax

Stock redeemed under § 303 ordinarily is held by the decedent's estate. Beneficiaries of stock included in the decedent's gross estate also may qualify to the extent that their interests are reduced by an obligation to pay death taxes or administrative expenses. § 303(b)(3).

3. Consequences to Distributing Corporation

A corporation that distributes property in a § 303 redemption must recognize gain under § 311(b) but may not recognize loss under § 311(a). The effect of a § 303 redemption on the distributing corporation's E & P is determined under § 312(n)(7). See VII.D.2.b.3. at page 141, *supra*.

G. Redemptions and Related Transactions

1. Redemptions and Sales

If a redemption and sale are part of an integrated transaction to dispose of a shareholder's entire interest in the corporation, the redemption will qualify as a complete termination under § 302(b)(3) whether it occurs before or after the sale. *Zenz v. Quinlivan*, 213 F.2d 914 (6th Cir.1954). Historically, this technique was used by individual shareholders to remove liquid assets from a corporation and sell the remaining stock at a reduced price in a transaction known as a "bootstrap acquisition." A sale and redemption also may be combined to qualify the redemption as "substantially disproportionate" under § 302(b)(2). Rev. Rul. 75–447, 1975–2 C.B. 113. When dividends and long-term capital gains are taxed at the same rate, this type of planning may be less significant or unnecessary for noncorporate shareholders.

Example (1): A owns all 100 outstanding shares of X Corp in which she has a basis of $30,000. The value of X Corp. is $100,000, including $20,000 in cash and $80,000 of operating assets. X Corp. has $50,000 of E & P. B wishes to acquire X Corp. (without the cash) for $80,000. X first distributes $20,000 to A in redemption of 20 shares, and A then sells her remaining 80 shares to B for $80,000. If the redemption and sale are part of an integrated plan, A is considered to have completely terminated her interest in X and the redemption qualifies for exchange treatment under § 302(b)(3). Allocating A's stock basis 20% to the redemption and 80% to the sale, A recognizes $14,000 long-term capital gain on the redemption and $56,000 long-term capital gain on the sale.

Example (2): Same as Example (1), except X Corp. first makes a $20,000 distribution to A (not in a redemption) and then A sells all 100 shares to B for $80,000. A has a $20,000 dividend (likely a qualified dividend taxable at 15% or 20%) and a $50,000 long-term capital gain on the sale. A's tax liability (tax paid at capital gains rates) is the same as in Example (1).

Example (3):   A and B, who are unrelated, each own 50 of X Corp.'s 100 outstanding shares. To bring C (also unrelated) into the business and rearrange control, X issues 25 new common shares to C and, pursuant to the same plan, X redeems 25 shares of its stock from A and B, respectively. Viewing the transactions as a whole, A and B's interests were reduced from 50% ($^{50}/_{100}$ shares) to 33⅓% ($^{25}/_{75}$ shares), and the redemptions qualify as substantially disproportionate under § 302(b)(2).

2. Redemptions Pursuant to Buy-Sell Agreements

a. Buy-Sell Agreements

Closely held corporations frequently use buy-sell stock purchase agreements to provide for the continuity of a business, to satisfy economic and tax goals when a shareholder dies or retires, and to resolve shareholder disputes. Under a "cross-purchase" agreement, the departing shareholder or his estate sells the stock to the continuing shareholders. Under an "entity-purchase" agreement, the corporation redeems the departing shareholder's stock. The obligation to buy (or sell) may be mandatory or optional, as the parties agree. Buy-sell agreements also typically include other restrictions on the transfer of shares and provisions to determine the value of any stock purchased pursuant to the agreement.

b. Constructive Dividend Issues

Constructive dividend issues may arise when a continuing shareholder is personally and unconditionally obligated to purchase stock pursuant to a buy-sell agreement and that obligation is assumed by the corporation. See, e.g., *Wall v. United States*, 164 F.2d 462 (4th Cir.1947); *Sullivan v. United States*, 363 F.2d 724 (8th Cir.1966), *cert. denied*, 387 U.S. 905, 87 S.Ct. 1683 (1967). A mere assignment to the corporation of an option (or other contractual right) to purchase stock from another shareholder does not result in a constructive dividend. *Holsey v. Comm'r*, 258 F.2d 865 (3d Cir.1958).

Example (1):   A and B, who are unrelated, own all 100 shares of X Corp. They agree that upon the death of either shareholder, the survivor will be unconditionally obligated to purchase the decedent's X stock from his estate. After B dies, A causes the corporation to assume his obligation and redeem the stock from B's estate. The redemption results in a constructive distribution to A. Rev. Rul. 69–608, 1969–2 C.B. 42, Situations 1 & 2.

Example (2):   Same as Example (1), except that the agreement provides that upon the death of either shareholder, X Corp. has an option to purchase the decedent's stock. If X chooses not to exercise the option, the surviving shareholder is obligated to purchase any unredeemed shares. If B dies and X redeems all of B's stock, the redemption is not a constructive distribution to A because A was not primarily obligated to buy the stock. Rev. Rul. 69–608, *supra*, Situation 5.

Example (3):   Same as Example (1), except that the agreement provides that either shareholder has an option to purchase the stock of the other on the occurrence of certain events but is free to assign the option to others. At B's retirement, A assigns his option to X Corp., which redeems all of B's stock. The redemption is not a constructive distribution to A because A had no unconditional obligation to buy the stock. Rev. Rul. 69–608, *supra*, Situation 4.

c. Redemptions Incident to Divorce

1) The Problem

Constructive dividend issues also may arise when a closely held corporation redeems stock in connection with a divorce settlement. Assume, for example, that H and W each own 50% each of the highly appreciated stock of X Corp., and H agrees to buy W's 50% interest upon their divorce. If H buys W's stock for cash, the transfer is governed by § 1041; W does not recognize gain, and H takes a transferred basis in the stock. But what if H's (unconditional?) obligation is fulfilled by a redemption of W's stock by X, Corp., leaving H as the sole shareholder? Is that transaction still governed by § 1041; does H (or W) have a constructive dividend; or is neither party taxable? Because the case law on these questions was unsettled, the Service issued regulations providing guidance and flexibility to taxpayers.

2) Case Law

The Ninth Circuit has held that when Husband ("H") and Wife ("W") each own 50% of the stock of Corporation, and Corporation redeems W's stock pursuant to a divorce settlement, the transaction should be treated as a tax-free § 1041 transfer of W's stock to H (see Reg. § 1.1041–1T(c), Q & A 9, treating such a transfer as made by W "on behalf of" H), followed by a redemption from H. In so holding, the court suggested that the subsequent redemption of half of H's stock results in a § 301 distribution and possible dividend to H. *Arnes v. United States,* 981 F.2d 456 (9th Cir.1992). See also *Hayes v. Comm'r,* 101 T.C. 593 (1993). In a related case, the Tax Court, addressing the same transaction, held that H did not have a constructive dividend because he was not unconditionally obligated to buy W's stock. *Arnes v. Comm'r,* 102 T.C. 522 (1994). In a later case, the Tax Court held (on similar facts where the agreement allowed H to buy W's stock or cause the corporation to do so in a redemption) that § 1041 applied to W's transfer because it was made "on behalf of" H and suggested that, as a result, H had a constructive dividend. *Read v. Comm'r,* 114 T.C. 14 (2000).

3) Regulations

The Service has issued regulations to clarify this area and harmonize the "primary and unconditional" standard for constructive dividends with the policy of § 1041. If a divorce-related redemption results in a constructive distribution to the nontransferor spouse under "applicable tax law" (applying the primary and unconditional standard), the redeemed stock is treated as if it were transferred by the transferor spouse (i.e., the spouse whose stock is being redeemed) in a tax-free § 1041 transaction (if all the § 1041 requirements are met) and then retransferred by the nontransferor spouse to the corporation in a redemption. Reg. § 1.1041–2(a)(2), (b)(2). If the redemption does not satisfy a primary and unconditional obligation of the nontransferor spouse, the form of the transaction is respected—i.e., the corporation is treated as directly redeeming the transferor spouse's stock and § 1041 does not apply. Reg. § 1.1041–2(a)(1), (b)(1). The spouses may agree in writing to treat a divorce-related redemption as a constructive distribution to the transferor spouse (even without a primary and unconditional obligation) and a tax-free § 1041 transfer, or as a direct redemption of the transferor spouse's stock and not a constructive distribution to the nontransferor spouse even if that spouse had a primary and unconditional obligation. Reg. § 1.1041–2(c).

Example (1): H and W each own 50 shares of X Corp. which has ample E & P. Pursuant to a divorce agreement, H is unconditionally obligated to purchase W's stock for cash. H is short of funds, however, and causes X Corp. to fulfill his obligation by redeeming W's stock for cash. Under the regulations, the transaction is treated as a tax-free § 1041 transfer of W's stock from W to H followed by a redemption that results in a constructive dividend to H.

Example (2): Same as Example (1), except the agreement gave H the option to purchase W's stock or to request X Corp. to redeem the stock. Since H did not have a primary and unconditional obligation to buy W's stock, the form of the transaction is respected for tax purposes under the regulations. Because the redemption terminates W's interest in X Corp. (and there is no family attribution after their divorce), the redemption likely qualifies as an exchange to W under § 302(b)(3), and H is not taxable.

Example (3): Same as Example (2), except H and W agree in writing to treat the redemption as a constructive dividend to H and a tax-free § 1041 transfer by W. Under the regulations, the tax results are the same as in Example (1). Similarly, the parties could agree in Example (1) to treat the transaction as a redemption of the transferor spouse's stock and not a constructive distribution to the nontransferor spouse.

3. Charitable Contribution Followed by Redemption

A shareholder of a closely held corporation may indirectly withdraw earnings but avoid dividend treatment by contributing stock to a charity and causing the corporation to redeem the stock from the charitable donee. The Service was unsuccessful in reclassifying this type of transaction as a constructive dividend followed by a charitable gift of cash. See *Grove v. Comm'r,* 490 F.2d 241 (2d Cir.1973). It subsequently ruled that a contribution of stock followed by a redemption shall be treated as a dividend to the donor only if the charitable donee is legally bound or can be compelled by the corporation to surrender the shares for redemption. Rev. Rul. 78–197, 1978–1 C.B. 83.

H. Review Questions

1. X Corp. has 1,000 shares of stock outstanding which are owned as follows:

Husband ("H")	200 shares
Wife ("W")	100 shares
Trust for H and W's Children	100 shares

| HYZ Partnership | 300 shares |
| Y (W's Father) | 300 shares |

H and W are married. The equal general partners of the HYZ Partnership are H, Y (W's Father) and Z (unrelated). How many shares of X Corp. are constructively owned by: H, H and W's children, Z, and Y?

2. Incorporate the facts of question 1, above, and assume that X Corp. redeems all 100 shares from the Trust. X Corp. has ample E & P. What are the tax consequences of the redemption to the Trust?

3. Individuals A, B and C are unrelated equal shareholders of X Corp. X has operated a nationwide restaurant chain for the past 10 years. Three years ago, it opened a restaurant division in the State of Depression but, because of adverse economic conditions, X has decided to sell the Depression division and distribute the proceeds pro rata to its shareholders. X has ample earnings and profits. What are the tax consequences of the distribution to the shareholders? What if shareholder A were a corporation?

4. A owns 700 shares of X Corp.'s 1,000 shares of common stock in which A has a $700 basis. A also owns 500 shares of Y Corp.'s 1,000 shares of common stock in which A has a $500 basis. X has $10,000 of E & P and Y has $15,000 of E & P. A sells 300 shares of X in which A has a $300 basis to Y for $30,000. What are the tax consequences of this transaction to A, X and Y?

Chapter VIII

Stock Distributions and § 306 Stock

■ ANALYSIS

A. Stock Distributions

1. Introduction

a. Types of Stock Distributions

A corporation makes a stock distribution when it distributes its own stock to some or all of its shareholders. Stock distributions include "stock dividends" and "stock splits." Under corporate law and accounting practice, a stock dividend may differ from a "split." Stock splits result in an increase in the number of outstanding shares of the same class. Stock dividends usually are smaller in degree than splits and may be of another class of stock—e.g., preferred stock distributed to common shareholders.

Example (1): X Corp. has 1,000 shares of common stock outstanding. A owns 200 shares. X declares a 10% common stock dividend. Each shareholder will receive one new share of common stock for each 10 shares held. Thus, A will receive 20 shares. Cash normally will be distributed in lieu of fractional shares.

Example (2): Same as Example (1), except X declares a 2-for-1 stock split and issues one new common share for each share held. After the split, X has 2,000 shares of common stock outstanding, and A owns 400 shares.

b. History of Taxation of Stock Distributions

In *Eisner v. Macomber,* 252 U.S. 189, 40 S.Ct. 189 (1920), the Supreme Court held that a "common on common" stock dividend was not taxable because it did not constitute gross income within the meaning of the Sixteenth Amendment to the Constitution. In a later case, the Court held that a "common on preferred" stock dividend was taxable because the shareholder received an interest different from her former stock holdings. *Koshland v. Helvering,* 298 U.S. 441, 56 S.Ct. 767 (1936). From these and other cases, a test evolved under which a stock dividend was taxable only if it increased a shareholder's proportionate ownership interest in the corporation. When Congress and the Treasury abandoned this approach in 1954, tax advisors devised methods that offered shareholders a choice between receiving taxable cash dividends or increasing their proportionate interests in the corporation through nontaxable distributions. Section 305, as amended in 1969 and accompanied by detailed regulations, is Congress's response.

c. Policy of § 305

Section 305 has two underlying policies. A stock dividend generally is not taxable if it does not increase a shareholder's proportionate ownership interest in the corporation. If a stock distribution increases the interests of some shareholders, however, or results in some shareholders receiving cash or property while others increase their proportionate interests, the distribution is usually taxable.

2. Nontaxable Stock Distributions

a. General Rule

Section 305(a) provides that stock distributions are not includible in gross income unless an exception in § 305(b) applies. Examples of nontaxable stock dividends include: "common on common" and "preferred on common" stock dividends where no other classes of stock are outstanding.

b. Allocation of Basis

If a stock distribution ("new stock") is not taxable, the shareholder's basis in the stock held prior to the distribution ("old stock") is allocated between the old and new stock in proportion to the relative fair market values of each on the date of the distribution. § 307(a).

Example (1): A owns 100 shares of X Corp. common stock with a basis of $12,000 ($120 per share). As a result of a 2-for-1 split, A receives 100 additional shares of X common stock. The stock distribution is not taxable, and A allocates his $12,000 basis between the old and new shares, leaving him with a basis of $60 per share after the distribution.

Example (2): A owns 100 shares of X Corp. common stock with a basis of $12,000 ($120 per share). X declares a preferred stock dividend on its common stock, and A receives 25 preferred shares with a value of $25,000. The value of A's common stock after the distribution is $75,000. A allocates his $12,000 basis in the common between the common and preferred based on their relative fair market values (75% common, 25% preferred), and thus takes a $9,000 basis ($90 per share) in the common stock and a $3,000 basis ($120 per share) in the preferred stock.

c. Holding Period

The holding period of the new stock includes the holding period of the old stock. § 1223(5).

d. Consequences to Distributing Corporation

The distributing corporation recognizes no gain or loss on a nontaxable stock distribution (§ 311(a)(1)), and it may not reduce its E & P (§ 312(d)(1)(B)).

3. Taxable Stock Distributions

Stock distributions described in § 305(b) are treated as distributions to which § 301 applies and thus are dividends to the extent of the distributing corporation's available E & P. The amount of the distribution is the fair market value of the distributed stock. Reg. § 1.305–1(b)(1). Stock distributions are taxable in the situations described below.

a. Election of Stock or Property

If a stock distribution is, at *any* shareholder's election, payable either in stock of the distributing corporation or in cash or other property, the stock distribution is taxable to all shareholders regardless of whether any shareholder exercises the election. § 305(b)(1).

Shareholders who participate in stock reinvestment plans by acquiring stock in lieu of cash dividends are taxable under § 305(b)(1) on the fair market value of the stock received. Rev. Rul. 78–375, 1978–2 C.B. 130.

Example: X Corp. has only common stock outstanding. X declares a cash dividend of $10 per share, or a shareholder may elect to receive additional common stock with a value of $10 per share for each share held. Shareholders who elect to receive stock are treated as receiving a § 301 distribution of $10 per share, even if all shareholders elect stock. Reg. § 1.305–2(a).

b.   Disproportionate Distributions

If the result of a distribution (or series of distributions) is that some shareholders receive cash or other property while others increase their proportionate interest in the earnings or assets of the corporation, those who increase their proportionate interest are taxed on the value of the increased interest. § 305(b)(2). Cash and stock distributions can have a disproportionate effect even if they are not pursuant to a plan and are unrelated. If distributions are separated by more than 36 months, however, they are presumed to be beyond the reach of § 305(b)(2) unless they are made pursuant to an integrated plan. Reg. § 1.305–3(b)(2), (4).

Example (1):   X Corp. has two classes of common stock outstanding: Class A and Class B. Each class has equal rights. X pays a cash dividend of $10 per share on the Class A stock and a dividend on the Class B stock payable in additional shares of Class B stock with a value of $10 per share. The stock distribution is taxable because the Class B shareholders increase their proportionate interest in earnings and assets of X while the Class A shareholders receive cash. Reg. § 1.305–3(e) Example (1).

Example (2):   X Corp. has two classes of stock outstanding: common and preferred. X declares a dividend on the common payable in additional common stock and pays a cash dividend on the preferred stock. The cash dividend is taxable, but the common on common stock dividend is not because it does not increase the proportionate interests of the common shareholders as a class. Reg. § 1.305–3(e) Example (2).

Example (3):   Same facts as Example (2) except that X Corp. declares a dividend on the common stock payable in shares of the preferred. Since the interests of the common shareholders in the assets and earnings of the corporation have increased (they have new rights and preferences as preferred shareholders), the preferred stock dividend is taxable. If the dividend had been payable in a new class of preferred stock that was subordinated in all respects to the old preferred, however, the distribution would not be taxable because it would not increase the proportionate interests of the common shareholders. The issuance of the junior preferred stock does not give the common shareholders more than they had before the distribution. Reg. § 1.305–3(e) Example (3).

c. Distributions of Common and Preferred Stock

If a distribution (or series of distributions) has the result of some common shareholders receiving preferred stock and others receiving common stock, all the distributions are taxable. § 305(b)(3). The rationale is that the shareholders who receive common stock increase their proportionate interest in earnings and assets while the other shareholders receive a relatively fixed interest akin to cash.

Example: X Corp. has two classes of common stock outstanding: Class A and Class B. Each class has equal rights. X declares a dividend on Class A stock payable in additional shares of Class A and a dividend on Class B stock payable in a new issue of preferred stock. Both stock distributions are taxable. Reg. § 1.305–4(b) Example (1).

d. Distributions on Preferred Stock

All distributions on preferred stock are taxable except for an increase in the conversion ratio of convertible preferred stock that is made solely to take account of a stock dividend or split. § 305(b)(4). For this purpose, "preferred stock" is any stock which does not participate in corporate growth to any significant extent and has limited rights and privileges. Reg. § 1.305–5(a).

Example (1):   X Corp. has two classes of stock outstanding: common and nonconvertible preferred. X declares a dividend on both the common and preferred, in each case payable in additional shares of the common. The distribution is taxable to the preferred shareholders but not to the common shareholders.

Example (2):   X Corp. has two classes of stock outstanding: common and preferred. Each share of preferred is convertible into two shares of common. X pays a dividend of one share of common stock for each common share held and doubles the conversion ratio of the preferred. Neither the common stock distribution nor the doubling of the conversion ratio is taxable.

e. Distributions of Convertible Preferred

A distribution of convertible preferred stock is taxable unless the taxpayer establishes to the satisfaction of the Service that it will not have the result of a disproportionate distribution. § 305(b)(5). A distribution of convertible preferred is likely to have a disproportionate effect if the right to convert must be exercised within a relatively short period and it is likely that some shareholders will convert and others will not, taking into account factors such as the dividend rate and market conditions. If the right may be exercised over many years and the extent of conversion cannot be predicted, the corporation probably can establish that the distribution will not have a disproportionate effect. Reg. § 1.305–6(a)(2).

Example: X Corp. has only common stock outstanding. It declares a convertible dividend payable in a new issue of preferred stock convertible into common for a period of 20 years. If the corporation can show that it is impossible to predict the extent to which the preferred will be converted, the distribution will not be taxable. If, however, the preferred were convertible over a short period of time and, on the facts, it was likely that some shareholders would convert while others would sell their stock, the distribution is taxable because it results in the receipt of cash by some shareholders and an increase in the proportionate interests of others. Reg. § 1.305–6(b) Examples (1), (2).

f. Deemed Stock Distributions

1) In General

Many transactions that are not distributions in form have the effect of increasing the proportionate interests of one group of shareholders while other shareholders are receiving cash or other property. Because these transactions may have the same effect as the taxable stock distributions described in § 305(b), § 305(c) and the regulations treat them as § 301 distributions to the shareholders whose equity interests have been increased. A few basic deemed distributions are illustrated below.

2) Change in Conversion Ratio

A "conversion ratio" is the rate at which a security may be converted into a security of another class. Most convertible securities have an "antidilution provision" which prevents the dilution that otherwise would result from stock dividends or splits on the security into which the convertible security may be converted. Changes in a conversion ratio to prevent dilution are not deemed stock distributions under § 305(c), but a conversion ratio adjustment that has the effect of increasing the proportionate interest of a class of shareholders will be treated as a taxable stock distribution.

Example: X Corp. has two classes of common stock outstanding: Class A and Class B. Both classes have the same rights to earnings and assets. Each share of Class B stock is convertible into one share of Class A stock. If cash dividends are paid on Class A stock, the Class B conversion ratio is increased. X declares a cash dividend of $10 per share on the Class A stock and simultaneously increases the Class B conversion ratio so that each share of Class B stock is convertible into 1.05 shares of Class A. The increase in conversion ratio of the Class B stock is a § 305(c) deemed distribution to the Class B shareholders because their proportionate interest in the corporation has been increased while the Class A shareholders receive cash. Reg. § 1.305–3(e) Example (7).

3) Dividend Equivalent Periodic Redemption Plans

If a redemption pursuant to an ongoing plan is treated as a § 301 distribution and has the effect of increasing the proportionate interests of other shareholders, the corporation is deemed to have made a stock distribution to the shareholders whose interests have been increased. Reg. § 1.305–7(a). An "isolated" redemption, however, even if it is treated as a dividend, will not cause § 305 to apply to those shareholders who have increased their proportionate interests. Reg. § 1.305–3(b)(3).

Example (1): X Corp. has one class of common stock outstanding, owned by five equal related shareholders. X adopts an annual redemption plan that enables shareholders to sell a limited amount of their stock back to the company. Pursuant to the plan, X distributes cash in redemption of a portion of the stock held by two shareholders. The redemptions are treated as § 301 distributions. The three shareholders whose stock is not redeemed increase their proportionate interests in X as a result of the redemptions of the others. The nonredeemed shareholders are treated as having received stock distributions to which § 305(b)(2) and § 301 apply. Rev. Rul. 78–60, 1978–1 C.B. 81. For the method of computing the amount of the deemed distribution, see Reg. § 1.305–3(e) Examples (8) and (9).

Example (2): Same facts as Example (1), except the redemptions are not pursuant to a periodic plan but rather are made to shift control from older to younger shareholders. Because this is an "isolated" redemption, § 305(b)(2) does not apply to the shareholders whose proportionate interests have increased.

g. Basis and Holding Period

The basis to a shareholder who receives a taxable stock dividend is the fair market value of the distributed stock. § 301(d). The holding period of the stock commences as of the date of the distribution.

h. Consequences to the Distributing Corporation

The distributing corporation recognizes no gain or loss on a taxable stock distribution. § 311(a)(1). The corporation may reduce its E & P by the fair market value of the distributed stock. Reg. § 1.312–1(d).

4. Distributions of Stock Rights

a. "Rights" Defined

"Rights" are options to purchase shares from an issuing corporation at a fixed price during a relatively short period of time.

b. Nontaxable Rights

1) In General

A distribution by a corporation of rights to acquire its stock is generally not includible in gross income unless the distribution has one of the effects described in § 305(b)—e.g., some shareholders get cash while others receive rights that have the effect of increasing their proportionate interest in earnings and assets.

2) Allocation of Basis

If a distribution of rights is nontaxable and the rights are later exercised or sold, § 307(a) requires an allocation of basis between the underlying stock and the rights in proportion to their relative fair market values on the date of distribution. If the rights are exercised, the basis allocated to the rights is added to the cost of the new stock acquired. If the rights lapse, no loss may be recognized and the underlying stock retains its same basis. Reg. § 1.307–1(a).

3) De Minimis Rule

Rights take a zero basis if their fair market value is less than 15% of the stock with respect to which they were distributed unless the shareholder elects to use the allocation method prescribed by § 307(a). § 307(b).

4) Holding Period

The holding period of nontaxable rights includes the holding period of the underlying stock. § 1223(5).

c. **Taxable Rights**

Taxable rights are treated as § 301 distributions. § 305(b). As such, assuming they have a value, they are taxed as dividends to the extent of the distributing corporation's E & P. The basis of taxable rights is their fair market value on the date of the distribution, and the shareholder's holding period begins as of that date. A lapse of taxable rights results in a deductible loss.

B. § 306 Stock

1. The Preferred Stock Bailout

a. Background

The "preferred stock bailout" was a device used by shareholders many years ago to withdraw corporate earnings at then very favorable long-term capital gains rates as compared to the much higher ordinary income rates on dividends. A profitable corporation would make a tax-free distribution of preferred stock to its common shareholders. The shareholders then sold the preferred stock to an investor, reporting a long-term capital gain. In computing the gain, a portion of the shareholder's basis in the common was allocated to the preferred. The corporation later redeemed the preferred stock from the investor. The net effect was that the shareholders received cash without reducing their proportionate interest in the corporation—the essence of a dividend. The Service contended that the preferred stock dividend was taxable on these facts, but its argument was rejected in *Chamberlin v. Comm'r,* 207 F.2d 462 (6th Cir.1953), cert. denied, 347 U.S. 918, 74 S.Ct. 516 (1954). Congress responded by enacting § 306.

b. Overview of § 306

Congress decided not to tax the receipt of a preferred stock dividend but rather to identify stock with bailout potential, label it as "§ 306 stock," and generally require a shareholder to recognize ordinary income rather than capital gain on a sale, redemption or other disposition of the stock. Another disadvantage of § 306 treatment is that a shareholder may not offset her stock basis against the amount realized on a disposition of § 306 stock. Exceptions are provided for dispositions, such as a complete termination of a shareholder's interest in the corporation, that do not have bailout potential.

c. Importance of § 306

Like several other provisions in Subchapter C that were designed to patrol against bailouts of corporate earnings at capital gains rates, § 306 is much less important when qualified dividends received by noncorporate shareholders are taxed at the same preferential rates as long-term capital gains.

2. Definition of § 306 Stock
a. In General

The principal category of § 306 stock is preferred stock distributed to a shareholder as a tax-free stock dividend under § 305(a). Common stock is not included because it participates in corporate growth and thus lacks bailout potential. § 306(c)(1)(A). If stock has either a limited right to dividends or a limited right to assets upon liquidation, it is not "common" stock for this purpose. Rev. Rul. 79–163, 1979–1 C.B. 131. Voting common stock that is subject to the issuing corporation's right of first refusal at net book value is "common" stock. Rev. Rul. 76–386, 1976–2 C.B. 95.

b. No Earnings and Profits

Section 306 stock does not include stock distributed by a corporation with no current or accumulated E & P for the year of the distribution. The test is whether no part of a tax-free stock distribution would have been a dividend if cash had been distributed instead of stock. § 306(c)(2). If even a small part of a cash distribution would have been a dividend, then all the stock is § 306 stock.

Example: X Corp., a calendar year taxpayer, makes a tax-free distribution of preferred stock with a value of $25,000 to its common shareholders on July 1. X has no accumulated E & P. On July 1, X has $10,000 current E & P, but by the end of the year it has a $1,000 current E & P deficit. The preferred stock is not § 306 stock because a distribution of cash in lieu of the stock would not have been a dividend. If X had ended the year with $20 of current E & P, however, all the preferred stock would be § 306 stock.

c. Stock with Transferred or Substituted Basis

Section 306 stock includes stock which has a transferred or exchanged basis determined by reference to the basis of § 306 stock. § 306(c)(1)(C). Examples include stock received as a gift (with a § 1015 transferred basis from the donor), or stock (of whatever class) received in exchange for § 306 stock in a tax-free § 351 transaction. The § 306 taint is removed on the death of a shareholder, however, because the stock will take a date-of-death basis under § 1014.

Example (1):   Parent gives 100 shares of X Corp. preferred stock, which is § 306 stock to Child. The stock remains § 306 stock in Child's hands. If Parent were to die and bequeath the stock to Child, it would no longer be § 306 stock.

Example (2):   A transfers 100 shares of X Corp. preferred stock, which is § 306 stock, to Y Corp. in exchange for 100 shares of Y Corp. common stock in a transaction that qualifies as tax-free under § 351(a). The X Corp. preferred stock (which has a § 362(a) transferred basis) and the Y Corp. common stock (which has a substituted basis determined by reference to the Y Corp. stock under § 358(a)) are each § 306 stock.

d.   Stock Received in a Reorganization or Division

Stock other than common stock which is received in a tax-free corporate reorganization or division is § 306 stock if the effect of the transaction is substantially the same as receipt of a stock dividend, or if the stock was received in exchange for § 306 stock. § 306(c)(1)(B). This aspect of § 306 is discussed in the context of reorganizations (see XI.B.8.b.6, at page 233, *infra*) and divisions (see Chapter XII, *infra*).

e.   Certain Stock Acquired in § 351 Exchange

Preferred stock acquired in a § 351 exchange is § 306 stock if the receipt of money instead of the stock would have been treated as a dividend to any extent. § 306(c)(3). In determining whether the receipt of money would have been equivalent to a dividend, rules similar to those in § 304 (dealing with redemptions through the use of related corporations) are applied. See § 304(b)(3), discussed at VII.E.4.a., at page 147, *supra*. This exception is intended to prevent shareholders from avoiding § 306 by contributing common stock of a profitable company to a newly organized holding company (with no E & P) in a § 351 transaction in exchange for common and preferred stock of the holding company. Such preferred stock has bailout potential but, without a special rule, it would not be § 306 stock because the holding company has no E & P.

Example: A is the sole common shareholder of X Corp., which has ample E & P. A transfers her X common stock to newly formed Y Corp. in exchange for Y common and preferred stock. The Y preferred stock will be § 306 stock because a transfer of cash to A in lieu of the preferred stock would have been treated as a dividend under § 304(a)(1). In applying § 304, recall that even if the acquiring corporation (Y) has no E & P, the E & P of the issuing corporation (X) may result in dividend treatment. § 304(b)(2)(B). See VII.E.2.b, at page 144, *supra*.

3.   Dispositions of § 306 Stock

a.   Redemptions

If § 306 stock is redeemed, the amount realized by the redeemed shareholder is treated as a distribution to which § 301 applies and thus is taxable as a dividend to the extent of the corporation's current or accumulated E & P at the time of the redemption. § 306(a)(2). The balance, if any, of the amount realized is first treated as a reduction of basis and then, if necessary, as capital gain under the rules generally applicable to distributions. See VI.A.3.d., at page 113, *supra*.

Example: X Corp. makes a tax-free distribution of preferred stock with a value of $20,000 to its sole common shareholder, A. X has $5,000 of E & P at the time of the distribution. A's allocable basis in the preferred stock (which is § 306 stock) is $10,000. Two years later, X redeems A's preferred stock for $20,000, at a time when X has $30,000 of E & P. A continues to own 100% of X's common stock. The entire $20,000 amount realized on the redemption is a dividend. A's basis in the preferred stock probably is added back to the basis of A's common stock. If X had no E & P at the time of the redemption, the entire $20,000 would be a return of capital under § 301(c)(2). Although the law is unsettled, A could make a reasonable argument that he may reduce his basis in both the preferred and the common stock before recognizing any gain under § 301(c)(3).

b. Sales and Other Dispositions

1) In General

On a sale or other disposition of § 306 stock, the amount realized is first treated as ordinary income to the extent of the stock's "ratable share" of the amount that would have been a dividend at the time of the distribution if cash rather than stock had been distributed. The balance, if any, of the amount realized first reduces the basis of the § 306 stock, and any excess is treated as gain from the sale or exchange of the stock. § 306(a)(1)(B). No loss may be recognized on a disposition of § 306 stock, but any unrecovered basis is allocated back to the stock with respect to which the § 306 stock was distributed. § 306(a)(1)(C); Reg. § 1.306–1(b)(2) Examples (2), (3).

2) Treatment of Ordinary Income as Qualified Dividend

The ordinary income realized by a noncorporate shareholder on a sale of § 306 stock is generally treated as a qualified dividend and thus is taxed at preferential capital gains rates. For other purposes, however, dividend treatment is available only if the Service so "specifies," which it had not done as of early 2019. As a result, it is likely that corporate shareholders are not allowed a § 243 dividends received deduction if they realize ordinary income on a sale of § 306 stock, and the corporation may not reduce its E & P on a disposition of § 306 stock that is not a redemption. Reg. § 1.306–1(b)(1).

Example (1):   X Corp. makes a tax-free distribution of preferred stock with a value of $20,000 to its sole common shareholder, A, who is an individual. X has $50,000 of E & P at the time of the distribution. A's allocable basis in the preferred stock (which is § 306 stock) is $2,000. Two years later, at a time when X has no E & P, A sells the § 306 stock for $24,000. Of this amount, $20,000 is treated as ordinary income that is a dividend (and likely a "qualified dividend," taxable at capital gains rates). The ordinary income is the amount that would have been a taxable dividend if cash rather than stock had been distributed at the time of the distribution. Of the balance, $2,000 is a reduction of A's basis in the preferred stock, and $2,000 is treated as gain from a sale of the stock.

Example (2):   If X's E & P in Example (1) had been $8,000 at the time of the distribution, only $8,000 of A's amount realized on the sale of the § 306 stock is a dividend; $2,000 is a reduction of basis; and $14,000 is treated as gain from a sale of the stock.

Example (3):   Same facts as Example (1), except A sells the § 306 stock for $21,000. Of this amount, $20,000 is treated as ordinary income and $1,000 is a reduction of A's $2,000 basis in the preferred stock. No loss will be allowed. A may add the remaining $1,000 basis in the preferred back to his basis in the X common stock. Reg. § 1.306–1(b)(2) Example (2).

c. Exempt Dispositions

Four types of dispositions are exempted from the punitive general rule of § 306(a) because they do not present any opportunity for a bailout.

1) Complete Terminations and Partial Liquidations

A disposition of § 306 stock in a transaction (other than a redemption) that terminates the shareholder's entire stock interest in the corporation is exempt if the shareholder does not transfer the stock to a § 318 related person or entity. § 306(b)(1)(A)(i), (ii). In determining whether the shareholder has completely terminated her interest, the § 318 attribution rules apply. § 306(b)(1)(A)(iii). Redemptions of § 306 stock that result in a complete termination of the shareholder's interest under § 302(b)(3) or qualify as a partial liquidation under § 302(b)(4) also are exempt. § 306(b)(1)(B).

Example: A owns 500 shares of X Corp. common stock and 250 shares of X Corp. preferred stock, which is § 306 stock. She owns no X stock constructively. A sells all of her common and preferred stock to an unrelated person. A's sale of the preferred stock is not subject to § 306(a) because she completely terminates her interest in the corporation.

2) Complete Liquidations

Section 306(a) does not apply to a redemption of § 306 stock in a complete liquidation. § 306(b)(2).

3) Nonrecognition Transactions

Dispositions that qualify for nonrecognition treatment, such as § 351 transfers, contributions to capital and tax-free exchanges of stock under § 1036, are exempt. § 306(b)(3). Any stock received in a tax-free exchange, however, becomes § 306 stock. § 306(c)(1)(C).

4) Transactions Not in Avoidance of Tax

Section 306(a) does not apply if the taxpayer satisfies the Service that either: (a) the distribution and the subsequent disposition or redemption of § 306 stock, or (b) in the case of a prior or simultaneous disposition (or redemption) of the underlying stock with respect to which the § 306 stock was issued, the disposition or redemption of the § 306 stock was not made pursuant to a plan having federal tax avoidance as one of its principal purposes. § 306(b)(4). The Service has ruled that § 306(b)(4) relief is not automatically available on dispositions of preferred stock of widely held corporations. Rev. Rul. 89–63, 1989–1 C.B. 90.

Example (1): Minority Shareholder, who holds both common and preferred (§ 306) stock in X Corp., sells her § 306 stock in an isolated transaction. The sale qualifies for relief under § 306(b)(4)(A) unless (unlikely on these facts) the distribution of the § 306 stock and Minority Shareholder's sale were pursuant to a tax avoidance plan. Reg. § 1.306–2(b)(3).

Example (2): In year 1, A receives a distribution of 100 shares of preferred (§ 306) stock with respect to her holding of 100 shares of common stock of X Corp. In year 3, A sells all her common stock. In year 4, A sells all her § 306 stock but continues to own X Corp. common stock by § 318 attribution. A's disposition of her § 306 stock ordinarily is not considered a tax avoidance transaction because she previously disposed of the common stock that allowed her to participate in the ownership and growth of the business. § 306(b)(4)(B); Reg. § 1.306–2(b)(3).

Example (3): Same as Example (2), above, except A only sold 50 shares of her common stock in year 3 and, although she substantially reduced her proportionate interest in the common stock, A retained effective control pursuant to X Corp.'s bylaws. A is not entitled to relief on the disposition of her § 306 stock because she retained effective control of the corporation. *Fireoved v. United States,* 462 F.2d 1281 (3d Cir.1972).

Example (4): Same as Example (2), above, except A simultaneously sold 50 shares of her common stock and 50 shares of her § 306 stock in year 3, and she did not retain effective control of the corporation. Absent any facts indicating a tax avoidance plan, A's sale of the § 306 stock should qualify for relief under § 306(b)(4)(B). But see Rev. Rul. 75–247, 1975–1 C.B. 104, holding that a similar simultaneous disposition did not, in itself, establish the requisite non-tax avoidance purpose.

C. Review Questions

1. Why do "common on common" and "preferred on common" stock distributions made by a corporation with no other classes of stock outstanding qualify as tax-free distributions?

2.   X Corp. distributes one share of nonconvertible $10 preferred stock for every 10 shares of common held by its shareholders. X has 1,000 shares of common stock outstanding. A owns 100 shares of common with a basis of $1,000 and receives 10 shares of preferred with a value of $100 after the distribution. The value of A's common stock after the distribution is $1,900. X has $100,000 of current and no accumulated E & P at the end of the year in which the distribution takes place. What are the tax consequences of the distribution to A and X Corp.?

3.   Assume the same facts as in question 2, above, except that the shareholders have the option of taking cash in lieu of the preferred stock. If none of the X shareholders exercise this option, what are the tax consequences of the distribution to A?

4.   Assume the same facts as in question 2, above, except that some of the X shareholders receive common stock and others receive preferred stock. Assume that A receives preferred stock. In general, what are the tax consequences of the distribution to A?

5.   Using the same facts as in question 2, above, assume that A sells all of her preferred stock for $250 one year after the distribution. What are the tax consequences of the sale to A?

6.   Same facts as question 5, above, except that A sells all the preferred stock for $80.

7.   Same facts as question 5, above, except that A previously sold all of her common stock and now sells all her preferred for $250.

Chapter IX

Complete Liquidations and Taxable Corporate Acquisitions

■ ANALYSIS

A. Complete Liquidation Defined

On a complete liquidation, a corporation distributes all of its assets (or the proceeds of their sale), subject to any liabilities, to its shareholders in exchange for all their stock. The corporation then usually dissolves under state law. A corporation liquidates for tax purposes when it ceases to be a going concern and its activities are merely for the purpose of winding up its affairs, paying its debts and distributing any remaining balance to its shareholders. Cf. Reg. § 1.332–2(c). Legal dissolution under state law is not required for a liquidation to be complete, and the corporation may retain a nominal amount of assets to pay remaining debts and preserve its legal existence. Rev. Rul. 54–518, 1954–2 C.B. 142.

A complete liquidation typically is evidenced by a formal "plan," which may be nothing more than a shareholders' or directors' resolution stating the corporation's intention to liquidate. Even in the absence of a formal written plan, an informal plan of liquidation may be found to exist when the shareholders or directors manifest their intent to liquidate the corporation.

B. Complete Liquidations Under § 331

1. Consequences to the Shareholders

a. Recognition of Gain or Loss

1) General Rule

Amounts distributed to a shareholder in complete liquidation are treated as in full payment in exchange for the shareholder's stock. § 331(a). The difference between the amount realized and the shareholder's adjusted basis in the stock is treated as capital gain or loss in the usual case where the stock is a capital asset. The shareholder's amount realized is the amount of money and the fair market value of all other property received from the liquidating corporation, less any liabilities assumed by the shareholder or encumbering the distributed property.

2) Different Blocks of Stock

A shareholder who holds several blocks of stock with different bases and acquisition dates determines his gain or loss separately for each block rather than on an aggregate basis. Reg. § 1.331–1(e).

Example: A holds 40 shares of X Corp. stock short-term with a $50,000 basis and 60 shares long-term with a $30,000 basis. X distributes $100,000 to A in complete liquidation. A allocates the $100,000 distribution pro rata between the two blocks of stock and recognizes $10,000 of short-term capital loss ($50,000 basis less $40,000 amount realized) on the 40 shares and $30,000 of long-term capital gain ($60,000 amount realized less $30,000 basis) on the 60 shares.

3) Series of Distributions

A distribution in complete liquidation includes one of a series of distributions in redemption of all the stock of a corporation pursuant to a plan. § 346(a). If liquidating distributions are made in two or more taxable years, the Service permits the shareholders first to recover their basis before recognizing any gain or loss. Rev. Rul. 85–48, 1985–1 C.B. 126. If a distribution is made before liquidation status exists, it will be treated as a nonliquidating distribution (and thus potentially a dividend) under § 301. When dividends were taxed at a higher rate than capital gains, this risk was eliminated by adopting a formal plan of liquidation before making the first of a series of liquidating distributions. Under current law, with most dividends taxed at the same rate as long-term capital gains, the distinction is of limited significance for noncorporate shareholders.

> ***Example:*** A has a $30,000 basis in 100 shares of X Corp., which adopts a plan of complete liquidation in Year 1. X distributes $30,000 in Year 1 and $20,000 in Year 2. A may recover her entire $30,000 basis before reporting any gain. She thus has no gain in Year 1 and $20,000 long-term capital gain in Year 2. If X did not adopt a plan of liquidation in Year 1, the Year 1 distribution may be classified as a § 301 distribution.

4) Distribution of Disputed and Contingent Claims

If a liquidating corporation distributes disputed or contingent claims that do not have a readily ascertainable fair market value, the shareholder may be able to treat the liquidation as an "open transaction" and defer including these assets in the amount realized until their value is ascertainable. Open transaction treatment is limited, however, to "rare and extraordinary" cases. Rev. Rul. 58–402, 1958–2 C.B. 15; see also Reg. § 15A.453–1(d)(2)(iii). Treating the transaction as open rather than closed affects both the timing and character of the shareholder's gain or loss.

> ***Example (1):*** Pursuant to a plan of complete liquidation in Year 1, X Corp. distributes to its sole shareholder, A, $20,000 cash, $50,000 in tangible assets, and a disputed claim against B in the amount of $50,000 but with an uncertain value. A has an $80,000 basis in his X stock. Under the open transaction method, A has no gain in Year 1 because the $70,000 of distributed cash and property does not exceed A's basis in the stock. The claim is not included in A's amount realized until it is collected or has an ascertainable value. If A collects $40,000 on the claim in Year 3, he would recognize $30,000 LTCG ($110,000 total distributions less $80,000 basis) at that time.

> ***Example (2):*** Same as Example (1), except the disputed claim is valued at $25,000 when it is distributed to A in Year 1, but A collects the full $40,000 in Year 3. The transaction must be closed in Year 1 because the claim has an ascertainable value. A recognizes $15,000 LTCG ($95,000 total distributions less $80,000 basis) on the liquidation, and takes a $25,000 basis in the claim under § 334(a). A recognizes $15,000 ($40,000 received less $25,000 basis) on collection of the claim; the gain is ordinary income because a collection is not a sale or exchange.

5) Installment Sale Reporting

If a liquidating corporation sells assets on the installment method to a person who is not "related" within the meaning of § 1239(b) and then distributes the installment obligations to its shareholders, the shareholders may be able to report their § 331(a) gain on the installment method. Installment sale reporting is accomplished by treating the shareholders' receipt of payments on the installment obligations as if they were payments in exchange for their stock. § 453(h)(1)(A). The installment obligations must have been acquired by the corporation in respect of a sale or exchange of property during the 12 months beginning on the date of adoption of a plan of complete liquidation, and the liquidation must be completed within that 12-month period. Installment obligations arising from the sale of inventory do not qualify for deferral unless substantially all of the inventory is sold to one person in one transaction. § 453(h)(1)(B). Installment sale treatment is not available, however, on a liquidation of a publicly traded corporation (§ 453(k)(2)) or if the shareholder elects out of § 453 (§ 453(d)).

Example: A is the sole shareholder of X Corp. and has a $20,000 basis in his X stock (held long-term). X's only asset is undeveloped land with a value of $50,000. In Year 1, X adopts a liquidation plan and sells the land to an unrelated buyer for $10,000 cash and a $40,000 installment note payable in Year 4. Within 12 months of the adoption of the plan, X distributes the $10,000 cash and $40,000 note to A in complete liquidation. (Ignore any corporate tax liability that X may have incurred.) A's $30,000 gain may be reported on the installment method. A's gross profit is $30,000, the total contract price is $50,000, and thus $3/5$, or 60%, of each payment is long-term capital gain. § 453(c). A recognizes $6,000 gain in Year 1 and the remaining $24,000 in Year 4 when the note is paid.

b. Basis of Distributed Property

The basis of property received by a shareholder on a § 331 complete liquidation is the fair market value of the property on the date of distribution, without reduction for any liabilities to which the property is subject. § 334(a).

2. Consequences to the Distributing Corporation

a. Background

1) *General Utilities* Doctrine

Under the *General Utilities* doctrine, a corporation did not recognize gain or loss on a nonliquidating distribution of property even though the shareholder took a fair market value basis in the distributed property. See VI.D.1.a., at page 118, *supra*. This doctrine, which also applied to liquidating distributions, was once codified in § 336(a). Prior to 1954, however, *sales* of assets by a liquidating corporation were fully taxable.

2) *Court Holding* Doctrine

Because of the disparate tax treatment of liquidating distributions (nontaxable) and sales (taxable) prior to 1954, *corporate*-level gain on the sale of a business could be avoided by a tax-free distribution in kind to the shareholders, who would take the assets with a fair market value basis and then sell them to the buyer without recognizing gain on the sale. In contrast, a corporation recognized gain when it sold an asset and then distributed the proceeds in complete liquidation. (In either case, the shareholders would recognize gain or loss on their stock.) If the sale were negotiated by the corporation but formally consummated by the shareholders, controversies arose over whether in substance the sale had been made by the corporation or the shareholders. Compare *Comm'r v. Court Holding Co.*, 324 U.S. 331, 65 S.Ct. 707 (1945) (sale attributed to corporation under step transaction doctrine) with *United States v. Cumberland Public Service Co.*, 338 U.S. 451, 70 S.Ct. 280 (1950) (sale made by shareholders rather than corporation).

3) Former §§ 336 and 337

In response to the disparate results under the pre-1954 law, Congress enacted former § 337, which extended the *General Utilities* doctrine to most liquidating sales and made it unnecessary to determine whether the corporation or the shareholders made the sale. Under former §§ 336 and 337, a corporation generally did not recognize gain on either a distribution of property in complete liquidation or a sale pursuant to a complete liquidation plan. Exceptions were provided for recapture income, certain sales of inventory and tax benefit items.

4) *General Utilities* Repeal

After chipping away at the *General Utilities* doctrine over many years, Congress rejected it completely in 1986 by repealing old §§ 336 and 337.

b. Recognition of Gain or Loss

Under current law, a corporation recognizes gain or loss when it distributes property in complete liquidation as if it had sold the property to the distributee for its fair market value. § 336(a). Gain or loss is determined separately on each asset. If the distributed property is subject to a liability or a shareholder assumes a corporate liability in connection with the distribution, the fair market value of the property is treated as not less than the amount of the liability. § 336(b).

Example (1):   A is the sole shareholder of X Corp., whose only asset is land with an adjusted basis of $40,000 and a fair market value of $100,000. X recognizes $60,000 gain if it distributes the land to A in complete liquidation.

Example (2):   Same as Example (1), except the fair market value of the land is only $80,000 but it is subject to a $100,000 mortgage. For purposes of determining the gain under § 336(a), the land is treated as having a fair market value of not less than the

$100,000 liability. X thus recognizes $60,000 gain on a distribution of the land in complete liquidation.

c. Limitations on Recognition of Loss

Losses on transactions between related taxpayers generally are disallowed under § 267(a)(1), but § 267 does not apply to any loss realized by a distributing corporation (or distributee shareholder) on a distribution in complete liquidation. Section 336(d), however, limits the recognition of loss by the distributing corporation in the three situations described below. These "outbound" loss limitations are less significant since the enactment of the "inbound" limitations in § 362(e) on the transfer of built-in losses in § 351 transactions or as contributions to capital. See IV.B.8., at page 78, *supra*.

1) Distributions to Related Persons

A liquidating corporation may not recognize loss on the distribution of any property to a § 267 "related person" if the distribution is not pro rata or is of "disqualified property" as defined in § 336(d)(1)(B).

a) Related Person

An individual shareholder is "related" to a corporation under § 267(b)(2) if the shareholder owns directly or indirectly (through attribution rules in § 267(c)) more than 50% in value of the corporation's outstanding stock.

b) Non Pro Rata

A distribution of loss property is non pro rata for purposes of § 336(d)(1)(A)(i) if it is not distributed to the shareholders in the same proportion as their stock ownership in the corporation.

c) Disqualified Property

"Disqualified property" is any property acquired by the liquidating corporation in a § 351 transaction or as a contribution to capital during the 5-year period ending on the date of the distribution. § 336(d)(1)(B).

Example (1): X Corp. has 100 outstanding shares, of which A owns 60 and B owns 40. A and B are unrelated. X's only assets are Gainacre (basis—$10,000; value—$40,000), Lossacre (basis—$80,000; value—$40,000), and $20,000 cash. Both parcels were acquired by X more than five years ago and thus neither is "disqualified property." X adopts a plan of complete liquidation and distributes 60% of each asset to A and 40% of each asset to B. Because the distribution is pro rata, § 336(d)(1) does not apply, and X recognizes $30,000 gain on Gainacre and $40,000 loss on Lossacre.

Example (2): Same as Example (1), except X distributes Lossacre and the cash to A and Gainacre to B. X recognizes $30,000 gain on Gainacre, but it may not recognize the

$40,000 loss because Lossacre was distributed to A, a related person, and the distribution was not pro rata.

Example (3): Same as Example (1), except X distributes Gainacre and the cash to A and Lossacre to B. X recognizes $30,000 gain on Gainacre and $40,000 loss on Lossacre. Although Lossacre is not distributed pro rata, B is not a related person and thus § 336(d)(1)(A) does not apply.

Example (4): Same as Example (1), except that X acquired Lossacre three years ago in a § 351 transaction at a time when the fair market value of Lossacre exceeded its basis. Although the distribution is pro rata, Lossacre is "disqualified property" and X may not recognize the $24,000 loss on the 60% interest in Lossacre that it distributes to A, a related person. X may recognize the $16,000 loss on the distribution of the 40% interest to B because B is not a related person. It is irrelevant under § 336(d)(1) that Lossacre had no built-in loss when it was contributed to X.

2) Property Acquired for Tax Avoidance Purpose

a) General Rule

Section 336(d)(2) limits recognition of loss if property distributed, sold or exchanged by a liquidating corporation was acquired in a § 351 transaction or as a contribution to capital as part of a plan the principal purpose of which was to recognize loss by the liquidating corporation in connection with the liquidation. Section 336(d)(2) only disallows the loss that accrued before the corporation acquired the property. This is accomplished by a rule that requires the corporation to reduce its basis for determining loss (but not below zero) by the precontribution built-in loss—i.e., the excess of the adjusted basis of the property when it was acquired over the fair market value of the property at that time. In the case of contributions of property subject to the limitation on transfer of built-in losses in § 362(e)(2), the corporation's basis usually will have been reduced to its fair market value on the date it was contributed. In that event, § 336(d)(2) will no longer have any impact when that property is distributed in a complete liquidation.

b) Plans to Recognize Loss

Except as provided by regulations, any property acquired by the liquidating corporation after a date that is two years before the adoption of the liquidation plan (or after the adoption of that plan) is treated as acquired as part of a plan to recognize loss. § 336(d)(2)(B)(ii). No regulations have yet been issued, but Congress indicated in the legislative history that this presumption will be limited to cases where there is no clear and substantial relationship between the contributed property and the conduct of the corporation's current or future business. Only in "rare and unusual cases" will a tax avoidance plan be found if the property is contributed more than two years before the adoption of the liquidation plan. See H.R.Rep. No. 99–841, 99th Cong., 2d Sess. II–200–201 (1986).

c)   Recapture in Lieu of Disallowance

Section 336(d)(2) is broad enough to apply to a disposition of property in a taxable year ending prior to the year in which the liquidation plan is adopted. If the corporation deducted the loss in the prior year and it is later disallowed, the Service may permit the corporation to "recapture" the disallowed loss by treating it as income in the later year in lieu of filing an amended return for the year the loss was reported. § 336(d)(2)(C).

d)   Overlap with § 336(d)(1)

If both §§ 336(d)(1) and (2) apply to the same transaction, § 336(d)(1) takes precedence.

Example (1): X Corp. has 100 outstanding shares, of which A owns 60 and B owns 40. X's only assets are Gainacre (basis—$10,000; value—$40,000), Lossacre (basis—$70,000; value—$40,000), and $20,000 cash. Lossacre, which has no relationship to X's business, was contributed to X in a § 351 transaction one year ago when it had a value of $60,000 and a basis of $70,000. X adopts a plan of complete liquidation and distributes Gainacre and the cash to A and Lossacre to B. Because Lossacre was contributed to X less than two years prior to the adoption of the liquidation plan and has no relationship to X's business, it is presumed to have been contributed in a plan to recognize loss. Assuming that X Corp. was not required by § 362(e)(2) to reduce its basis in Lossacre to $60,000 when it was contributed to the corporation (e.g., because the shareholder and X elected to reduce the shareholder's basis in the stock received for Lossacre), X must reduce its adjusted basis by $10,000 (the built-in loss when X acquired Lossacre) and recognizes only a $20,000 loss ($60,000 basis less $40,000 value) on the distribution. Section 336(d)(1) does not apply because the distribution was not made to a related person.

Example (2): Same as Example (1), except X planned to subdivide the land as part of its business. If X can show there was a clear and substantial relationship between Lossacre and its business, § 336(d)(2) will not apply and X may recognize the entire $30,000 loss on the distribution to B.

3)   Distributions in § 332 Liquidations

A liquidating corporation may not recognize loss on a distribution to a minority shareholder on a § 332 liquidation of a subsidiary and in certain other specialized situations. See IX.C.3., at page 179, *infra*.

d. Distributions Pursuant to Reorganization Plan

Section 336 does not apply to liquidating distributions made pursuant to a tax-free reorganization plan under § 368. §§ 336(c), 361(c)(4). See XI.B.8.c., at page 234, *infra*.

C. Liquidation of a Subsidiary

1. Introduction

Congress views the liquidation of a subsidiary as a mere change in the form of the corporate structure. As a result, §§ 332 and 337 generally provide that neither the parent shareholder nor the liquidating subsidiary recognizes gain or loss. In keeping with the policy of nonrecognition provisions, the subsidiary's asset bases and other tax attributes (such as earnings and profits) transfer to the parent.

2. Consequences to the Shareholders

a. Requirements for Nonrecognition Under § 332

A parent corporation does not recognize gain on the receipt of distributions in complete liquidation of a subsidiary if the following requirements under § 332(b) are met. § 332(a).

1) Cancellation of Stock Pursuant to Plan

The subsidiary must distribute property to its parent in complete cancellation or redemption of its stock pursuant to a plan of liquidation. §§ 332(b)(2), (3).

2) Control

The parent must own at least 80% of the total voting power and 80% of the total value of all outstanding stock of the subsidiary on the date of the adoption of the plan of complete liquidation and at all times thereafter until the liquidation is completed. §§ 332(b)(1); 1504(a)(2). Certain nonvoting preferred stock is ignored for purposes of these 80% tests.

3) Timing

The distributions must occur within one taxable year (even if it is not the same year that the liquidation plan is adopted), in which case the plan need not specify when the liquidation will be complete. § 332(b)(2). Alternatively, in the case of a series of distributions, the plan must provide that all the subsidiary's property will be distributed to the parent within three years after the close of the taxable year of the subsidiary in which the first distribution is made. Failure to meet the 3-year deadline will retroactively disqualify the liquidation under § 332. § 332(b)(3). If the parties rely on the 3-year timing rule, the parent must file a waiver of the statute of limitations and may be required to post a bond. § 332(b).

4) Parent's Gain or Loss on Stock Eliminated

Section 332 has the effect of permanently eliminating the parent's "outside" gain or loss on its subsidiary's stock. The parent inherits the subsidiary's "inside" gain or loss on its assets and other tax attributes under §§ 334(b)(1) and 381.

5) Intentionally Avoiding § 332

On rare occasions, such as where the parent wishes to recognize a current loss on its stock in the subsidiary or avoid inheriting the subsidiary's E & P, the parties may attempt to avoid § 332 by intentionally violating one of its requirements. One avoidance technique that has been upheld by the courts is the sale of sufficient stock after the adoption of a liquidation plan to bring the parent's ownership below 80%. *Comm'r v. Day & Zimmermann, Inc.,* 151 F.2d 517 (3d Cir.1945).

6) Backing into Control

A controlling corporation that does not meet the 80% control test may seek to qualify under § 332 by acquiring more stock or by causing the subsidiary to redeem stock held by minority shareholders shortly before a liquidation. If the sale or redemption occurs prior to the adoption of a liquidation plan, this technique has been upheld. See *George L. Riggs, Inc. v. Comm'r,* 64 T.C. 474 (1975); Rev. Rul. 75–521, 1975–2 C.B. 120. A possible risk is that the Service may determine that control is lacking because the acquisition or redemption was part of an integrated liquidation plan that was adopted before the parent had 80% control. See Rev. Rul. 70–106, 1970–1 C.B. 70.

7) Subsidiary Insolvent

If a liquidating subsidiary is insolvent and the parent receives nothing in exchange for its common stock, § 332 does not apply. In that case, the parent shareholder may take a worthless security deduction on its common stock under § 165(g)(2) unless the stock became worthless in a prior year. Because the corporations are "affiliated," the deduction likely is an ordinary loss. § 165(g)(3). *H.K. Porter Co., Inc. v. Comm'r,* 87 T.C. 689 (1986).

b. Basis and Holding Period of Distributed Property

The parent corporation takes a transferred basis and a tacked holding period in any property received from the subsidiary in a § 332 liquidation. § 334(b)(1). If the liquidating subsidiary is not subject to U.S. tax with respect to the distributed property (e.g., because it is a foreign corporation) and the distributee parent is subject to U.S. tax, the distributee's aggregate adjusted basis of the distributed property, if it otherwise would exceed its fair market value, is limited to fair market value. § 334(b)(1)(B).

c. Treatment of Minority Shareholders

Even if a liquidation qualifies under § 332, minority shareholders recognize gain or loss under the general rule in § 331(a) and take a fair market value basis in any distributed property under § 334(a).

Example: P Corp. owns 90% of the stock of S Corp. and has a $20,000 basis in its S stock. The remaining 10% of S is owned by individual ("I"), who has a $3,000 basis in her S stock. S's only assets are $10,000 cash and Gainacre (value—$90,000, basis—$40,000). S adopts a plan of complete liquidation and distributes Gainacre to P and the cash to I. P recognizes no gain on the liquidation, but I recognizes $7,000 LTCG. P takes a $40,000 transferred basis in Gainacre. P's basis in its S stock disappears, and its $70,000 realized gain on its S stock is never recognized.

d. Carryover of Tax Attributes

On a § 332 liquidation, the liquidating subsidiary's tax attributes (e.g., earnings and profits, net operating loss carryovers) carry over to the parent subject to certain limitations in § 381. See Chapter XIII, *infra*.

3. Consequences to the Liquidating Subsidiary

a. Distributions to Parent

A liquidating subsidiary does not recognize gain or loss on distributions of property to its parent (referred to in the Code as "the 80% distributee") in a complete liquidation to which § 332 applies. § 337(a).

b. Distributions to Minority Shareholders

The subsidiary recognizes gain but not loss on a distribution of property to a minority shareholder (i.e., a shareholder other than "the 80% distributee") in a § 332 liquidation. § 336(a), (d)(3).

c. Distributions to Satisfy Debt of Subsidiary to Parent

If a subsidiary owes a debt to its parent on the date of the adoption of a § 332 liquidation plan, any transfer of property by the subsidiary to satisfy the debt is treated as a distribution subject to the general nonrecognition rule of § 337(a). § 337(b)(1).

Example (1): P Corp. owns 90% of the stock of S Corp. and has a $20,000 basis in its S stock. The remaining 10% of S is owned by individual ("I"), who has a $3,000 basis in her S stock. S owes $10,000 to P. S's only assets are $10,000 cash, Gainacre (value—$90,000, basis—$30,000), and Lossacre (value—$10,000, basis—$40,000). Pursuant to a plan of complete liquidation, S distributes Gainacre to P, Lossacre to I, and S uses the $10,000 cash to satisfy its debt to P. Under § 337(a), S does not recognize gain on the distribution of Gainacre, and P takes a $30,000 transferred basis under § 334(b)(1). Under § 336(d)(3), S may not recognize loss on the distribution of Lossacre, and I takes a $10,000 fair market value basis under § 334(a). Distribution of a loss asset to a minority shareholder thus results in permanent elimination of the loss.

Example (2): Same as Example (1), except S distributes the $10,000 cash to I and distributes Lossacre to P in satisfaction of the $10,000 debt. S recognizes neither gain nor loss on the distribution of Gainacre and Lossacre, and P takes a transferred basis in each asset.

d. Distributions to Tax-Exempt and Foreign Parents

To prevent the nonrecognition provided by § 337 from becoming a permanent exemption from corporate-level tax, § 337(b)(2) provides (with specialized exceptions) that a liquidating subsidiary recognizes gain or loss on distributions of property to certain tax-exempt or foreign parent corporations. In that event, the parent takes a fair market value basis in the distributed property. § 334(b)(1)(A).

D. Taxable Acquisitions of a Corporate Business

1. Introduction

When a corporate business is acquired, the transaction may be structured as a purchase of either the corporation's assets or the shareholder's stock. For the remainder of this chapter, a corporation whose assets or stock are acquired will be referred to as the "target," or "T," and the purchaser (usually another corporation) will be referred to as "P." This chapter discusses *taxable* acquisitions; tax-free acquisitions (known as "reorganizations") are discussed in Chapter XI, *infra*.

2. Asset Acquisitions

Asset acquisitions include T's direct sale of its assets to P or a "cash merger" of T into P (or a P subsidiary), where T's assets are automatically transferred to P (or a P subsidiary) under state law and T's shareholders receive cash or a combination of cash and P debt obligations, and T disappears.

a. Tax Consequences to T

T recognizes gain or loss on the sale of its assets under general tax principles whether or not the sale is followed by a complete liquidation of T. P's assumption of T's liabilities is included in T's amount realized. Section 336(d)(2) may disallow precontribution built-in loss on a liquidating sale of property acquired by T in a § 351 transaction or as a contribution to capital if the property was acquired as part of a tax-avoidance plan. See IX.B.2.c.2., at page 175, *supra*.

b. Tax Consequences to the T Shareholders

1) T Liquidates

If T liquidates after selling its assets, T's shareholders recognize capital gain or loss on their stock under § 331(a) (see IX.B.1.a. at page 170, *supra*) unless T is an 80% or more subsidiary of another corporation (the "parent") in which case the liquidation is tax-free to the parent under § 332 and taxable to any minority shareholders under § 331(a) (see IX.C., at page 177, *supra*). In a taxable liquidation, the shareholders may defer all or part of their gain on the § 453 installment method to the extent that T sold its assets for installment obligations of the buyer and distributed those obligations to the shareholders in the liquidation. See § 453(h) and IX.B.1.a.5, at page 172, *supra*.

2) T Does Not Liquidate

If T does not liquidate after its assets are acquired, its shareholders do not recognize any gain or loss. Shareholder-level gain can be avoided by holding the stock until death, when the shareholder's estate will take a stepped-up basis in the stock under § 1014. A C corporation that remains in existence as an investment company, however, is likely to be classified as a "personal holding company" and will be subject to a penalty tax if it does not distribute its net income to its shareholders. See §§ 541 et seq. and X.D., at page 201, *infra*. In view of the ongoing problem of the double tax, staying alive may be more expensive than liquidating, although less expensive when, as under current law, most dividends are taxed at preferential capital gains rates rather than as ordinary income.

c. Tax Consequences to P

P takes a § 1012 cost basis in assets that it purchases in a taxable acquisition. P's cost includes the price paid for the assets (in cash or notes) plus any T liabilities transferred to P and acquisition expenses.

d. Allocation of Purchase Price and Basis

1) In General

A sale of assets of a going business for a lump sum is treated for tax purposes as a sale of each individual asset of the business. The parties must allocate the aggregate purchase price among the assets sold. Under § 1060, which applies to any "applicable asset acquisition" including taxable corporate asset acquisitions, this allocation of total "consideration" is made using the "residual method." Reg. § 1.1060–1(a)(1). Consideration received is the seller's aggregate amount realized from the sale of its assets determined under general tax principles. Consideration paid is the buyer's aggregate cost of purchasing the assets that is properly taken into account in determining basis. Reg. § 1.1060–1(c)(1). Aggregate consideration is then allocated by assigning all "acquisition date assets" among seven classes and allocating the consideration among those classes in a prescribed order. Reg. § 1.1060–1(c)(2), incorporating by reference Reg. § 1.338–6. No asset in any class (except the final "residual" category) is allocated more than its fair market value. Reg. § 1.338–6(c)(1).

2) Applying the Residual Method of Allocation

In applying the residual method of allocation, the "consideration" is first reduced by cash and cash equivalents (known as "Class I acquisition date assets") transferred by the seller. Reg. § 1.338–6(b)(1). The remaining consideration then is allocated first to highly liquid assets, such as certificates of deposit, U.S. Government and other marketable securities ("Class II assets") in proportion to their gross fair market values, then to accounts receivable, mortgages and credit card receivables (Class III), then to inventory and other dealer-type property (Class IV), then to all assets other than those in the preceding categories (Class V, which includes most tangible assets such as equipment and real estate), then to § 197 intangibles (including a covenant not to compete entered into in connection with acquisition of all or a substantial part of a trade or business but excluding goodwill and going concern value) (Class VI) to the extent of their fair market values, and finally any remaining consideration is allocated to goodwill and going concern value (Class VII). Reg. § 1.338–6(b)(2).

Example: On July 1 of the current year, P purchases all of T's assets for $300,000. T's assets include: $20,000 cash; marketable securities (value—$50,000); land and building (value—$100,000); and a § 197 intangible asset (value—$40,000). Total consideration of $300,000 is first reduced by the $20,000 cash to $280,000 and then allocated $50,000 to Class II assets (the securities), $100,000 to Class III assets (land and building), $40,000 to Class VI assets (the § 197 intangible), and the $90,000 "residue" to Class VII (goodwill and going concern value).

3) Effect of Agreement Between the Parties

A written agreement between the buyer and seller allocating the consideration among the assets of the business is binding on both parties unless the Service determines that the allocation is not appropriate or one party can prove that the agreement is unenforceable due to mistake, undue influence, fraud or duress. Reg. § 1.1060–1(c)(4).

3. Stock Acquisitions

Stock acquisitions include P's purchase of T stock directly from T's shareholders or a "reverse cash merger" in which T merges into a subsidiary of P and T's shareholders receive cash or a combination of cash and P notes.

a. Background

An acquisition of T stock for cash or notes of P is a taxable event to the selling T shareholders, who recognize capital gain or loss. P takes a cost basis in the acquired T stock. The difficult conceptual questions are whether T also should recognize corporate-level gain or loss and whether the basis of T's assets should remain unchanged or be determined by reference to the amount paid by P for the T stock. If the form of the transaction is respected, T would not recognize gain, and its asset bases and other tax attributes would not change.

1) *Kimbell-Diamond* Case

Prior to 1954, the courts held that when P acquires the stock of T with the intent of obtaining T's assets by a prompt liquidation, P should be treated as having made a direct purchase of those assets, resulting in an asset basis equal to the amount paid by P for the stock. *Kimbell-Diamond Milling Co. v. Comm'r*, 14 T.C. 74 (1950), *aff'd per curiam*, 187 F.2d 718 (5th Cir.1951), cert. denied, 342 U.S. 827, 72 S.Ct. 50 (1951).

2) Former § 334(b)(2)

The *Kimbell-Diamond* concept was refined and codified in 1954 Code § 334(b)(2), which treated P's purchase of 80% or more of T's stock within a 12-month period as a purchase of assets if T were liquidated within two years after completion of the stock purchase. This mandatory rule enabled P to obtain a cost basis for T's assets and to avoid inheriting T's E & P and other tax attributes, but only if P liquidated T. If T stayed alive, it retained its old asset bases and other tax attributes.

3) History and Enactment of § 338

Congress enacted § 338 to further refine the original *Kimbell-Diamond* concept, eliminate subjective determinations of a purchaser's "intent," and provide greater parity between stock and asset acquisitions. Section 338 generally applies only to an electing corporate purchaser of at least 80% of T's stock within a 12-month period. If elected, it treats T as having sold all of its assets in a single transaction for their fair market value to a hypothetical "new" T, which takes an aggregate basis in those assets in an amount generally equal to what P paid for T's stock. There is no requirement that T be liquidated. The role of § 338 is more limited under current law than it was when first enacted. Prior to the Tax Reform Act of 1986, a § 338 election was attractive because T generally did not recognize gain or loss on the deemed sale of its assets under "old" § 337. See IX.B.2.a.3., at page 173, *supra.* Since the repeal of the *General Utilities* doctrine, however, T recognizes gain or loss on the deemed sale, just as it would on an actual sale of assets. See IX.B.2.b., at page 173, *supra.* This change makes a § 338 election far less desirable in most cases.

b. Operation of § 338: Basic Requirements

1) Qualified Stock Purchase Requirement

The § 338 election is available only when P makes a "qualified stock purchase" of the stock of T.

a) A "qualified stock purchase" is a transaction or series of transactions in which P acquires by "purchase" at least 80% of the total voting power and value of T during a 12-month "acquisition period." § 338(d)(3). Nonvoting preferred stock is generally ignored in applying the 80% tests. § 1504(a)(4).

b) A "purchase" is generally an acquisition from an unrelated person in a transaction where P takes a cost rather than a transferred basis in the acquired stock—e.g., an acquisition for cash or notes of P from a person whose stock is not attributable to P under § 318. § 338(h)(3).

c) The first day that the "qualified stock purchase" requirement is met is known as the "acquisition date." § 338(h)(2). P must acquire 80% of T during the 12-month "acquisition period." Stock acquired during this period and held on the acquisition date is "recently purchased stock." § 338(b)(6)(A). Stock purchased prior to the 12-month period does not count in meeting the 80% test and is "nonrecently purchased stock." § 338(b)(6)(B).

Example (1): T has 100 shares of common stock outstanding. On January 1 of the current year, P purchases 90 shares for cash. Individual A continues to own the other 10 shares. P has made a qualified stock purchase and is eligible to make the § 338 election.

Example (2): Same as Example (1), except P purchases 40 shares on February 1 of Year 1, 30 shares on August 1, and 20 shares on January 1 of Year 2. P has made a qualified stock purchase because it acquired at least 80% of T stock by purchase during a 12-month period. The acquisition date is January 1 of Year 2.

Example (3): Same as Example (1), except P purchased 20 shares five years ago and 80 shares on January 1 of the current year. P has made a qualified stock purchase, but the 20 shares purchased five years ago are "nonrecently purchased stock."

Example (4): Same as Example (3), except P purchased only 70 shares on January 1 of the current year and the remaining 10 shares on February 1 of Year 2. P has not made a qualified stock purchase.

2) The § 338 Election

P must make the § 338 election no later than the 15th day of the ninth month beginning after the month in which the "acquisition date" occurs. § 338(g)(1). Once P has acquired the requisite 80% interest within a 12-month period, it may not create a new acquisition date and thus extend the election deadline by acquiring additional stock. Once made, a § 338 election is irrevocable. § 338(g)(3).

Example: P Corp. purchases 10% of T Corp. stock on February 1 of the current year, 60% on July 1, 10% on August 1 and 20% on November 1. The 12-month acquisition period begins on February 1; the acquisition date (the date within the acquisition period on which the 80% qualified stock purchase is completed) is August 1. The § 338 election must be made no later than May 15 of the following year.

c. The Deemed Sale of T's Assets

If P makes a valid § 338 election, T is treated as having sold all of its assets at the close of the acquisition date for their fair market value in a single transaction to a new corporation ("new T"). § 338(a)(1). The deemed sale has tax consequences to both "old T" and "new T."

1) Consequences to Old T

a) Determination of Aggregate Deemed Sale Price

Old T recognizes gain or loss on the deemed sale, just as if it actually had sold its assets. Old T is deemed to have sold *all* its assets even if P acquires less than 100% of the T stock. The regulations treat T as selling its assets for their "aggregate deemed sales price" ("ADSP"), which is the sum of: (1) the grossed-up amount realized on the sale to P of P's recently purchased T stock, and (2) old T's liabilities, including any tax liabilities resulting from the deemed sale. Reg. § 1.338–4(b). The grossed-up amount realized on the sale of P's recently purchased stock is an amount equal to the amount realized on the sale to P of P's recently purchased T stock (without regard to costs of sale), divided by the percentage of T stock (by value, determined on the acquisition date) attributable to that recently purchased stock, less any selling costs (e.g., brokerage commissions) incurred by the selling T shareholders. Reg. § 1.338–4(c).

In the simple case where P purchases 100% of T's stock during the 12-month acquisition period, the ADSP is P's cost for the stock plus liabilities of old T. The gain or loss from the deemed § 338 sale is reported on old T's tax return and may not be included in any consolidated return filed by P and its other subsidiaries. § 338(h)(9). But the economic burden of old T's tax liability ordinarily is borne by P, which will take it into account in determining the price paid for the T stock. Old T's E & P and other tax attributes terminate after the deemed asset sale.

b)   Liabilities of Old T: Special Problems

As discussed above, the ADSP includes the liabilities of old T, determined as of the beginning of the day after the acquisition date, and including tax liabilities arising from the deemed asset sale. Reg. § 1.338–4(d)(1). A T liability must be one that is properly taken into account under general principles. (In some cases, this may require inclusion of contingent liabilities at the time of sale.) The inclusion of tax liabilities from the deemed sale in determining the ADSP causes a potentially circular calculation because T's tax liability depends on the ADSP, and vice versa. The regulations resolve this dilemma by providing the following (simpler than it seems) formula, where G is the grossed-up amount realized on the sale to P of P's recently purchased T stock, L is T's liabilities (other than deemed sale tax liabilities), T_r is the applicable corporate tax rate, and B is the adjusted basis of the assets deemed sold:

$$ADSP = G + L + T_r (ADSP - B)$$

Reg. § 1.338–4(g) Examples.

2)   Consequences to New T

a)   Adjusted Grossed-up Basis

New T is treated as having purchased old T's assets as of the beginning of the day after the "acquisition date." New T's aggregate basis in the acquired assets is the "adjusted grossed-up basis" ("AGUB"), which is defined as the sum of: (1) "the grossed-up basis" of P's recently purchased stock, (2) P's basis in its nonrecently purchased T stock, and (3) the liabilities of new T. Reg. § 1.338–5(a), (b). The grossed-up basis of P's recently purchased T stock is generally P's cost basis in that stock multiplied by a fraction the numerator of which is 100% minus the percentage attributable to P's nonrecently purchased stock, and the denominator of which is P's percentage ownership of recently purchased stock. Reg. § 1.338–5(c). AGUB is similar but not identical to ADSP. The principal difference arises from the fact that, although the AGUB calculation grosses up the basis of T stock not owned by P, it does not "gross up" the basis of P's *nonrecently* purchased stock. P, however, may elect to recognize the gain on its nonrecently purchased stock as if it had sold that stock for the average price paid by P for the recently purchased T stock. In that case, P may increase the AGUB of T's assets by the amount of such recognized gain. § 338(b)(3); Reg. § 1.338–5(d). If P holds only recently purchased T stock, the AGUB and the ADSP are usually the same.

b)   Allocation of AGUB

New T's aggregate AGUB is allocated among its assets using the residual method prescribed by Reg. § 1.338–6. See IX.D.2.d.2., *supra*, at page 181.

3)   Examples

In the following examples, assume (for computational convenience) that the applicable corporate income tax rate for any ordinary income or capital gain arising from T's deemed asset sale is 20%.

Example (1):   T has 1,000 shares of common stock outstanding. T's only asset is Gainacre (basis—$50,000, value—$300,000). P buys all of T's stock for $250,000 and makes a § 338 election. All the T stock acquired by P is recently purchased, and thus the grossed-up amount realized is $250,000. The ADSP is $250,000 plus T's tax liability on the deemed sale. Under the formula in the regulations, where G is the grossed-up amount realized ($250,000), L is liabilities other than the deemed sale tax liability (0), T_r is the corporate tax rate (.20), and B is the adjusted basis of T's assets deemed sold ($50,000), ADSP is determined as follows:

$$ADSP = G + L + T_r (ADSP - B)$$

$$ADSP = \$250,000 + 0 + .20 \, (ADSP - \$50,000)$$

$$ADSP = \$250,000 + .20 \, ADSP - \$10,000$$

$$.80 \, ADSP = \$240,000$$

$$ADSP = \$300,000$$

T thus recognizes $250,000 gain on the sale of Gainacre, and T's tax liability is $50,0000 (20% × $250,000).

New T's adjusted grossed-up basis ("AGUB") is the $250,000 paid for all of T's stock plus the $50,000 tax liability on the deemed sale, for a total of $300,000 all of which is allocated to Gainacre.

Example (2):   Same as Example (1), except P buys only 900 shares of T stock for $225,000. The remaining 100 shares are owned by Individual ("I"). T's grossed-up amount realized on the sale to P of the 900 shares of recently purchased T stock is the $225,000 amount realized divided by .90 (the percentage of total T stock attributable to recently purchased stock), or $250,000. The analysis is then identical to Example 1, above.

Example (3):   Same as Example (1), except P purchased 100 shares of T five years ago for $10,000 and 900 shares in the current year for $225,000. As in Examples 1 and 2, above, T's grossed-up amount realized on the sale to P of the 900 shares of recently purchased T stock is $250,000, P's ADSP is $300,000, and the gain on the deemed sale of Gainacre is $250,000, resulting in a $50,000 tax liability.

New T's AGUB is the sum of: (1) the cost basis to P of its 900 shares of recently purchased stock ($225,000), which is not grossed-up in this case since P owns 100% of T, (2) the basis of P's nonrecently purchased stock ($10,000), and (3) T's tax liability on the deemed sale ($50,000), for a total AGUB of $285,000. T could increase its basis to $300,000 if it elected to recognize gain under § 338(b)(3) on a hypothetical sale of the nonrecently purchased stock for the average price paid for the recently purchased stock ($250 per share). This election would cause P to recognize $15,000 gain ($25,000 amount realized less $10,000 basis).

d. The Consistency Period Requirements

The consistency period requirements were originally designed to prevent P from selectively (and opportunistically) obtaining disparate favorable tax treatment for different assets acquired from the same corporate enterprise—e.g., a cost basis for some of T's assets and a transferred basis for others. These rules are far less significant after the repeal of the *General Utilities* doctrine. As currently interpreted by the Service in regulations, the consistency period rules now apply only where T is a member of a group of affiliated corporations that file a consolidated return and in a few other very specialized situations. See Reg. § 1.338–8.

1) The Consistency Period

The consistency period generally begins one year before the first purchase of T stock that is included in a "qualified stock purchase" and ends one year after the "acquisition date." § 338(h)(4)(A). The Service may extend the period to prevent plans to circumvent its restrictions. § 338(h)(4)(B).

Example (1): P buys 80% of T's stock on July 1, Year 2 (which is the "acquisition date") and the remaining 20% on September 1, Year 2. The consistency period begins on July 1, Year 1 and ends on June 30, Year 3.

Example (2): Same as Example (1), except P buys 40% of T's stock on July 1, Year 2, 20% on August 1, Year 2, and the remaining 40% on October 1, Year 2 (which is the "acquisition date"). The consistency period begins on July 1, Year 1 and ends on September 30, Year 3.

2) Asset Acquisition Consistency Rules

Under the regulations, the asset acquisition consistency rules generally apply only if: (1) P acquires an asset directly from T during the consistency period, (2) T is a subsidiary of another corporation ("S"), and (3) T and S file a consolidated corporate tax return. Reg. § 1.338–8(a)(2). In this situation, unless a § 338 election is made, P generally takes a carryover (rather than cost) basis in any asset purchased from T during the consistency period. The purpose of the rule is to prevent P from exploiting the consolidated return investment basis adjustment rules by acquiring assets from T with a stepped-up cost basis and then acquiring T stock from S at no additional tax cost to the S consolidated group. See XIV.D.3.a., at page 288, *infra*. The mandatory carryover basis rule does not apply, however, if T sold the asset in the ordinary course of its business and in certain other narrow situations. Reg. § 1.338–8(d)(2).

> *Example:*   S and T, S's 100% subsidiary, file a consolidated return. S has a $100 basis in its T stock, which has a fair market value of $180. On January 1, Year 1, T sells Asset (basis—$20, value—$100) to P and recognizes $80 of gain. Under the consolidated return regulations, S may increase its T stock basis from $100 to $180. On March 1, Year 1, S sells the T stock to P for $180 and recognizes no gain or loss. Because P acquired Asset from T during the consistency period and T's gain is reflected in S's basis in its T stock, P must take an $80 carryover basis for Asset.

3) Stock Acquisition Consistency Rules

The stock acquisition consistency rules in § 338(f) have become virtually irrelevant and are now applied only when necessary to prevent avoidance of the asset consistency rules. Reg. § 1.338–8(a)(6).

4. Sales and Distributions of Stock of a Subsidiary

a. The § 338(h)(10) Election

If T is a subsidiary of another corporation ("S"), whether or not T and S file a consolidated tax return (they normally would) and P wishes to acquire T, S can avoid recognizing gain on its T stock if T sells its assets directly to P and then distributes the sales proceeds to S in a tax-free § 332 liquidation, or if T first liquidates, distributes its assets to S and then S sells the assets to P. A corporate parent and its subsidiary-target can achieve the same result on a sale of T stock to P by making a joint election with P under §§ 338 and 338(h)(10) to treat T as if it sold all of its assets for fair market value to "new T" while a member of the S consolidated group and then T distributed the sales proceeds to S in a tax-free § 332 liquidation. S does not recognize gain or loss on the sale of its stock, S inherits T's tax attributes (e.g., earnings and profits), T is treated as having sold its assets for fair market value in a taxable transaction with any gain or loss included in the consolidated tax return filed by S and its affiliates, and new T is treated as having acquired old T's assets for an amount equal to their adjusted grossed-up basis as determined by a formula prescribed in the regulations. Reg. § 1.338(h)(10)–1(d). Like §§ 332 and 337, the purpose of § 338(h)(10) is to prevent the imposition of two tiers of corporate-level tax.

Situations in which a § 338(h)(10) election may be desirable include: (1) when S's "outside" gain on its stock exceeds T's "inside" gain on its assets (the election eliminates the outside gain); and (2) S's consolidated group has losses that can be used to offset any gain recognized by T on the deemed sale of its assets.

Example: S, Inc. owns all 100 outstanding shares of T, Inc. stock and has a $20,000 basis in its T stock. S and T file a consolidated return. T's only asset is Gainacre (basis—$40,000, value—$100,000). P purchases the T stock for $100,000 cash, and the parties jointly make the § 338 and § 338(h)(10) elections. T is treated as having sold Gainacre for $100,000 and recognizes $60,000 gain, which is includible on S and T's consolidated return. S recognizes no gain on the sale of its T stock. P takes a $100,000 basis in the T stock, and "new T" takes a $100,000 basis in Gainacre.

b. The § 336(e) Election

Section 336(e), as implemented by final regulations issued in 2013, permits a corporation that owns at least 80% of the voting power and value of a subsidiary to elect to treat a sale, exchange or distribution of that subsidiary's stock as if it were a disposition by the subsidiary of its assets. If a § 336(e) election is made, the parent corporation does not recognize gain or loss on the disposition of its stock in the subsidiary. Unlike § 338(h)(10), § 336(e) applies to distributions as well as sales, and to combinations of sales, exchanges and distributions, and in the case of sales and exchanges a § 336(e) election is permitted even when the buyer is not a corporation. A § 336(e) election may be made when an S corporation is the target. See generally Reg. § 1.336–1(b). If a transaction is a "qualified stock purchase" within the meaning of § 338(d)(3), it is governed exclusively by § 338 and does not qualify for a § 336(e) election. Reg. § 1.336–1(b)(6)(ii). A § 336(e) election generally is made jointly by both the seller and the target (acting as a proxy for the purchasers). Reg. § 1.336–2(h).

Example (1):   Individual A owns all the stock of P Corp., which owns all the stock of S Corp. A has a $10,000 basis in her P stock and P has a $10,000 basis in its S stock. S owns one asset, Gainacre (basis—$10,000, value—$30,000). P liquidates and distributes the S stock to A. Under § 336(a), P recognizes $20,000 gain on the distribution of the S stock to A, and A recognizes $20,000 gain (less tax paid by P on its gain) on the liquidation under § 331(a). Although A takes a $30,000 basis in the S stock, S still has a built-in gain of $20,000 on Gainacre. Section 336(e) permits P to elect to treat the distribution of S stock as a disposition of S's assets and to ignore any gain or loss on the distribution of the S stock. Under a § 336(e) election, S recognizes $20,000 gain on the constructive disposition of its assets and takes a $30,000 basis in Gainacre. P recognizes no gain or loss on the distribution of the S stock. A recognizes $20,000 gain on receipt of the S stock in the liquidation and takes a fair market value basis in the S stock.

Example (2):   Same as Example (1), except P sells the S stock to B, an individual, in anticipation of the liquidation. Section 338(h)(10) does not apply because the buyer, B, is not a corporation. Under § 336(e), P and S may elect to treat the sale of S stock as a disposition by S of Gainacre and ignore the gain on the actual sale of S stock. S recognizes $20,000 gain and "new S" takes a $30,000 fair market value basis in Gainacre. P must pay the tax on S's gain.

5. Comparison of Acquisition Methods

From a tax standpoint, the preferred method for a taxable acquisition of a profitable company is usually a stock purchase with no § 338 election because T may defer any gain inherent in its assets. An asset purchase, or a stock purchase coupled with a § 338 election, results in gain at both the corporate and shareholder levels. On a stock purchase, a § 338 election may be desirable, however, when T has net operating loss carryovers that will offset the gain recognized on T's deemed asset sale, or where T is a subsidiary and the parties also jointly make a § 338(h)(10) election. Changes made in 2017 by the Tax Cuts and Jobs Act may change this analysis. The lower corporate income tax rate and the opportunity under § 168(k) to deduct 100% of the cost of the purchase price allocable to most tangible depreciable personal property may make an actual or deemed asset acquisition more attractive in some situations.

E. Review Questions

1. X Corp. has 100 shares of common stock outstanding, of which 80 shares are owned by individual A (stock basis—$300,000) and 20 shares are owned by individual B (stock basis—$600,000). X's only assets are:

Asset	Adj. Basis	F. Mkt. Value
Gainacre	$100,000	$500,000
Lossacre	$800,000	$500,000

Both assets were transferred to X 18 months ago in a § 351 transaction. At that time, Lossacre had an adjusted basis of $800,000 and a fair market value of $900,000. In the current year, before taking into account any of the transactions below, X had accumulated E & P of $100,000 and no current E & P.

(a) Pursuant to a plan of complete liquidation, X distributes each asset pro rata to its shareholders. What are the tax consequences to X, A and B? (In determining the shareholder-level tax consequences, ignore any adjustment resulting from the corporate-level tax imposed on X on the distribution.)

(b) Same as (a), above, except Lossacre had an $800,000 adjusted basis and a $700,000 fair market value at the time it was transferred to X in a § 351 transaction and § 362(e)(2) did not apply to that transfer.

(c) Same as (a), above, except the § 351 transfers occurred six years prior to the liquidation.

(d) Same as (a), above, except that shareholder A is a corporation which has held its X stock continuously for the past three years.

2. S Corp. has 100 shares of common stock outstanding, of which 90 shares are owned by P Corp. (stock basis—$50,000) and 10 shares are owned by individual B (stock basis—$2,000). Pursuant to a plan of complete liquidation, S distributes Gainacre, its only asset (adjusted basis—$70,000; fair market value—$100,000), pro rata to its shareholders. What are the tax consequences to S, P and B?

3. Target Corporation ("T") has 100 shares of common stock outstanding, of which 80 shares are owned by Mr. S (stock basis—$100,000) and 20 shares are owned by Ms. I (stock basis—$50,000). T owns the following assets subject to no liabilities:

Asset	Adj. Basis	F. Mkt. Value
Cash	$120,000	$120,000
Inventory	30,000	50,000
Land	100,000	300,000
Goodwill	0	30,000
Total	$250,000	$500,000

P Corporation ("P") wishes to acquire T's business for cash.

(a) Identify three principal methods for structuring P's acquisition of T.

(b) In general, what are the tax consequences of each of the principal acquisition methods? Assume for convenience that T is subject to a 20% flat corporate income tax rate.

(c) What is the most desirable acquisition method from a tax standpoint?

(d) Would your answer to (c), above, change if S were a corporation that filed a consolidated tax return with T, and S had $2,000,000 of unexpired net operating loss carryforwards? Assume that T is a wholly-owned subsidiary of S.

Chapter X

Anti-Avoidance Rules

■ ANALYSIS

A. Introduction

Subchapter C is predicated on the double taxation of corporate profits. Historically, taxpayers have pursued various strategies to mitigate the impact of the double tax and take advantage of disparities between the corporate and individual rates by accumulating income at the corporate level rather than paying dividends. Congress has responded from time to time by enacting statutory rules to combat these tax-avoidance maneuvers. This chapter examines three such weapons: the economic substance doctrine, a longstanding judicial principle that has been codified along with a strict no fault penalty imposed on corporate tax shelter transactions that lack economic substance; the accumulated earnings tax; and the personal holding company tax.

B. Economic Substance Doctrine

1. Common Law Roots

The economic substance doctrine is one of several doctrines developed by courts to deny tax benefits to transactions that may satisfy the literal requirements of the Code but are largely motivated by the goal of reducing federal income taxes without resulting in any meaningful change to a taxpayer's economic position apart from tax savings. See I.E., at page 52, *supra*, for an overview of all the judicial doctrines.

2. Applications by Courts

The courts have applied the economic substance doctrine in cases involving a variety of complex transactions known as corporate tax shelters. The doctrine has not been applied uniformly or clearly, contributing to much confusion.

a. Economic Substance Tests

Some courts apply a rigorous conjunctive test requiring taxpayers to establish the presence of both economic substance and business purpose. See, e.g., *Pasternak v. Comm'r*, 990 F.2d 893 (6th Cir.1993). Others employ a narrower approach under which a demonstration of either a business purpose or economic substance is sufficient for a transaction to be respected. See, e.g., *Rice's Toyota World v. Comm'r*, 752 F.2d 89 (4th Cir.1985). Another approach treats business purpose and economic substance as "simply more precise factors to consider" in determining if a transfer has practical economic effect apart from tax benefits. See, e.g., *ACM Partnership v. Comm'r*, 157 F.3d 231 (3d Cir.1998). A more recent case respected the form chosen by the taxpayers despite the absence of a nontax business purpose. In so doing, the court limited the application of the economic substance doctrine to situations where "the taxpayer's financial characterization of a transaction fails to capture economic reality and would distort the meaning of the Code in the process." *Summa Holdings, Inc. v. Comm'r*, 848 F.3d 779, 787 (6th Cir. 2017).

b. Nontax Economic Benefits

The courts also disagree about the type of nontax economic benefit that must be established to demonstrate economic substance. Some deny tax benefits based on a finding that the stated business benefit of the taxpayer's chosen structure was not in fact obtained. Others do not respect transactions that lack any profit potential or where the economic risks and profit potential are insignificant when compared to tax benefits, or they require an objective determination of whether a "reasonable possibility of profit" exists apart from tax benefits.

c. Financial Accounting Benefits as Nontax Business Purpose

The cases also conflict on whether financial accounting benefits arising from tax benefits, which can have a positive impact on a public company's stock price, qualify as a nontax business purpose.

3. Codification

a. In General

Section 7701(o) codifies the economic substance doctrine and is accompanied by a no-fault penalty. It employs the stricter conjunctive (two-pronged) test. Any transaction to which the economic substance doctrine is "relevant" will be treated as having economic substance only if, apart from the effect of federal income taxes, it changes the taxpayer's economic position in a meaningful way and the taxpayer has a substantial purpose for engaging in the transaction. § 7701(o)(1). Whether or not the economic substance doctrine is "relevant" apparently is determined by reference to standards developed by the courts. § 7701(o)(5)(C). For individual taxpayers, the codified doctrine applies to transactions entered into in connection with a trade or business or an activity engaged in for the production of income but not to personal transactions. § 7701(o)(5)(B).

b. Determination of Nontax Purpose

In determining whether a nontax purpose is "substantial," a purpose of achieving favorable financial accounting treatment may not be taken into account if the origin of that benefit is a reduction of federal income tax. § 7701(o)(4).

c. Profit Potential

A taxpayer relying on profit potential to meet the two-pronged statutory test must demonstrate that the value of the reasonably expected pre-tax profit is substantial in relation to the present value of the expected net tax benefits that would be allowed if the transaction is respected. § 7701(o)(2)(A). Fees, other transaction costs, and possibly foreign taxes (subject to regulations not yet issued) must be considered in determining pre-tax profit. § 7701(o)(2)(B).

d. Strict Liability Penalty

A penalty of 20% of the amount of any underpayment attributable to any disallowance of claimed tax benefits is imposed if a transaction lacks economic substance under § 7701(o) or fails to meet the requirements of "any similar rule of law." § 6662(b)(6). The penalty is increased to 40% if the taxpayer does not adequately disclose the relevant facts in its timely filed original tax returns. § 6662(i). Taxpayers may not rely on a reasonable cause or good faith exception to escape the penalty and thus reliance on an outside opinion of counsel is not a defense. § 6664(c)(2). The IRS only will impose this penalty when it invokes the codified economic substance doctrine, not when it relies on other judicial doctrines (e.g., the step transaction doctrine). IRS Notice 2014–58, 2014–44 I.R.B. 746.

e. Exempted Transactions

Congress did not intend the codified economic substance doctrine to prevent accepted tax planning techniques, such as the choice to capitalize a corporation with a reasonable amount of debt, or to structure an acquisition to qualify as a certain type of tax-free reorganization. The doctrine also is not likely to be applied to tax-motivated transactions that Congress intended to encourage through incentives such as credits for low-income housing, research and development, and clean energy.

f. IRS Guidance

The IRS has resisted requests for guidance on the meaning and scope of the codified economic substance doctrine. It will continue to rely on relevant case law, will not issue rulings on whether or not the doctrine is "relevant" to a transaction, and will not issue a list of specific protected transactions. IRS Notice 2010–62, 2010–40 C.B. 411; see also IRS Notice 2014–58, 2014–44 I.R.B. 746.

C. Accumulated Earnings Tax

1. Introduction

For most of U.S. tax history, the marginal rates applied to the taxable ordinary income of individuals were significantly higher than the corporate rates. The lower rates on corporate taxable income made corporations attractive vehicles for accumulating income. High-bracket shareholders could allow corporate income to accumulate and compound at lower rates in corporate solution. The accumulation strategy also had the benefit of deferring imposition of a second level of tax on corporate distributions. Shareholders needing to realize corporate profits could sell stock and recognize capital gains while shareholders with no immediate need for cash could wait and leave the stock to their heirs, who would take a stepped-up § 1014 basis.

The accumulated earnings tax was enacted to combat the accumulation strategy. It applies to corporations formed or availed of to avoid the individual income tax rather than distributing the corporation's earnings and profits. § 532(a). The importance of the accumulated earnings tax was greatly reduced under the rate structure in effect for many years prior to 2018, when ordinary income of high-income individuals and C corporations was taxed at close to the same top marginal rates, with a much lower rate for qualified dividends received by noncorporate shareholders. During this period, the primary role of the penalty was to combat accumulation strategies designed to avoid the double tax of Subchapter C. Under current law, however, the wide differential between the 21% corporate rate and the 37% top marginal individual rate has restored the incentive to accumulate business income in a C corporation in some situations, breathing new life into the accumulated earnings tax.

The accumulated earnings tax is paid in addition to other taxes imposed on the corporation and generally applies to every C corporation formed or availed of for the purpose of avoiding the individual income tax by accumulating rather than distributing earnings and profits. §§ 531, 532(a). Publicly held, as well as closely held, corporations are subject to the tax, although it rarely has been applied to public companies. § 532(c). The tax is determined by applying a 20% rate to a C corporation's "accumulated taxable income." § 531. Personal holding companies, tax-exempt corporations and passive foreign investment companies are not subject to the tax. § 532(b).

2. The Prohibited Tax Avoidance Purpose

The accumulated earnings tax only applies to a corporation that is formed or availed of for a tax avoidance purpose. The statutory standard is met if tax avoidance is one of several factors which motivated corporate accumulations. *United States v. Donruss Co.,* 393 U.S. 297, 89 S.Ct. 501 (1969). The existence of a tax avoidance purpose depends upon the particular circumstances of each case, including (1) dealings between the corporation and its shareholders, such as personal loans to the shareholders or expenditures by the corporation for the personal benefit of the shareholders, (2) investments having no reasonable relationship to the corporation's business, and (3) the extent to which the corporation distributes its earnings and profits. Reg. § 1.533–1(a)(2).

The fact that a corporation accumulates its earnings and profits "beyond the reasonable needs of the business" establishes a presumption of tax avoidance purpose unless the corporation rebuts the presumption by a preponderance of the evidence. § 533(a). This presumption adds still more weight to the general presumption of correctness that attaches to a determination of tax liability by the Service. Reg. § 1.533–1(b). A taxpayer may shift the burden of proof on the reasonableness of its accumulations to the Service in a Tax Court proceeding if, in response to the Service's notice proposing an accumulated earnings tax deficiency, it submits a statement and alleges facts sufficient to show that the accumulation was reasonable. § 534(a)(2), (c). Under § 533(b), the fact that a corporation is a "mere holding or investment company" is prima facie evidence of a tax avoidance purpose.

3. Reasonable Needs of the Business

a. In General

If a corporation permits its earnings and profits to accumulate beyond the reasonable needs of its business, that fact establishes a tax avoidance purpose unless the corporation proves it does not have such a purpose by a preponderance of the evidence. § 533(a). While it is possible for a corporation with unreasonable accumulations to rebut the presumption of a tax avoidance purpose, that situation rarely occurs. Thus, the critical question in accumulated earnings cases usually is whether corporate accumulations are beyond the reasonable needs of the business.

The regulations provide that the question of whether there is an accumulation beyond the reasonable needs of the business depends on the circumstances of each case. Thus, the issue is essentially factual in nature and the corporation normally will put forward several business needs which it claims justified its accumulation of profits. Courts typically are reluctant to question the business judgment of corporate management if the plans for an accumulation have substance and are not a facade for retaining corporate earnings. See generally, *Myron's Enterprises v. United States,* 548 F.2d 331 (9th Cir.1977), in which accumulations for the purchase and improvement of business property were justified as being for the reasonable needs of the business. This longstanding body of case law has weakened the effectiveness of the accumulated earnings tax.

b. Examples of Reasonable Business Needs

The regulations provide the following list of grounds which, if supported by sufficient facts, may indicate that earnings and profits have been accumulated for the reasonable needs of the business. Reg. § 1.537–2(b).

1) To provide for bona fide expansion of business or replacement of plant;

2) To acquire a business enterprise through a stock or assets purchase;

3) To provide for retirement of bona fide business indebtedness;

4) To provide necessary business working capital;

5) To provide for investments or loans to suppliers or customers in order to maintain the corporation's business; and

6) To provide for payment of reasonably anticipated product liability losses.

c. Examples of Unreasonable Accumulations

Accumulations for the following nonexclusive list of objectives may indicate that earnings and profits are being accumulated beyond the reasonable needs of the business. Reg. § 1.537–2(c).

1) Loans to shareholders or the expenditure of corporate funds for the personal benefit of the shareholders;

2) Loans to relatives or friends of shareholders, or to other persons, having no reasonable relation to the conduct of the business;

3) Loans to another corporation engaged in a different business which is controlled by the controlling shareholders of the corporation;

4) Investments in properties or securities unrelated to the corporation's business; and

5) Retention of earnings and profits to provide against unrealistic hazards.

d. Anticipated Needs of the Business

Section 537(a)(1) provides that the reasonable needs of the business include the "reasonably anticipated" needs of the business. The regulations state that to justify an accumulation for anticipated needs, a corporation must show a business need for the accumulation and it must have "specific, definite, and feasible plans for the use of such accumulation." The accumulation does not have to be for immediate use or even use within a short period so long as it will be used within a reasonable time depending on all the facts and circumstances relating to the future needs of the business. Reg. § 1.537–1(b)(1). Because reasonably anticipated needs of the business are determined at year end, subsequent events are not used to show that retention of profits was unreasonable at the close of the taxable year. Subsequent events, however, may be considered to determine whether the taxpayer actually intended to consummate or has actually consummated the plan for which earnings and profits were accumulated. If an accumulation justified for future needs is never consummated, the amount of the accumulation is considered in determining the reasonableness of subsequent accumulations. Reg. § 1.537–1(b)(2).

e. The "Business" of the Corporation

The business of a corporation is not merely the one it has previously carried on but includes, in general, "any line of business it may undertake." Reg. § 1.537–3(a). Thus, reasonable needs include expansions of existing businesses and acquisition of related businesses. Accumulations to acquire entirely unrelated businesses run the risk of being labeled "investments in properties, or securities which are unrelated to the activities of the business of the taxpayer," which may indicate the accumulation is beyond the reasonable needs of the business. Reg. § 1.537–2(c)(4). In the case of investments in a subsidiary corporation, reasonable needs of the parent include the needs of an 80% or more subsidiary. Otherwise, the determination of whether the subsidiary's business needs are attributed to the parent depends on the particular circumstances. Reg. § 1.537–3(b).

f. Working Capital Needs of the Corporation

Accumulations to provide necessary business working capital may indicate that accumulations are for the reasonable needs of the business. Reg. § 1.537–2(b)(4). The courts have approached this question by attempting to determine the capital requirements of the corporation for one operating cycle, which in general is the time it takes to purchase raw materials, make finished goods, sell the product, and collect any outstanding receivables so the process may be repeated. The analysis, which is called the *Bardahl* formula after *Bardahl Manufacturing Corp. v. Comm'r,* 24 T.C.M. 1030 (1965), provides an approximation of the corporation's working capital needs.

g. Stock Redemptions

Section 537(a)(2) provides that accumulations designed to meet the reasonably anticipated needs of the corporation for § 303 redemptions to pay death taxes which are made in the year a shareholder dies or any taxable year thereafter are for the reasonable needs of the business. See § 537(b)(1). The treatment of accumulations for other types of non pro rata redemptions varies. In theory, the tax treatment of the accumulation should depend upon whether the redemption is motivated by *corporate* purposes or personal needs of the shareholders. Thus, accumulations to redeem the stock of dissenting minority shareholders or to prevent stock from falling into the hands of antagonistic shareholders have been determined to be for the reasonable needs of the business. For example, in *Gazette Publishing Co. v. Self,* 103 F.Supp. 779 (E.D.Ark.1952), the court determined that the redemption of a shareholder's voting stock in a newspaper publisher to prevent the stock from being owned by special interests who might oppose the paper's editorial policy was a reasonable need of the business.

4. Accumulated Taxable Income

a. In General

A corporation subject to the accumulated earnings tax must pay a tax determined by applying a 20% rate to the corporation's "accumulated taxable income." § 531. Accumulated taxable income is taxable income adjusted under

§ 535(b), minus the § 561 dividends paid deduction and the § 535(c) accumulated earnings credit. § 535(a).

b.   § 535(b) Adjustments to Taxable Income

The corporation's taxable income is adjusted under § 535(b) to arrive at a more accurate determination of the corporation's economic success. Thus, certain nondeductible taxes and charitable contributions in excess of the 10% limitation are permitted as reductions to taxable income. § 535(b)(1), (2). The dividends received deduction and net operating loss deduction are not allowed and must be added back to taxable income in arriving at accumulated taxable income. § 535(b)(3), (4).

Net capital gain, less attributable taxes, is deducted from taxable income. § 535(b)(6). For purposes of determining net capital gain, net capital loss from prior taxable years is treated as short-term capital loss. § 535(b)(7)(A). A corporation also may deduct its net capital loss for the year but the deduction is limited to the lesser of the "nonrecaptured capital gains deduction" (as defined in § 535(b)(5)(C)) or the corporation's accumulated earnings and profits at the end of the year. § 535(b)(5)(A), (B).

c.   § 561 Dividends Paid Deduction

A corporation may reduce its accumulated taxable income by the amount of the dividends it pays during the year and the amount of the "consent dividends" for the year. §§ 535(a); 561(a)(1), (2); 562(a). For this purpose, the amount of a dividend paid in property other than money is the corporation's adjusted basis in the property. Reg. § 1.562–1(a); *Fulman v. United States*, 434 U.S. 528, 98 S.Ct. 841 (1978). To be eligible for the dividends paid deduction, the distribution generally must be pro rata among the shareholders. § 562(c). A portion of a liquidating distribution or a distribution in redemption of stock also may qualify for the dividends paid deduction. § 562(b)(1). Dividends paid on or before the 15th day of the fourth month following the taxable year are considered as paid in such year for purposes of the accumulated earnings tax. § 563(a).

"Consent dividends" are amounts which the shareholders agree to consider to have been distributed even though there was no actual distribution. Consent dividends must be pro rata in order to be deductible and must be for amounts which would have been dividends if actually distributed. § 565(b). Under § 565(c), consent dividends are considered to be distributed in money to the shareholder on the last day of the corporation's taxable year, thereby producing a dividend, and recontributed to the corporation on the same day.

d.   § 535(c) Accumulated Earnings Credit

Under § 535(c)(1), a corporation, other than a mere holding or investment company, is entitled to a deduction equal to the portion of its earnings and profits retained for the reasonable needs of its business less the deduction for net capital gains. Under § 535(c)(2), the amount of this deduction can not be less than the amount by which $250,000 ($150,000 for service corporations in certain businesses) exceeds the accumulated earnings and profits at the close of the year. This provision, in effect, permits every corporation to accumulate $250,000, regardless of the purpose for the accumulation.

D. Personal Holding Company Tax

1. Introduction

The accumulated earnings tax has certain limitations. Its application depends upon determining a prohibited tax avoidance purpose for accumulations, and the accumulated earnings credit permits corporations to accumulate substantial amounts of corporate earnings. Congress enacted the personal holding company tax, in part, to respond to these deficiencies in the accumulated earnings tax and to address other tax avoidance strategies.

The original targets of the personal holding company tax were the so-called "incorporated pocketbooks," "incorporated talents," and "incorporated properties" strategies. Incorporated pocketbooks involved the transfer of investment assets (stocks, bonds, etc.) to a corporation which was taxed at rates significantly lower than the rates paid by individual taxpayers. Passive investment income could be earned and compounded subject only to the lower corporate tax rates, and dividends received by the corporation would be eligible for the dividends received deduction. The shareholders could defer recognition of income until needed, at which time it could be realized in transactions producing capital gain. Alternatively, the shareholders could leave the stock to their heirs who would take a stepped-up § 1014 basis. In the "incorporated talents" strategy, a highly compensated individual would form a corporation which would then contract out the services of its owner. The shareholder could receive enough salary to meet personal needs and allow the remainder of the income to accumulate in the corporation at lower corporate tax rates. The "incorporated properties" strategy involved the transfer of a nonbusiness asset, such as a yacht or home, to a corporation which would then rent the property back to the shareholder. The goal was to deduct depreciation on the nonbusiness asset to offset the rent payment and other corporate income.

The significance of these tax avoidance strategies is diminished when the top individual and corporate rates are very close to one another, but the personal holding company rules remained in the Code through an extended period of tax rate instability and reassumed greater importance in 2018 when the corporate tax rate was reduced to 21%.

Section 541 imposes a tax of 20% on the "undistributed personal holding company income" of a personal holding company. The tax is imposed in addition to other taxes paid by the corporation. Certain corporations subject to special tax rules are not subject to the personal holding company tax.

2. Definition of Personal Holding Company

Under § 542(a), a "personal holding company" is a company which meets both a stock ownership requirement and an income requirement.

a. Stock Ownership Requirement

More than 50% in value of a corporation's stock must be owned, directly or indirectly, at any time during the last half of the taxable year by five or fewer individuals. § 542(a)(2). Attribution rules are applied to test stock ownership. Stock owned by a corporation, partnership, estate or trust is considered owned proportionately by its shareholders, partners or beneficiaries. § 544(a)(1). An individual also is considered to own stock owned by or for her family (brothers, sisters, ancestors and lineal descendants) or by or for her partner. § 544(a)(2).

Stock subject to an option to purchase is considered to be owned by the option holder. § 544(a)(3). Securities convertible into stock are considered stock for purposes of the stock ownership test if the effect of such inclusion is to make the corporation a personal holding company. § 544(b)(1).

b. Income Requirement

At least 60% of a corporation's adjusted ordinary gross income ("AOGI") for the taxable year must be personal holding company income. § 542(a)(1). AOGI is equal to the corporation's ordinary gross income ("OGI") with certain adjustments. OGI is equal to the corporation's gross income less its gains from the sale or other disposition of capital assets and § 1231(b) property. § 543(b)(1). The adjustments to OGI in arriving at AOGI are designed to take into account the costs of earning certain forms of gross income so corporations cannot easily generate gross receipts to avoid the personal holding company tax. Thus, AOGI includes the corporation's income from rents and mineral, oil and gas royalties after adjustments for cost recovery, property taxes, interest and rents. § 543(b)(2)(A), (B). Copyright royalties, produced film rents, and active business computer software royalties, however, are not adjusted in determining AOGI. § 543(b)(2)(A), (3). Interest on U.S. obligations held by dealers and interest on condemnation awards, judgments and tax refunds are excluded from AOGI. § 543(b)(2)(C).

c. Definition of Personal Holding Company Income

Section 543(a) defines "personal holding company income" as the portion of AOGI consisting of specified types of income. The definition of personal holding company income focuses on passive investment income and income from personal services contracts. Section 543(a) is extremely complex because it contains a number of statutory tests which, in general, are designed to distinguish between passive forms of income and income earned in pursuit of the corporation's business.

1) Passive Investment Income

Dividends, interest, and royalties (other than mineral, oil or gas royalties or copyright royalties) included in AOGI are personal holding company income. § 543(a)(1). Active computer software royalties (as defined) also are excluded from the general passive income category. § 543(a)(1)(C). But royalties from patents, secret processes and formulas, goodwill, trademarks, trade brands, franchises and comparable properties are included in personal holding company income. Reg. § 1.543–1(b)(3).

2) Rents

Under § 543(a)(2), rents are personal holding company income unless the adjusted income from rents (as defined in § 543(b)(3)) constitutes 50% or more of AOGI. § 543(a)(2)(A). The theory of this test is that where rental income represents the major activity of the corporation that activity is more likely to be of an active rather than passive nature. In general, a corporation with adjusted gross income from rents equal to 50% or more of its AOGI may have its rents classified as personal holding company income if it has large amounts of other forms of personal holding company income which it does not distribute to its shareholders. § 543(a)(2)(B).

3) Mineral, Oil and Gas Royalties

The adjusted income from mineral, oil, and gas royalties (as defined in § 543(b)(4)) is personal holding company income unless (1) it constitutes 50% or more of AOGI, (2) certain other types of personal holding company income are not more than 10% of OGI, and (3) the corporation's § 162 trade or business deductions (other than for shareholder provided services and deductions allowable under other sections) are 15% or more of AOGI. § 543(a)(3).

4) Copyright Royalties

Under § 543(a)(4), copyright royalties are personal holding company income unless (1) they constitute 50% or more of OGI, (2) certain other personal holding company income is not more than 10% of OGI, and (3) the corporation's § 162 trade or business deductions allocable to such royalties (other than for shareholder provided services, amounts paid or incurred for royalties, and deductions allowable under other sections) equals or exceeds 25% of OGI less the sum of the royalties paid or accrued and the amounts allowed under § 167 as depreciation for copyright royalties.

5) Produced Film Rents

"Produced film rents" (as defined in § 543(a)(5)(B)) are personal holding company income unless they constitute 50% or more of OGI. § 543(a)(5)(A).

6) Use of Corporate Property by Shareholder

Under certain conditions, rents received from 25% or more shareholders (by value) are personal holding company income. § 543(a)(6). This provision is designed to attack the "incorporated properties" strategy.

7) Personal Service Contracts

Amounts received by a corporation under a contract for personal services, or a sale of the contract, are personal holding company income under § 543(a)(7) if some person other than the corporation has the right to designate by name or description the individual who performs such services or the individual who will perform the services is designated in the contract. This provision only applies to amounts received for services if a 25% or more shareholder (by value) is the individual who has performed, is to perform, or may be designated to perform the services. Section 543(a)(7) is the provision which deals with the "incorporated talents" strategy.

In Revenue Ruling 75–67, 1975–1 C.B. 169, the Service applied § 543(a)(7) to a professional service corporation which was 80% owned by a doctor who was the only doctor employed by the corporation. Typically, a physician-patient relationship arises from a general agreement of treatment between a physician and patient. Either party generally may terminate the relationship at will. A physician who is unable to treat the patient when services are needed may provide a qualified and competent substitute physician to render the services. Because of the special nature of the physician-patient relationship, Rev. Rul. 75–67 concluded that the establishment of the relationship does not constitute a designation under § 543(a)(7). But if the physician contracts to provide particular services with no right of substitution, or if the nature of the physician's services are so unique as to preclude substitution, there is a designation for purposes of § 543(a)(7).

8)   Amounts Received from Estates and Trusts

Amounts included in a corporation's taxable income as a result of it being a beneficiary of an estate or trust are personal holding company income. § 543(a)(8).

9)   Active Computer Software Royalties

Personal holding company income does not include "active computer software royalties." § 543(a)(1)(C), (4). "Active computer software royalties" are defined as royalties received in connection with the licensing of computer software, if: (1) the royalties are received by a corporation engaged in the active conduct of the trade or business of developing, manufacturing, or producing computer software and are attributable to software developed, manufactured, or produced in connection with the business or directly related to such business; (2) the royalties must constitute at least 50% of OGI; (3) the corporation's expenses under § 162 (other than compensation paid to certain shareholders and expenses allowable under other sections), § 174, and § 195 for the year properly allocable to the software business must be equal to at least 25% of OGI or the average of such deductions for the past five years (or the life of the corporation if shorter) must be at least 25% of the average OGI for such period; and (4) the dividends paid during the year (including dividends considered paid on the last day under § 563 and consent dividends under § 565) must equal or exceed the corporation's other personal holding company income (with adjustments) less 10% of OGI. § 543(d).

3. Undistributed Personal Holding Company Income

The personal holding company tax is 20% of the corporation's "undistributed personal holding company income" ("UPHCI"). § 541. UPHCI is defined in § 545(a) as taxable income with adjustments minus the § 561 dividends paid deduction.

a. Adjustments to Taxable Income

In calculating UPHCI, several adjustments are required to reach a more accurate measure of the corporation's economic performance. A deduction for certain nondeductible items, such as federal income taxes and excess charitable contributions, is allowed. § 545(b)(1), (2). The dividends received deduction is not allowed and there are special rules for net operating losses. § 545(b)(3), (4). In order to eliminate capital gains from the base of the personal holding company tax, a deduction equal to the corporation's net capital gain minus allocable taxes is allowed in computing UPHCI. § 545(b)(5). In the case of property leased by the corporation, § 162 and § 167 deductions allocable to the operation and maintenance of such property are allowed only to the extent of the rent or compensation generated by the property unless the taxpayer establishes that (1) the rent or other compensation was the highest obtainable, (2) the property was held in the course of a business carried on bona fide for profit, and (3) either there was a reasonable expectation of profit from the operation of the property or the property was necessary to the conduct of the business. § 545(b)(6).

b. § 561 Dividends Paid Deduction

1) In General

A corporation may reduce its UPHCI by the amount of the dividends it pays during the year, the consent dividends for the year under § 565, and the dividend carryover in § 564. §§ 545(a), 561(a). To be eligible for the dividends paid deduction, the distribution generally must be pro rata among the shareholders. § 562(c). The amount of any dividend paid in property other than money is the corporation's adjusted basis in the distributed property. Reg. § 1.562–1(a); *Fulman v. United States*, 434 U.S. 528, 98 S.Ct. 841 (1978).

Generally, operating distributions and distributions characterized as § 301 distributions (e.g., certain redemptions and stock dividends) produce dividends to the extent of the corporation's earnings and profits. In addition, under § 316(b)(2) any distribution by a personal holding company is a dividend to the extent of its UPHCI for the year. This rule also applies to distributions which are considered made in the year under § 563(b) and deficiency dividends under § 547.

2) § 563(b) Election

In the case of dividends paid on or before the 15th day of the fourth month following the taxable year, the corporation may elect to have the dividend be considered as paid during the year. § 563(b). This election is limited to an amount of dividends which does not exceed either the corporation's UPHCI for the year or 20% of the dividends otherwise paid during the year.

3) Consent Dividends

"Consent dividends" are amounts which the shareholders agree to consider to have been distributed even though there was no actual distribution. Consent dividends must be pro rata in order to be deductible and must be for amounts which would have been dividends if actually distributed. § 565(b)(1). Under § 565(c), consent dividends are considered to be distributed in money on the last day of the corporation's taxable year thereby producing a dividend, and then to be recontributed to the corporation on the same day.

4) § 564 Dividend Carryover

Corporations also are potentially eligible for a dividend carryover from the preceding two years which will reduce UPHCI. The amount of the dividend carryover from each of those years is the excess of the dividends paid deduction (without carryovers) for the year over taxable income computed with the adjustments provided in § 545. If there is such an excess in the earlier of the two years, that excess is offset by the excess, if any, of taxable income over the dividends paid deduction (without carryovers) in the later year. § 564(b)(4), (5).

5) Liquidating Distributions

Under § 562(b)(2), liquidating distributions to corporate distributees within 24 months of the adoption of a plan of liquidation are treated as dividends paid to the extent of the corporate distributee's allocable share of UPHCI for the year. Under § 316(b)(2)(B), distributions in complete liquidation to noncorporate shareholders may be designated as dividend distributions to the extent of the distributee's allocable share of UPHCI. If a payment to a noncorporate shareholder is so designated, the shareholder must treat that portion of the distribution as a dividend.

6) § 547 Deficiency Dividends

If a determination is made that a corporation is liable for the personal holding company tax, § 547 permits a deduction for "deficiency deductions" for purposes of determining UPHCI and tax liability, but not interest and penalties. "Deficiency dividends" are dividends paid within 90 days of a determination of liability for personal holding company tax which would have been included in the § 561 dividends paid deduction in the year to which the liability exists if distributed in that year. § 547(d)(1). A claim for a deficiency dividend deduction must be filed within 120 days after the determination of liability for personal holding company tax. § 547(e).

E. Review Questions

1. If a corporation permits its earnings and profits to accumulate beyond the reasonable needs of its business, it is conclusively presumed to have been formed for a tax avoidance purpose. True or False?

2. What requirements must be met for a corporation to be classified as a "personal holding company"?

Chapter XI

Tax-Free Reorganizations

■ ANALYSIS

A. Introduction

1. Policy

The term "reorganization" is used in the Internal Revenue Code to describe a variety of transactions that result in a fundamental change in the ownership or structure of one or more corporations. Transactions that qualify as reorganizations under § 368 are wholly or partially tax free to the corporations and their shareholders. The rationale for nonrecognition is that a reorganization is merely a readjustment of a continuing corporate enterprise, resulting in a continuity of investment. See Reg. § 1.368–1(b). In keeping with nonrecognition principles, the gain or loss of the corporate parties to a reorganization and their shareholders is not permanently forgiven but merely deferred through transferred and exchanged bases for the corporation's assets and the shareholders' stock.

2. Types of Corporate Reorganizations

Corporate reorganizations fall into three broad categories:

a. Acquisitive Reorganizations

Acquisitive reorganizations are transactions where one corporation (the "acquiring corporation," hereafter referred to as "P") acquires the assets or stock of another corporation ("the target corporation," hereafter "T"). Included in this category are statutory mergers or consolidations (Type A); stock-for-stock acquisitions (Type B); stock-for-assets acquisitions (Type C); variations, known as "triangular reorganizations," which involve the use of a subsidiary; and certain transfers of substantially all of the assets of one corporation to another commonly controlled corporation followed by a liquidation of the first corporation (nondivisive Type D).

b. Nonacquisitive, Nondivisive Reorganizations

Nonacquisitive, nondivisive reorganizations are adjustments to the corporate structure of a single, continuing corporate enterprise. This category includes recapitalizations (Type E); changes in the identity, form or place of incorporation (Type F); and transfers of a corporation's assets to another corporation in connection with a bankruptcy reorganization plan (Type G).

c. Divisive Reorganizations

Divisive reorganizations are divisions of a single corporation into two or more separate corporate entities. Corporate divisions are covered in Chapter XII, *infra*.

3. Guide to Analyzing a Reorganization

A student should first determine if a transaction qualifies as a reorganization. To qualify, a transaction must satisfy both the literal statutory requirements for one of the reorganization "types" in § 368 and also meet other requirements derived from case law (continuity of proprietary interest, continuity of business enterprise and business purpose) that are incorporated in the regulations and referred to below as "nonstatutory" requirements. Reg. § 1.368–1(b). See XI.A.4., at pages 209–210, *infra*. Depending on the facts, other judicial doctrines, such as substance over form and the step transaction doctrine, also may be applied by the Service and the courts in analyzing a reorganization. Reg. § 1.368–1(a), (c). See I.E., at pages 52–54, *supra*. If a transaction qualifies as a reorganization, the specific tax consequences to the parties are determined by "operative provisions" that govern recognition of gain or loss, treatment of liabilities, basis, and carryover of tax attributes (e.g., earnings and profits and net operating losses). See XI.B.8., at pages 230–236, *infra*. If a transaction fails to qualify as a reorganization, the tax consequences are determined under general Subchapter C principles. See XI.B.9., at page 236, *infra*.

4. Nonstatutory Requirements

a. Continuity of Shareholder Proprietary Interest

The purpose of the continuity of interest doctrine is to prevent transactions that resemble sales from qualifying as tax-free reorganizations. Continuity of interest requires that a substantial part of the proprietary interest in T be preserved through an equity interest in P. Reg. § 1.368–1(e)(1). Put differently, P must acquire T by using consideration that represents a proprietary interest in P's affairs—i.e., stock—and that stock must be a substantial part of the value of the consideration used in the reorganization. Reg. § 1.368–2(e)(1)(i). Debt instruments, including convertible debt, do not confer the requisite proprietary interest. Id. The continuity of interest requirement has been incorporated into most of the statutory definitions in § 368. For example, the only permissible consideration in a Type B reorganization is voting stock. Where the statutory definition is imprecise as to consideration, as with Type A reorganizations, satisfying the judicial requirement becomes critical. See XI.B.1.b., at page 211, *infra*, for specific applications.

b. Continuity of Business Enterprise

To qualify as an acquisitive reorganization, the regulations require "continuity of business enterprise" under the modified corporate form. Reg. § 1.368–1(b). P either must continue T's historic business or continue to use a "significant portion" of T's "historic business assets" in a business. Reg. § 1.368–1(d)(1). The fact that P and T are in the same line of business tends to establish the requisite continuity but is not alone sufficient. If T has more than one business, P only must continue a "significant" line of T's business. Reg. § 1.368–1(d)(2)(ii). T's "historic business assets" are the assets used in its historic business. All the facts and circumstances are considered in evaluating whether a line of business is "significant". In general, the portion of those assets that are considered "significant" is based on their relative importance to the operation of the business. Reg. § 1.368–1(d)(2)(iii), (iv), –1(d)(3)(iii). The continuity of business enterprise requirement does not apply to the business or business assets of P prior to the reorganization. Rev. Rul. 81–25, 1981–1 C.B. 132. The regulations include extensive guidance on whether the continuation of T's historic business in tiered entities and through partnerships satisfies continuity of business enterprise. See Reg. § 1.368–1(d)(5) Examples (7)–(12).

Caveat: Some older cases, decided prior to the current regulations, have held that P need not continue T's historic business or use its business assets but merely must engage in some type of business activity. See, e.g., *Bentsen v. Phinney,* 199 F.Supp. 363 (S.D. Tex. 1961).

Example (1): T conducts three separate lines of business which are of equal value. T disposes of two of the businesses for cash and, six months later, T merges into P, with T shareholders receiving P stock. If P continues T's remaining business, the continuity of business enterprise test is met because P is continuing a "significant line" of T's business. Reg. § 1.368–1(d)(5) Example (1).

Example (2): T is a manufacturer and P operates a lumber mill. T merges into P, which disposes of T's assets immediately after the merger and does not continue T's manufacturing business. Continuity of business enterprise is lacking because T neither continues T's historic business nor uses its historic business assets. Reg. § 1.368–1(d)(5) Example (5).

Example (3): Same as Example (2), except after the merger P sells its lumber mill and uses the proceeds to expand the manufacturing business formerly conducted by T. The continuity of business enterprise requirement is met because P continues T's historic business. It is irrelevant that P sold the business it conducted prior to the merger. Rev. Rul. 81–25, 1981–1 C.B. 132.

c. Business Purpose

A transaction will not qualify as a reorganization unless it is motivated by a business or corporate purpose apart from tax avoidance. Reg. § 1.368–1(c). This requirement is most significant in connection with divisive reorganizations and will be discussed in detail in Chapter XII, *infra*.

5. Ruling Guidelines

Historically, most tax-free reorganizations would not be consummated unless the parties first received a favorable advance ruling from the Internal Revenue Service. Many transactions were planned in reliance on the Service's extensive advance ruling guidelines. More recently, the Service has announced that it will not grant "comfort" rulings on whether a transaction qualifies as a reorganization, but it will rule on a particular aspect of the transaction if the issue is "significant." Rev. Proc. 2013–32, §§ 4.01(1) & (3), 2013–28 I.R.B. 55. The Service's ruling guidelines remain an influential source of law, however, and they will be noted below when relevant to a specific transaction.

B. Acquisitive Reorganizations

1. Type A Reorganizations (Statutory Merger or Consolidation)

a. Merger and Consolidation Defined

1) In General

A Type A reorganization is a statutory merger or consolidation that meets the requirements of applicable state corporate law. In a typical merger, the assets and liabilities of T are transferred to P, and T dissolves by operation of law. The consideration received by T's shareholders is determined by the merger agreement. A consolidation is a transfer of assets and liabilities of two or more existing corporations to a newly created corporation. The transferor corporations dissolve by operation of law and their shareholders own stock of the new company.

2) Divisive Mergers

A "divisive" merger is a transaction that is a merger under state law where a corporation's assets are divided among two or more corporations. A divisive merger where only some of T's assets are transferred and T remains in existence does not qualify as a Type A reorganization. Rev. Rul. 2000–5, 2000–1 C.B. 436 (Situation 1). Similarly, T's transfer of assets and liabilities to two acquiring corporations followed by T's dissolution, with T's shareholders receiving stock of both acquiring corporations, does not qualify. Id. (Situation 2). See also Reg. § 1.368–2(b)(1)(iii) Example 1.

3) Mergers Involving Disregarded Entities

A single-member limited liability company ("SMLLC") is a disregarded entity for tax purposes and thus is treated as a division of its corporate owner unless it elects to be taxed as a separate corporation. Reg. § 301.7701–2(a). A merger of an SMLLC owned by a corporation ("X") into another corporation ("P") in exchange for P stock does not qualify as a Type A reorganization because it results in X's assets and liabilities being divided between X and P. Reg. § 1.368–2(b)(1)(iii) Example 6. But a merger of a corporation ("T") into an SMLLC may qualify as a Type A reorganization if the continuity of interest and business enterprise requirements are met and T's legal existence terminates. Reg. § 1.368–2(b)(1)(iii) Example 2.

b. Continuity of Shareholder Proprietary Interest Requirement

Section 368(a)(1)(A) does not expressly limit the permissible consideration in a merger or consolidation. It is settled, however, that a transaction will not qualify as a Type A reorganization unless the continuity of shareholder proprietary interest requirement is met. See *Southwest Natural Gas Co. v. Comm'r,* 189 F.2d 332 (5th Cir.1951). The test focuses on the quality of consideration received by T's shareholders (stock maintains continuity, debt or cash does not) and the percentage (by value) of equity consideration paid by P in the reorganization relative to the total consideration. For ruling purposes, the Service historically required at least 50% of the consideration paid by P to consist of P stock, which may be common or preferred and need not be voting stock. Rev. Proc. 77–37, 1977–2 C.B. 568. Some old cases held that the continuity of interest requirement is met by lesser percentages, and an example in the regulations confirms the Service's new view that 40% continuity is acceptable. See, e.g., *John A. Nelson Co. v. Helvering,* 296 U.S. 374, 56 S.Ct. 273 (1935) (38% preferred stock sufficient); Reg. § 1.368–1(e)(2)(v) Example 1. The test is met even if some T shareholders receive only cash or P debt as long as the T shareholders as a group maintain continuity of interest. Rev. Rul. 66–224, 1966–2 C.B. 114.

Example (1): T merges into P under state law. T shareholders receive a combination of cash and short-term P notes. The merger fails to qualify as a Type A reorganization because there is no continuity of interest. Such a cash merger is treated as a taxable sale of T's assets followed by a complete liquidation of T.

Example (2):   Same as Example (1), except T shareholders receive P nonvoting preferred stock. There is 100% continuity and the merger qualifies as a Type A reorganization.

Example (3):   Same as Example (1), except each T shareholder receives 40% P preferred stock and 60% cash. There is 40% continuity and the merger qualifies, but the T shareholders must recognize their realized gain, if any, to the extent of the cash received.

Example (4):   Same as Example (1), except shareholders owning 60% of T stock receive P preferred stock and the remaining T shareholders receive cash. Even though some T shareholders only receive cash, the shareholders as a group have 60% continuity, and thus the transaction qualifies as a Type A reorganization. But the T shareholders who receive only cash will recognize gain. See XI.B.8.b. at page 231, *infra.*

c. Measuring Continuity of Interest

1) Consideration Is "Fixed": Signing Date Rule

In determining if the requisite continuity of interest is preserved for a potential reorganization where the consideration is "fixed," the issuing corporation (P) stock received by T's shareholders is valued as of the close of the "signing date"—i.e., the last business day before the first date that the parties enter into a binding commitment to consummate the transaction. Reg. § 1.368–1(e)(2)(i). Consideration is "fixed" if the contract recites the number of shares of P stock and the amount of nonstock consideration to be received by T's shareholders and does not include contingent adjustments that prevent T's shareholders from being subject to the economic benefits and burdens of ownership of P as of the signing date. Reg. § 1.368–1(e)(2)(iii)(A). This Signing Date Rule ensures that value fluctuations (e.g., a decline in value of P's stock between the signing date and the date the merger is completed) will not cause the transaction to fail the continuity of interest test.

Example: On January 3 of Year 1, when the value of publicly traded P stock is $1 per share, P and T sign a binding contract pursuant to which T will merge into P on June 1 of the same year. The contract provides that T shareholders will receive 50 P shares and $50 cash in exchange for all the outstanding stock of T. On June 1, when the merger is consummated, the value of P stock is 25 cents per share. Because the transaction provides for fixed consideration pursuant to a binding contract, the determination of whether the continuity of interest requirement is met is made as of the end of January 2, the last business day before the first date that the merger contract is binding. As a result, the merger qualifies as a Type A reorganization even though the consideration received by the T shareholders on June 1 is $12.50 in P stock and $50 cash. See Reg. § 1.368–1(e)(2)(v) Example 1.

2) Consideration Not "Fixed": Closing Date Rule

If the consideration received in a potential reorganization is not fixed, the determination of whether the continuity of interest requirement is satisfied is based on the value of the P stock as of "the effective date" of the transaction. Rev. Proc. 77–37, 1977–2 C.B. 568; Reg. § 1.368–1(e)(2)(i). Under this Closing Date Rule, a decline in the value of the P stock between the signing and closing dates could cause a transaction to fail the continuity of interest requirement.

3) Valuation Safe Harbors

In valuing stock for continuity of interest purposes in most real-world transactions, the parties usually prefer to hedge against market volatility by using an average price over a period of time rather than a closing price on a single date. If either the Signing Date or Closing Date rule applies, the IRS authorizes three safe harbor valuation methods using average trading prices over a range of measuring periods if: (1) shares of one or more classes of issuing corporation stock are traded on a national securities exchange, (2) all parties to the potential reorganization treat the transaction in a consistent manner, and (3) the transaction is pursuant to a binding agreement specifying the safe harbor method, the measuring period (which generally must include at least 5 but not more than 35 consecutive trading days), and the national securities exchange and reporting source to determine the trading prices. Rev. Proc. 2018–12, 2018–6 I.R.B. 349.

d. Preacquisition Continuity by Historic T Shareholders

1) In General

At one time, the continuity of interest doctrine required that a substantial part of the consideration paid by P in an acquisitive reorganization must have consisted of P stock paid to "historic" shareholders of T. In tax jargon, a "historic shareholder" was a person whose T stock was "old and cold" when acquired by P. Historic shareholders generally must have held their T stock prior to the time P commenced its efforts to acquire control of T in a reorganization. Identification of historic shareholders often was problematic in the case of acquisitions of publicly traded companies because of numerous open market transactions that occur after a merger is announced but before it is consummated.

2) Erosion of Historic Shareholder Concept

The importance of the historic shareholder concept diminished, at least in the context of publicly traded corporations, after the Tax Court's decision in *J.E. Seagram Corp. v. Comm'r*, 104 T.C. 75 (1995). The fact pattern and holding are illustrated in the example below.

Example: X Corp. wishes to acquire T Corp. but is unable to negotiate a friendly takeover. P Corp. also wishes to acquire T. X, P, and T are all publicly traded companies. On January 1 of Year 1, X commences a cash tender offer to T shareholders. On January 15, P commences a competing tender offer to acquire all of T's stock for a combination of cash and P stock. As of March 1, X acquires 32% of T's stock for cash, and P acquires 46% of T's stock for cash. P emerges as the successful bidder and negotiates a merger with T's board of directors. On April 1, P acquires in the merger the 54% of T stock that it did not own (including the 32% acquired by X in its tender offer) in exchange for P stock. X realizes a loss on the exchange of its T stock for P stock, and it seeks to deduct the loss on the theory that the merger was not a tax-free reorganization because 78% of the "historic" T shareholders received cash for their T stock. In *J.E. Seagram Corp., supra*, the Tax Court denied X's loss, holding that the merger satisfied the continuity of interest doctrine and thus qualified as a tax-free reorganization. Noting that X's purchase of 32% of T stock for cash was independent of P's competing offer, the court suggested that X had become a "historic" shareholder of T. The opinion also can be read as holding that the continuity of interest test should be applied by focusing on the extent of equity consideration used by P without the necessity of identifying historic T shareholders. The court also noted that it was difficult to apply the historic shareholder concept in cases involving public companies because of frequent market transactions (e.g., arbitrage activity) after a takeover bid is announced. Thus, *J.E. Seagram* can be interpreted as a narrow holding only applicable to transactions involving widely-held companies.

3) **Regulations**

The regulations eliminate the relevance of historic shareholders in acquisitive reorganizations except in limited situations. They provide that a "mere disposition" of T stock prior to a potential reorganization to buyers unrelated to T or P is disregarded in applying the continuity of interest doctrine. Reg. § 1.368–1(e)(1)(i).

Example (1): A owns 100% of the stock of T, Inc. (value—$100,000), which has negotiated a merger with P. Shortly before the merger is consummated, B, who is unrelated to T or P, purchases all of A's T stock for $100,000. Then, in the merger, B receives $50,000 cash and $50,000 P stock in exchange for her T stock. Continuity of interest is satisfied because B's T stock was exchanged for a sufficient amount of P stock (50% of total consideration) to preserve a substantial part of the value of the proprietary interest in T. The fact that B was not a "historic" T shareholder is irrelevant. Reg. § 1.368–1(e)(6) Example 1(ii).

Example (2): A owns 60% and B owns 40% of the stock of T, which has negotiated a merger with P. Because A does not wish to own P stock, T redeems all of A's T shares in exchange for cash, none of which is provided by P. T then merges into P, and B receives solely P stock. T's prereorganization redemption is not considered in determining if continuity of interest is preserved. The merger qualifies as a Type A reorganization because B's proprietary interest is preserved. Reg. § 1.368–1(e)(6) Example 9.

e. Postacquisition Continuity

1) Prior Law

T's shareholders have never been required to maintain continuity of interest in P for any particular period of time after a Type A reorganization. But in determining if the continuity of interest requirement has been met, the Service historically considered sales and other dispositions of stock occurring subsequent to a merger which are part of the same overall "plan." Rev. Proc. 77–37, 1977–2 C.B. 568. For example, where the former T shareholders sold P stock pursuant to a binding commitment made prior to the merger, the merger and sale have been treated as one integrated transaction that may fail the continuity of interest test. The courts have disagreed over whether a pre-merger intent to sell (without any binding commitment) will defeat continuity of interest. See, e.g., *McDonald's Restaurants of Illinois, Inc. v. Comm'r,* 688 F.2d 520 (7th Cir.1982), rev'g, 76 T.C. 972 (1981), where the Tax Court treated a post-merger sale as a separate transaction because the former T shareholders were not contractually bound to sell, but the Seventh Circuit reversed, holding that a binding commitment was not required for application of the step transaction doctrine.

> ***Example:*** T merges into P, and T's sole shareholder, A, receives 1,000 shares of P stock. If A sells 700 of his P shares after the merger pursuant to a binding commitment, the continuity of interest test was not met under the historical case law. Some courts would reach the same result if A intended from the outset to sell more than 50% of his P stock or if the merger would not have been consummated unless A had been guaranteed the opportunity to make the sale.

2) Regulations

The regulations change the rules discussed above by providing that subsequent dispositions of P stock by former T shareholders generally are not considered in determining whether the continuity of shareholder interest requirement is met, even if the dispositions are pursuant to a preexisting binding contract. Reg. § 1.368–1(e)(1)(i). If the facts demonstrate that T shareholders have sold their P stock for cash to P or a related party (e.g., a P subsidiary) before the transaction, the continuity of interest requirement may not be satisfied. Reg. § 1.368–1(e)(1)(ii), –1(e)(2). But if, after a reorganization, P initiates an open market stock repurchase program that was not previously negotiated with T or its shareholders, and some former T shareholders sell their P stock to P for cash in the open market, the sales will not be treated as "in connection with" the merger and thus will not have a negative effect on continuity of interest. Rev. Rul. 99–58, 1999–2 C.B. 701.

Example (1): T merges into P, and T's sole shareholder, A, receives $50,000 cash and $50,000 of P common stock. One month later, pursuant to a preexisting binding contract negotiated by A, A sells all the P stock received in the merger to B, a party unrelated to P. The merger satisfies the continuity of interest requirement because, in the merger, A received stock of P representing a substantial part of the value of the total consideration transferred in the acquisition. Reg. § 1.368–1(e)(6) Example 1(i). As a result of the merger and subsequent sale, A would be fully taxable on the disposition of his T stock, but T would not recognize gain on the transfer of its assets, and P would take a transferred basis in those assets. §§ 361(a); 362(b).

Example (2): Same as Example (1) except one month after the merger S, a P subsidiary, buys the P stock received by A for cash. On these facts, the cash is treated as furnished by P, and the merger does not satisfy the continuity of interest requirement. Reg. § 1.368–1(e)(6) Example 4(iii).

f. Relationship to Taxable Stock Acquisitions

When P acquires 80% or more of T stock for cash or notes within a 12-month period and no § 338 election is made, the regulations treat P as owning the T stock for continuity of interest purposes if T later transfers its assets to P or a P subsidiary in a transaction (e.g., a merger) that otherwise qualifies as a tax-free reorganization. See Reg. § 1.338–3(d), reversing the result in *Yoc Heating Corp. v. Comm'r,* 61 T.C. 168 (1973). In other words, P's exchange of T stock for a direct interest in T is treated as preserving continuity of interest for purposes of determining the *corporate-level* consequences of the merger. Some older case law held that P may not be treated as a historic T shareholder in determining the tax consequences to minority shareholders who receive P stock when T merges into P (or a P subsidiary). *Kass v. Comm'r,* 60 T.C. 218 (1973), aff'd without opinion, 491 F.2d 749 (3d Cir.1974). The current regulations continue to follow this case law. Reg. § 1.338–3(d). The purpose of these confusing regulations is to reinforce the policy of § 338 by ensuring that P may not obtain a cost basis in T's assets after a qualified stock purchase unless a § 338 election is made even if P acquired all of T's stock for cash and T then liquidates or merges into P or a P subsidiary.

Example: P acquires 90 of T's 100 outstanding shares for cash on January 1 and does not make a § 338 election. On July 1 of the same year, T merges into S, a subsidiary of P. In the July 1 merger, T's minority shareholder, A, receives P stock in exchange for her 10 shares of T stock. As to P and T, the merger qualifies as a tax-free reorganization because the T stock acquired by P for cash may be counted for continuity of interest purposes. Thus, T does not recognize gain or loss on the transfer of its assets, P does not recognize gain or loss on the exchange, and the assets take a transferred basis in S's hands. Reg. § 1.338–3(d)(5) Example (i)–(iv). The merger does not qualify as a Type A reorganization as to A, however, because continuity of interest is tested by reference to T's "historic" shareholders prior to P's acquisition of 90 shares. A thus must recognize gain or loss on her T stock. Reg. § 1.338–3(d)(5) Example (v).

g. Drop Downs and Remote Continuity

A transaction otherwise qualifying as a Type A reorganization is not disqualified if P transfers all or part of the T assets that it acquires to a controlled subsidiary of P. § 368(a)(2)(C). The regulations also permit successive post-reorganization transfers to lower-tier controlled subsidiaries and other controlled entities of P provided that the continuity of business enterprise requirement is met. Reg. § 1.368–2(k)(1).

2. Type B Reorganizations (Stock-for-Stock Acquisition)

a. Definition

A Type B reorganization is P's acquisition of T stock solely in exchange for P voting stock (or voting stock of P's parent) provided that P is in "control" of T immediately after the acquisition. § 368(a)(1)(B). For this purpose, "control" is ownership of 80% or more of T's voting power and 80% or more of the total shares of each class of T's nonvoting stock. § 368(c). T remains alive as a subsidiary of P after a Type B reorganization.

Example (1): P transfers its voting stock to all of T's shareholders in exchange for their T stock. The acquisition qualifies as a Type B reorganization.

Example (2): Same as Example (1), except that P only acquires 90% of the T stock. Because P is in "control" of T immediately after the exchange, the transaction qualifies as a Type B reorganization.

b. Solely for Voting Stock Requirement

Voting stock is the only permissible consideration in a Type B reorganization. With some minor exceptions noted below, even an insignificant amount of boot (including any nonvoting stock) will disqualify the exchange. To qualify as voting stock, shareholders must have an unconditional right to vote on routine corporate matters, not merely extraordinary events such as mergers and liquidations. Cf. Reg. § 1.302–3(a).

1) Fractional Shares

The payment of cash in lieu of fractional shares in an otherwise qualifying stock-for-stock exchange will not violate the solely for voting stock requirement. Rev. Rul. 66–365, 1966–2 C.B. 116.

2) P's Payment of Expenses

P may pay T's expenses (e.g., legal and accounting fees, registration fees) related to the reorganization without violating the solely for voting stock requirement, but P's payment of expenses of T's shareholders is impermissible consideration and will disqualify the exchange. Rev. Rul. 73–54, 1973–1 C.B. 187.

3) Buyouts of Dissenting Minority Shareholders

If shareholders of T object to a stock-for-stock exchange, T may redeem their shares for cash prior to the exchange with P without violating the solely for voting stock requirement provided that the consideration is not provided by P. Rev. Rul. 55–440, 1955–2 C.B. 226. Alternatively, other T shareholders may purchase shares from dissenters for cash prior to a Type B reorganization. If a shareholder participates in the exchange and her new P voting stock is then redeemed by P for cash, the post-exchange redemption may disqualify the entire transaction if P was obligated to redeem the stock from the outset.

c. Creeping Acquisitions

To satisfy the "control" requirement in § 368(a)(1)(B), P must be in control after the stock-for-stock exchange, but P is not required to acquire 80% or more of T's stock in a Type B reorganization. The final step of a "creeping" acquisition thus may qualify as a Type B reorganization if P uses solely voting stock and any earlier cash acquisitions of voting stock are "old and cold." Whether or not an earlier cash acquisition is "old and cold" is usually a factual question, but the regulations assume acquisitions are related if they take place over a relatively short time span (e.g., 12 months) but not if they are separated by a very long interval (e.g., 16 years). Reg. § 1.368–2(c).

Example (1): P acquired 60% of the stock of T for cash in Year 1. P acquired an additional 30% of T stock in Year 16 solely for P voting stock. Assuming, as is likely, that the cash acquisition is old and cold, the stock-for-stock exchange qualifies as a Type B reorganization because P has control of T after the transaction.

Example (2): Same as Example (1), except P acquired 60% of T for cash in Year 15 as a first step to acquiring control of T. It is likely that the cash and stock acquisitions will be integrated and, if so, the stock-for-stock exchange does not qualify as a Type B reorganization.

Example (3): Same as Example (2), except P acquired only 10% of T for cash and, one year later, pursuant to the same overall plan, P acquired the remaining 90% solely for P voting stock. The stock-for-stock exchange does not qualify as a Type B reorganization even though more than 80% of T was acquired for voting stock. But if the 10% cash acquisition had been unrelated ("old and cold"), the later acquisition of 90% for stock would qualify. See *Chapman v. Comm'r,* 618 F.2d 856 (1st Cir.1980).

Example (4): Same as Example (3), except P sold its 10% interest in T to an unrelated buyer and then acquired 100% of the T stock solely for P voting stock. If the earlier sale was unconditional, the stock-for-stock acquisition qualifies as a Type B reorganization. Rev. Rul. 72–354, 1972–2 C.B. 216.

d. Contingent Consideration

A Type B reorganization will not lose its tax-free status if, as part of the plan, P agrees to transfer additional P voting stock to the former T shareholders based on future earnings or other subsequent events. Contingent consideration will not disqualify the transaction if the additional stock is not evidenced by a negotiable instrument and certain other detailed requirements imposed by the Service are met. See Rev. Proc. 84–42, 1984–1 C.B. 521, § 3.03. Alternatively, P may place some of its stock in escrow on the condition that it be transferred to the T shareholders only if certain conditions (e.g., T's attaining specified earnings) are met. Id. at § 3.06.

e. Drop Downs

A transaction otherwise qualifying as a Type B reorganization is not disqualified if P transfers all or part of the T stock it acquires to a controlled subsidiary of P. § 368(a)(2)(C). The Service also permits successive drop downs of the T stock to lower-tier controlled P subsidiaries. See, e.g., Reg. § 1.368–2(k)(3) Example 5.

f. Subsequent Liquidation of T

If P acquires T stock in a stock-for-stock acquisition that qualifies as a Type B reorganization and then liquidates T pursuant to the same plan, the transaction is treated as an asset acquisition and is tested under the rules applicable to Type C reorganizations. Rev. Rul. 67–274, 1967–2 C.B. 141. See XI.B.3.h., at page 222, *infra*.

3. Type C Reorganizations (Stock-for-Assets Acquisition)

a. Definition

With a few exceptions described below, a Type C reorganization generally is P's acquisition of substantially all of T's assets solely in exchange for P voting stock (or voting stock of P's parent). A Type C stock-for-assets acquisition differs from a merger in that T's assets and liabilities are not automatically transferred to P by operation of law, and T does not immediately dissolve but must distribute the consideration it receives from P (and any assets it retains) to its shareholders in a complete liquidation.

b. "Substantially All of the Properties" Requirement

P must acquire substantially all of the properties of T. For advance ruling purposes, the Service has required a transfer of assets representing at least 90% of the fair market value of T's "net assets" (i.e., assets less liabilities) and at least 70% of the fair market value of the gross assets held by T immediately prior to the transfer. Rev. Proc. 77–37, 1977–2 C.B. 568. For this purpose, assets distributed by T to redeem stock held by dissenting and other minority shareholders and unwanted assets sold by T to other buyers are considered as assets held by T if the distributions are part of the reorganization plan. Id. The ruling policy is merely a safe harbor, not operative law. Some authorities interpret this requirement more flexibly by stating that no particular percentage is controlling and by looking to the type of assets retained by T and the purpose for the retention. For example, it may be permissible for T to retain nonoperating liquid assets (e.g., cash) to pay liabilities. Rev. Rul. 57–518, 1957–2 C.B. 253. If

T sells 50% of its historic assets to unrelated parties for cash and then transfers all its assets (including the sales proceeds) to P, the "substantially all" requirement is met because T transfers all its assets and the effect of the transaction was not divisive. Rev. Rul. 88–48, 1988–1 C.B. 117.

Example (1): T has $100,000 of assets and $20,000 of liabilities. T's gross assets are $100,000 (70% = $70,000) and its net assets are $80,000 (90% = $72,000). To satisfy the "substantially all" requirement under the Service's ruling guidelines, P must acquire at least $72,000 of T's assets.

Example (2): T has $100,000 of assets, consisting of $70,000 of operating assets and $30,000 cash, and no liabilities. It distributes the cash to A, a 30% shareholder, in redemption of A's T stock. P then acquires the operating assets from T solely in exchange for P voting stock. If the pre-exchange redemption is part of the reorganization plan, the cash is considered a T asset for purposes of the "substantially all" test, and the acquisition fails the Service's guidelines because P has not acquired 90% ($90,000) of T's net assets. Under the case law, however, the transaction may qualify as a Type C reorganization because T has not retained operating assets.

c. Assumption of Liabilities

In applying the solely for voting stock requirement in § 368(a)(1)(C), P's assumption of T's liabilities, or taking of property subject to liabilities, is disregarded.

Example: T has $100,000 of assets and $20,000 of liabilities. P acquires all of T's assets and assumes its liabilities in exchange for $80,000 of P voting stock. The exchange qualifies as a Type C reorganization.

d. Boot Relaxation Rule

P's use of consideration other than its voting stock will not disqualify an exchange provided that P acquires at least 80% of the fair market value of *all* of T's assets solely for voting stock. For this purpose, T liabilities assumed (or taken subject to) by P are treated as cash consideration. § 368(a)(2)(B). As a result, a combination of liabilities assumed and other boot likely will disqualify an exchange.

Example (1): T has $100,000 of assets and no liabilities. P acquires all of T's assets in exchange for $80,000 of P voting stock and $20,000 cash. The transaction qualifies because P has acquired at least 80% of T's assets solely for P voting stock.

Example (2): Same as Example (1), except P acquires $90,000 of T's assets for $75,000 of P voting stock and $15,000 cash, and T retains $10,000 of its assets. The transaction does not satisfy the boot relaxation rule because P only acquires 75% of T's assets for P voting stock.

Example (3): Same as Example (1), except that T has $100,000 of assets and $20,000 of liabilities, and P acquires all of T's assets in exchange for $79,000 of P voting stock, $1,000 cash, and the assumption of all $20,000 of T's liabilities. The transaction does not satisfy the boot relaxation rule because the liability assumption is treated as cash consideration and thus P only acquires 79% of T's assets for P voting stock.

e. Liquidation Requirement

In a Type C reorganization, T must distribute all of the stock or securities it receives from P and all of its other assets pursuant to the reorganization plan unless the Service agrees to waive this requirement. § 368(a)(2)(G). As a practical matter, this means that T must completely liquidate after its exchange with P. In the rare case where the Service waives the distribution requirement, T is treated for tax purposes as if it had distributed its assets and recontributed them to the capital of a new corporation. H.R.Rep. No. 98–861, 98th Cong., 2d Sess. 845–846 (1984).

f. Creeping Acquisitions

If P previously acquired more than 20% of T's stock (even in an unrelated transaction) and then acquires all of T's assets solely in exchange for P voting stock, and T distributes the P voting stock to its shareholders (other than P) in complete liquidation, one old case held that the transaction failed to qualify as a Type C reorganization. *Bausch & Lomb Optical Co. v. Comm'r*, 267 F.2d 75 (2d Cir.1959), cert. denied, 361 U.S. 835, 80 S.Ct. 88 (1959). The questionable rationale was that P acquired more than 20% of T's assets in the liquidation of T in exchange for the *T* stock that P previously owned. The Service followed *Bausch & Lomb* for many years, but ultimately rejected its rationale. The regulations now provide that P's prior ownership of some T stock does not by itself prevent the "solely for voting stock" requirement from being met. The theory is that a transaction in which P converts an indirect interest in T's assets (through ownership of T stock) to a direct interest does not necessarily resemble a taxable sale of T's assets. Reg. § 1.368–2(d)(4)(i). But if the § 368(a)(2)(B) boot relaxation rule applies to the final step of a creeping C reorganization, the sum of: (1) the boot distributed to T's shareholders other than P and to T's creditors, and (2) the liabilities of T assumed by P, may not exceed 20% of the value of all of T's assets. Id. Finally, if in connection with potential C reorganization, P acquires T *stock* for cash or other boot from a T shareholder or T itself, that consideration is treated as boot exchanged by P for T's assets. As a result, the overall transaction will not qualify as a Type C reorganization unless at least 80% of the consideration consists of P voting stock. Id.

Example (1): Several years ago, in an unrelated transaction, P acquired 60% of T's stock for cash. The other 40% of T stock is owned by A. T has assets with a fair market value of $110,000 and a $10,000 liability. T transfers all of its assets to P in exchange for $30,000 of P voting stock and $10,000 cash. T then distributes the P voting stock and cash to A and liquidates. Applying the boot relaxation rule, the transaction qualifies as a Type C reorganization because the $10,000 cash and $10,000 liability assumption does not exceed $22,000 (20% of the value of T's assets). P's prior ownership of 60% of T stock does not adversely affect qualification. Reg. § 1.368–2(d)(4)(ii) Example (1).

Example (2): Same as Example (1), except P purchased its 60% stock interest in T for $60,000 cash as the first step in an overall plan to acquire T's assets—i.e., the 60% stock acquisition was not "unrelated" to the subsequent asset acquisition. The asset acquisition does not qualify as a Type C reorganization because P is treated as having acquired all of T's assets for consideration consisting of $70,000 cash ($60,000 for T stock and $10,000 in the later asset acquisition), $10,000 of liability assumption, and $30,000 of P voting stock. Reg. § 1.368–2(d)(4)(ii) Example (2).

g. Drop Downs

A transaction otherwise qualifying as a Type C reorganization is not disqualified if P transfers all or part of the T assets it acquires to a controlled subsidiary of P. § 368(a)(2)(C). The Service also permits successive drop downs to lower-tier P subsidiaries. See, e.g., Reg. § 1.368–2(k)(3) Example 1.

h. Overlap Issues

To prevent the use of Type C reorganizations to accomplish a tax-free corporate division without satisfying § 355 (see Chapter XII, *infra*), a transaction that qualifies as both a Type C and Type D reorganization is treated (and tested) as a Type D. § 368(a)(2)(A). If P acquires T stock in a stock-for-stock acquisition that qualifies as a Type B reorganization and then liquidates T pursuant to the same plan, the transaction is treated as an asset acquisition and is tested under the rules applicable to Type C reorganizations. Rev. Rul. 67–274, 1967–2 C.B. 141.

4. Forward Triangular Mergers

a. Background

If P wishes to acquire T's assets in a tax-free acquisitive reorganization, it may be unwilling to incur the risk of T's unknown or contingent liabilities. This risk might continue even if P drops down T's assets and liabilities to a P subsidiary after a merger of T into P. P also may not wish to incur the expense and delay of securing formal approval of its shareholders to a merger or direct asset acquisition. The "forward triangular merger" solves many of these nontax problems. In its simplest form, a forward triangular merger consists of the following steps:

1)   P forms a new subsidiary, S, by transferring P stock (and perhaps other consideration) for S stock in an exchange that is tax free under § 351.

2)   T is merged into S under state law. T shareholders receive P stock and any other consideration provided by the merger agreement. P ordinarily does not need to secure approval from its shareholders because S is the party to the merger and P is the only shareholder of S. All of T's assets and liabilities are automatically transferred to S, which remains a wholly owned subsidiary of P.

b. Qualification Requirements

A forward triangular merger qualifies as a tax-free reorganization under § 368(a)(2)(D) if the following requirements are met:

1) S must acquire substantially all of the properties of T. This is the same requirement imposed on Type C reorganizations, and similar standards are applied. See XI.B.3.b., at page 219, *supra*.

2) No stock of S may be used as consideration in the merger. Use of S debt securities is not prohibited.

3) The transaction must have qualified as a Type A reorganization if T had merged directly into P. This means that the transaction must satisfy the judicial continuity of interest requirement as interpreted by the regulations—i.e., under Reg. § 1.368–1(e)(2)(v) Example 1, P must acquire T using at least 40% P stock (voting or nonvoting).

Example (1): T merges into S, a wholly owned subsidiary of P. Under the merger agreement, T shareholders as a group receive $100,000 of P nonvoting stock and $100,000 of P notes. The transaction qualifies as a forward triangular merger.

Example (2): Same as Example (1), except the T shareholders receive $100,000 of P nonvoting stock and $100,000 of S voting stock. The transaction does not qualify because stock of S was used as consideration.

Example (3): Same as Example (1), except prior to the merger T distributes 35% of its operating assets to shareholder A in redemption of all of A's T stock. T then merges into S, and the remaining T shareholders receive solely P voting stock. If the redemption was part of the reorganization plan, the transaction will not qualify because it fails the "substantially all of the properties" test.

c. Subsequent Transfers of S Stock to P Subsidiary

If, after a valid forward triangular merger in which T merges into S (a P subsidiary), P transfers its S stock to S-1 as part of an overall reorganization plan, the transfer will not cause P to be treated as not in "control" of S (now a second-tier subsidiary) for purposes of § 368(a)(2)(D), and thus the transaction continues to qualify as a reorganization. Rev. Rul. 2001–24, 2001–1 C.B. 1290. Note that if the transaction were recast under the step transaction doctrine, T's assets would be treated as having been acquired by a second-tier P subsidiary (S) and the transaction would not qualify under § 368(a)(2)(D) because P would not directly "control" S (S-1 would control S).

5. Reverse Triangular Mergers

a. Background

P may wish to acquire the stock of T in a tax-free reorganization and keep T alive as a subsidiary in order to preserve certain rights under state law or valuable assets (e.g., a lease or franchise) that might be lost if T liquidated. A Type B reorganization may not be feasible, however, if P wishes to use consideration other than its voting stock. The "reverse triangular merger" was developed to accommodate these objectives. It consists of the following steps:

1) P forms a new subsidiary, S, by transferring P voting stock and other consideration for S stock in an exchange that is tax free under § 351. (Alternatively, P could make the transfer to an existing subsidiary.)

2) S merges into T under state law. T shareholders receive P voting stock and any other consideration provided by the merger agreement. P exchanges its S stock for T stock. S disappears and T survives as a wholly owned subsidiary of P. The end result is similar to a Type B reorganization.

b. Qualification Requirements

A reverse triangular merger qualifies as a tax-free reorganization under § 368(a)(2)(E) if the following requirements are met:

1) After the merger, T must hold substantially all of its properties and the properties of S (other than the stock of P distributed in the transaction and any boot used by S to acquire shares of minority shareholders). If, as is likely, S is a transitory subsidiary, it will not have any properties other than the consideration used to acquire T.

2) In the merger transaction, P must acquire 80% "control" of T in exchange for P voting stock. The remaining 20% of T may be acquired for cash or other boot. Note that 80% of T stock must be acquired for P voting stock in a single merger transaction; prior T stock held by P will not help to meet this requirement. Thus, the permissible consideration in a reverse triangular merger is more restrictive than in a forward triangular merger, and creeping acquisitions will not qualify.

Example (1): S, a wholly owned subsidiary of P, has no assets other than P voting stock and cash. P owns no stock of T. S merges into T. In the merger, T shareholders owning 90% of T stock receive P voting stock and holders of the remaining 10% of T stock receive cash. T continues to hold all of its own assets. The transaction qualifies as a reverse triangular merger.

Example (2): Same as Example (1), except P had acquired 21% of T five years ago in an unrelated transaction. In the merger of S into T, shareholders holding the remaining 79% of T stock receive P voting stock in exchange for their T stock. P does not acquire "control" of T in one transaction in exchange for P voting stock, and thus the transaction does not qualify as a reverse triangular merger. If S is a transitory corporation formed solely to effectuate the merger, the transaction will qualify as a Type B reorganization where, as here, the sole consideration used is P voting stock. See Reg. § 1.368–2(j)(7) Example (4).

c. Payments to Dissenting Shareholders

For purposes of the "control" requirement, T stock that is redeemed for cash or T property prior to a reverse merger is not treated as outstanding prior to the reorganization even if the redemption is related to the merger. Reg. § 1.368–2(j)(3)(i). But cash and property of T used to redeem stock of dissenting shareholders is taken into account in applying the "substantially all of the properties" requirement. Reg. § 1.368–2(j)(3)(iii).

Example: T has 1,000 shares of common stock outstanding, of which 800 shares are owned by A and 200 by B. S, a wholly owned subsidiary of P, merges into T. In a related transaction prior to the merger, T distributed cash in redemption of B's 200 shares. In the merger, P acquired 640 of A's shares for P voting stock and the remaining 160 shares for cash. Since B's shares are not treated as outstanding for purposes of determining whether P has acquired "control" of T with P voting stock, the acquisition satisfies the control requirement. But the cash used by T to redeem B's stock is treated as a T asset in applying the "substantially all of the properties" test. Reg. § 1.368–2(j)(7) Example (3).

d. Subsequent Sale of T Assets

If, following a qualified reverse triangular merger and as part of an overall acquisition plan, T sells 50% of its operating assets to an unrelated buyer and retains the cash proceeds, the asset sale will not cause the transaction to fail the requirement in § 368(a)(2)(E) that the surviving corporation "holds" substantially all of its properties. Rev. Rul. 2001–25, 2001–1 C.B. 1291. Compare Rev. Rul. 88–48, 1988–1 C.B. 117 ("substantially all" requirement met for Type C reorganization where T sells for cash one of two historic businesses representing 50% of its operating assets and then transfers cash and remaining assets to P in exchange for P voting stock and assumption of liabilities). The policy underlying these rulings is that the sale of 50% of T's assets to an unrelated buyer for cash, even if part of the overall plan, did not effect a divisive reorganization where former T shareholders sold part of T for cash and part for P stock.

6. Multi-Step Acquisitions: Special Problems

For nontax and strategical reasons, the parties to a corporate acquisition may desire to employ a multi-step structure. As discussed above, the tax consequences of multi-step ("creeping") acquisitions often turn on whether or not the various steps are analyzed separately or are treated as one integrated transaction. The Service has shown an increasing inclination to apply the step transaction doctrine to qualify multi-step acquisitions as reorganizations except when doing so violates a clear statutory policy (e.g., § 338). This complex area is best explained through a series of examples based on selected cases, regulations, and published rulings.

Example (1): As part of an integrated acquisition plan where P intends to acquire T's assets, P first acquires all of T's stock from T's shareholders for consideration consisting of 51% P stock and 49% cash. T then promptly merges into P. Viewed in isolation, the first step does not qualify as a Type B reorganization because it fails the "solely for voting stock" requirement. Applying the step transaction doctrine, however, the overall acquisition qualifies as a Type A reorganization because at 51% of the total consideration consists of P stock. *King Enterprises v. United States*, 418 F.2d 511 (Ct. Cl.1969).

Example (2): As a first step in a plan to acquire T, P initiates a tender offer for at least 51% of T stock, to be acquired solely for P voting stock. After acquiring the requisite 51% of T stock, P then forms Y Corp., and Y merges into T. In the merger, T's remaining shareholders (holding 49% of T stock) exchange their T stock for a combination of consideration consisting of $2/3$ P voting stock and $1/3$ cash. Overall, T's shareholders have received 83.7% P stock and 16.3% cash for their T stock, and P owns 100% of T. If all the other requirements are met, the two steps will be integrated and will qualify as a § 368(a)(2)(E) reverse triangular merger even though neither step, viewed separately, qualifies as a reorganization. Rev. Rul. 2001–26, 2001–1 C.B. 1297. Note that the Service will apply the step transaction doctrine to these facts only if there is a factual basis to do so—e.g., the first step tender and the second step merger are announced as a package.

Example (3):   Pursuant to an integrated plan to acquire T's assets, P first forms a subsidiary, Y, and Y merges into T. In the merger, T shareholders receive solely cash. Shortly thereafter, T merges upstream into P. The Service treats these steps as, first, P's "qualified stock purchase" of T (as defined in § 338(d)(3)) followed by a tax-free § 332 liquidation of T. As a result, if P does not make a § 338 election, it takes a transferred (rather than cost) basis in T's assets. Even though the step transaction doctrine properly could be applied here to disregard the existence of transitory Y and treat the transaction as P's direct taxable acquisition of T's assets, the Service respects the form of the two steps in deference to Congress's intent to replace the *Kimbell-Diamond* doctrine (treating a stock purchase followed by an upstream merger or liquidation of T as an asset purchase) with a more precise statutory regime (§ 338) which allows P to elect the tax treatment of the transaction at the corporate level. Rev. Rul. 90–95, 1990–2 C.B. 67. See IX.D.3.a., at pages 182–183, *supra.*

Example (4):   Same as Example (3), except in the reverse merger T shareholders exchange their T stock for consideration consisting of 70% P stock and 30% cash. Shortly thereafter, T merges into P. Viewed in isolation, the first step (the merger of Y into T) does not qualify as a § 368(a)(2)(E) reverse triangular merger because too much cash (more than 20%) was used as consideration. If, however, the two steps are treated as an integrated transaction—i.e., a single statutory merger of T into P—the overall acquisition qualifies as a Type A reorganization because the 30% cash does not violate continuity of interest. Rev. Rul. 2001–46, 2001–2 C.B. 321. Note that application of the step transaction doctrine to these facts does not violate the policy underlying § 338 because the integrated transaction qualifies as a reorganization in which P acquires T's assets with a transferred basis under § 362. As a result, the Service has ruled that a unilateral § 338 election may not be made in such a situation.

Example (5):   T, which is owned by individual A, has $150 of assets and $50 of liabilities. P, which is unrelated to T or A, has net assets of $410. Pursuant to an integrated plan to acquire T's assets, P first forms a subsidiary, Y, and Y merges into T, which becomes a subsidiary of P. In the merger, T shareholders exchange their T stock for consideration consisting of $90 of P voting stock and $10 cash. T then liquidates into P in a transaction that is not a statutory merger under state law. In the liquidation, T distributes all its assets to P and P assumes T's liabilities and continues to conduct T's former business after the liquidation. Viewed separately, the merger of Y into T qualifies as a § 368(a)(2)(E) reverse triangular merger, and the liquidation of T qualifies as tax-free under § 332. In Revenue Ruling 2008–25, 2008–1 C.B. 986, however, the Service collapsed the two steps and treated the entire transaction as an acquisition by P of T's assets that did not qualify as a Type C reorganization because only 60% of the $150 consideration paid for the assets was P voting stock ($90). The transaction also failed to qualify as a § 368(a)(2)(E) reverse triangular merger because T did not hold substantially all of its properties and the properties of Y immediately after the transaction. As a result, the ruling required A to recognize gain or loss on his sale of T stock. To protect the integrity of § 338, it also held that P's acquisition of T stock (the first step) was a qualified stock purchase under § 338 followed by a tax-free liquidation of a subsidiary under § 332 so that, if P does not make a § 338 election, T does not recognize gain on the transfer of its assets, and P takes those assets with a carryover basis.

Example (6): T is a wholly owned subsidiary of S Corp. Pursuant to an integrated plan to acquire T's assets, P forms a subsidiary, Y, and Y merges into T. In the merger, S receives consideration consisting of 50% P voting stock and 50% cash and then, pursuant to a prearranged plan, T merges into P. Viewed independently of any other step, P's acquisition of T stock constitutes a qualified stock purchase under § 338(d)(3). If P and S jointly make a § 338(h)(10) election, the Service will "turn off" the step transaction doctrine and respect the form of the separate steps. As a result, T will recognize gain or loss on the deemed sale of its assets, S will not recognize any gain or loss on the sale of its T stock, and P will take a fair market value ("cost") basis in T's assets. Reg. § 1.338(h)(10)–1(c)(2), –1(e) Example 12. If P and S do not make a § 338(h)(10) election, the two steps will be integrated, and the overall acquisition will qualify as a Type A reorganization, and P will take a transferred basis in T's assets. Reg. § 1.338(h)(10)–1(e) Example 11.

Example (7): Same as Example (6), except in the merger of Y into T, S receives only P voting stock. On these facts, no § 338(h)(10) election can be made because P's acquisition of T stock does not constitute a qualified stock purchase. Applying the step transaction doctrine, the overall transaction is treated as a statutory merger of T into P that qualifies as a Type A reorganization. Reg. § 1.338(h)(10)–1(e) Example 14. See also Rev. Rul. 2001–46, in Example (4), *supra*, at page 226.

7. Nondivisive Type D Reorganizations (Transfer to Controlled Corporation)

A nondivisive Type D reorganization is a transfer by one corporation ("R" for transferor) of all or part of its assets to another corporation ("E" for transferee) controlled immediately after the transfer by R or its shareholders (or any combination) provided that the stock or securities of E are distributed in pursuance of the plan in a transaction that qualifies under § 354.

a. Control

For purposes of nondivisive D reorganizations, the definition of "control" is borrowed from § 304(c)—i.e. 50% of voting power or value. § 368(a)(2)(H).

b.   Distribution Requirement

Section 354(b) requires that R must transfer "substantially all" of its assets to E and must distribute all of its properties (including the E stock and securities) to its shareholders.

c.   Historical Application: Liquidation-Reincorporation

The Service historically used the nondivisive D provisions to attack the now outmoded liquidation-reincorporation strategy, which was used by taxpayers to bail out corporate earnings at capital gains rates without paying corporate-level tax. A corporation with liquid and operating assets would distribute all its assets to its shareholders in complete liquidation and then recontribute the operating assets to a new corporation that would continue to operate the same business. If the strategy worked, the corporation would not recognize gain on the liquidation, and the shareholders would recognize capital gain under § 331. The new corporation would obtain a fair market value basis in the recontributed operating assets. This technique has largely been rendered obsolete by repeal of the *General Utilities* doctrine and the reduced tax rates on qualified dividends. The Service's principal line of attack was to apply the step transaction doctrine and classify the distribution of liquid assets as a dividend to the shareholders. To reach this result, it often argued that liquidation-reincorporation transactions were nondivisive Type D reorganizations. The Service generally was successful when the new corporation acquired substantially all of the old corporation's assets, as required by § 354(b). In applying the "substantially all" test for this purpose, the courts tended to focus on operating assets and ignore nonessential liquid assets. See, e.g., *Smothers v. United States,* 642 F.2d 894 (5th Cir.1981). The Service sometimes argued that a liquidation-reincorporation was really an F reorganization in which the shareholders realized a "boot dividend" to the extent of the liquid assets received on the "liquidation."

Liquidation-reincorporation transactions are rarely desirable under current law because the liquidation will trigger corporate-level gain under § 336. In most cases, any benefits from this strategy will be outweighed by the acceleration of the corporate-level gain.

d.   All-Cash D Reorganizations

A transaction may qualify as a Type D reorganization even where no stock or securities of the transferee corporation are issued and distributed if the same person or persons own, directly or indirectly, all the stock of the transferor and transferee corporations or there is only a de minimis variation in shareholder identity or proportionality of ownership. Reg. § 1.368–2(l)(2)(i), (ii). For this purpose, an individual and all members of his family with a relationship described in § 318(a)(1) are treated as one individual. Reg. § 1.368–2(l)(2)(ii). In such cases, the transferee corporation is deemed to have issued a nominal share of stock in addition to the actual consideration exchanged for the transferor's assets and the transferor is deemed to have distributed that stock to its shareholders and, when appropriate, to have further transferred it to the extent necessary to reflect the actual ownership of the two corporations. Reg. § 1.368–2(l)(3)(i).

Example (1):   A owns all the stock of R, Inc. and E, Inc. The fair market value of the R stock is $100,000, and A's adjusted basis in the stock is $20,000. R sells all its assets to E for $100,000 cash and liquidates, distributing the cash to A. The transaction qualifies as a Type D reorganization. E is deemed to have issued a nominal share of its stock to R in addition to the cash, and R is deemed to have distributed the $100,000 cash and the E stock to A. Reg. § 1.368–2(*l*)(3) Example 1. A recognizes $80,000 gain under §§ 354 and 356. R does not recognize gain on the transfer of its assets, and E takes those assets with a transferred basis. §§ 361; 362(b).

Example (2):   Assume the same facts as Example 1, except C, A's son, owns all the stock of E. Because A and C are treated as one individual and thus there is complete shareholder identity and proportionality of ownership in both corporations, the tax results are the same as in Example 1.

e.   Internal Restructuring Transactions

The Service has issued two revenue rulings that apply § 368(a)(1)(D) to provide flexibility and certainty with respect to certain internal restructuring transactions known as a "drop and sideways merger" and a "triple drop and check."

Example (1):   P, a domestic corporation, owned all the stock of two foreign subsidiaries, S-1 and S-2. S-1 directly operated a business and S-2 was a holding company that owned all the stock of three foreign operating companies (X, Y and Z). All P's subsidiaries were incorporated in the same country. As part of a prearranged plan with a valid business purpose, P wished to combine the operating companies (S-1, X, Y, and Z) into N, a new foreign subsidiary of S-2. To achieve that result, P first transferred all the stock of S-1 to S-2 in exchange for additional shares of S-2 stock. Immediately after that transfer, S-1, X, Y, and Z transferred substantially all their assets to N in exchange for N stock. S-1, X, Y, and Z then liquidated, distributing all the N stock to S-2. The IRS ruled that the first step of the transaction (P's transfer of its S-1 stock to S-2) was a nontaxable § 351 exchange. The subsequent transfers and liquidation by S-1, X, Y, and Z were treated as tax-free reorganizations under § 368(a)(1)(D). Rev. Rul. 2015–9, 2015–21 I.R.B. 972.

Example (2):   P, a domestic corporation, transferred its interest in a limited liability company that had elected to be taxed as a corporation, to a subsidiary, S-1, in exchange for S-1 stock. S-1 then transferred the LLC interest to another subsidiary, S-2, for S-2 stock, and S-2 transferred the LLC interest to S-3 for S-3 stock. The LLC then "checked the box," electing to be a disregarded entity. The IRS ruled that the transfers by P and S-1 qualified for nonrecognition under § 351. The election by the LLC to be a disregarded entity and the transfer by S-2 of its LLC interest to S-3 were characterized as an acquisitive Type D reorganization followed by a tax-free liquidation of a subsidiary under § 332. Rev. Rul. 2015–10, 2015–21 I.R.B. 973.

Perspective: In both these transactions, no assets were removed from corporate solution and control of P was unchanged. The IRS's reasoning in the rulings reflects its policy to respect the form of a § 351 exchange even if it is followed by subsequent transfers of the contributed property as part of a prearranged integrated plan. The rulings also warn, however, that the IRS is prepared to apply the step transaction to deny § 351 nonrecognition or otherwise recast the separate steps of an integrated transaction if "a different treatment is warranted to reflect the substance of the transaction as a whole." We are not sure what this means either without a specific fact pattern, but the best explanation is that the IRS does not want to be precluded from using a different approach to avoid what it believes to be an improper tax outcome.

8. Treatment of the Parties to an Acquisitive Reorganization

If a transaction qualifies as a reorganization under § 368, the tax consequences to T's shareholders and any corporation that is a "party to a reorganization" are governed by the various operative provisions discussed below. Carryover of tax attributes (other than basis) in a reorganization is discussed in Chapter XIII, *infra*.

a. Operative Provisions Glossary

1) The operative provisions apply only if "stock or securities" are issued by a "party to a reorganization." A "party" includes the acquiring and target corporations, the controlling parent corporation in a triangular reorganization, and the surviving corporation in a consolidation. § 368(b).

2) "Stock" is an equity interest in the corporation but does not include rights, warrants or options to purchase stock. Reg. § 1.354–1(e). Debt convertible into stock is treated as debt until the holder actually converts.

3) "Securities" are debt obligations that represent a degree of continuing participation in the corporation that falls short of an equity interest but is greater than an interest held by a short-term creditor. See *Camp Wolters Enterprises, Inc. v. Comm'r,* 22 T.C. 737 (1954), aff'd, 230 F.2d 555 (5th Cir.1956), cert. denied, 352 U.S. 826, 77 S.Ct. 39 (1956). Long-term bonds (10 years or more) generally qualify as securities but short-term notes (5 years or less) do not.

4) "Boot" is tax jargon for cash, short-term notes, the excess of securities received over securities surrendered by the taxpayer, and other property that does not qualify for nonrecognition. It often is referred to in the Code as "other property."

5) "Nonqualified preferred stock" is preferred stock with certain debt-like characteristics specified in § 351(g). See IV.B.3.b., at page 72, *supra*. Nonqualified preferred stock is treated as boot except to the extent it is exchanged for other nonqualified preferred stock. §§ 354(a)(2)(C)(i); 356(e).

b. Consequences to T Shareholders and Security Holders

The rules described in this section generally apply to all types of acquisitive reorganizations.

1) Recognition of Gain or Loss

T shareholders do not recognize gain or loss on an exchange of their T stock solely for P stock. § 354(a)(1). Realized gain must be recognized, however, to the extent that a T shareholder receives boot. § 356(a). A security holder of T does not recognize gain on the receipt of P securities in at least the same principal amount as the securities surrendered by the holder. But if the principal amount of P debt securities received exceeds the principal amount of T debt securities surrendered, the fair market value of the excess is treated as boot, and the security holder's realized gain is recognized to the extent of that boot. § 354(a)(2). In all events, a T shareholder or security holder who receives boot may not recognize any realized loss. § 356(c).

2) Character of Gain

Gain recognized by a T shareholder on an acquisitive reorganization is treated as a dividend if the exchange "has the effect of the distribution of a dividend" to the extent of the shareholder's ratable share of post-1913 earnings and profits "of the corporation." § 356(a)(2). In determining dividend equivalency, the principles of § 302 (see VII.C, at pages 131–139, *supra*) and the § 318 attribution rules apply. For this purpose, each T shareholder is treated as having initially received only P stock, a portion of which is then considered to be redeemed by P for an amount equal to the boot received. *Comm'r v. Clark,* 489 U.S. 726, 109 S.Ct. 1455 (1989); Rev. Rul. 93–61, 1993–2 C.B. 118. If this hypothetical redemption meets any of the tests for exchange treatment in § 302(b), the receipt of boot does not have the effect of a dividend and the shareholder recognizes capital gain. If the hypothetical redemption does not qualify for exchange treatment, the amount of recognized gain is a dividend to the extent of the shareholder's "ratable share" of "the corporation's" accumulated earnings and profits, and any remaining gain is capital gain. This rule is often referred to as the "dividend within gain" limitation. Although the statute is unclear, the majority view seems to be that the dividend determination is made by looking to T's earnings and profits. Any capital gain attributable to installment boot (e.g., a P note or bond that is not readily tradable) may be reported on the § 453 installment method unless the T stock surrendered was publicly traded. § 453(f)(6), (k)(2). See Prop. Reg. § 1.453–1(f)(2).

Example: A, an individual, is the sole shareholder of T Corp., which has $150,000 of accumulated E & P. A has a $60,000 basis in her T stock. P Corp. has 100,000 shares of common stock outstanding with a fair market value of $10 per share. T merges into P in a Type A reorganization. A receives 20,000 shares of P stock (value—$200,000) and $100,000 cash. A realizes $240,000 gain ($300,000 amount realized less A's $60,000 basis). A must recognize $100,000 of that gain under § 356(a)(1) (to the extent of the $100,000 cash boot). In determining dividend equivalency, A is treated as having received 30,000 shares of P stock (value—$300,000), of which 10,000 shares are redeemed by P in exchange for $100,000 cash. Before this hypothetical redemption, A is treated as owning 30,000 out of P's 130,000 outstanding shares (23.1%). After the redemption, A actually owned 20,000 out of P's 120,000 outstanding shares (16.67%). The redemption thus qualifies as substantially disproportionate under § 302(b)(2) (A's percentage ownership after the redemption is less than 80% of her ownership before), and A's $100,000 gain is capital gain because it does not have the effect of a dividend.

3) Allocation of Boot

The regulations provide detailed guidance for situations where T shareholders receive boot in a reorganization and surrender more than one block of stock (i.e., shares of stock acquired at different times for different prices) or more than one class of stock or securities. If the receipt of boot does not have the effect of a dividend, the terms of the agreement may specify how the boot is to be allocated among multiple blocks or different classes of stock if the specification is economically reasonable. If no specification is made, the types of consideration received by T shareholders must be allocated pro rata to the shares surrendered based on relative fair market values at the time of the exchange. Reg. § 1.356–1(b).

Example (1):   A owns 20 shares of T stock (10 shares each in Blocks 1 and 2, respectively). A's basis for Block 1 is $30, and her basis for Block 2 is $90. P acquires T in a merger that qualifies as a Type A reorganization. On the date of the exchange, the fair market value of the T stock was $10 per share. In exchange for her T stock, A receives $100 of P stock and $100 cash, the receipt of cash does not have the effect of a dividend, and the terms of the exchange do not specify how the consideration received by A is to be allocated. A realizes $70 of gain on Block 1 and $10 of gain on Block 2. Under the default rule in the regulations, the $100 boot is allocated pro rata to Blocks 1 and 2 (50%, or $50 to each block). A thus recognizes $50 of gain on Block 1 and $10 of gain on Block 2.

Example (2):   Same as Example 1, except the terms of the agreement specify that A receives $100 of P stock in exchange for A's Block 1 shares and $100 cash in exchange for A's Block 2 shares. The specification is economically reasonable because each block has a value of $100. A does not recognize any gain on Block 1 (because none of the boot was allocated to that block) and $10 gain on Block 2. If the receipt of boot had the effect of a dividend, this specification would not be respected and a pro rata allocation would be required.

4) Tax Stakes

Because dividend treatment under § 356(a)(2) is limited to a shareholder's recognized gain, noncorporate shareholders suffer little or no tax disadvantage if boot is characterized as a dividend when, as under current law, dividends and long-term capital gains are taxed at the same preferential rates. Corporate shareholders generally prefer to characterize boot received in a reorganization as a dividend because of the dividends received deduction and the absence of any preferential rate on corporate capital gains.

5) Basis and Holding Period

The basis of "nonrecognition property"—i.e., stock or nonboot securities received by former T shareholders or security holders in an exchange to which § 354 applies—is the same as the T stock or securities surrendered, decreased by the cash and the fair market value of any other boot received, and increased by the amount treated as a dividend and any other gain recognized. § 358(a)(1); Reg. § 1.358–1(a). Nonrecognition property takes a tacked holding period. § 1223(1). If different types of nonrecognition property are received (e.g., two classes of P stock), the aggregate § 358(a)(1) exchanged basis is allocated in proportion to their relative fair market values on the date of the exchange. § 358(b)(1); Reg. § 1.358–2. Any boot received takes a fair market value basis and its holding period begins as of the date of the exchange. § 358(a)(2). If a T shareholder surrenders multiple "tax lots" of T stock acquired at different times and for different per-share prices in exchange for P stock, the regulations require the shareholder to use a tracing approach that, to the greatest extent possible, matches the T shares surrendered to an appropriate number of P shares received in determining the basis and holding period of the P shares. Reg. § 1.358–2(a)(2). These regulations reject a simpler approach under which former T shareholders could use the average basis of their surrendered T shares to determine the basis of each share of P stock received.

> ***Example:*** A acquired 20 shares of T stock on Date 1 for $3 per share and 10 shares of T stock on Date 2 for $6 per share. On Date 3, P acquired all of T's assets in a tax-free Type A reorganization pursuant to which T shareholders received 2 shares of P stock for each share of T stock surrendered. A thus received 60 shares of P stock in which A takes a basis of $1.50 per share for 40 shares treated as acquired on Date 1 and a basis of $3 per share for 20 shares treated as acquired on Date 2. On or before the date that A's basis in the P stock becomes relevant (e.g., a sale of a portion of A's holdings), A may designate which of the P shares have a basis of $1.50 per share and which have a basis of $3 per share. Reg. § 1.358–2(c) Example 1.

6) § 306 Stock

Preferred stock received in a reorganization may be § 306 stock if: (a) it is received in exchange for § 306 stock, or (b) the effect of the transaction was substantially the same as the receipt of a stock dividend and the taxpayer would have realized dividend income under § 356(a)(2) if cash, rather than preferred stock, had been received. § 306(c)(1)(B), (c)(2); Reg. § 1.306–3(d). See VIII.B.3., at page 164, *supra*. In view of the decision in the *Clark* case, it is less likely that cash received in an acquisitive reorganization will be equivalent to a dividend and, as a result, preferred stock is unlikely to constitute § 306 stock. The Service nonetheless has ruled that where shareholders of publicly traded T receive both common and preferred stock of publicly traded P, the preferred stock is § 306 stock and the § 306(b)(4) no tax avoidance exception does not apply. Rev. Rul. 89–63, 1989–1 C.B. 90. Preferred stock is not § 306 stock if the shareholder surrenders preferred stock that was not § 306 stock and the stock received and surrendered are of equal value and have comparable terms.

c. Consequences to T

The rules described below apply to T's transfer of its assets in a Type A or Type C reorganization or a forward triangular merger, and to T's distribution to its shareholders of the consideration it receives from P, along with any assets that it retains, in a complete liquidation pursuant to the reorganization plan.

1) Treatment of the Reorganization Exchange

T recognizes no gain or loss on an exchange of property, pursuant to a reorganization plan, solely for stock or securities of P. § 361(a). P's assumption of T liabilities is not treated as boot and does not prevent the exchange from qualifying as tax-free to T except in the rare case where the liability assumption is motivated by tax avoidance or lacks a business purpose. § 357(a), (b). If T receives boot, it must recognize its realized gain (but may not recognize loss) to the extent of the cash and the fair market value of any boot that T does not distribute to its shareholders or creditors pursuant to the reorganization plan. § 361(b), (c). Since any boot passes directly to the T shareholders in a merger and must be distributed to the T shareholders in a Type C reorganization, T will rarely recognize gain or loss on a reorganization exchange.

2) Treatment of Distributions by T

T does not recognize gain or loss when it distributes "qualified property" to its shareholders pursuant to a reorganization plan. § 361(c). In this context, "qualified property" includes P stock or debt obligations received by T in the reorganization exchange. A transfer of "qualified property" directly to creditors to satisfy T liabilities is treated as a "distribution" for this purpose. § 361(c)(3). If T distributes an asset other than qualified property, such as unwanted T assets not acquired by P in the reorganization, or boot received from P that appreciates between its receipt and later distribution, T recognizes gain (but not loss) as if the property had been sold for its fair market value. § 361(c)(1), (2).

3) Sales Prior to Liquidation of T

After a reorganization exchange with P but prior to liquidating, T may sell some of the P stock or securities it receives to third parties. These sales are fully taxable events even if they were necessary to raise funds to pay off creditors. If T transfers the stock or securities directly to creditors, however, no gain is recognized because the transfer is treated as a "distribution" of "qualified property" under § 361(c).

4) Basis and Holding Period

T is generally unconcerned with the basis and holding period of the P stock or securities received in an acquisitive reorganization because those properties ordinarily will be distributed tax free under § 361(c) to T's shareholders, who will determine their basis and holding period by reference to their former T stock under §§ 358 and 1223. See XI.B.8.b.5., at page 233, *supra*. Even in a Type C reorganization where the Commissioner waives the distribution requirement, T is deemed to have distributed its assets to its shareholders, who are then treated as having recontributed the property to a "new" corporation which takes over the shareholders' basis and holding period. T takes a fair market value basis in any boot received from P. § 358(a)(2).

Example (1): In a Type C reorganization, T transfers assets worth $100,000 with an aggregate adjusted basis of $65,000 to P in exchange for $100,000 of P voting stock. T immediately distributes the P stock to its shareholders in complete liquidation of T. T recognizes no gain on either the transfer of its assets or the distribution of the P stock.

Example (2): Same as Example (1), except T receives $90,000 of P voting stock and $10,000 cash in exchange for its assets, and T immediately distributes the P stock and cash to its shareholders. T recognizes no gain on either the transfer of its assets or the distribution. The result is the same if T uses the cash to pay debts not assumed by P.

Example (3): Same as Example (1), except T receives $90,000 of P voting stock and a $10,000 parcel of land (Gainacre) in exchange for its assets, and Gainacre is worth $12,000 when T distributes it along with the P stock to its shareholders. T recognizes no gain on the transfer of its assets to P. T recognizes no gain on the distribution of the P voting stock but recognizes $2,000 gain ($12,000 value less $10,000 § 358(a)(2) basis) on the distribution of Gainacre.

Example (4): Same as Example (1), except that T transfers $10,000 of the P stock received in exchange for its assets to a T creditor in full satisfaction of a $10,000 T debt that P did not assume. T recognizes no gain because a transfer of "qualified property" (the P stock) directly to a creditor is treated as a tax-free distribution under § 361(c). T would recognize gain if it sold the P stock and used the proceeds to pay the debt.

d. Consequences to P

1) Recognition of Gain or Loss

P does not recognize gain or loss on the issuance of its stock (or the stock of its parent) in an acquisitive reorganization. § 1032(a). P recognizes no gain if it issues securities or other debt consideration because the issuance is treated as a purchase. Reg. § 1.61–12(c)(1). If P transfers other "boot" property in connection with a reorganization exchange, it recognizes gain or loss under general tax principles. Rev. Rul. 72–327, 1972–2 C.B. 197. In a triangular reorganization, a subsidiary does not recognize gain on the acquisition of property in exchange for the stock of its parent. Rev. Rul. 57–278, 1957–1 C.B. 124.

2)   Basis and Holding Period of T Assets Received

P's basis in T assets received in a Type A or Type C reorganization or a forward triangular merger generally is the same as T's basis in those assets increased by any gain recognized by T on the reorganization exchange. § 362(b). Since T rarely recognizes gain (see XI.B.8.c., at page 234, *supra*), P almost always takes a transferred basis. In certain specialized situations, such as where P acquires property with a built-in loss (i.e., the basis of the property exceeds its fair market value) from a transferor not subject to U.S. tax (such as a foreign corporation or tax-exempt organization), the basis of such property must be reduced to its fair market value immediately after the transaction. § 362(e)(1); see Reg. §§ 1.358–6, 1.362–3. P takes a tacked holding period for capital and § 1231 assets that it receives from T. § 1223(2). In a Type B reorganization or reverse triangular merger, the bases of T's assets are unaffected.

3)   Basis and Holding Period of T Stock Received

In a Type B reorganization, P's basis in the T stock equals the aggregate bases of the former T shareholders. §§ 362(b); 1223(2). In a forward triangular merger in which T merges into S (a P subsidiary), P may increase its basis in its S stock (usually zero, if S is newly formed) by the "net basis" (aggregate basis of assets less liabilities assumed) of T's assets. Reg. § 1.358–6(c)(1). In a reverse triangular merger, where S, a subsidiary of P, merges into T, P's basis in the T stock that it holds after the merger is generally the same as T's "net basis" in its assets increased by P's basis, if any, in its S stock. If S is a transitory subsidiary formed solely to carry out the merger, P likely will not have any basis in its S stock. Reg. § 1.358–6(c)(2).

9.   Failed Reorganizations

An acquisition that fails to qualify as a reorganization under § 368 is treated as a taxable acquisition of T's assets or stock. See IX.D., at pages 180–190, *supra*. In the case of a failed Type A or C reorganization or a forward triangular merger, T recognizes gain or loss on the transfer of its assets and T's shareholders are treated as receiving a distribution in complete liquidation that is taxable under § 331. P obtains a cost basis in T's assets. In the case of a failed Type B reorganization or reverse triangular merger, T's shareholders recognize gain or loss on the sale of their stock. T does not recognize gain and retains its same asset bases unless P makes a § 338 election.

C. Nonacquisitive, Nondivisive Reorganizations

1. Type E Reorganizations (Recapitalizations)

a. Introduction

A Type E reorganization is a recapitalization. "Recapitalization" is not defined in the Code but has been described by the Supreme Court as a "reshuffling of a capital structure within the framework of an existing corporation." *Helvering v. Southwest Consolidated Corp.*, 315 U.S. 194, 202, 62 S.Ct. 546, 551 (1942). In a recapitalization, a corporation's shareholders or creditors exchange their interests for other equity or debt interests. The assets of the corporation generally remain unchanged.

b. Judicial Requirements

Because a recapitalization involves only a single corporation, the Service has ruled that neither continuity of proprietary interest nor continuity of business enterprise is required for a recapitalization to qualify as a Type E reorganization. Rev. Rul. 77–415, 1977–2 C.B. 311; Rev. Rul. 82–34, 1982–1 C.B. 59. A recapitalization still must serve some corporate business purpose to qualify for nonrecognition. Reg. § 1.368–1(b).

c. Stock for Stock

Virtually all stock-for-stock exchanges, including preferred for common and common for preferred, will qualify as Type E reorganizations if they are carried out pursuant to a plan. Reg. § 1.368–2(e)(2)–(4). A stock-for-stock exchange also may qualify as tax-free under § 1036.

1) Receipt of Boot

A shareholder does not recognize gain on a Type E stock-for-stock recapitalization unless boot is received. In that event, realized gain is recognized to the extent of the boot. See §§ 354; 356; and XI.B.8.b., at pages 231–233, *supra*. The gain is capital gain unless the transaction has the effect of the distribution of a dividend, in which case the dividend income is limited by both the shareholder's recognized gain and his ratable share of the corporation's E & P. § 356(a)(2). As with acquisitive reorganizations, § 302 principles are used in determining dividend equivalence. See XI.C.1.f., at page 238, *infra*, for additional issues raised when a shareholder receives a combination of stock and bonds for stock.

2) § 305 Aspects

A recapitalization may result in a deemed stock distribution under § 305(c) (see VIII.A.3.f., at pages 160–161, *supra*) if it is: (a) pursuant to a plan to periodically increase a shareholder's proportionate interest in the assets or earnings and profits of the corporation, or (b) is with respect to preferred stock with dividend arrearages and the preferred shareholder increases his proportionate interest in the corporation as a result of the exchange. Reg. § 1.305–7(c). In these cases, the dividend (assuming sufficient E & P) is the amount of the increase in the shareholder's liquidation preference or the amount of the dividend arrearages that were eliminated. Reg. § 1.368–2(e)(5).

3) § 306 Aspects

Stock received in a recapitalization will constitute § 306 stock if: (a) it is not common stock, (b) it was received pursuant to a plan of reorganization, (c) no gain or loss was recognized on its receipt under §§ 354 and 356, and (d) the effect of the transaction was substantially the same as the receipt of a stock dividend or the stock was received in exchange for § 306 stock. § 306(c)(1)(B). Dividend equivalence results if cash received in lieu of the preferred stock received in a recapitalization would have been a dividend under § 356(a)(2). See Reg. § 1.306–3(d).

4) Nonqualified Preferred Stock

Although nonqualified preferred stock is generally treated as boot for purposes of § 368 reorganizations (see XI.B.8.a., at page 230, *supra*), it is not so treated in the case of an otherwise qualified recapitalization of certain "family-owned" corporations. § 354(a)(2)(C)(ii).

d. Bonds for Bonds

A creditor's exchange of outstanding bonds for newly issued bonds of the same corporation qualifies as a Type E reorganization. Rev. Rul. 77–415, 1977–2 C.B. 311. The creditor may recognize income, however, insofar as the bonds received are attributable to accrued or unpaid interest or the principal amount of the bonds received in the exchange exceeds the principal amount of the bonds surrendered. §§ 354(a)(2); 356(d). In some cases, a bonds-for-bonds recapitalization may result in discharge of indebtedness income to the corporation. The new bonds also may give rise to original issue discount.

e. Bonds Exchanged for Stock

When a creditor of a corporation exchanges old bonds for new stock in the debtor corporation, the exchange generally qualifies as a tax-free Type E reorganization. Reg. § 1.368–2(e)(1). Such exchanges commonly occur when a financially distressed corporation pays off outstanding bonds by transferring preferred or common stock to the creditor. If the principal amount of the surrendered bonds exceeds the fair market value of the stock, the corporation may recognize discharge of indebtedness income.

f. Stock Exchanged for Bonds or Stock and Bonds

A shareholder who surrenders old stock in exchange for new bonds, or a combination of new stock and bonds, has fundamentally altered his investment to the extent that new debt replaces old equity.

1) Stock for Bonds

An exchange of old stock solely for new bonds is treated as a redemption and is tested for dividend equivalency under §§ 301 and 302 whether or not the overall transaction is a Type E reorganization. See Reg. §§ 1.354–1(d) Example (3); 1.301–1(*l*).

2) Stock for Stock and Bonds

An exchange of old stock for new stock and bonds may qualify as a Type E reorganization. If so, the bonds constitute boot, and the shareholder's realized gain is recognized to the extent of the fair market value of the bonds received. § 354(a)(2)(A)(ii), (d). If the bonds are issued pro rata to all the shareholders, this gain likely will be characterized as a dividend under § 356(a)(2) to the extent of each shareholder's ratable share of E & P. If the bonds are not issued pro rata, the gain is more likely to be capital gain.

3) Securities Bailouts

In *Bazley v. Comm'r*, 331 U.S. 737, 67 S.Ct. 1489 (1947), the Supreme Court held that an exchange of old stock for a combination of new stock and bonds was not a recapitalization and that the shareholders realized dividend income (to the extent of E & P) under § 301 in an amount equal to the fair market value of the bonds received. *Bazley* was decided prior to enactment of the rule in § 354(a)(2)(A), which treats securities received in a recapitalization as boot if no securities are surrendered. The difference between the result in *Bazley* and the current statutory scheme is that under *Bazley* the entire value of the bonds is a dividend (even if the shareholder has no recognized gain), while under §§ 354 and 356 the dividend is limited to the shareholder's recognized gain on the stock. The extent to which *Bazley* still applies to a recapitalization is unsettled.

2. Type F Reorganizations (Change in Form)

a. Introduction

A Type F reorganization is a mere change in identity, form, or place of organization of one corporation, however effected. § 368(a)(1)(F). Some courts once held that an F reorganization could include a combination of two or more active corporations. Although these transactions also qualified as Type A reorganizations, Type F status was preferable because postacquisition net operating losses of the new corporation could be carried back to offset profits earned by the previous corporation that conducted the same business. § 381(b). Congress eventually amended the Code to make it clear that F reorganizations are limited to transactions involving only a single operating corporation.

Example: X Corp., which is incorporated in California, wishes to change its state of incorporation to Delaware. To that end, X merges into newly formed Y Corp., a Delaware corporation. Pursuant to the merger, the X shareholders receive Y stock in proportion to their holdings of X stock and X dissolves by operation of law. The merger qualifies as an F reorganization.

b. Qualification Requirements

Under the regulations, a transaction must satisfy six requirements to qualify as an F reorganization. The regulations refer to the corporations involved in the transaction as the "transferor corporation" ("T"), and the "resulting corporation" ("R"). In general, the six requirements are:

(1) All the stock of R must have been exchanged for stock of T;

(2) The same shareholders generally must own T before the transaction and R immediately after the transaction in identical proportions;

(3) R generally may not hold any property or have any tax attributes immediately before the transaction;

(4) T must completely liquidate;

(5) Immediately after the transaction, R must be the only corporation holding the property of T; and

(6) Immediately after the transaction, R may not hold property acquired from a corporation other than T.

Reg. § 1.368–2(m)(1).

c. Application of Judicial Doctrines

Since only one operating corporation is involved, a transaction does not have to satisfy the continuity of interest and continuity of business enterprise doctrines to qualify as an F reorganization. Reg. § 1.368–2(m)(2). The step transaction doctrine may apply to a series of related transactions that together meet the requirement of an F reorganization. Reg. § 1.368–2(m)(3)(i). An F reorganization also may occur before, within, or after other transactions. The related events that precede or follow the F reorganization generally will not cause it to fail the requirements of § 368(a)(1)(F).

d. Overlap Situations

If a transaction qualifies as both an F reorganization and either an A, C or D asset reorganization, it is treated as an F reorganization except where the transaction (or a step thereof) is one of the various types of § 368 triangular reorganizations, such as a § 368(a)(2)(D) forward triangular merger. Reg. § 1.368–2(m)(3)(iv).

3. Type G Reorganizations (Insolvency)

A Type G reorganization is a transfer by one corporation of all or part of its assets to another corporation in a bankruptcy proceeding under Title 11 of the U.S. Code or a similar proceeding (e.g., receivership, foreclosure) in federal or state court, provided that the stock or securities of the transferee corporation are distributed pursuant to a plan of reorganization in a transaction that qualifies under §§ 354, 355 or 356. § 368(a)(1)(G). In overlap situations, the Type G rules take precedence. § 368(a)(3)(C).

D. Review Questions

1. Determine whether or not the transactions described below qualify as a reorganization under § 368:

    (a) T, Inc. has 200 shares of common stock outstanding, owned 81% by A and 19% by B. In a single transaction, P, Inc. acquires all the stock of T in a stock-for-stock exchange in which A receives P voting stock and B receives P nonvoting preferred stock that is not nonqualified preferred stock.

    (b) Same as (a), above, except that P liquidates T one week after acquiring the T stock.

(c) Same as (a), above, except that P acquired 21% of the T stock for cash 15 years ago and acquired the remaining 79% upon the merger of S, a transitory subsidiary of P formed to effect the transaction, into T. In the merger, T's shareholders (other than P) received P voting stock for their T stock.

(d) T, Inc., a computer software manufacturer, merges into P, Inc., a book publisher. T shareholders receive P voting stock (75% of the consideration) and P long-term bonds (25% of the consideration). One month after the merger, P sells T's assets and uses the proceeds to expand its book publishing business.

(e) T, Inc. owns operating assets with a fair market value of $200,000 subject to liabilities of $50,000. P, Inc. acquires the assets of T (subject to $25,000 of liabilities) in exchange for P voting stock worth $150,000 and $25,000 cash. T uses the cash to pay off its remaining liabilities and then liquidates, distributing the P voting stock to its shareholders.

2. T, Inc. is a closely held corporation with 100 shares of common stock outstanding, owned 50 shares by A (basis—$200,000) and 50 shares by B (basis—$400,000). T has the following assets:

	Adj. Basis	Fair Mkt. Value
Operating Assets	$600,000	$1,000,000
Liquid Assets	100,000	200,000
Total	$700,000	$1,200,000

T has $200,000 of liabilities and $300,000 of accumulated earnings and profits.

Determine the tax consequences to all relevant parties if P, Inc., a publicly traded company with 2 million shares of common stock outstanding, acquires T's assets, in the following alternative transactions:

(a) T merges into P. A and B each receive $500,000 of P nonvoting preferred stock

(b) Same as (a), above, except P acquires all of T's assets subject to its liabilities in exchange for $1,000,000 of P nonvoting preferred stock, and T promptly liquidates, distributing the P stock pro rata to A and B.

(c) Same as (a), above, except A and B each receive $300,000 of P voting stock and $200,000 of P long-term bonds.

(d) P acquires T's operating assets in exchange for $1,000,000 of P voting stock. T transfers $200,000 of the P voting stock to its creditors to pay off its liabilities, and then liquidates, distributing $800,000 of P voting stock and its $200,000 of liquid assets to its shareholders.

(e) P forms a new subsidiary, Y, and Y merges into T. In the merger, A and B receive only cash and P notes. Shortly thereafter, as part of the same overall plan, T merges into P. No § 338 election is made.

(f) Same as (e), above, except in the initial merger, A and B each receive consideration consisting of 60% P stock and 40% cash.

(g) Same as (f), above, except T is a wholly owned subsidiary of S, Inc., and in the initial reverse merger, S receives consideration consisting of 50% P stock and 50% cash. P and S jointly make a § 338(h)(10) election.

Chapter XII

Corporate Divisions

■ ANALYSIS

A. Introduction

Corporate divisions are transactions in which a single corporate enterprise is divided into two or more separate corporations that remain under the same ownership. A division is accomplished when a parent corporation—known as "the distributing corporation"—distributes to its shareholders stock or securities of one or more controlled subsidiaries. If various judicial and statutory requirements are met, the transaction is generally tax free to the distributing corporation and its shareholders. The rationale is that a corporate division is merely a change in the form of businesses which continue to be owned and operated by the same shareholders. As with other nonrecognition provisions, gain or loss is preserved through transferred and exchanged bases. In this chapter, the parent distributing corporation will be referred to as "P" and the controlled subsidiary corporations will be referred to as "S," "S-1," "S-2," etc. P shareholders receiving S stock sometimes will be referred to as "distributees."

1. Types of Corporate Divisions

a. Spin-offs

A spin-off is a pro rata distribution of S stock by P to its shareholders. S may be a preexisting subsidiary or a corporation that was formed by P immediately prior to the distribution. A spin-off resembles a dividend.

Example: P operates hotel and restaurant chains as separate divisions. P transfers the assets of the hotel division to a newly formed subsidiary, S, and distributes the S stock pro rata to its shareholders. After the distribution, the P shareholders own all the stock of both P and S.

b. Split-offs

A split-off is a non pro rata distribution of S stock by P to some of its shareholders in exchange for all or part of their P stock. A split-off resembles a redemption.

Example: A and B are two equal shareholders of P, which operates hotel and restaurant chains as separate divisions. P transfers the hotel division assets to a newly formed subsidiary, S, and distributes the S stock to A in redemption of all of her P stock. After the distribution, A owns all the stock of S, and B owns all the stock of P.

c. Split-ups

A split-up is a distribution of S-1 and S-2 stock, either pro rata or non pro rata, by P (which owns no other assets) to all of its shareholders. A split-up resembles a complete liquidation.

Example: A and B are two equal shareholders of P, which operates hotel and restaurant chains as separate divisions. P transfers the hotel division assets to a newly formed subsidiary, S-1, and the restaurant division assets to a newly formed subsidiary, S-2. P distributes the S-1 stock to A and the S-2 stock to B in complete liquidation. Alternatively, P might distribute the S-1 and S-2 stock pro rata to A and B. In either case, the transaction would be a split-up.

2. Type D Reorganization Preceding a Division

As illustrated above, the first step in a corporate division may involve P's transfer of the assets of a distinct trade or business to a controlled subsidiary, S, in exchange for S stock followed by P's distribution of the S stock to P's shareholders in a spin-off, split-off or split-up. This first step qualifies as a divisive Type D reorganization if (as is likely) immediately after the transfer P or one or more of its shareholders (including persons who were shareholders immediately before the transfer) or any combination thereof is in "control" (using the 80% tests in § 368(c)) of S and the subsequent distribution of S stock is pursuant to a plan that meets the requirements of § 355. § 368(a)(1)(D). In testing for "control," the fact that the P shareholders dispose of part or all of the distributed stock, or the fact that the corporation whose stock was distributed issues additional stock, shall not be taken into account. § 368(a)(2)(H)(ii). The resulting tax consequences of a divisive Type D reorganization are:

a.   P recognizes no gain or loss on the transfer of assets to newly formed S. § 361(a).

b.   P's basis in its S stock is the same as the aggregate basis in the P assets transferred to S. § 358(a).

c.   S takes a transferred basis in the assets contributed to it by P. § 362(b).

Note that the same tax consequences generally would result on the formation of S under §§ 351, 358 and 362(a). See Chapter IV, *supra*. In a divisive Type D reorganization, however, the earnings and profits of P are allocated between P and S, and there are some other minor differences on collateral matters. See Reg. § 1.312–10 and XII.I.2.e., at page 266, *infra*.

3. Summary of Requirements for Tax-Free Division

P's distribution of S stock to P's shareholders will be tax free to P and its shareholders if the following statutory and judicial requirements are satisfied:

a.   P must control S immediately before the distribution—i.e., P must own at least 80% of S's voting power and 80% of each class of outstanding S nonvoting stock. §§ 355(a)(1)(A); 368(c).

b.   P must distribute either all of the S stock or securities held by P immediately before the distribution or distribute an amount of stock representing § 368(c) "control" of S and establish to the Service's satisfaction that the retention of S stock or securities was not part of a tax avoidance plan. § 355(a)(1)(D).

c.   Immediately after a spin-off or split-off distribution, both P and S must be engaged or treated as engaged (e.g., through a subsidiary) in the active conduct of a trade or business. § 355(b)(1)(A). In applying this rule, all members of each corporation's separate affiliated group—generally, subsidiaries in which the parent owns 80% or more of the voting power and total value—are treated as one corporation. § 355(b)(3)(A). In a split-up, P must own no assets other than stock or securities of two or more subsidiaries immediately prior to the distribution, and each of those subsidiaries must engage in the active conduct of a trade or business after the distribution. § 355(b)(1)(B).

d.   Each postdistribution active trade or business must have been actively conducted throughout the five-year period preceding the distribution, must not have been acquired during that period in a transaction in which gain or loss was recognized in whole or in part, and must not have been conducted by a corporation the control of which was acquired by P, or by any corporate distributee shareholder of P, in a taxable transaction during the five-year predistribution period. § 355(b)(2)(B)–(D).

e. P's distribution of S stock and securities must not have been used principally as a "device" for the distribution of earnings and profits of P or S, or both. § 355(a)(1)(B).

f. The division must be carried out for a bona fide corporate business purpose. Reg. § 1.355–2(b). Section 355 also contemplates the continued operation of the business or businesses existing prior to the separation. Reg. § 1.355–1(b).

g. The shareholders of P prior to the distribution must maintain sufficient continuity of proprietary interest in both P and S following the distribution. Reg. § 1.355–2(c).

h. Immediately after the distribution, neither P nor S may be a "disqualified investment corporation" (generally, a corporation with two-thirds or more of its assets consisting of liquid investments such as cash and securities), and no person who did not hold a 50% interest in the disqualified investment corporation immediately before the distribution may hold such an interest immediately after the distribution. § 355(g).

i. The anti-avoidance rules in §§ 355(d) and 355(e) must not be violated; if they are, P (but not its shareholders) may recognize gain on the distribution.

j. Neither the distributing nor controlled corporations may be a real estate investment trust ("REIT") except spin-offs of one REIT by another REIT are not disqualified. § 355(h).

4. IRS Ruling Policy

The IRS's position on issuing rulings in § 355 transactions continues to evolve. The Service will rule on one or more "significant issues" presented in a § 355 transaction. Rev. Proc. 2019–3, § 3.01(55), 2019–1 I.R.B. 130. For this purpose, an issue generally is "significant" if it is "a germane and specific issue of law," provided that in a ruling on the issue "the conclusion . . . otherwise would not be essentially free from doubt." Id. The Service also will issue letter rulings pertaining to the corporate business purpose requirement and the device limitation provided the issue is not inherently factual in nature. Id. at § 3.01(58). More broadly, in Rev. Proc. 2017–52, 2017–41 I.R.B. 283, the Service introduced a pilot program expanding the scope of its letter rulings to include rulings on the tax consequences of a distribution of stock, or stock or securities, of a controlled corporation under § 355. This new pilot program is an expansion of the IRS's more limited general ruling position.

B. Active Trade or Business

To qualify as a tax-free corporate division, P and S (or, in a split-up, S-1 and S-2) each must be engaged in the active conduct of a trade or business immediately after the distribution. These trades or businesses must have been actively conducted throughout the five-year period preceding the distribution and generally must not have been acquired by P or S in a taxable transaction within that five-year period. In 2007, the Service issued extensive proposed regulations (including 51 examples) that provide updated guidance on the active trade or business test. REG–123365–03, 2007–1 C.B. 1357. When finalized, they will have a significant influence on the interpretation of § 355. The proposed regulations are referred to selectively below.

1. Trade or Business

A "trade or business" is a specific group of activities carried on by the corporation for the purpose of earning income or profit. The activities must include every operation that forms a part of the process of earning income, including the collection of income and payment of expenses. Reg. § 1.355–3(b)(2)(ii). Passive investment activities do not constitute a trade or business.

2. Active Conduct

"Active conduct" of a trade or business requires the corporation itself to perform "active and substantial management and operational functions." Reg. § 1.355–3(b)(2)(iii). Proposed regulations would permit the corporation's activities to be performed by others, such as employees, shareholders, affiliated corporations, and certain partnerships in which the corporation is a partner. Prop. Reg. § 1.355–3(b)(2)(ii). Activities performed by outsiders, such as independent contractors, generally are not considered as performed by the corporation. Id. "Active conduct" does not include the holding of stock, securities, raw land or other purely passive investments, or the ownership (including leasing) of real or personal property used in a trade or business unless the owner performs significant services with respect to the operation and management of the property. Reg. § 1.355–3(b)(2)(iv). Real estate management services are "active" if a corporation provides them in its capacity as a corporate general partner or as a member-manager of a limited liability company. Rev. Rul. 92–17, 1992–1 C.B. 142; Rev. Rul. 2002–49, 2002–2 C.B. 288.

Example (1): P has discovered oil on land which it uses in a ranching business. If P has not engaged in any significant development activities with respect to its mineral rights, the holding of those rights is not an active business. Reg. § 1.355–3(c) Example (3).

Example (2): P owns real estate that it leases to others. P performs no services with respect to the property apart from collection of rent. P's rental activities do not constitute the active conduct of a trade or business. See, e.g., *Rafferty v. Comm'r,* 452 F.2d 767 (1st Cir.1971).

Example (3): Same as Example (2), except that P actively manages and maintains its rental properties. The activity is an active trade or business because P performs significant services with respect to the operation and management of the property. Reg. § 1.355–3(c) Example (12).

3. Relative Size of Active Trade or Business

In interpreting the active trade or business test, the IRS has taken the position that no specific percentage of the value of the distributing or controlled corporation's assets must be devoted to any particular active trade or business but the percentage is a factor in determining whether the transaction is being used as a device for the distribution of earnings and profits. Rev. Rul. 73–44, 1973–1 C.B. 182. Relying on this position, some taxpayers try to satisfy the test by combining a relatively small trade or business in a subsidiary with substantially more valuable investment assets, such as stock, securities, or real estate. Their goal is to distribute the investment assets to shareholders or sell them without payment of any corporate-level tax. In response, the IRS has announced that it will no longer rule on the application of § 355 to transactions in which the value of the business assets relied upon by either the distributing or controlled corporation to satisfy the active trade or business requirement is less than 5% of the value of the total gross assets of such corporation.

Rev. Proc. 2019–3, § 4.01(30), 2019–1 I.R.B. 130. For proposed regulations dealing with these issues, see XII.G.3., *infra,* at page 260.

4. Divisions of a Single Integrated Business

a. Vertical Divisions

Section 355 does not require two distinct predistribution businesses. The active business test is met if P vertically divides an integrated business by transferring a portion of its assets and liabilities to S and then distributing the S stock to one or more of P's shareholders.

Example: A and B each own 50% of the stock of P. For more than five years, P has engaged in a construction business. P transfers one of its two major construction contracts, along with cash and equipment, to a new subsidiary, S, and distributes the S stock to A in redemption of A's P stock. After the distribution, P (now wholly owned by B) owns the other construction contract and the remaining equipment and cash. The distribution satisfies the active business requirement even though P conducted only one predistribution trade or business. *Comm'r v. Coady,* 289 F.2d 490 (6th Cir.1961); Reg. § 1.355–3(c) Example (4).

b. Horizontal (or Functional) Divisions

The active business test is not necessarily violated on a distribution of certain distinct functions of a single business enterprise—e.g., the separation of manufacturing and research departments. A functional division, however, may present evidence of a device. Reg. § 1.355–2(d)(2)(iv)(C).

Example: For more than five years, P has engaged in a manufacturing business and maintained a research department in connection with its manufacturing activities. P transfers the assets of the research department to a new subsidiary, S, and distributes the S stock pro rata to P's shareholders. After the distribution, S continues its research activities, furnishing services only to P. The division satisfies the active business test. The result is the same if S performed services for P and outsiders after the distribution. Reg. § 1.355–3(c) Example (9). Proposed regulations would reach the same result provided the research department has significant assets and goodwill. Prop. Reg. § 1.355–3(d) Example 16. Even though the active business test is met, the distribution may be evidence of a device if S serves only P. See XII.C.2.c., at page 254, *infra.*

5. Five-Year Business History Rule

The postdistribution trades or businesses must have been actively conducted throughout the five-year period preceding the distribution. § 355(b)(2)(B). The assets of the business must not have been acquired within that period in a transaction in which gain or loss is recognized by the seller (§ 355(b)(2)(C)), and the business must not have been conducted by a corporation the control (as defined by using the 80% tests in § 368(c)) of which was acquired by P or a distributee corporation in a taxable transaction (§ 355(b)(2)(D)) within the five-year period. These rules have engendered controversies over whether a particular activity is a separate business requiring its own five-year history or is simply part of an integrated business which has been actively conducted for more than five years.

a. Expansion of Existing Trade or Business

In determining whether a corporation has conducted an active trade or business throughout the five-year period preceding a distribution, the fact that a trade or business underwent changes during that period is disregarded provided the changes are not of such a character as to constitute the acquisition of a new or different business. Reg. § 1.355–3(b)(3)(ii). For example, if P has engaged in a trade or business for more than five years and expands that business to other geographical locations within the five-year predistribution period, each location is considered part of an integrated trade or business with a more-than-five-year history. If P acquired the assets of a new branch in the same line of business within the five-year predistribution period in a taxable transaction, the new branch will be treated as an expansion of P's original business unless the acquisition effects such a change in character that it constitutes the acquisition of a new or different business. Id.; *Lockwood's Estate v. Comm'r,* 350 F.2d 712 (8th Cir.1965).

Example (1):   P has been engaged in the operation of a department store in City for more than five years. Two years ago, it opened a second store in Suburb. P transfers the assets of the suburban store to a new subsidiary, S, and distributes the S stock pro rata to P's shareholders. Both P and S are considered to satisfy the five-year business history rule. Reg. § 1.355–3(c) Example (7).

Example (2):   P has been engaged in the manufacture of farm machinery in Nebraska for more than five years. Two years ago, it acquired the assets of a similar manufacturing plant in Maine, where P had not previously conducted business. P transfers the assets of the Maine facility to a new subsidiary, S, and distributes the S stock pro rata to P's shareholders. Both P and S satisfy the five-year business history rule because the acquisition of the Maine plant was an expansion of an existing trade or business rather than an acquisition of a new business. Reg. § 1.355–3(c) Example (8).

Example (3):   P has been engaged in a retail shoe store business for more than five years. P's business enjoys favorable name recognition and goodwill. Three years ago, P created a web site and began selling shoes over the Internet. The web site takes advantage of P's name recognition and goodwill. In the current year, P transfers all the assets and liabilities of the web site to a new subsidiary, S, and distributes the S stock pro rata to the P shareholders. Because the retail stores and the web site draw to a significant extent upon P's experience and know-how and the web site's success is largely dependent on the goodwill associated with P, the creation of the web site does not constitute the acquisition of a new trade or business but is an expansion of P's retail shoe store business. Both P and S satisfy the five-year business history rule. Rev. Rul. 2003–38, 2003–1 C.B. 811; Prop. Reg. § 1.355–3(d)(2) Example 19.

b. Acquisition of a New Trade or Business in a Taxable Transaction

The active business test is violated if P acquired the assets (§ 355(b)(2)(C)) or if P or a distributee corporation acquired a controlling stock interest (§ 355(b)(2)(D)) in the business in a taxable transaction within the five years preceding the distribution. A "taxable" transaction is one in which gain or loss was recognized to the seller in whole or in part—i.e., almost any acquisition other than a wholly tax-free reorganization under § 368 or a liquidation of a subsidiary under § 332. Reg. § 1.355–3(b)(4)(i). If P's acquisition of S stock causes S to become a member of P's "separate affiliated group" (see XII.B.8., at page 252, *infra*), the transaction is treated as an acquisition of assets, reducing the significance of § 355(b)(2)(D). Prop. Reg. § 1.355–3(b)(1)(ii), —3(b)(4)(iv)(F).

Example (1):   P has been engaged in the apparel business for more than five years. Two years ago, it acquired for cash all the assets of a hardware business. P transfers the hardware assets to a newly formed subsidiary, S, and distributes the S stock pro rata to the P shareholders. The distribution fails the active business test because P acquired the hardware assets in a taxable transaction within five years prior to the distribution.

Example (2):   Same as Example (1), except P acquired the hardware assets two years ago in a Type A reorganization in which some of the former shareholders of the hardware business recognized gain because they received boot. The distribution would not qualify because the hardware assets were acquired in a partially taxable transaction.

Example (3):   Same as Example (2), except P acquired the hardware assets in a Type C reorganization from an unrelated corporation which had operated the business for more than five years. No gain or loss was recognized by any of the parties to the transaction. The distribution qualifies under the active business test because S has been engaged in the hardware business for more than five years and P did not acquire the assets in a taxable transaction.

6. Disposition of a Recently Acquired Business

A distribution will fail the active business test if a controlling interest in P was acquired by a corporate distributee (i.e., a corporate shareholder of P) in a taxable transaction within the five-year predistribution period. § 355(b)(2)(D). The purpose of this requirement is to prevent a corporation from using § 355 to dispose of a recently acquired subsidiary without paying a corporate-level tax.

Example: P and its wholly owned subsidiary, S, each have been engaged in the active conduct of a trade or business for more than five years. Two years ago, X Inc. purchased 100% of the stock of P and did not make a § 338 election. X wishes to sell the business operated by S without recognizing gain. Even if the other § 355 requirements are met, P's distribution of its S stock to X will not satisfy the active business test because X acquired control of P in a taxable transaction within the five years preceding the distribution. (In any event, it is doubtful whether this transaction would satisfy the business purpose or continuity of interest requirements.)

7. Activities Conducted by a Partnership

For purposes of the active trade or business test, a corporation that owns a meaningful (at least 20%) interest in a partnership or LLC is treated as engaged in the conduct of the partnership's or LLC's trade or business if the corporation itself or through its officers performs active and substantial management functions for the partnership's business even if another partner also performs such functions. Rev. Rul. 92–17, 1992–1 C.B. 142; Rev. Rul. 2002–49, 2002–2 C.B. 288. A corporation that owns a significant (at least one-third) interest in a partnership or LLC is treated as engaged in the partnership's or LLC's business even if it does not directly conduct any activities relating to that business. Rev. Rul. 2007–42, 2007–2 C.B. 44.

8. Treatment of Separate Affiliated Groups

a. In General

In determining whether the distributing or controlled corporation is engaged in the active conduct of a trade or business, all members of either corporation's "separate affiliated group" ("SAG") are treated as one corporation. § 355(b)(3)(A). With minor modifications, the definition of an SAG is borrowed from the rules governing consolidated tax returns in § 1504(a). In general, an SAG consists of one or more chains of corporations in which a common parent owns at least 80% of the voting power and 80% of the total value of at least one other corporation and at least 80% (by vote and value) of each corporation is owned by another corporation in the chain. Note that this definition of control differs from the benchmark in § 368(c) (voting power and total number of shares of other classes of stock) that is used for acquisitive reorganizations and other § 355 control tests.

Example: For more than five years, P has owned 85% of the voting power and total value of S-1 and 100% of the only class of stock of S-2. Throughout this period, S-1 and S-2 have engaged in the active conduct of separate trades or businesses (ATB 1 and ATB 2). In Year 8, P distributes the S-2 stock to its shareholders. Because P has § 1504(a)(2) control of S-1 and S-2, P, S-1 and S-2 are treated as one corporation in determining whether P is engaged in an active trade or business, and thus P is considered to engage in ATB 1 and ATB 2 throughout the five-year predistribution period and continues to be engaged in ATB 1 immediately after the distribution. Prop. Reg. § 1.355–3(d)(2) Example 3.

b. Impact on Certain Stock Acquisitions

The proposed regulations apply the SAG rules in determining if the active trade or business requirement has been satisfied during the five-year predistribution period and immediately after the distribution. For this purpose, an acquisition of stock of a corporation that becomes a subsidiary member of a SAG is treated as an acquisition of the acquired corporation's assets. Prop. Reg. § 1.355–3(b)(1)(ii). This treatment may have an impact on whether the acquisition qualifies as an expansion of an existing trade or business and in certain other contexts.

Example (1):   For more than five years, P has owned all the stock of S and, throughout this period, S and unrelated T each have engaged in the active conduct of a computer software business. In Year 6, P purchases all the stock of T, causing T to become a member of P's separate affiliated group. Under the separate affiliated group rules of § 355(b)(3), P is treated as having acquired T's assets for purposes of the active trade or business test. In Year 8, P distributes all the S stock to P's shareholders but continues to own T as a 100% subsidiary. P's acquisition of T is considered to be an expansion of the computer software business. P and S thus both satisfy the five-year business history rule, and P is treated as engaged in that active trade or business (through T) immediately after the distribution. Prop. Reg. § 1.355–3(d)(2) Example 20.

Example (2):   P has been engaged in the apparel business for more than five years. Two years ago, P acquired for cash 100% of the stock of S, which has operated a hardware business for more than five years, in a transaction that was taxable to the former S shareholders. The transaction caused S to become a member of P's "separate affiliated group" and thus is treated as an acquisition of assets. The distribution fails the active business test under § 355(b)(2)(C) (rather than § 355(b)(2)(D)) because P is treated as having acquired the assets of S in a taxable transaction within the five-year predistribution period.

C. Device Limitation

A distribution does not qualify as tax-free under § 355 if it is used principally as a device for the distribution of the earnings and profits of P, S, or both corporations. § 355(a)(1)(B).

1. Introduction

Historically, the purpose of the device limitation was to prevent bailouts of corporate earnings at preferential capital gains rates where P distributed its S stock pro rata to the P shareholders, who then sold the P or S stock. When dividends and long-term capital gains are taxed at the same rates, the device limitation is much less significant. In the absence of a rate differential between dividends and capital gains, the device limitation serves primarily to prevent tax avoidance through a recovery of basis. Reg. § 1.355–2(d)(1). The regulations provide that the determination of whether a transaction was used principally as a device is a factual question, and they identify certain factors that constitute evidence of a device or a nondevice. Reg. § 1.355–2(d)(1). Section 355(a)(1)(B) provides that the "mere fact" that stock or securities of either P or S are sold subsequent to the distribution shall not be construed to mean that the distribution was used principally as a device unless the sale was negotiated or agreed upon prior to the distribution. The regulations nonetheless emphasize that subsequent sales of P or S stock may be evidence of a device. Reg. § 1.355–2(d)(2)(iii). See XII.C.2.b., at page 254, *infra*.

2. Device Factors

The presence of any of the following factors is evidence of a device, the strength of which depends on the facts and circumstances. Reg. § 1.355–2(d)(2)(i).

a. Pro Rata Distribution

Because a pro rata or substantially pro rata distribution of S stock presents the greatest potential for a bailout, pro rata distributions (e.g., spin-offs) are evidence of a device. Reg. § 1.355–2(d)(2)(ii).

b. Subsequent Sale or Exchange of P or S Stock

A sale or exchange of either P or S stock after the distribution is evidence of a device. The strength of the evidence increases as more stock of P or S is sold and decreases as more time passes between the distribution and subsequent sale. Reg. § 1.355–2(d)(2)(iii)(A). The strength of the evidence also depends upon whether the sale or exchange is pursuant to an arrangement negotiated or agreed upon before the distribution—i.e., if enforceable rights to buy or sell existed before the distribution or if the sale was discussed by the parties and was reasonably to be anticipated before the distribution. Reg. § 1.355–2(d)(2)(iii)(D). A subsequent sale that was prearranged is *substantial* evidence of a device, while other subsequent sales are only evidence. A subsequent exchange of P or S stock in a wholly tax-free reorganization, or a reorganization where only an insubstantial amount of gain is recognized, is not treated as a subsequent sale or exchange. Reg. § 1.355–2(d)(2)(iii)(E).

c. Nature and Use of Assets

Evidence of a device exists if either P or S holds assets, such as cash or portfolio securities, that are not used in or related to the reasonable needs of the qualifying active business. The strength of this evidence depends on all the facts and circumstances, including the ratio for P and S of the nonbusiness assets to the value of the active businesses. Reg. § 1.355–2(d)(2)(iv)(B). Evidence of a device also exists if the business of P or S is a "secondary business" that principally services the business of the other corporation and which can be sold without adversely affecting the business that it serves. Reg. § 1.355–2(d)(2)(iv)(C).

Example (1): P and its wholly owned subsidiary, S, each engage in the active conduct of a trade or business. P distributes its S stock pro rata to the P shareholders. Prior to the distribution, P transferred to S excess cash not reasonably related to the conduct of either business. The result of this transfer is that the percentage of unrelated liquid assets is substantially greater for S than for P. The transfer of cash by P to S in connection with the distribution is relatively strong evidence of a device. Reg. § 1.355–2(d)(4) Example (3). If P and S held liquid assets in amounts proportional to the values of their businesses after a transfer of cash by P to S, the transaction would be relatively weak evidence of device. Reg. § 1.355–2(d)(4) Example (2).

Example (2): P engages in the manufacture and sale of steel. Its wholly owned subsidiary, S, operates a coal mine solely to supply P's needs for coal. If P distributes the S stock pro rata to the P shareholders and S continues to supply coal exclusively to P, the relationship of P and S after the distribution constitutes evidence of a device if it can be demonstrated that the coal mine could be sold without adversely affecting P's steel business. Reg. § 1.355–2(d)(2)(iv)(C).

3. Nondevice Factors

The presence of any of the following factors is evidence of a "nondevice," the strength of which depends on the facts and circumstances. Reg. § 1.355–3(d)(3)(i).

a. Corporate Business Purpose

The corporate business purpose for P's distribution is evidence of a nondevice, the strength of which depends on all the facts and circumstances, including but not limited to:

1)   The importance of achieving the purpose to the success of the business.

2)   The extent to which the transaction is prompted by a person not having a proprietary interest in either corporation, or by other outside factors beyond the control of P.

3)   The immediacy of the conditions prompting the transaction. Reg. § 1.355–2(d)(3)(ii).

The stronger the evidence of device, the stronger the corporate business purpose must be to prevent the distribution from failing the device test. Id.

b. P Is Publicly Traded and Widely Held

The fact that P is publicly traded and has no shareholder that directly or indirectly owns more than 5% of any class of P stock is evidence of nondevice. Reg. § 1.355–2(d)(3)(iii).

c. Distributions to Domestic Corporate Shareholders

The fact that the stock of S is distributed to a domestic corporate distributee which, without § 355, would be entitled to an 65% or 100% dividends received deduction under § 243, is evidence of nondevice. Reg. § 1.355–2(d)(3)(iv). Note that distributions to corporate shareholders that would be entitled to only the 50% dividends received deduction are not evidence of nondevice.

4. Presumptive Nondevice Transactions

The following types of distributions "ordinarily" are not treated as a device notwithstanding the presence or absence of any device factors. Reg. § 1.355–2(d)(5)(i).

a. Absence of Earnings and Profits

A distribution in which P and S have neither accumulated nor current E & P as of the date of the distribution, taking into account the possibility that a distribution by P would create E & P if § 355 did not apply. Reg. § 1.355–2(d)(5)(ii).

b. § 302 or 303 Exchange Redemption

In the absence of § 355, the distribution would qualify, with respect to each distributee shareholder, as an exchange redemption under § 302(a) (see VII.C., at pages 131–139, *supra*) or a redemption to pay death taxes under § 303 (see VII.F., at pages 147–149, *supra*). Reg. § 1.355–2(d)(5)(iii), (iv). This nondevice presumption does not apply, however, if P distributes the stock of two or more subsidiaries and the distribution facilitates avoidance of the dividend provisions through the subsequent sale of stock of one subsidiary and the retention of stock of another. Reg. § 1.355–2(d)(5)(i).

D. Distribution of Control Requirement

P must distribute either all the S stock or securities that it holds immediately before the distribution or an amount of S stock constituting "control," as defined in § 368(c) (i.e., 80% of voting power and total shares of each class of nonvoting stock) and establish to the satisfaction of the Service that the retention of S stock or securities is not part of a plan having tax avoidance as one of its principal purposes. § 355(a)(1)(D). For this purpose, "stock" does not include "rights" to acquire stock. Reg. § 1.355–1(b). The stock does not have to be distributed pro rata among the shareholders to satisfy this requirement. § 355(a)(2)(A). Ordinarily, the business purpose for the division will require P to distribute all of the S stock or securities. Reg. § 1.355–2(e)(2). In practice, the Service has permitted P to retains stock or securities only when retention was required by loan agreements with outside lenders (e.g., the stock was collateral for a loan). Rev. Rul. 75–321, 1975–2 C.B. 123. A series of distributions of S stock over several years will not meet this requirement unless P was under a binding commitment to distribute all the S stock or securities from the outset. *Comm'r v. Gordon,* 391 U.S. 83, 88 S.Ct. 1517 (1968).

E. Business Purpose

To qualify as tax free under § 355, a corporate division must be motivated by a "real and substantial non-Federal tax purpose" germane to the business of P or S. Reg. § 1.355–2(b)(1)–(2). Business purpose is a judicially created requirement that is now incorporated in the regulations and published rulings. It is independent of the other requirements under § 355.

1. Background

The business purpose requirement is generally applicable to tax-free reorganizations but assumes its greatest significance when applied to corporate divisions. It originated in the case of *Gregory v. Helvering,* 293 U.S. 465, 55 S.Ct. 266 (1935), where the Supreme Court held that a transaction that literally satisfied the requirements for tax-free treatment did not qualify as a reorganization because it had "no business or corporate purpose" and was a "mere device" to bail out earnings at capital gains rates. *Gregory* also was one of the first articulations of the substance over form doctrine. See I.E.1., at page 53, *supra.*

2. Corporate Business Purpose

A § 355 distribution must be motivated by a corporate rather than a shareholder business purpose. In cases where a shareholder purpose is so nearly coextensive with a corporate business purpose as to preclude any distinction between them, the requirement will be satisfied. Reg. § 1.355–2(b)(2).

Example: P is a family farm that grows grain and raises livestock. The two principal shareholders are siblings who disagree over the future direction of the business. To permit these shareholders to devote their undivided attention to the businesses in which they are most involved and to further the estate planning goals of their parents, who are also shareholders, P wishes to divide the business into two separate corporations. Since the principal motivation for the transaction is to benefit the grain and livestock businesses, there is a valid corporate business purpose even though the division also promotes family harmony and facilitates personal estate planning goals of the shareholders. Rev. Rul. 2003–52, 2003–1 C.B. 960.

3. Substantial Nontax Business Purpose

A distribution must be motivated by a substantial non-federal tax purpose germane to the business of the distributing corporation. Reg. § 1.355–2(b)(2). The fact that qualifying a distribution under § 355 permits P to distribute S stock to P's shareholders without recognition of gain does not, in itself, present the potential for avoidance of federal taxes and is not considered in determining if a transaction has a business purpose. Rev. Rul. 2003–110, 2003–2 C.B. 1083. A distribution substantially motivated by a corporate business purpose satisfies the business purpose requirement even though a federal tax purpose also exists. Reg. § 1.355–2(b)(5) Example (8).

4. Examples of Valid Business Purposes

The regulations and published rulings include the following examples of valid business purposes:

a. To comply with a law or court decree requiring a division of P's businesses—e.g., an antitrust decree. Reg. § 1.355–2(b)(5) Example (1).

b. A split-up to resolve a shareholder dispute or to enable shareholders with different expertise to devote their undivided attention to separate parts of the business. Reg. § 1.355–2(b)(5) Example (2).

c. To enable a key employee to acquire an equity interest in either P or S. Reg. § 1.355–2(b)(5) Example (8); Rev. Rul. 88–34, 1988–1 C.B. 115.

d. To dispose of a business that is unwanted by a corporation seeking to acquire P. See, e.g., Rev. Rul. 70–434, 1970–2 C.B. 83.

e. To reduce state or local taxes provided that the transaction does not also result in a comparable or greater reduction of Federal taxes. Reg. §§ 1.355–2(b)(2), –2(b)(5) Examples (6) and (7).

f. To help P secure needed additional debt capital. Rev. Rul. 85–122, 1985–2 C.B. 118.

g. To improve corporate "fit and focus" by allowing senior management of a public company to concentrate on separate dissimilar businesses (e.g., paper products and software). Rev. Rul. 2003–74, 2003–2 C.B. 77.

h. To resolve disputes among senior management of a public company over capital allocation where internal competition for new capital has prevented separate businesses from pursuing development strategies that management of each business believes are appropriate. Rev. Rul. 2003–75, 2003–2 C.B. 79.

5. Business Purpose for Distribution

The business purpose requirement is not satisfied if P's goals could have been achieved through a nontaxable transaction that: (a) would not have required the distribution of S stock and (b) was neither impractical nor unduly expensive. Reg. § 1.355–2(b)(3).

Example: P actively conducts a candy business and a toy business. To protect the candy business from the risks of the toy business, P transfers the toy assets to a newly formed subsidiary, S, and distributes the S stock to the P shareholders. The business purpose requirement is not met because P could have achieved its purposes simply by transferring the toy assets to S. Reg. § 1.355–2(b)(5) Example (3).

6. Relationship to Device Limitation

The corporate business purpose for a transaction is used as evidence in determining whether the transaction was used principally as a device for the distribution of E & P. See XII.C.3.a., at page 255, *supra*.

F. Continuity of Interest

The § 355 regulations incorporate the judicial continuity of interest requirement by providing that, after P's distribution of S stock, one or more of the historic predistribution P shareholders must maintain, in the aggregate, continuity of interest in both P and S. Reg. § 1.355–2(c)(1). The regulations indicate that this requirement is met if one or more of the predistribution P shareholders own at least 50% (by value) of both P and S after the division, and it is likely that 40% ownership will suffice based on the continuity of interest regulations for acquisitive reorganizations. Some historic shareholders may own P stock and others may own S stock provided that, in the aggregate, the historic P shareholders maintain continuity in both P and S. Reg. § 1.355–2(c)(2) Examples (2) and (4).

Example (1): A and B each own 50% of the stock of P. P and its wholly owned subsidiary, S, each conduct an active business. P and S are equal in value. For a valid corporate business purpose, P distributes the S stock to B in exchange for all of his P stock, and A continues as the sole shareholder of P. The continuity of interest requirement is met because the prior owners of P (A and B), in the aggregate, retain sufficient continuity in P and S after the distribution. Reg. § 1.355–2(c) Example (1).

Example (2): Same as Example (1), except that pursuant to a plan to acquire a stock interest in P, unrelated individual C purchases all of A's stock in P before the distribution. After the distribution, C owns 100% of P and B owns 100% of S. The continuity of interest requirement is not met. Even though historic P shareholders (i.e., B) own 50% of the overall enterprise, they have not maintained a 50% interest in P. C is not considered a historic P shareholder because he acquired his P stock shortly before and in anticipation of the distribution. Reg. § 1.355–2(c) Example (3).

G. Distributions Involving Significant Cash and Investment Assets

1. Background

In a transaction known as a "cash-rich split-off," a corporation with a significant but not controlling interest in another corporation seeks to use § 355 to facilitate a sale of its investment for cash without paying any current tax. A related transaction is where a corporation combines a small (by value) active trade or business with significant investment assets, such as a large highly appreciated stock holding or real estate, in a new subsidiary and then spins off the subsidiary's stock to its shareholders with the hope of not paying any corporate-level tax while providing the shareholders with more value as a result of the division. These strategies, which are best illustrated by examples, have attracted the attention of Congress and the IRS.

Example (1): For more than five years, Investor Corp. ("I") has owned a highly appreciated 30% interest in Distributing Corp. ("D"). I wishes to sell its D stock for cash without paying any current tax, and D wishes to repurchase some of its stock. D transfers a small five-year active business and a large amount of cash to Controlled Corp. ("C"), a new subsidiary, in exchange for all of the C stock. D then redeems I's D stock in a transaction intended to qualify under § 355 by distributing its C stock to I, and I then liquidates C in a tax-free liquidation of a subsidiary under § 332. Prior to the enactment of § 355(g), discussed below, the split-off likely qualified under § 355. The transaction did not violate the active trade or business test because historically that test has not required a particular active business with a five-year history to constitute any minimum percentage (by value) of either the distributing or controlled corporation. The device test was not violated because I completely terminated its interest in D.

Example (2): Distributing Corp. ("D") is a publicly traded company which has conducted several active trades or businesses for more than five years and also owns 30% of the stock of Bigco, Inc. ("B"). D contributes one of its small active businesses (value—$10x) and its Bigco stock (value—$1,000x; basis—$1x) to Controlled Corp. ("C") in exchange for all of C's common stock and then D distributes the C stock to its shareholders. D's goal is to avoid corporate-level tax on the distribution of its Bigco stock by qualifying the transaction under § 355.

2. Denial of Tax-Free Treatment to Certain Cash-Rich Split-offs

a. General Rule

Section 355(g) denies tax-free treatment to certain divisions involving "disqualified investment corporations." A distribution does not qualify under § 355 if: (1) either the distributing or controlled corporation is, immediately after the transaction, a "disqualified investment corporation," and (2) any person holds, immediately after the transaction, a 50% or greater interest (measured by voting power and value) in any disqualified investment corporation if such person did not hold such an interest in such a corporation immediately before the transaction. § 355(g)(1).

b. Disqualified Investment Corporation Defined

A corporation is a "disqualified investment corporation" if the fair market value of its "investment assets" is two-thirds or more of the fair market value of all its assets. § 355(g)(2)(A)(i). Investment assets include cash, stock or securities, partnership interests, debt instruments, options, foreign currency, and similar liquid financial assets. § 355(g)(2)(B)(i).

c. Some Cash-Rich Split-offs Still Viable

Despite § 355(g), somewhat less aggressive cash-rich split-offs are still viable if neither the distributing nor controlled corporations are "disqualified"—i.e., if the fair market value of their cash and other liquid assets is less than two-thirds of the value of their assets.

3. Proposed Regulations

a. In General

As noted above, some cash-rich split-offs are not disqualified by § 355(g), which also does not apply to *spin-offs* where the distributing or controlled corporation ends up owning investment assets (e.g., cash, stock, real estate) having substantial value relative to its business assets. The IRS is concerned that these transactions may violate the active trade or business requirement, present evidence of a device for distribution of earnings and profits, or lack an adequate business purpose. To address these concerns, the IRS has issued proposed regulations that would: (1) add a new active business requirement, and (2) modify the device factors.

b. Active Business Requirement

The proposed regulations provide that, for the active trade or business requirements of § 355(a)(1)(C) and (b) to be satisfied with respect to a distribution, a five-year-active-business percentage test must be met. Basically, the percentage determined by dividing the fair market value of the five-year-active-business assets by the fair market value of total assets for both the distributing corporation and the controlled corporation must be at least 5%. Prop. Reg. § 1.355–9(b). Five-year-active-business assets are a corporation's gross assets used in a five-year-active business and include reasonable amounts of cash and cash equivalents held for working capital and assets required to be held to provide for exigencies or for regulatory purposes. Prop. Reg. § 1.355–9(a)(3). See XII.B.3., at page 248, *supra*, for a related no ruling policy regarding whether this type of transaction satisfies the active trade or business test.

c. Nature and Use of Assets Device Factor

In general, device potential exists under the proposed regulations if the distributing or controlled corporation owns a large percentage of assets not used in business operations compared to total assets, or if the distributing corporation and controlled corporation's percentages of these assets differ substantially. In making those determinations, the proposed regulations focus on the "business assets" and "nonbusiness assets" of the corporations. Business assets are the gross assets used in a business, including reasonable amounts of cash and cash equivalents held for working capital and assets required (by binding commitment or legal requirements) to be held to provide for exigencies related to a business or for regulatory purposes with respect to a business. Nonbusiness assets are the corporation's gross assets that are not business assets. The larger the percentage of nonbusiness assets of either corporation, the stronger the evidence of device. If neither the distributing nor the controlled corporation has nonbusiness assets that comprise 20% or more of its total assets, the ownership of nonbusiness assets ordinarily would not be evidence of device. Prop. Reg. § 1.355–2(d)(2)(iv)(C)(1). A difference in the nonbusiness asset percentages (nonbusiness assets divided by total assets) for the distributing corporation and controlled corporation ordinarily would not be evidence of device if such difference is less than 10%, or the distribution is not pro rata and the difference is attributable to a need to equalize the value of the controlled corporation stock and securities distributed and the consideration exchanged therefore by the distributees. Prop. Reg. § 1.355–2(d)(2)(iv)(C)(2).

d.   Corporate Business Purpose as Evidence of Nondevice

The proposed regulations also revise the nondevice factor which relates to corporate business purpose for a transaction as evidence of nondevice. Evidence of a device presented by ownership of nonbusiness assets can be outweighed by a corporate business purpose for the ownership. Evidence of device presented by a difference between nonbusiness asset percentages of the distributing and controlled corporations can be outweighed by a corporate business purpose for the difference. Under the change, a corporate business purpose that relates to a separation of nonbusiness assets from one or more businesses or from business assets would not be evidence of nondevice, unless the business purpose involves an exigency that requires an investment or other use of the nonbusiness assets in a business. Prop. Reg. § 1.355–2(d)(3)(ii). The proposed regulations illustrate this rule with an example where there is a nonproportionate division of nonbusiness assets because the lease of one corporation will expire in six months and it retains the nonbusiness assets to purchase a building for relocation. The need to buy the building is an exigency which is a business purpose and evidence of a nondevice. Prop. Reg. § 1.355–2(d)(4) Example 4.

e.   Per Se Device Test

The proposed regulations also add a two-pronged per se device test. The first prong is satisfied if either the distributing or controlled corporation has a nonbusiness asset percentage (nonbusiness assets divided by total assets) of $66^{2}/_{3}\%$ or more. Also, if $66^{2}/_{3}\%$ or more of the total assets of either corporation consist of nonbusiness assets, a strong device potential exists. Prop. Reg. § 1.355–2(d)(5)(iii)(A). The second prong compares the nonbusiness percentages of the distributing and controlled corporations. The second prong is satisfied if the nonbusiness percentage (1) of one corporation is $66^{2}/_{3}\%$ or more but less than 80%, and the other's is less than 30%, (2) of one corporation is 80% or more but less than 90%, and the other's is less than 40%, or (3) of one corporation is more than 90%, and the other's is less than 50%. Prop. Reg. § 1.355–2(d)(5)(iii)(B). If the per se test is not satisfied the general facts and circumstances test applies to determine if the transaction was a device. The only exceptions to this per se device rule are if the distribution is to a corporate distributee entitled to a dividends received deduction or is a transaction ordinarily not considered to be a device. Prop. Reg. § 1.355–2(d)(5)(i).

H. Real Estate Investment Trusts

1. Background

During the 2010s, companies such as hotels, casinos, restaurants and shopping malls that owned valuable real estate came under pressure from activist investors to "unlock" the value of their assets by spinning off the real estate into a separate publicly traded real estate investment trust ("REIT"). The economics of the transaction depended on it qualifying as tax-free under § 355. The operating business often would lease back the real estate, and the rental income paid to the REIT would pass through to its shareholders without incurring corporate-level tax. (Under a special tax regime, REITs are not subject to corporate tax if they pass through most of their income to shareholders.) The proposed regulations addressing the active trade or business requirement and the device prohibition potentially apply to transactions involving REITs. See XII.G.3, at page 260, supra.

2. Restrictions on Tax-Free Spin-offs

To curb tax-free REIT spin-offs, Congress enacted legislation providing that a transaction will not qualify under § 355 if either the distributing or controlled corporation is a REIT. § 355(h)(1). If a corporation that is not a REIT was a distributing or controlled corporation in a qualified § 355 distribution, it is not eligible to elect tax treatment under the special REIT regime for any taxable year beginning before the end of the 10-year period beginning on the date of the distribution. § 856(c)(8).

3. Exceptions

The general disqualification rule does not apply if, immediately after the distribution, both the distributing and the controlled corporation are REITS or in a specialized situation involving a spin-off of a taxable REIT subsidiary. § 355(h)(2).

I. Tax Treatment of the Parties to a Corporate Division

1. Shareholders and Security Holders

a. No Boot Received

With exceptions noted below, P's shareholders and security holders generally do not recognize gain or loss on the receipt of S stock or securities if the requirements of § 355 are met. § 355(a)(1). The shareholders allocate their old basis in the P stock between the P and S stock in proportion to their relative fair market values, and they may tack the holding period of their P stock to the S stock received from P. Shareholders who receive S stock in exchange for all their P stock (e.g., in a split-up) take a basis in the new S stock equal to the basis in their old P stock. §§ 358(a); 1223(1).

Example: A is the sole shareholder of P and has a $12,000 basis in her P stock. P distributes all the stock of its 100% subsidiary, S, to A in a spin-off that qualifies under § 355. After the distribution, the fair market values of A's P and S stock were $40,000 and $20,000, respectively. A allocates her $12,000 basis as follows: ⅔ ($8,000) to the P stock and ⅓ ($4,000) to the S stock.

b. Boot Received

1) Boot Defined

For purposes of § 355 transactions, boot includes any property other than S stock or securities (e.g., cash or short-term debt obligations), S securities (e.g., debt obligations with a longer term) to the extent that their principal amount exceeds the principal amount of any securities surrendered, and any stock of S (known as "hot stock") that was acquired by P (or a subsidiary of P) in a taxable transaction within the five-year period preceding the distribution. §§ 355(a)(3)(B); 356(a), (b), (d)(2)(C). For purposes of measuring boot, stock rights generally are considered "securities" with a zero principal value. Reg. § 1.355–1(c). "Hot stock" is not boot under § 355(a)(3)(B), however, in the case of any acquisition of the stock of S in the five years prior to the distribution if S becomes a member of P's separate affiliated group (i.e., where P owns at least 80% of the voting power and value of S) at any time after the stock is acquired and before it is distributed. Reg. § 1.355–2(g)(2)(i). The purpose of this relief provision is to harmonize the treatment of boot with the more liberal treatment of separate affiliated groups under the active trade or business test. Boot also may include nonqualified preferred stock, as defined in § 351(g). See IV.B.3.b., at page 72, *supra*.

Example (1): For more than five years, P has owned 80% of the voting power and 80% of the total number of shares of all other classes of stock of S (i.e., § 368(c) control) but not 80% of the *value* of S (so it does not have § 1504(a)(2) control). In Year 6, P purchases additional S stock from A but it still does not own 80% or more of the value of S. D distributes all its S stock to its shareholders within five years of the Year 6 purchase in a transaction that meets all the requirements of § 355. The S stock purchased in Year 6 is boot under § 355(a)(3)(B). Reg. § 1.355–2(g)(5) Example 1.

Example (2): Same as Example 1, except P's total ownership of S after the Year 6 purchase causes P to own more than 80% of the value of S. The S stock purchased in Year 6 is not boot because S became a member of P's separate affiliated group at the time of that purchase. Reg. § 1.355–2(g)(5) Example 2.

2) Spin-offs

In a spin-off, the receipt of boot is treated as a § 301 distribution (without regard to the shareholder's realized gain) and is thus a dividend to the extent of P's E & P. Any remaining portion of the distribution first reduces the shareholder's basis in his P stock and then is treated as capital gain under the rules in § 301(c). § 356(b).

3) Split-offs and Split-ups

A P shareholder who receives boot in a split-off or split-up recognizes her realized gain to the extent of the boot. § 356(a)(1). If the exchange has "the effect of the distribution of a dividend," the recognized gain is a dividend to the extent of the shareholder's ratable share of P's accumulated E & P. § 356(a)(2). Any remaining recognized gain is gain from an exchange of property—usually capital gain. Reg. § 1.356–1(b)(2). Dividend equivalence is tested by applying § 302 principles (reduction of proportionate interest) prior to the exchange by treating the recipient shareholder as having received the boot in redemption of an amount of P stock equal to the value of the boot and by then comparing the shareholder's interest in P before the exchange with the interest the shareholder would have retained if she had surrendered only an amount of P stock equal in value to the boot. Rev. Rul. 93–62, 1993–2 C.B. 118. In no event may loss be recognized. § 356(c).

Example: A owns 100 shares of P stock with a fair market value of $1,000 ($10 per share) and a basis of $200 ($2 per share). P has 1,000 shares of stock outstanding. In a split-off that qualifies under § 355, P distributes all the stock in its 100% subsidiary, S (value—$500) and $250 cash in redemption of 75 shares of A's P stock. A recognizes $250 of gain on the distribution. To determine if that gain is a dividend, it is assumed that P only distributed $250 to A in redemption of 25 P shares. Under this analysis, A owned 10% of P ($100/1000$ shares) before and 7.7% ($75/975$ shares) after the redemption. The hypothetical redemption qualifies as substantially disproportionate under § 302(b)(2) and A's $250 gain is capital gain.

4) Basis and Holding Period

The aggregate basis of the P and S stock (or, in a split-up, the S-1 and S-2 stock) after a corporate division is the same as the basis of the shareholder's P stock (prior to the exchange), reduced by the cash and the fair market value of any boot property received, and increased by the shareholder's recognized gain (including any dividend income). That amount is then allocated between the P and S stock (or, in a split-up, the S-1 and S-2 stock) in proportion to their relative fair market values. § 358(b)(2), (c); Reg. § 1.358–2. If the "old" P stock was acquired at different times or for different prices, proposed regulations would require the distributee shareholders to trace their bases in the various blocks of old stock rather than using an average basis in determining the basis of the "new" S stock. If tracing is impossible, the shareholder may designate how the § 358 basis is to be allocated among the different lots. Prop. Reg. § 1.358–2(a)(2)(i), –2(c) Example 7. The S stock takes a tacked holding period. § 1223(1). The boot received takes a fair market value basis, and its holding period begins on the date of the exchange. § 358(a)(2).

2. The Distributing Corporation

a. Distribution Preceded by Reorganization

1) P's Formation of S in Type D Reorganization

In general, P does not recognize gain or loss on the transfer of assets to S solely in exchange for stock or securities of S in a divisive Type D reorganization (see XII.A.2., at page 246, *supra*). § 361(a). P does recognize gain, however, if the liabilities assumed by S exceed the aggregate adjusted basis of the assets transferred to it by P, or if it otherwise receives boot that is not distributed to shareholders, security holders or creditors as part of the reorganization plan. § 361(b). The amount of cash and property that P may distribute to creditors without gain recognition is limited to the aggregate adjusted basis of the assets contributed to S in the Type D reorganization. § 361(b)(3).

2) P's Distribution of Qualified and Other Property

P does not recognize gain when it distributes S stock or S debt obligations ("qualified property") to P shareholders. § 361(c)(1), (2). P recognizes gain, however, on a distribution of appreciated boot in a § 355 transaction. § 361(c)(2). In no event may P recognize loss.

b. Distribution Not Preceded by Reorganization

If a § 355 distribution is not preceded by a reorganization—e.g., where S is not a newly formed subsidiary of P—P recognizes no gain or loss on a distribution of S stock or securities ("qualified property") to the P shareholders. P recognizes gain on a distribution of property other than S stock or securities. § 355(c).

c. Certain Disqualified Distributions

The nonrecognition rules of §§ 355(c) and 361(c) do not apply to a "disqualified distribution" of S stock or securities. § 355(d)(1). This rule is designed to prevent the use of § 355 to facilitate a tax-free sale of part of a business following a corporate takeover.

1) Disqualified Distribution

A distribution is "disqualified" if, immediately after the distribution, any person holds "disqualified stock" in either P or any controlled subsidiary of P that constitutes a 50% or greater interest (measured by voting power or value) in that corporation. § 355(d)(2). Aggregation rules are used in applying the 50% ownership test. § 355(d)(7), (8). For example, two or more otherwise unrelated persons who act pursuant to a plan to acquire P or S stock are treated as a single person for purposes of § 355(d). § 355(d)(7)(B). The § 318 attribution rules also apply, as modified to provide that stock is attributed from a corporation to 10% (rather than 50%) shareholders. § 355(d)(8).

2) Disqualified Stock

"Disqualified stock" is any stock in either P or any controlled subsidiary of P that is acquired by purchase during the five-year period preceding the distribution. A "purchase" is a transaction where the acquirer takes a cost basis in the stock of P or P's subsidiary. Stock with a § 1014 date-of-death basis or a transferred basis is generally not acquired by purchase. § 355(d)(5)(A). The five-year holding period is suspended whenever the holder's risk of loss is substantially diminished (e.g., by an option or special class of stock). § 355(d)(6).

Example: T Corp. has actively conducted four distinct businesses (of equal size) for more than five years through wholly owned subsidiaries. A, B, C and D are four unrelated corporations, each of which wishes to acquire one of the T subsidiaries. A, B, C and D each acquires 25% of T's stock and, after waiting a sufficient time to establish their status as historic T shareholders for continuity of interest purposes (but before five years), T distributes 100% of the stock of a subsidiary to A, B, C and D, respectively, in exchange for their T stock. The distribution is "disqualified" because the distributees each hold "disqualified stock" representing a 100% interest in the distributed subsidiary. Although the split-up may qualify as tax-free to the distributee shareholders, T recognizes gain on the distribution of the stock of its subsidiaries.

d. § 355 Distributions Related to Acquisition Plan

The nonrecognition rules of §§ 355(c) and 361(c) do not apply to certain distributions of S stock or securities that are made in connection with related acquisitions of one or more businesses controlled by P. § 355(e). See XII.J.3., at pages 267–269, *infra*.

e. Tax Attributes

All of P's tax attributes, except E & P, stay with P following a § 355 distribution even if the division is pursuant to a reorganization plan. Section 381 does not apply to divisive Type D reorganizations. (See XIII.B.3., at page 274, *infra*). All of P's tax attributes thus disappear when P liquidates following a split-up. If a § 355 distribution is part of a Type D reorganization, P's E & P are allocated between P and S in proportion to the relative fair market value of the assets held by each corporation after the distribution. Reg. § 1.312–10(a). Different rules may apply if P and S file a consolidated return.

J. Corporate Division Combined with Tax-Free Reorganization

1. Background

Corporate divisions historically have been used to facilitate an acquisition of one of several corporate businesses in a tax efficient manner. For example, one corporation ("P") operating two separate businesses as divisions would contribute the assets of the unwanted business to a newly created subsidiary ("S") and spin off the stock of S prior to a tax-free acquisition of P's remaining business. Or P would retain direct ownership of the unwanted business, transfer the wanted assets to S, and spin off the S stock to the P shareholders to set the stage for X's acquisition of S in a reorganization. The tax consequences of these transactions often depended on the form used by the parties. Under current law, § 355 distributions made in conjunction with an attempted tax-free acquisition of part of P's business may cause P (but not necessarily its shareholders) to recognize gain under § 355(e). It is possible that the same transaction may be subject to both § 355(d) and § 355(e). If so, § 355(d) takes precedence. § 355(e)(2)(D). Section 355(e) was enacted to prevent avoidance of corporate-level gain on the sale of part of a business. Its reach is very broad and it may extend to transactions that previously were viewed as appropriate for tax-free treatment. The Service, however, has issued regulations narrowing the scope of § 355(e).

2. Historical Opportunities and Pitfalls

a. The *Morris Trust* Technique

Prior to enactment of § 355(e), the preferred planning technique was to spin-off the unwanted business and then transfer the wanted business in a tax-free Type A or Type B reorganization. If both businesses satisfied the active trade or business test and the other requirements of §§ 355 and 368 were met, the spin-off was tax-free to the distributing corporation and its shareholders under § 355, and the acquisition qualified as tax-free under § 368. *Comm'r v. Morris Trust*, 367 F.2d 794 (4th Cir.1966); Rev. Rul. 70–434, 1970–2 C.B. 83.

b. Historical Pitfalls

A spin-off of unwanted assets followed by a Type C reorganization or triangular merger was likely to be treated as an integrated transaction, with the result that the unwanted assets were considered in determining whether P transferred substantially all of its assets. If the unwanted assets were a substantial part of P's business, the acquisition did not qualify as a reorganization, and the spin-off probably was not tax-free under § 355. *Helvering v. Elkhorn Coal Co.*, 95 F.2d 732 (4th Cir.1937), cert. denied, 305 U.S. 605, 59 S.Ct. 65 (1938). If the transaction was structured as a spin-off of the wanted business followed by an attempted tax-free acquisition of that business and the steps were prearranged, the Service historically took the position that neither the spin-off nor the reorganization qualified for tax-free treatment. Rev. Rul. 70–225, 1970–1 C.B. 80. In taking that position, the Service applied the step transaction doctrine and treated the transaction as if the distributing corporation exchanged the stock of the controlled subsidiary for stock of the acquiring corporation and then distributed the acquiring corporation stock to its shareholders. This "recasting" caused the distribution to fail to qualify under § 355 because the distributing corporation was not in "control" of the acquiring corporation at the time of the deemed distribution. Rev. Rul. 96–30, 1996–1 C.B. 36, obsoleted by Rev. Rul. 98–27, 1998–1 C.B. 1159.

c. IRS Changes of Position

1) § 355 Qualification

In a significant about face, the Service retreated from its application of the step transaction doctrine to deny § 355 treatment because of postdistribution "restructurings" or acquisitions of the controlled subsidiary. Rev. Rul. 98–27, 1998–1 C.B. 1159. It now will patrol any abuse from these transactions through the device limitation (at the shareholder level) and § 355(e) (at the corporate level).

2) Qualification of Acquisitive Reorganization

The Service has ruled that P's transfer of wanted business assets to a newly formed subsidiary, S, followed by P's distribution of the S stock to its shareholders and the acquisition of S's assets in exchange for voting stock of an unrelated acquiring corporation will not violate the "substantially all of the properties" requirement. The asset acquisition thus qualifies as a Type C reorganization. But an acquisition of those same assets from P after P's spin off of the unwanted assets still does not qualify as a Type C reorganization. Rev. Rul. 2003–79, 2003–2 C.B. 80.

3. Corporate-Level Gain Recognition: § 355(e)

a. Recognition of Gain by Distributing Corporation

Section 355(e) requires recognition of gain by the distributing corporation (but not the distributee shareholder) on a distribution of appreciated stock or securities in a transaction that otherwise qualifies as a tax-free corporate division. Specifically, the distributing (parent) corporation must recognize gain as if it had sold the stock of the distributed controlled subsidiary for its fair market value on the date of the distribution if, as part of a "plan" or series of related transactions, one or more persons acquires (directly or indirectly) a 50% or greater interest in either the distributing or controlled corporation within two years before or after the distribution. § 355(e)(1), (2). Technically, this result is achieved by excluding the stock or securities in the distributed controlled subsidiary from the definition of "qualified property" for purposes of § 355(c)(2) or § 361(c)(2), causing gain to be recognized under § 311(b). Neither the distributing nor controlled corporations may adjust the basis of their assets or stock to reflect the recognition of gain under § 355(e).

b. Plan Requirement

Section 355(e) applies only if the transaction is part of a "plan" or series of related transactions to acquire 50% or more of the target corporation. Whether or not a "plan" exists is based on all the facts and circumstances, subject to the safe harbors and factors summarized below. Reg. § 1.355–7(b)(1). In general, in the case of an acquisition not involving a public offering after a distribution, the distribution will be treated as part of a "plan" only if there was an agreement, understanding, arrangement, or substantial negotiations regarding the acquisition (collectively referred to below as "Talks") at some time during the two-year period ending on the date of the distribution. Reg. § 1.355–7(b)(2). If the distribution is motivated in whole or substantial part by a corporate business purpose other than to facilitate the acquisition and it would have occurred at approximately the same time and in a similar form regardless of whether the acquisition was effected, the taxpayer has a better chance of establishing that a "plan" does not exist. Id.

c. Two-Year Presumption

If one or more persons directly or indirectly acquire a 50% or greater interest in the distributing corporation or any controlled corporation during the four-year period beginning two years before the distribution, the acquisition is presumed to be pursuant to a plan unless the taxpayer establishes that such a plan did not exist. § 355(e)(2)(B).

d. Rebutting the Presumption

1) Plan and Nonplan Factors

In the absence of a safe harbor, the regulations contain an extensive nonexclusive list of plan and nonplan factors to consider in making the facts and circumstances determination. Examples of "plan factors" include Talks during the two-year period ending on the date of the distribution and a business purpose to facilitate the acquisition. Reg. § 1.355–7(b)(3). Examples of "nonplan factors" include unexpected changes in market or business conditions occurring after the distribution that influenced the acquisition and the absence of Talks with the acquiring corporation during the two-year period ending on the date of the distribution. Reg. § 1.355–7(b)(4).

2) Safe Harbors

If any one of nine safe harbors in the regulations is met, the existence of a plan is negated without further inquiry. A key factor under most of the safe harbors is whether there were Talks concerning an acquisition during a specified time period. See Reg. § 1.355–7(d).

e. Examples

Example (1): T Corp. manufactures video games. Its wholly owned subsidiary, S Corp., manufactures parts for wireless phones. T Corp. is relatively small in its industry. T wants to combine with P Corp., a large video game company. T and P begin negotiating for P to acquire T, but P is not interested in acquiring S. To facilitate its acquisition, T agrees to distribute all of its S stock pro rata to its shareholders before the acquisition. Prior to this distribution, T and P enter into a contract for T to merge into P. One month thereafter, T distributes the S stock and, the next day, T's merger into P is completed, with T shareholders receiving P stock (representing less than 50% of P's outstanding stock) in the merger. Under the regulations, the agreement between T and P regarding the acquisition and the fact that the distribution was motivated by a business purpose to facilitate the merger are "plan factors." Since there are no "nonplan factors," the distribution of S and the merger of T into P are considered part of a plan. As a result, T will recognize gain on the distribution of its S stock. Reg. § 1.355–7(j) Example 1. If the requirements of §§ 355 and 368 are met, however, T's shareholders will not recognize gain on the spin-off or the merger.

Example (2): Same as Example (1), except after the merger of T into P, T's former shareholders own more than 50% of P. Section 355(e) would not apply to this fact pattern because a 50% interest in T or S was not acquired in the transaction.

Example (3): Same as Example (1), except T's spin-off of S was motivated by a corporate business purpose unrelated to the acquisition of T, and the acquisition occurred more than six months after the distribution, and there were no Talks concerning the acquisition of T during the one-year period before and six-month period after the distribution. This fact pattern would be covered by Safe Harbor I in the regulations and thus the distribution and acquisition will not be considered part of a plan. Reg. § 1.355–7(d)(1).

K. Review Questions

1. A tax-free corporate division under § 355 must be pursuant to a Type D reorganization plan. True or False?

2. P Corp. has been engaged in two separate businesses as divisions for more than five years. It wishes to separate the assets of one business from the risks and liabilities of the other. Will this constitute a sufficient corporate business purpose for a spin-off under § 355?

3. Consider whether the following distributions qualify under the active business test:

   (a) P Corp. has been engaged in a manufacturing business for six years. It distributes the stock of its 100% subsidiary, S Corp., which has owned investment securities for seven years.

   (b) P Corp. has been engaged in the business of manufacturing men's pants for 20 years. It wishes to distribute the stock of a hat business that it started two years ago.

   (c) P Corp. has been engaged in the newspaper business for 10 years. Three years ago, in a Type B reorganization, it acquired the stock of a corporation that has operated a radio station for 15 years.

4. Federal law requires that P Corp., a television station, divest itself of its 100% subsidiary, S Corp., which publishes a newspaper. Under what circumstances will a spin-off of S Corp., followed by a sale of the S Corp. stock by its new shareholders constitute a forbidden device to distribute earnings and profits for purposes of § 355?

5. A is the sole shareholder of P Corp. and has a $100,000 basis in his P stock. P Corp. has a $40,000 basis in the stock of its 100% subsidiary, S Corp. In a spin-off that qualifies under § 355, P Corp. distributes the stock of S Corp. to A. After the distribution, the fair market value of the P stock is $600,000 and the fair market value of the S stock is $200,000. What are the tax consequences of the transaction to both corporations and to A?

6. P Corporation has 1,000 shares of common stock (its only class) outstanding. Each share has a fair market value of $1. A, one of P's five unrelated individual shareholders, owns 400 shares of P stock. P owns all the outstanding stock of S. The S stock has a total fair market value of $200. P distributes all the S stock plus $200 cash to A in exchange for all of A's P stock. But for the receipt of the cash, the exchange satisfies the requirements of § 355. What are the tax consequences of the exchange to A?

Chapter XIII

Carryovers of Corporate Tax Attributes

■ ANALYSIS

A. Introduction

The Code contains a comprehensive set of rules governing the impact of various corporate transactions, such as reorganizations, on the tax attributes (earnings and profits, net operating losses, etc.) of a target corporation. In general, § 381(a) provides that in an acquisition of a target's assets by another corporation in a liquidation under § 332 or in a reorganization (other than a Type B or E reorganization), the acquiring corporation "shall succeed to and take into account" the target's tax attributes.

Carryovers of the target's tax attributes are limited by rules in § 381 and by the provisions of § 382, § 383, § 384, § 269 and the rules governing consolidated tax returns. The purpose of these limitations is to prevent profitable corporations from acquiring loss corporations in order to use the loss corporation's earnings and profits deficit and net operating losses to offset its positive earnings and profits account and future taxable income.

B. Operation of § 381

1. In General

Section 381(a) provides for the carryover of corporate tax attributes specified in § 381(c) on a liquidation of a controlled subsidiary under § 332 and on Type A, Type C and Type F reorganizations and nondivisive Type D and Type G reorganizations. These tax attributes are transferred to the parent or acquiring corporation as of the close of the day of distribution or transfer of assets. The principal carryover items are earnings and profits and net operating losses. Other items specified in § 381(c) include capital loss carryovers, accounting methods, inventories and depreciation methods. The list of items specified in § 381(c) is not exclusive, and some items not listed may carry over under principles developed in the case law.

The general § 381 carryover rules do not apply to Type B and Type E reorganizations (and presumably reverse triangular reorganizations) because in those transactions the target or recapitalized corporation remains in existence and retains all of its tax attributes.

Only a single corporation may be an "acquiring corporation" with respect to the tax attributes governed by § 381. In a § 332 liquidation, the corporation that acquires the assets of a subsidiary is the acquiring corporation. In a Type A, C, D, F, or G reorganization, the acquiring corporation is the corporation that directly acquires the transferred assets even if it ultimately retains none of them, such as where it drops down all or part of the assets to a controlled subsidiary. Reg. § 1.381(a)–1(b)(2)(i).

Example: X Co. acquires all the assets of Z Co in a Type C reorganization. As part of the reorganization, X Co. transfers all of the assets acquired from Z Co. to Y Co., its wholly owned subsidiary. X Co. is the acquiring corporation for purposes of § 381. Reg. § 1.381(a)–1(b)(2)(ii) Example 2.

2. § 381 Limitations on Carryovers

a. Earnings and Profits (E & P) Deficits

Section 381(c)(2)(B) provides that if the acquiring corporation or the target has an E & P deficit, the deficit only may offset E & P accumulated after the transfer and not preacquisition E & P. For purposes of this rule, the E & P of the acquiring corporation in the year of the acquisition are deemed to accumulate pro rata over the year.

Example (1):   P acquires T on December 31, Year 1, in a Type C reorganization. At the time of the acquisition, P has $10,000 of accumulated E & P and T has a $30,000 E & P deficit.

Assume that in Year 2 the combined P has $5,000 of current E & P and it distributes $5,000 to its shareholders. The $5,000 distribution is a dividend since it is out of current E & P. § 316(a)(2). The distribution would eliminate P's $5,000 of current E & P and it would begin Year 3 with $10,000 of accumulated E & P and T's $30,000 preacquisition deficit.

Assume that in Year 2 the combined P has $5,000 of current E & P and makes no distributions to its shareholders. In that case, T's preacquisition deficit may offset the $5,000 of postacquisition accumulated E & P. Beginning in Year 3, P would have $10,000 of accumulated E & P and $25,000 of T's preacquisition deficit.

Example (2):   T merges into P midway through the current year. For the year of the merger, T has a $20,000 E & P deficit and P has $30,000 of current E & P. Under § 381(b)(2)(B), P has $15,000 of preacquisition accumulated E & P and $15,000 of postacquisition E & P. T's deficit can be used to eliminate the $15,000 of postacquisition E & P and the combined P will begin the next year with $15,000 of preacquisition accumulated E & P and $5,000 of T's preacquisition deficit.

b. Net Operating Losses

Under § 172, a corporation's net operating losses ("NOLs") generally may be used to offset 80% of taxable income by being carried forward to subsequent taxable years. § 172(b)(1)(A)(ii). Two-year carrybacks are permitted in the case of farming losses and losses of property and casualty insurance companies. § 172(b)(1)(B) & (C). Prior to 2018, an NOL generally would offset taxable income without limitation and could be carried back two years and carried forward 20 years. Various other special carryback rules also applied prior to 2018. The revised rules regarding NOLs apply to taxable years beginning after 2017.

Under § 381(c)(1), a target's NOLs carry over to an acquiring corporation, but only to taxable years ending after the acquisition date. In the year of the acquisition, the acquiring corporation may deduct an NOL inherited from the target only against the portion of its income (determined on a per day basis) attributable to the postacquisition period. Note that while § 381 may permit the carryover of a target's NOLs to an acquiring corporation, other Code sections (primarily § 382) may limit the acquiring corporation's use of those NOLs.

If a loss corporation with NOLs acquires a profitable corporation, § 381 and other Code sections may limit the loss corporation's ability to use preacquisition NOLs against taxable income generated by the profitable business. Section 381(b)(3) provides that, except in the case of Type B, E and F reorganizations, an acquiring corporation cannot carry back an NOL incurred after the acquisition to a taxable year of the profitable target. As a result of the general prohibition on NOL carrybacks in § 172, the restriction on carrybacks in § 381(b)(3) should rarely apply.

3. Carryovers in Divisive Reorganizations

Section 381 does not apply to divisive reorganizations. In general, the tax attributes of the distributing corporation are not altered by the transaction except in the case of a split-up, where the tax attributes of the distributing corporation do not survive its liquidation. See XII.I.2.e., at page 266, *supra*, for further details.

C. Limitations on Carryovers of Corporate Tax Attributes

1. Introduction

Without restrictions, § 381 would allow any acquiring corporation to use a target corporation's NOLs to offset its future income. Congress has long sought to prevent the "trafficking in loss corporations" which would result from unlimited carryforward of a target's NOLs. The principal limitation is in § 382, which restricts the use of NOL carryforwards. Other sections also potentially limit the carryforward of capital losses, deductions, credits, and other tax allowances. See, e.g., § 383.

2. Limitation on Net Operating Loss Carryforwards: § 382

Section 382 limits the use of a loss corporation's NOL carryforwards if there is a substantial change in ownership of the corporation. If the new corporation does not continue the business enterprise of the old loss corporation for at least two years after an "ownership change," the preacquisition NOLs are disallowed. § 382(c). If the continuity of business requirement is met, the taxable income permitted to be offset by preacquisition NOLs is limited to the value of the loss corporation multiplied by the "long-term tax-exempt rate." § 382(b). The theory of this limitation is that after a substantial ownership change the preacquisition NOLs should only be permitted to offset the future income of the business which generated the losses. That income figure is arbitrarily determined by multiplying the fair market value of the old loss business by an assumed rate of return that is periodically adjusted.

a. Ownership Change Requirement

1) In General

The § 382 limitation is triggered only after an "ownership change" occurs with respect to a corporation that has net operating loss carryovers. § 382(a), (g), (k)(3). An "ownership change" takes place if, immediately after any "owner shift involving a 5-percent shareholder" or an "equity structure shift," the percentage of stock of a loss corporation owned by one or more "5-percent shareholders" increases by more than 50% over the lowest percentage of stock in the corporation owned by such shareholders during the "testing period" (generally the prior three years if the corporation has NOL carryovers). § 382(g)(1), (i). The percentage of stock held by a person is determined on the basis of the stock's fair market value, and nonvoting, nonconvertible preferred stock is not counted. § 382(k)(5), (6).

2) Owner Shifts Involving 5% Shareholders

An owner shift involving a 5% shareholder is any change in stock ownership of a corporation which affects the percentage ownership of a person who is a 5% shareholder before or after the change. § 382(g)(2). Examples include stock purchases, redemptions, § 351 transfers and recapitalizations. A few special rules apply. All less than 5% shareholders are treated as one 5% shareholder for purposes of determining whether an ownership shift has occurred. § 382(g)(4)(A). Gifts, transfers at death and transfers between spouses are disregarded and the transferee is treated as having owned the stock during the period it was owned by the transferor. § 382(*l*)(3)(B). Changes in proportionate ownership attributable solely to fluctuations in value of different classes of stock also are disregarded, except as provided in regulations. § 382(*l*)(3)(C).

Example (1): Loss Co. has a large NOL which it can carry forward to future years. If Buyer purchases 51% of Loss Co. she will be a 5% shareholder and an owner shift involving a 5% shareholder has occurred. The owner shift increases Buyer's percentage ownership in Loss Co. by more than 50%, producing an "ownership change" which triggers the § 382 limitation. The result is the same if Buyer acquires 51% of Loss Co. in a series of transactions stretching over the three-year testing period. These transactions could include the redemption of stock from other Loss Co. shareholders which have the result of increasing Buyer's ownership interest above the 50% threshold.

Example (2): Buyer purchases 40% of Loss Co. and, within the three-year testing period, Other Buyer purchases 15% of Loss Co. In that situation, both Buyer and Other Buyer are 5% shareholders. An ownership change has occurred which triggers § 382 since the percentage ownership of one or more 5% shareholders has increased by more than 50% during the testing period.

Example (3): Loss Co. is publicly traded and has a large NOL which it can carry over to future years. No single shareholder owns 5% or more of Loss Co. If more than 50% of Loss Co. is traded to other less than 5% shareholders during the testing period, the § 382 limitations are not triggered. Since all less than 5% shareholders are treated as one 5% shareholder, that single hypothetical shareholder has continued to own 100% of Loss Co. at all times and no ownership change has taken place.

Example (4): A, an individual, owns 100% of Loss Co. If A sells 2% of Loss Co. to each of 50 buyers during the testing period, there will be an ownership change that triggers the § 382 limitation. The 50 buyers will be treated as a single 5% shareholder whose interest in Loss Co. has increased from zero percent to 100%.

3) Equity Structure Shifts

An "equity structure" shift is defined as any reorganization other than a Type F reorganization or Type D and Type G reorganizations which are divisive. The term also includes taxable reorganization-type transactions and public offerings. § 382(g)(3)(B). In determining the change of ownership in a reorganization involving a loss corporation, the prereorganization ownership of the loss corporation is compared with the post-reorganization ownership of the surviving corporation. § 382(k)(1), (3). In a reorganization setting the less than 5% shareholders of each corporation are treated as one 5% shareholder in that corporation. § 382(g)(4)(B)(i). In virtually all cases, an equity structure shift also will be an owner shift involving a 5% shareholder and, apart from specialized transitional rules, the distinction appears to have no substantive significance.

Example: Loss Co. is owned 20% by A, 30% by B and 50% by the public. Profit Co. is publicly owned. If Loss Co. merges into Profit Co. with the Loss Co. shareholders receiving 40% of the outstanding Profit Co. stock, an equity structure shift and ownership change will occur and the § 382 limitation will apply. The ownership of the Profit Co. shareholders in Loss Co. before the merger (zero percent) is compared with their ownership interest in the surviving corporation, Profit Co. (60%), which is now the "loss corporation." § 382(k)(1), (3). Thus, the percentage ownership of one or more 5% shareholders has increased by more than 50% during the testing period. If, instead, Profit Co. merged into Loss Co. and received 60% of the outstanding stock of Loss Co., an equity structure and an ownership change again would result. The ownership of the Profit Co. shareholders in Loss Co. (zero percent) is compared with their ownership interest in Loss Co. after the reorganization (60%).

In both situations, the less than 5% shareholders in Loss Co. and Profit Co. are treated as a single more than 5% shareholder in their respective corporations. The two groups are not aggregated into a single more than 5% shareholder. § 382(g)(4)(B)(i).

4)   Attribution Rules

In testing stock ownership to determine whether an ownership change has occurred, § 382(*l*)(3) applies modified § 318 attribution rules. In general, these rules provide that: (1) an individual and all members of his family (as described in § 318(a)(1)) are treated as one individual, (2) stock owned by a partnership, trust, estate or corporation is treated as owned proportionately by the beneficial owners and the entity's actual ownership is disregarded, and (3) attribution to entities is disregarded. The impact of these rules is to disregard transfers within a family and to focus the § 382 ownership test on corporate ownership by individuals.

b.   Effect of an Ownership Change

1)   Continuity of Business Enterprise Requirement

If an ownership change takes place, § 382(c) provides that all NOLs are disallowed if the new loss corporation does not continue the business enterprise of the old loss corporation at all times during the two-year period following the date of the ownership change. § 382(c)(1), (j). This provision requires the new loss corporation to either continue the business of the loss corporation or use a significant portion of its historic business assets in one of its businesses for the two-year period. Reg. § 1.368–1(d)(2). See XI.A.4.b., at page 209, *supra*.

2) The § 382 Limitation

a) In General

If there is an ownership change and the continuity of business enterprise requirement is satisfied, the new loss corporation may use NOLs in any "post-change year" (a year after the ownership change) only in an amount equal to the value of the old loss corporation multiplied by the long-term tax-exempt rate. § 382(a), (b)(1). If the amount of this limitation exceeds the taxable income of the new loss corporation for the year, the excess carries over and increases the next year's limitation. § 382(b)(2). If an ownership change takes place mid-year and the § 382 limitation applies, the limit is prorated over the year by time. § 382(b)(3)(B).

Example: Assume Loss Co. has a value of $1,000,000 and losses of $300,000. If Loss Co. is subject to § 382 and the long-term tax exempt rate is 5%, it may use its loss carryforwards only to the extent of $50,000 ($1,000,000 multiplied by 5%). If it only had $40,000 of taxable income in the year, the $10,000 excess of the limitation over its taxable income carries over and increases the § 382 limitation in the next year. If the ownership change triggering § 382 did not occur on the first day of the loss corporation's taxable year, the § 382 limitation would have to be prorated over the year of the ownership change. For example, if the § 382 limitation for the full year were $50,000 and the ownership change took place three-fourths of the way through the year, the § 382 limitation for the remainder of the year would be $12,500. The § 382 limitation does not apply to the portion of the taxable year prior to the ownership change and taxable income during the year of the ownership change is allocated ratably to each day in the year. § 382(b)(3)(A).

b) Long-Term Tax-Exempt Rate

The § 382 limitation is determined by multiplying the long-term tax-exempt rate by the value of the company. § 382(b)(1). The long-term tax-exempt rate is the highest federal long-term rate under § 1274(d) in effect for any month in the three-month period ending with the calendar month in which the ownership change occurs, adjusted for the differences between long-term taxable and tax-exempt rates. § 382(f).

c)   Value of the Company

The value of the old loss corporation is the value of its stock, including preferred stock, immediately before the ownership change. § 382(e)(1), (k)(6)(A). Section 382 has rules to prevent manipulation of the value either before or after the ownership change. If a redemption or corporate contraction takes place in connection with an ownership change, the loss corporation's value is determined after taking the redemption or contraction into account. § 382(e)(2). Any contribution to the loss corporation as part of a plan to avoid or increase the § 382 limitation is ignored in determining the corporation's value, and a contribution made within two years before the date of the ownership change is treated as part of such a plan, unless it is exempted by the regulations. § 382(*l*)(1). This later rule prevents preownership-change "stuffing" contributions designed to increase the corporation's value and its § 382 limitation. In certain instances the value of a corporation also may be reduced by a portion of its nonbusiness, i.e., investment, assets. If at least one-third of a loss corporation's assets are nonbusiness assets, its value is reduced by the percentage of its net value represented by the fair market value of nonbusiness assets, less a proportionate amount of corporate indebtedness. § 382(*l*)(4).

Example (1):   P Corp. purchases 80% of the stock of Loss Corp. when the Loss stock is worth $20 million. As part of the acquisition plan, the other 20% of the Loss stock is later redeemed for $4 million. Under § 382(e)(2), the redemption is taken into account in determining the value of Loss for purposes of the § 382 limitation. Thus, the value of Loss is $16 million for § 382 purposes, not $20 million.

Example (2):   In anticipation of an ownership change, the shareholders of Loss Corp. make a $1,000,000 capital contribution to the corporation. The value of Loss Corp. for purposes of the § 382 limitation will be determined without regard to the additional stock value attributable to the contribution. If the contribution were made within two years of the ownership change, it is presumed to be part of a prohibited plan.

3)   Special Rules for Built-in Gains and Losses

If a loss corporation has a "net unrealized built-in gain"—that is, on the date of the ownership change the fair market value of its assets (other than cash and certain cash equivalents) exceeds their aggregate adjusted basis— the § 382 limitation is increased by any *recognized* built-in gain during the five-year period after the ownership change. § 382(h)(1)(A)(i). This rule applies only if the corporation's net unrealized gain exceeds either 15% of the fair market value of its assets (other than cash and certain cash equivalents) or $10 million. § 382(h)(3)(B). The total amount of recognized built-in gain eligible for this preferred treatment is limited to the amount of net unrealized built-in gain. § 382(h)(1)(A)(ii). The corporation has the burden of showing that a recognized built-in gain accrued before the ownership change. § 382(h)(2)(A). If applicable, this rule permits a corporation to increase its § 382 limitation so it is able to deduct losses against built-in gains from asset sales or deemed asset sales resulting from a § 338 election.

If a loss corporation has a "net unrealized built-in loss"—that is, on the date of the ownership change the aggregate basis of its assets (other than cash and certain cash equivalents) exceeds their fair market value—the corporation's recognized built-in loss during the five-year period after the ownership change is subject to the § 382 limitation in the same manner as if it were a carryover NOL. § 382(h)(1)(B)(i). This rule applies only if the corporation's net unrealized built-in loss exceeds either 15% of the fair market value of its assets (other than cash and certain cash equivalents) or $10 million. § 382(h)(3)(B). The total amount of recognized built-in loss subject to this rule is limited to the amount of the net unrealized built-in loss. § 382(h)(1)(B)(ii). The corporation has the burden of showing that a loss recognized during the five-year period is not a built-in loss by establishing that the asset disposed of was not held by the loss company immediately before the change date or that the loss exceeds the loss which had accrued at the time of the ownership change. Depreciation or other cost recovery during the five-year period attributable to the excess of an asset's adjusted basis over its fair market value on the change date is considered a recognized built-in loss and subject to the limitation. § 382(h)(2)(B).

Example (1): Loss Co., a calendar year taxpayer, has $2 million of loss carryforwards. On January 1 of the current year, P Co. acquired all of Loss's assets for $5 million of P Co. stock in a Type C reorganization and Loss liquidated. After the reorganization, the Loss shareholders own 20% of the P Co. stock. The Loss assets, other than cash and cash equivalents, had a $4.5 million aggregate fair market value and a $3 million basis at the time of P's acquisition. Loss had held all of its assets for more than two years. A parcel of real estate owned by Loss at that time had a fair market value of $300,000 and a basis of $200,000. The long-term tax-exempt rate is 5%. P Co. sells the real estate for $300,000 in September of this year.

There has been an ownership change since before the acquisition the P Co. shareholders owned no Loss stock and after they own 80% of P Co., the surviving corporation. § 382(g)(1), (3). Since Loss Co. is worth $5 million on the change date, its loss carryforwards can be deducted to the extent of 5% of $5 million, or $250,000.

There is net unrealized built-in gain in the Loss Co. assets since the fair market value of the assets, less cash and cash equivalents, exceeds their aggregate basis. The net unrealized built-in gain is $1.5 million which exceeds 15% of their fair market value. Under § 382(h)(1)(A), when P Co. recognizes its $100,000 gain on the sale of the real estate, its § 382 limitation for the year will be increased by that gain to $350,000. If P Co. sold the land for more than

$300,000, its increase in the § 382 limitation would still be limited to $100,000, the appreciation in the parcel of real estate on the change date. § 382(h)(2)(A)(ii).

Example (2): Assume the same facts as in Example (1) except that Loss's assets had an aggregate basis of $6 million and the parcel of real estate had a basis of $400,000. In that case, there is a net unrealized built-in loss in the Loss Co. assets since the aggregate basis of the assets, less cash and cash equivalents, exceeds their fair market value. The net unrealized built-in loss is $1.5 million which again exceeds the 15% threshold. Under § 382(h)(1)(B), the $100,000 loss on the sale of the real estate is treated as a loss carryforward and is subject to the § 382 limitation. If the real estate were sold for less than $300,000, the loss in excess of the $100,000 loss on the change date is not subject to this limitation and would be fully deductible.

3. Special Limitations on Other Tax Attributes: § 383

Under the authority of § 383, the Treasury has issued regulations which will apply the principles of § 382 following an ownership change to the general business credit under § 39, the foreign tax credit carryover under § 904, and capital losses. Thus, a change of ownership under § 382 will result in a limitation in these tax attributes as well as NOLs. Section 383(b) requires that the § 382 limitation be further reduced by any net capital loss permitted to be deducted under § 383.

4. Limitation on Use of Preacquisition Losses to Offset Built-in Gains: § 384

Section 384 prevents a loss corporation from applying its preacquisition losses against recognized built-in gains of another corporation. The section, which employs many of the definitions developed in § 382, applies if: (1) a corporation acquires directly or through other corporations "control" (defined as 80% ownership under the affiliated corporation rules in § 1504(a)(2)) of another corporation or the assets of another corporation in a Type A, C or D reorganization, and (2) either corporation is a "gain corporation," that is, a corporation with a net unrealized built-in gain as defined in § 382(h)(3). § 384(a), (c)(4). If those requirements are met, income attributable to recognized built-in gains of one of the corporations may not be offset by a preacquisition loss of the other corporation during the five-year period following the acquisition. § 384(a). The limitation does not apply to the preacquisition loss of a corporation if it and the gain corporation were members of the same controlled group (generally, more than 50% common ownership by vote and value) for five years prior to the acquisition. § 384(b)(1). Section 384 also applies to certain other tax attributes. § 384(d).

Example: Loss Co. has substantial NOL carryovers. In the current year, Loss acquires all of the assets of Profit Co. in a Type C reorganization. After the reorganization, the preacquisition Loss Co. shareholders still own 60% of the Loss Co. stock. Thus, § 382 will not apply to Loss Co. But if Profit Co. had a net unrealized built-in gain, i.e., it is a "gain corporation," the combined corporation will not be able to use Loss's preacquisition NOLs to offset any recognized built-in gains attributable to the acquired Profit assets during the five-year period after the acquisition.

5. Acquisitions to Evade or Avoid Income Tax: § 269

Section 269(a) permits the Service to disallow a deduction, credit or other allowance following a corporate acquisition if the principal purpose of the acquisition was the evasion or avoidance of federal income tax by having the acquiring party secure a tax benefit which would not otherwise have been enjoyed. § 269(a). The provision applies to acquisitions in which either (1) a person or persons acquire, directly or indirectly, control of a corporation, or (2) a corporation acquires, directly or indirectly, property with a transferred basis from a corporation which is not controlled. "Control" is defined as ownership of stock which has either 50% of the total voting power or 50% of the total value of the corporation. Thus, § 269(a) potentially applies to the various types of acquisitive reorganizations, provided the transaction is motivated by a prohibited purpose. Under § 269(b) the Service's power to disallow tax benefits is extended to liquidations motivated by a prohibited tax purpose if the liquidation occurs within two years of a qualified stock purchase in which no § 338 election was made.

Because § 269 employs a subjective tax avoidance standard, its principal role in the area of corporate tax attribute carryovers is to act as a backstop to the various other statutory limitations, such as §§ 382 and 383, which may come into play. For example, the Service might invoke § 269 in a situation where there is a shift in corporate ownership which impacts control but which is not sufficient to trigger § 382. Section 269, however, is not limited to the carryover area; it can apply in a much wider range of settings.

6. Consolidated Return Rules

Because the consolidated return rules permit an affiliated group to combine the separate taxable income or loss figures of its members for purposes of determining the group's tax obligation, the potential exists for the improper deduction of losses of one member against the post-affiliation income of another. See XIV.D.3., at page 288–289, *infra*. To prevent that abuse, all of the various limitations on the carryover of tax attributes apply to corporations filing a consolidated return. See Reg. § 1.1502–91 through Reg. § 1.1502–99A. The consolidated return regulations contain an additional restriction on the use of a member's pre-affiliation NOLs: the separate return limitation year ("SRLY") limitation.

A separate return limitation year ("SRLY") of a member of an affiliated group is a year in which the member filed its taxes separately or as a member of another affiliated group. Reg. § 1.1502–1(e), (f). Under the consolidated return rules, the NOLs of a member of an affiliated group from a SRLY generally may be carried over and deducted only against the income of that member. Reg. § 1.1502–21(c).

Example: If Profit Co. acquires Loss Co. and the two file a consolidated tax return, Loss's NOLs from separate return limitation years can not be carried over to post-affiliation years and be deducted against Profit's income.

In general, the SRLY limitation does not apply when a corporation becomes a member of a consolidated group (where the limitation otherwise applies) within six months of the change date of a § 382(g) change of ownership. As a result, in many acquisitions the SRLY limitation relinquishes jurisdiction over NOLs as well as recognized built-in losses to § 382. Reg. §§ 1.1502–15(g), –21(g)(1) & (2).

D. Review Questions

1. In what ways does § 382 limit the carryover of a target's tax attributes following a reorganization?

2. P Co. is considering acquiring an interest in T Co., which has substantial NOLs. Which of the following acquisitions will be an ownership change which triggers the § 382 limitation?

    (a) P Co. acquires 80% of the T Co. stock pursuant to a cash tender offer for T shares.

    (b) Same as (a), except P Co. acquires 50% of the T Co. stock.

    (c) T Co. merges into P Co. in exchange for P Co. stock and following the merger the T Co. shareholders own 60% of P Co.

Chapter XIV

Affiliated Corporations

■ ANALYSIS

A. Introduction

A corporation generally determines its taxable income or loss without reference to the taxable income or loss of its shareholders or other entities. The theory that each corporation is a separate taxpayer is limited, however, in certain situations in which corporations are "affiliated" (i.e., subject to common control or joined through interlocking ownership). In the case of affiliated corporations, Code restrictions limit the ability to obtain multiple tax benefits and to manipulate intercompany transactions to reduce tax liability. The Code also recognizes that the identities of affiliated corporations may merge at certain very high levels of common control. For tax purposes, it is permissible to treat the corporations as a single entity in which intercompany transactions are disregarded. For example, intercompany dividends may be eligible for a 100% dividends received deduction and an "affiliated group" of corporations, as defined in § 1504, is permitted to file a consolidated tax return in which it is treated as a single entity for tax purposes.

B. Restrictions on Multiple Tax Benefits

1. In General

Without restrictions, taxpayers would have an incentive to multiply the number of corporations employed in operating a business to take advantage of certain tax benefits. For example, absent a limitation, a business could be organized in several corporations with each corporation eligible to: (1) obtain a $250,000 accumulated earnings tax credit, or (2) expense depreciable business property under § 179, etc. Section 1561 contains a restriction on multiple accumulated earnings credits and many Code sections which authorize a deduction or credit contain similar limitations.

2. § 1561

a. Limitation on Accumulated Earnings Credit

Under § 1561(a), the "component members of a controlled group" are limited to one $250,000 (or $150,000 if any member is a "personal service corporation") accumulated earnings tax credit. The single credit is generally divided equally among the component members of the group on December 31. In certain situations the members may consent to an unequal allocation.

b. Component Members of a Controlled Group of Corporations

Under § 1563(a), a "controlled group of corporations" may be either a "parent-subsidiary" controlled group or a "brother-sister" controlled group. Combinations of parent-subsidiary and brother-sister groups also are possible. § 1563(a)(3).

1) Parent-Subsidiary Controlled Group

A parent-subsidiary controlled group exists if one or more chains of corporations are connected through stock ownership with a common parent and (1) each corporation (other than the parent) is at least 80% owned (by voting power or value) by one or more of the other corporations and (2) the parent directly owns at least 80% (by voting power or value) of at least one of the other corporations. § 1563(a)(1).

Example: P Co. owns 80% of the only class of stock of S Co. and T Co. S Co. owns 30% of the only class of stock of V Co. and T Co. owns 50% of the V Co. stock. P Co. is the common parent of a parent-subsidiary controlled group consisting of P Co., S Co., T Co. and V Co.

2) Brother-Sister Controlled Group

A brother-sister controlled group is two or more corporations having five or fewer persons who are individuals, estates, or trusts that own more than 50% (by voting power or value) of each corporation taking into account the stock ownership of each person only to the extent it is identical, or overlapping, in each corporation. § 1563(a)(2).

Example: A (an individual) owns 20% of the only class of stock of X Co. and 35% of the only class of stock of Y Co. B (an individual) owns 40% of X Co and 45% of Y Co. A's identical ownership of X Co. and Y Co. is 20%. B's identical ownership in those corporations is 40%. Thus, X Co. and Y Co. are a brother-sister controlled group because A's and B's identical ownership of those corporations totals more than 50%.

3) Other Rules

Nonvoting preferred stock, treasury stock and "excluded stock" (as defined) are not considered in applying the parent-subsidiary and brother-sister ownership tests. § 1563(c). Various constructive ownership rules also are applied to test stock ownership. § 1563(d), (e), (f). In general, every member of a controlled group of corporations on December 31 is a "component member" of the group. Special rules apply to corporations which are not members of the group for the full year and corporations taxed under other statutory schemes, such as tax-exempt and foreign corporations, are excluded from the group. § 1563(b).

3. Other Restrictions

Several other Code sections contain specific limitations on multiple tax benefits for affiliated corporations. For purposes of those other provisions, the Section 1563 definition of a brother-sister controlled group may be modified. See § 1563(f)(5). Some examples of provisions limiting tax benefits are:

a.   A controlled group, as defined in § 1563(a), is limited to one $25,000 amount for purposes of computing the general business credit limitation. § 38(c)(6)(B).

b.   All component members of a controlled group are treated as one taxpayer for purposes of expensing the cost of § 179 property. § 179(d)(6), (7).

c.   Section 269 gives the Service the discretion to disallow various tax benefits if any person or persons acquire, directly or indirectly, control of a corporation and the principal purpose for the acquisition is tax avoidance. "Control" is defined for this purpose as 50% of voting power and value. Although § 269 is more commonly applied to limit the use of preacquisition losses following a corporate acquisition (see XIII.C.5., at page 281, *supra*), the fact that a person or persons organize two or more corporations to secure multiple accumulated earnings tax credits indicates a tax avoidance purpose. Reg. § 1.269–3(b)(2).

C. Transactions Involving Related Corporations and Other Taxpayers

1. In General

Without some limitations, commonly controlled business organizations could engage in transactions designed to reduce their overall tax liability. Income shifting and recognition of losses in transactions between controlled entities are the most obvious avoidance strategies. The Code has a number of provisions designed to prevent tax avoidance in transactions between related taxpayers and many of those provisions apply to controlled and commonly owned corporations. For example, the loss disallowance and matching of income and deduction rules in § 267(a) apply to corporations which are members of the same controlled group as defined in § 267(f). § 267(b)(3). See III.A.7., at page 66, *supra*. Another example is the application of the related-party resale rules in § 453(e) which also apply to controlled groups defined in § 267(f). § 453(e), (f)(1)(B). In addition to the various statutory limitations applicable to specific transactions, § 482 empowers the Service to prevent tax evasion in transactions between controlled businesses.

2. Allocations of Income and Deductions: § 482

a. Purpose of § 482

Under § 482, the Service may distribute, apportion, or allocate tax items between or among organizations, trades, or businesses which are owned or controlled, directly or indirectly, by the same interests when the reallocation of the items is necessary to prevent evasion of taxes or clearly to reflect the income of any of the businesses. To illustrate the type of manipulation at which § 482 is directed, assume that one commonly controlled business is very profitable and another has sustained large losses. Transactions between the two businesses involving services, the leasing of property, transfers or use of intangible property, or sales of goods could be structured so as to shift income from the profitable business to the one with losses. Section 482 is frequently applied to transactions between a domestic corporation and a commonly controlled foreign corporation which are structured to shift income to more lightly taxed foreign jurisdictions. In these situations, § 482 is the Service's principal weapon for preventing abuse. The regulations state that the purpose of the section is to place a controlled taxpayer on a parity with an uncontrolled taxpayer by determining the controlled taxpayer's true taxable income using the standard of an uncontrolled taxpayer. Reg. § 1.482–1(b)(1).

b. Commonly Controlled Trades or Businesses

Section 482 applies to transactions involving two or more "organizations, trades, or businesses," regardless of whether they are incorporated, domestic or foreign, or file consolidated returns. "Organization" is defined expansively and includes sole proprietorships, partnerships, trusts, estates, associations and corporations. Reg. § 1.482–1(i)(1). Two or more organizations, trades or businesses are considered "controlled" for § 482 purposes if there is control of any kind, direct or indirect, whether legally enforceable or not. The regulations state that the "reality of the control" is the key question, "not its form or the mode of its exercise." Further, a presumption of control is created if income or deductions are arbitrarily shifted between two entities. Reg. § 1.482–1(i)(4).

c. The Arm's Length Standard

Transactions between controlled taxpayers are subjected to special scrutiny under § 482 and the Service has the authority to make adjustments in cases involving inadvertence as well as those motivated by tax avoidance considerations. Reg. § 1.482–1(f)(1)(i). In testing transactions under § 482, the standard applied is that of an uncontrolled taxpayer dealing at arm's length with another uncontrolled taxpayer. Reg. § 1.482–1(b)(1).

Whether a controlled transaction produces an arm's length result is generally evaluated by comparing the results of that transaction to those realized by uncontrolled taxpayers engaged in comparable transactions under comparable circumstances. The comparability of transactions and circumstances must be evaluated considering all factors that could affect prices or profits in arm's length dealings, including functions, contractual terms, risks, economic conditions, and property or services. Reg. § 1.482–1(d)(1). To be considered comparable to a controlled transaction, an uncontrolled transaction does not have to be identical to a controlled transaction, but it must be sufficiently similar that it provides a reliable measure of an arm's length result. Reg. § 1.482–1(d)(2). When an adjustment is made to the income of one member of a group of controlled taxpayers under this standard, an appropriate correlative adjustment must be made to other members involved in the adjustment. Reg. § 1.482–1(g)(1), (g)(2). The § 482 regulations provide guidance for the application of the arm's length standard in specific situations, such as loans and advances, performance of services, use of tangible property, sales of tangible property, and sales or use of intangible property. Reg. §§ 1.482–2(a) through (c), –3, –4.

> *Example:* Assume services are provided by a profitable controlled business to an unprofitable controlled business at a price below that which would have been paid in an arm's length arrangement. When additional income is allocated under § 482 to the profitable business, a correlative deduction must be provided to the unprofitable business, assuming payment for the services is currently deductible. Note that the deduction may simply increase the unprofitable business' losses and not provide a current tax benefit.

D. Consolidated Returns

1. Introduction

The Code permits commonly controlled corporations meeting certain requirements (i.e., an "affiliated group of corporations") to be treated as a single entity for tax purposes. The theory is that at very high levels of common ownership a family of corporations may be viewed as a single economic unit which should be eligible to compute joint, or "consolidated," tax liability. The principal advantages of filing a consolidated return are: (1) losses of one member of the group may be used to offset income of other members; (2) intercompany dividend distributions are eliminated from income; and (3) income from intercompany transactions is deferred. A principal disadvantage is that an election to file a consolidated return may not be revoked without the Service's approval. Other possible disadvantages include the fact that losses on intercompany transactions also are deferred.

2.　Eligibility to File a Consolidated Return

Under § 1501, an "affiliated group of corporations" is eligible to file a consolidated return in lieu of separate returns. All corporations who are members of the group must consent to application of all of the consolidated return regulations, which are issued by the Service under the authority granted it in § 1502.

An "affiliated group" is one or more chains of "includible corporations" in which a parent corporation owns directly at least 80% (by vote and value) of at least one includible corporation and at least 80% (by vote and value) of each includible corporation is owned directly by one or more other includible corporations. § 1504(a)(1), (2). For purposes of the ownership tests, nonvoting nonconvertible preferred stock which has redemption and liquidation rights limited to its issue price (plus a reasonable premium) is disregarded. § 1504(a)(4). "Includible corporations" generally are all corporations except those subject to certain special taxing schemes.

Example:　P Corp. owns 90% of X Co.'s only class of stock. X Co. owns 80% of the only class of stock of Y Co. and 60% of the only class of stock of Z Co. Y Co. owns the other 40% of Z Co.'s stock. Z Co. owns 75% of the class of stock of T Co. and 100% of Foreign Co., a corporation formed in Germany. The remaining 25% of T Co.'s stock is publicly traded. On these facts, P Corp., X Co., Y Co., and Z Co. are an affiliated group eligible to file a consolidated return. Foreign Co. is not an includible corporation and cannot be part of the affiliated group. If another 5% of the T Co. stock were owned by other members of the group, T Co. would then be part of the affiliated group. If filing a consolidated return were advantageous, each corporation in the group would have to consent to all the consolidated return regulations.

3.　Computing Consolidated Taxable Income

a.　In General

The consolidated taxable income for a consolidated group generally is determined by combining the separate taxable income or loss of each member of the group. Reg. § 1.1502–11(a)(1). In computing its separate taxable income, each member of the group uses the common parent's taxable year and its own accounting method. § 1.1502–17(a), –76(a). The separate taxable incomes of the members are aggregated and combined with certain items that must be determined on a consolidated basis, and tax liability is computed based upon consolidated taxable income. § 1.1502–2.

"Investment adjustments" are required to be made at the end of each consolidated return year to the basis of each member's stock in a subsidiary member of the group. In general, upward adjustments are made to stock to reflect undistributed earnings and profits of the subsidiaries and downward adjustments are made to reflect earnings and profits deficits. § 1.1502–32. The regulations permit these adjustments to result in a negative basis in the stock. § 1.1502–32(a)(3)(ii), –19(a)(2). These stock basis adjustments are designed to prevent double recognition of gain or loss on a disposition of the subsidiary's stock.

b. Intercompany Distributions

Since a consolidated group is considered a single tax entity, intercompany distributions generally are eliminated from the computation of consolidated taxable income. § 1.1502–13(f)(2)(ii). Intercompany dividends are reflected by a downward investment adjustment in the subsidiary's stock. § 1.1502–32(b)(2)(iv).

c. Intercompany Transactions

The consolidated return regulations have extensive and detailed rules for the taxation of intercompany transactions. Under the regulations, the selling member in a transaction is referred to as "S," and its items of income, gain, deduction, and loss from an intercompany transaction are referred to as "intercompany items." Reg. § 1.1502–13(b)(2)(i). The buying member in a transaction is referred to as "B" and its tax items from an intercompany transaction are referred to as "corresponding items." Reg. § 1.1502–13(b)(3)(i). A "recomputed corresponding item" is the corresponding item that B would take into account if S and B were divisions of a single corporation and the intercompany transaction were between those divisions. Reg. § 1.1502–13(b)(4). The following examples illustrate how the regulations employ these definitions in routine intercompany transactions.

Example (1): S and B are members of an affiliated group that files a consolidated return. S sells property with a $70 basis to B for $100 in year 1. In year 3, B sells the property to X for $110. S's gain on its sale to B is its intercompany item. B's $10 gain from its sale to X is its corresponding item. For each consolidated return year, S takes its intercompany item into account under a matching rule to reflect the difference for the year between B's corresponding item taken into account and the recomputed corresponding item. If S and B were divisions in the same corporation, B would have taken S's $70 basis and would have a $40 gain on the sale to X in year 3, instead of $10. Thus, S takes no gain into account in years 1 and 2 and takes the entire $30 gain into account in year 3, to reflect the $30 difference in that year between the $10 gain B takes into account and the $40 recomputed corresponding item. Reg. § 1.1502–13(c)(7) Example (1).

Example (2): Assume again that S and B are members of an affiliated group that files a consolidated return. S leases land to B for year 1 in exchange for a $100 rent payment that is deductible to B under its separate accounting method. S takes its $100 of rental income into account in year 1 to reflect the difference between B's rental deduction and the $0 recomputed rental deduction (the rental deduction if S and B were divisions of a single corporation). See Reg. § 1.1502–13(c)(7) Example (8).

E. Review Questions

1. The outstanding stock of W Co., X Co., Y Co. and Z Co. are owned as follows:

   A, an individual, owns 35% of W Co. and 25% of Y Co.

   B, an individual, owns 50% of X Co. and 35% of Z Co.

   C, an individual, owns 47% of W Co., 25% of X Co., 60% of Y Co. and 10% of Z Co.

   Twenty other unrelated individuals own the remaining shares in W Co., X Co., Y Co. and Z Co. A, B and C are not related to one another.

   Which, if any, of the corporations form a brother-sister controlled group under § 1563(a)(2)?

2. Under what circumstances will the Service most likely challenge intercompany transactions and what is its authority?

Chapter XV

S Corporations

■ ANALYSIS

A. Introduction

Profits distributed as dividends by a C corporation to its shareholders generally are subject to tax at both the corporate and shareholder levels. A C corporation is subject to the tax under § 11 on its taxable income at a flat rate of 21%. When the after-tax profits are distributed, noncorporate shareholders are taxed on most dividends as net capital gain at a maximum rate of 20% (23.8% for high-income taxpayers subject to the additional tax on net investment income). §§ 1(h)(11), 61(a)(7), 301, and 1411. In contrast, a partnership is generally treated as an aggregate of its partners rather than a taxable entity. § 701. The partners are taxed directly on the income from the enterprise, and partnership distributions generally do not produce additional taxable income. §§ 702; 731.

In 1958, Congress created a method for corporations to avoid the double tax by enacting Subchapter S, which allows the shareholders of a "small business corporation" to elect to be taxed directly on corporate-level profits. The S corporation taxing scheme was substantially improved by the Subchapter S Revision Act of 1982, which adopted a simplified pass-through approach. As a result, the taxation of S corporations and their shareholders became similar, but not identical, to the taxation of partnerships and their partners, and S corporations became a more attractive legal form for operating a business enterprise. Subsequent legislation has liberalized the eligibility requirements and made S corporations more accessible vehicles for operating a closely held business.

B. Eligibility for S Corporation Status

The special tax provisions in Subchapter S are available only to an "S corporation," which is defined as a "small business corporation" which has an election under § 1362(a) in effect for the year. § 1361(a)(1). Any corporation which is not an S corporation is referred to as a "C corporation." § 1361(a)(2). Despite the use of "small business" in the definition, there are no limits on the asset size or revenue of S corporations and, although most S corporations are relatively small and many have only one shareholder, some have net assets exceeding $100 million. A "small business corporation" is defined as a domestic corporation which meets the requirements set forth in § 1361 and outlined below.

1. Ineligible Corporations and Subsidiaries

a. In General

Ineligible corporations do not qualify as small business corporations. § 1361(b)(1). The "ineligible corporation" category includes four specialized types of corporations (such as banks and insurance companies) that are subject to their own taxing regimes under the Code. § 1361(b)(2). At one time, a corporation was "ineligible" if it was a member of an affiliated group—e.g., a parent with an 80% subsidiary.

b. Wholly Owned Subsidiaries

S corporations may have 80% or more subsidiaries under certain conditions.

1) C corporation subsidiaries are generally permitted, but the S corporation parent and the C corporation subsidiary may not file a consolidated return. § 1504(b)(6).

2) Parent-subsidiary relationships between two S corporations are permitted if the parent elects to treat the subsidiary as a "qualified subchapter S subsidiary" ("QSSS"). § 1361(b)(3)(A). To be "qualified," the subsidiary must

not be an ineligible corporation (see above) and 100% of the stock of such corporation must be held by an S corporation. § 1361(b)(3)(B). If this election is made, all the assets, liabilities, income, deductions, and credits are treated as belonging to the S parent. § 1361(b)(3)(A). In effect, even though the subsidiary is a separate corporation, it is treated as a division of its parent for tax purposes. The regulations provide detailed rules for making or revoking a QSSS election. See Reg. §§ 1.1361–3, –4, –5.

2. 100-Shareholder Limit

An S corporation may not have more than 100 shareholders. § 1361(b)(1)(A). If stock is owned (other than by a husband and wife) by tenants in common or joint tenants, each owner is considered to be a shareholder of the corporation. Reg. § 1.1361–1(e)(1). Stock held by a nominee, guardian, custodian or agent is considered to be held by the beneficial owner of the stock. Id.

A special rule treats a husband and wife (and their estates) and all members of a "family" (and their estates) as one shareholder for purposes of the 100-shareholder limit. § 1361(c)(1)(A). A family is defined as the lineal descendants (and their spouses or former spouses) of a common ancestor who is no more than six generations removed from the youngest generation shareholder as of the later of the date the S corporation election is made, the earliest date that a family member holds stock in the corporation, or October 22, 2004. § 1361(c)(1)(B). Adopted children and foster children are treated as children by blood. § 1361(c)(1)(C). If a husband and wife are members of a family they are counted as part of that family (rather than separately) for purposes of the shareholder limit. § 1361(c)(1)(A)(i).

Example (1): Assume 99 of 100 outstanding shares of stock in X Corp. are owned by 99 unrelated individuals. If the remaining share is owned in joint tenancy by Herman and Wanda, who are husband and wife, X is considered to have 100 shareholders and may qualify as a small business corporation. If Herman and Wanda were brother and sister, X again would have 100 shareholders because Herman and Wanda would be members of a family that is counted as one shareholder.

Example (2): Assume again that Herman and Wanda in Example (1) are husband and wife. If Herman dies, Wanda and his estate will continue to be considered as one shareholder until distribution of the stock by the estate to a beneficiary other than Wanda and who is not part of Wanda's family. If the stock were distributed by Herman's estate to another unrelated beneficiary, X would have 101 shareholders and would no longer qualify as an S corporation. § 1362(d)(2)(A). If Herman and Wanda get divorced, X will still have 100 shareholders because former spouses are considered part of a family.

3. Restrictions on Types of Shareholders

a. In General

An S corporation may not have as a shareholder a person (other than an estate and certain trusts) who is not an individual or a § 501(c)(3) tax-exempt charitable organization or qualified pension trust. § 1361(b)(1)(B). For this purpose, the term "estate" includes the bankruptcy estate of an individual. § 1361(c)(3). Thus, an S corporation cannot have another corporation or a partnership as a shareholder. Reg. § 1.1361–1(f).

b. Nonresident Alien Restriction

An S corporation may not have a nonresident alien as a shareholder. § 1361(b)(1)(C).

c. Trusts as Eligible Shareholders

The following types of domestic trusts are eligible S corporation shareholders:

1) Grantor trusts—i.e., domestic trusts treated for income tax purposes as owned by an individual who is a U.S. citizen or resident. § 1361(c)(2)(A)(i). The deemed owner of the trust is treated as the shareholder. § 1361(c)(2)(B)(i). If the deemed owner of a grantor trust dies and the trust continues in existence as a testamentary trust, it continues to be a permissible shareholder for the 2-year period following the deemed owner's death. § 1361(c)(2)(A)(ii). The estate of the deemed owner is considered to be the owner of the stock. § 1361(c)(2)(B)(ii).

2) Testamentary trusts to which stock has been transferred pursuant to a will, but only for the 2-year period beginning on the day of transfer. § 1361(c)(2)(A)(iii). The testator's estate is treated as the shareholder during this period. § 1361(c)(2)(B)(iii).

3) Voting trusts—i.e., trusts created to exercise the voting power of stock. Each beneficial owner is treated as a separate shareholder. § 1361(c)(2)(A)(iv); 1361(c)(2)(B)(iv).

   Example: Assume 95 of 100 outstanding shares of stock in Y Corp. are owned by 95 individuals. If the remaining 5 shares are owned by a voting trust, Y may qualify as a small business corporation as long as the trust does not have more than 5 beneficial owners.

4) Qualified Subchapter S Trusts and Electing Small Business Trusts, discussed below.

d. Qualified Subchapter S Trusts

Section 1361(d)(1) permits the beneficiary of a "qualified Subchapter S trust" to elect to have the trust treated as a qualified shareholder for Subchapter S purposes and to be treated as the owner of the portion of the trust consisting of S corporation stock. The owner of stock in a qualified Subchapter S trust may be included in a family that elects to be treated as one shareholder. A "qualified Subchapter S trust" is a trust the terms of which require that:

1) During the life of the current income beneficiary, the trust shall have only one income beneficiary;

2) Any corpus distributed during the life of the current income beneficiary may be distributed only to that beneficiary;

3) The income interest of the current income beneficiary shall terminate on the earlier of the beneficiary's death or the termination of the trust;

4) Upon the termination of the trust during the life of the current income beneficiary, the trust shall distribute all of its assets to such beneficiary; and

5) All of the income is or must be distributed currently to one individual who is a U.S. citizen or resident. § 1361(d)(3).

e. Electing Small Business Trusts

The electing small business trust ("ESBT") was added as an eligible shareholder to provide more flexibility in estate planning for businesses operated as S corporations. An ESBT, for example, may have more than one current income beneficiary, and the trustee may have discretion over distributions of income and corpus. The requirements for an ESBT are (§ 1361(e)(1)):

1) All the beneficiaries must be individuals, estates, or tax-exempt organizations that are eligible S corporation shareholders, nonresident aliens, or charitable organizations holding contingent remainder interests;

2) No interests in the trust may have been acquired by purchase; and

3) The trustee must elect ESBT status.

Each current income beneficiary of an ESBT is treated as a shareholder for purposes of the 100-shareholder limit. § 1361(c)(2)(B)(v). A beneficiary of an ESBT who is a shareholder may be included in a family that elects to be counted as one shareholder. An ESBT's pro rata share of S corporation income is taxable to the trust at the highest marginal rates in § 1(e) (for estates and trusts), whether or not the income is distributed. § 641(d).

4. One-Class-of-Stock Requirement

a. In General

An S corporation may not have more than one class of stock. § 1361(b)(1)(D). The purpose of this rule is to simplify the allocation of income and deductions among an S corporation's shareholders. An S corporation generally is treated as having one class of stock if all of its outstanding shares confer identical rights to distribution and liquidation proceeds. Differences in voting rights are disregarded. Thus, an S corporation may issue both voting and nonvoting common stock. Reg. § 1.1361–1(*l*)(1). Distributions that take into account varying interests in stock during the taxable year do not violate the "identical rights" requirement. Reg. § 1.1361–1(*l*)(2)(iv). For purposes of this requirement, outstanding stock does not include § 83 restricted stock that is not substantially vested unless the holder made a § 83(b) election. Reg. § 1.1361–1(*l*)(3).

b. Buy-Sell and Redemption Agreements

Buy-sell agreements among shareholders, stock transfer restriction agreements, and redemption agreements generally are disregarded in determining whether a corporation has more than one class of stock unless a principal purpose of the agreement is to circumvent the one-class-of-stock requirement and the agreement establishes a purchase price that, at the time the agreement is entered into, is significantly higher or lower than the fair market value of the stock. Reg. § 1.1361–1(*l*)(2)(iii).

c. Obligations Treated as Equity Under General Principles

Unless the § 1361(c)(5) straight debt safe harbor applies (see XV.B.4.d., below), S corporation debt instruments or obligations treated as equity under general tax principles are treated as a second class of stock if the principal purpose of issuing the instrument is to circumvent the identical-rights-to-distributions and liquidation-proceeds rule or the shareholder-limitation rules. Reg. § 1.1361–1(*l*)(4)(ii)(A).

d. Straight Debt Safe Harbor

1) Background

At one time, S corporations with debt instruments (e.g., bonds) outstanding risked losing their S status if their debt was reclassified as equity under general debt/equity principles because the Service argued that the corporation had more than one class of stock. That threat has diminished with the enactment of the § 1361(c)(5) "straight debt safe harbor" under which "straight debt" will not be treated as a second class of stock.

2) Straight Debt Defined

"Straight debt" is any written, unconditional obligation, whether or not embodied in a formal note, to pay a sum certain on demand or on a specified date, if:

a) The interest rate and payment dates are not contingent on profits, the borrower's discretion, the payment of dividends on common stock, or similar factors;

b) The instrument is not convertible (directly or indirectly) into stock; and

c) The creditor is an individual, estate or a trust that would be a permissible S corporation shareholder.

Reg. § 1.1361–1(*l*)(5)(i). The fact that an obligation is subordinated to other debt of the corporation does not prevent it from qualifying as straight debt. Reg. § 1.1361–1(*l*)(5)(ii).

3) Treatment of Straight Debt for Other Purposes

An obligation of an S corporation that satisfies the straight debt safe harbor will not be treated as a second class of stock even if it is considered equity under general tax principles. Straight debt generally will be treated as debt for other purposes of the Code (e.g., the interest deduction). But if a straight debt obligation bears an unreasonably high rate of interest, an appropriate portion of that interest may be recharacterized as a payment that is not interest. Reg. § 1.1361–1(*l*)(5)(iv). Such a recharacterization, however, does not result in a second class of stock. Id.

4) Treatment of Converted C Corporation Debt

If a C corporation has outstanding debt obligations that satisfy the straight debt safe harbor but might be classified as equity under general tax principles, the safe harbor ensures that the obligation will not be treated as a second class of stock if the C corporation elects to convert to S status. The conversion and change of status also is not treated as a taxable exchange of the debt instrument for stock. Reg. § 1.1361–1(*l*)(5)(v).

C. Election, Revocation and Termination of Subchapter S Status

1. Electing S Corporation Status

a. In General

In order to be an S corporation, a small business corporation must make an election to which all of its shareholders consent. § 1362(a). An S election is effective for the taxable year for which it is made and for all succeeding taxable years of the corporation until it is terminated. § 1362(c). The Service may waive the effect of an inadvertent invalid election (e.g., failure to obtain all necessary shareholder consents) under certain circumstances. § 1362(f).

b. Timing and Effective Date of Election

An S election may be made for a taxable year at any time during the preceding taxable year or on or before the fifteenth day of the third month of the taxable year. § 1362(b)(1).

Example (1): Assume Z Corp. qualifies as a small business corporation under § 1361(b). If the shareholders of Z wish to elect S corporation status for calendar Year 2, they must make the election either during Year 1 or before March 16 of Year 2.

An election made after the 15th day of the third month of the taxable year and before the same day in the following year is generally treated as made for the following year. § 1362(b)(3). If an election is made during a taxable year and on or before the 15th day of the third month of the year, but either (1) the corporation was not a small business corporation on one or more days before the election was made, or (2) one or more persons who held stock in the corporation prior to the time the election was made does not consent, then the election is treated as made for the following year. § 1362(b)(2). The Service, however, has the authority to treat a late election as timely for reasonable cause. § 1362(b)(5).

Example (2): Assume Z Corp. in Example (1) makes an election to be an S corporation on March 10, Year 2. If Z had a shareholder which was a partnership during January of Year 2, it could not elect S status for the Year 2 taxable year, because it had an ineligible shareholder during the period of the taxable year prior to the election. The election would be treated as made for Z's Year 3 taxable year.

Example (3): Assume that on January 1, Year 2, W Co., which is a C corporation, had 10 shareholders. On January 15, Year 2, one of W's shareholders, A, who is an individual, sells her W stock to B, who also is an individual. On March 5, Year 2, W files an election to be an S corporation for its Year 2 taxable year. Assuming W qualifies as a small business corporation, its election will be effective only if all of the shareholders as of March 5, Year 2, as well as former shareholder A, consent to the election. For W's election to be effective for its Year 3 taxable year, A would not have to consent to the election.

2. Revocation and Termination of S Corporation Status

a. Revocation

An S election may be revoked with the consent of more than one-half of the shares of the stock (including nonvoting stock) of the corporation on the day the revocation is made. § 1362(d)(1)(B); Reg. § 1.1362–2(a)(1). The corporation may specify any effective date on or after the day of the revocation. If an effective date is not selected, a revocation is effective: (1) on the first day of the taxable year if made before the sixteenth day of the third month of such year, or (2) on the first day of the next taxable year if it is made after the fifteenth day of the third month of the year. § 1362(d)(1)(C), (D).

b. Termination

1) Ceasing to Be a Small Business Corporation

An S corporation election terminates whenever the corporation ceases to be a small business corporation. The termination is effective on and after the day of the event that terminated its small business corporation status. § 1362(d)(2). Reg. § 1.1362–2(b).

Example: If an S corporation exceeds the 100-shareholder limit, has an impermissible shareholder, issues a second class of stock, or otherwise ceases to be a small business corporation, its Subchapter S election will terminate as of the day of the disqualifying event.

2) Passive Income Limitation for Certain S Corporations

An S corporation's election will terminate if it has Subchapter C accumulated earnings and profits (i.e., E & P from its pre-Subchapter S existence) at the close of each of three consecutive taxable years in which it was an S corporation and more than 25% of its gross receipts for each of those years consists of passive investment income. The termination is effective on the first day of the taxable year beginning after the three-year measuring period. § 1362(d)(3)(A)(i), (ii). An S corporation which has never been a C corporation or which was a C corporation but has no E & P from that period would not be concerned about a termination under this provision. "Passive investment income" generally includes gross receipts from royalties, rents, dividends, interest, and annuities but does not include gains from the disposition of property. § 1362(d)(3)(C)(i). For purposes of the overall gross receipts definition, gross receipts from sales or exchanges of stock or securities are taken into account only to the extent of gains and gross receipts from dispositions of capital assets other than stock or securities are taken into account only to the extent that capital gains from such dispositions exceed capital losses. § 1362(d)(3)(B). See also Reg. § 1.1362–2(c).

c. S Termination Year

If an S corporation's election is revoked or terminated, the corporation has an "S termination year," which consists of an S short year and a C short year. § 1362(e)(1), (4). In general, the tax results for the S termination year are assigned to the two short years on a pro rata basis unless all persons who were shareholders during the S short year and all of the shareholders on the first day of the C short year elect to make the allocation on the basis of normal tax accounting rules. § 1362(e)(2), (3). Since the C short year is subject to the full sting of the double tax on corporate profits, the corporation will be motivated to select the method which allocates the most income to the S short year. The pro rata method may not be used if there is a sale or exchange of 50% or more of the stock in the corporation during the year. § 1362(e)(6)(D). Once the allocation between the short years is made, the tax liability for the C short year is computed on an annualized basis. § 1362(e)(5). See Reg. § 1.1362–3.

d. Inadvertent Terminations

If an S corporation's election is revoked or terminated, the corporation generally is not eligible to reelect S corporation status for five years unless it receives the Treasury's consent to an earlier election. § 1362(g). Section 1362(f) provides relief for terminations that occur when the corporation ceases to be a small business corporation or violates the passive income limitation. If (1) the Treasury determines that the termination was inadvertent, (2) the corporation takes steps to rectify the problem within a reasonable period of time after discovery, and (3) the corporation and all of the persons who were shareholders during the relevant period agree to make certain adjustments required by the Treasury, then the corporation will retain its S corporation status. The fact that the terminating event was not reasonably within the control of the corporation and took place despite its due diligence tends to establish that a termination was inadvertent. Reg. § 1.1362–4(b). Section 1362(f) may also be used to obtain relief from ineffective elections to treat a subsidiary as a qualified Subchapter S subsidiary or to treat a family as one shareholder.

Example: X Corporation, in good faith, determined that it had no earnings and profits, but the Service later determined on audit that X's S election terminated because X violated the passive income test for three consecutive years by having accumulated earnings and profits. If the shareholders were to agree to treat the earnings as distributed and include the dividends in income, it may be appropriate to waive the terminating event, so X's election is treated as if it never terminated.

D. Tax Treatment of S Corporation Shareholders

1. Introduction

Except in a few situations discussed later in this chapter (See XV.F., at pages 315–318 *infra*), an S corporation is not a taxable entity. § 1363(a). Instead, the corporation's income, loss, deductions, and credits are taxed directly to its shareholders. § 1366(a). Even though aggregate principles are employed for the taxation of an S corporation's income or loss, entity principles generally are used for its computation.

2. Corporate Level Determination of Tax Results

An S corporation is required to calculate its gross income and taxable income in order to determine the tax items that pass through to the shareholders. §§ 1366(c); 1363(b).

An S corporation also must file its own tax return (Form 1120S) and is subject to audit and examination by the Internal Revenue Service. § 6037.

a. Accounting Method

An S corporation generally is free to select its own accounting method. If an S corporation is a "tax shelter" as defined in § 448, however, it may not use the cash method of accounting, but the corporation is, in effect, required by § 267 to use the cash method for purposes of taking deductions on payments to persons who own stock in the corporation either directly or by way of attribution. § 267(a)(2), (e).

b. Taxable Year

1) In General

The shareholders of an S corporation are required to include in income their pro rata share of S corporation income in the taxable year in which the S corporation's taxable year ends. § 1366(a). The calendar year shareholders of a profitable S corporation would prefer the corporation to adopt a January 31 taxable year so that they could wait 14½ months (until April 15 of the following year) to pay tax on the corporation's income. To preclude this type of deferral, § 1378 requires an S corporation's taxable year to be a "permitted year," which is defined as a calendar year or an accounting year for which the corporation establishes a business purpose. Deferral of income to the shareholders is not treated as a business purpose. § 1378(b). The legislative history provides that: (1) the use of a particular year for regulatory or financial accounting purposes, (2) hiring patterns of a business, (3) administrative considerations, such as compensation or retirement arrangements with staff or shareholders, and (4) the fact that the business uses price lists, model years, etc., which change on an annual basis, ordinarily are not sufficient to satisfy the business purpose requirement. H.R.Rep. No. 99–841, 99th Cong. 2d Sess. II–319 (1986).

Example: Assume W Corp. is an S corporation and its principal business is selling new automobiles. The fact that W's new model cars come out in late summer or fall ordinarily is not sufficient to establish a business purpose for it to use a taxable year ending at that time.

2) Natural Business Year

The business purpose standard is satisfied if the taxable year of an S corporation coincides with a "natural business year." The Service has quantified the natural-business-year concept by providing that a corporation will be deemed to have adopted a natural business year if in each of the prior three years its gross receipts for the last two months of the requested taxable year equaled or exceeded 25% of the gross receipts for the full requested year. Rev. Proc. 2006–46, 2006–2 C.B. 859. An S corporation unable to satisfy this standard still may demonstrate that a particular taxable year satisfies the business purpose standard under a facts and circumstances test. The Service, however, considers the tax consequences (i.e., deferral) of the year selected to be a fact and circumstance relevant to the question. Rev. Rul. 87–57, 1987–2 C.B. 117.

> ***Example:*** Y Co. desires to use a May 31 tax year. Y's reason for the requested tax year is that due to weather conditions its business is operational only during the period of September 1 through May 1. For its 10-year business history, Y has had insignificant gross receipts for the period of June 1 through August 31. Y's facility is not used for any other purpose during those months. Despite the fact that Y was unable to satisfy the mechanical "natural business year" test, the Service ruled in Revenue Ruling 87–57 that Y established a business purpose for a May 31 tax year.

3) § 444 Fiscal Year Election

Section 444 alleviates some of the harshness of the permitted year requirement. It permits an S corporation to adopt a taxable year other than the calendar year normally required by § 1378, provided the year selected results in no more than three months of tax deferral. As a cost for this relief, the corporation must make "required payments" under § 7519 which are designed to offset the financial benefits of the tax deferral provided by § 444. A § 444 election and § 7519 payments, however, are not required if an S corporation can establish a business purpose for the taxable year it selects. § 444(e).

> ***Example:*** Assume T Corp. is an S corporation which cannot establish a business purpose for using a taxable year other than a calendar year. T may elect under § 444 to select a fiscal year ending on September 30, October 31, or November 30. If it makes a § 444 election, T will have to make § 7519 required payments to, in effect, "pay back" the benefits of its shareholders being able to defer inclusion of its income for an additional one to three months. Section 7519 has a de minimis provision which would relieve T of this burden if its required payment for a taxable year is $500 or less. If T establishes a business purpose for adopting a taxable year other than a calendar year, it may adopt such a year without electing under § 444 and making § 7519 payments.

c. S Corporation Taxable Income

1) In General

An S corporation is required to compute its taxable income in the same manner as an individual except that it is not permitted certain deductions allowed only to individuals, such as personal exemptions, medical expenses, and expenses for the production or collection of income under § 212. §§ 1363(b)(2); 703(a)(2)(A), (E). Because an S corporation's losses pass through to its shareholders, the corporation is not permitted a net operating loss deduction. §§ 1363(b)(2); 703(a)(2)(D). Net operating losses from years in which the corporation was a C corporation also may not be carried over to a taxable year in which it is an S corporation. § 1371(b)(1).

2) Separately Stated Items

To preserve their unique character as they pass through to the shareholders, the corporation must separately report any item of income (including tax-exempt income) loss, deduction or credit the separate treatment of which could affect the tax liability of any shareholder. These are known as "separately stated" items. § 1363(b)(1). The characterization of items is determined at the corporate level. § 1366(b). Certain separately stated items, such as charitable contributions, foreign taxes, and depletion, are not deductible by the corporation in computing its taxable income, but they still pass through to the shareholders. §§ 1363(b)(2); 703(a)(2)(B), (C), (F). Examples of other separately stated items include: (1) capital gains and losses, so that the § 1211 limitation on capital losses may be applied at the shareholder level after consideration of each shareholder's other capital gains and losses; (2) § 1231 transactions, so the provisions of § 1231 are applied at the shareholder level taking into account all of the shareholder's § 1231 transactions; and (3) investment interest, so the § 163(d) investment interest limit is applied after taking into account each shareholder's personal tax situation. Reg. § 1.1366–1(a)(2).

3) Charitable Contributions

Unlike C corporations, S corporations are not subject to the 10% of taxable income limitation on charitable contributions. Rather, charitable contributions are categorized by the percentage limitations applicable to individuals in § 170(b) (e.g., 60% for cash contributions and 30% for contributions of long-term capital gain property to public charities) and pass through as such to the shareholders. Reg. § 1.1366–1(a)(2)(iii). Charitable contributions of appreciated capital gain property are generally deductible by the shareholders at their fair market value, subject to any reductions required by § 170(e).

Example: T Corp., which has an S election in effect, makes a charitable contribution during the year. Since T is not allowed a charitable deduction in computing taxable income, the special 10% limitation on corporate charitable deductions in § 170(b)(2) does not apply. Instead, the charitable contribution is a separately stated item which passes through to the shareholders who each combine their share of the deduction with their personal charitable contributions before applying the § 170 percentage limits on charitable contributions by individuals.

4) No Dividends Received Deduction

Because an S corporation generally must compute its taxable income as if it were an individual, it is not allowed deductions granted only to corporations such as the § 243 dividends received deduction.

5) Organizational Expenses

An S corporation is allowed to deduct and amortize its organizational expenses under § 248. § 1363(b)(3).

d. Tax Elections

Elections affecting the determination of taxable income generally are made by the S corporation rather than its shareholders. § 1363(c)(1); Reg. § 1.1363–1(c)(1).

Example: An election to deduct and amortize organizational expenditures under § 248 must be made by the S corporation, not on a shareholder-by-shareholder basis. An election to expense the cost of § 179 property must be made by the S corporation and the dollar limitations in § 179(b) apply at both the S corporation and shareholder levels. § 179(d)(8).

3. Tax Consequences to Shareholders

a. Timing and Character of Pass Through Items

S corporation shareholders are required to take into account their respective pro rata shares of the corporation's separately stated items and nonseparately computed income or loss (i.e., the net total of the items which are not separately stated) in the taxable year in which the S corporation's taxable year ends. § 1366(a). The separately stated items retain their character when reported by the shareholders. § 1366(b).

Example: Assume S Corp. (which is an S corporation) has properly adopted a November 30 taxable year and during its current year has the following income and expenses:

Business Income	$ 100,000
Salary Expense	$ 40,000
Depreciation	$ 10,000
Taxes	$ 5,000
§ 1245 Gain	$ 25,000
§ 1231 Gain	$ 20,000
LTCG from Stock Sale	$ 15,000
LTCL from Stock Sale	$ 4,000
STCL from Stock Sale	$ 6,000

Of these items, the § 1231 gain and capital gain and losses are separately stated items because their separate treatment could affect the tax liability of a particular shareholder depending on the results of the shareholder's other asset dispositions during the year. The regulations permit separate netting of long-and short-term capital gain transactions. Reg. § 1.1366–1(a)(2)(i) & (ii). Thus, S's separately stated items will be: § 1231 gain—$20,000; net LTCG—$11,000 ($15,000 of gain and $4,000 of loss); and STCL—$6,000. These items will retain their character when they are reported by the shareholders. S's nonseparately computed income will be $70,000 ($100,000 business income plus $25,000 § 1245 gain less $55,000 of deductions (salary, depreciation and taxes)). Because the § 1245 gain is ordinary income, its tax treatment cannot vary among shareholders so it is not a separately reported item. Each shareholder will have to take into account his or her pro rata share of the § 1231 gain, net LTCG,

STCL, and $70,000 of nonseparately computed income in the taxable year in which S's November 30 taxable year ends. Calendar year shareholders would report their pro rata shares of these items on April 15 of the following year.

b. Determining Each Shareholder's Pro Rata Share

1) In General

Each shareholder's pro rata share of S corporation tax items is determined on a per share, per day basis. § 1377(a)(1).

Example: Assume Z Co. is an S corporation and has 100 shares of stock outstanding. If shareholder A owns 30 shares of Z for the full year, he will be allocated 30% of each of Z's separately stated items and its nonseparately computed income or loss. If A sells 10 of his shares to D midway through the year, he would be allocated 25% of Z's separately stated items and nonseparately computed income or loss (30% for one-half the year, or 15%, plus 20% for one-half the year, or 10%, for a 25% total).

2) Special Rule for Termination of a Shareholder's Interest

If a shareholder's interest in the corporation is terminated, all shareholders during the year may agree to elect to treat the year as if it consisted of two taxable years with the first year ending on the day of termination. § 1377(a)(2).

Example: Assume X Corp. is an S corporation and has 100 shares of stock outstanding. During the year X earns $50,000 of nonseparately computed income and under its accounting method, $40,000 of the $50,000 was earned in the first half of the year. Assume shareholder B sells all 40 of her X shares midway through the year. Under the per share, per day method of allocation, B will report $10,000 of the nonseparately computed income (40% for one-half the year, or 20% of the $50,000). Alternatively, if all of the shareholders in the corporation agree, X's books can be treated as closing as of the day of B's sale and she will report $16,000 (40% of the $40,000 earned in the first half of X's year). Presumably, B will agree to this arrangement only if she has other losses or deductions to offset the additional income or she has some other reason (maybe a family relationship?) to help the other shareholders save taxes.

3) Special Rule for a Family Group

In order to prevent tax avoidance within a family group through the use of an S corporation, § 1366(e) authorizes the Service to reallocate an S corporation's income if an individual who is a member of the "family" (defined as including a spouse, ancestors and lineal descendants) of an S corporation shareholder renders services or provides capital to the corporation and does not receive reasonable compensation. Note that the service or capital provider to whom income is reallocated does not have to be a shareholder of the S corporation. The statute only requires that a family member of the service or capital provider be a shareholder. In applying § 1366(e), the courts look to what would be paid to obtain comparable services or capital from an unrelated party. *Davis v. Comm'r*, 64 T.C. 1034 (1975).

> *Example:* Assume W Co. is an S corporation with 100 shares of stock outstanding which are owned 20 shares by Dad, 40 shares by Daughter, and 40 shares by Son. If Dad performs $20,000 of deductible services without charge for W, the Service can step in and allocate $20,000 of W's income to Dad. The allocation would produce a $20,000 deduction for W which would reduce the income (or increase the loss) otherwise allocable to Daughter and Son.

c. Limitations on Losses

1) § 1366(d) Basis Limit

A shareholder's share of S corporation losses and deductions is limited to the shareholder's adjusted basis in the (1) stock of the corporation, and (2) indebtedness of the corporation to the shareholder. § 1366(d)(1). Losses or deductions disallowed by § 1366 carry over indefinitely and may be used when the shareholder obtains additional stock or debt basis by, for example, contributing or loaning additional funds to the corporation or buying more stock. § 1366(d)(2)(A). In the case of a transfer of stock of an S corporation to a spouse or former spouse under § 1041(a), the transferee-spouse is allowed to carry over disallowed losses or deductions until that shareholder obtains additional basis. § 1366(d)(2)(B).

> *Example (1):* C is a shareholder in an S corporation and has a $5,000 basis in her stock. C also loaned the corporation $4,000 in exchange for a corporate note. If C's share of the corporation's nonseparately computed loss for the year is $12,000, she will be limited to a $9,000 deduction (her combined basis in the stock and note) and will have $3,000 of suspended loss which will carry over until she obtains additional basis.

If the basis limitation is exceeded by a combination of different types of losses, the limit consists of a proportionate amount of each type of loss. See Reg. § 1.704–1(d)(2), which uses this approach in the analogous partnership setting.

> *Example (2):* D is a shareholder in an S corporation and has a $3,000 basis in his stock. D's share for the year of the corporation's long-term capital loss is $6,000 and his share of nonseparately computed operating loss is $3,000. Under § 1366(d)(1), D will be allowed a $3,000 loss deduction for the year which will be made up as follows:

$$\frac{6000}{9000} \times 3000 = 2000 \text{ LTCL}$$

$$\frac{3000}{9000} \times 3000 = 1000 \text{ OL}$$

D would have a $4,000 long-term capital loss carryover and a $2,000 operating loss carryover going into the next year. See Reg. § 1.1366–2(a)(4).

2) Basis of Indebtedness of S Corporation to a Shareholder

Treasury regulations provide general guidance on the basis of indebtedness of an S corporation to its shareholders. They provide that a shareholder receives basis credit in such indebtedness if the debt is "bona fide," a determination that is made under general tax principles and depends on all the facts and circumstances. For this purpose, relevant factors include evidence of intent to make a loan (e.g., proper documentation and adherence to a payment schedule), objective indicia of indebtedness, and economic reality (e.g., would a third-party lender loan money under similar circumstances). Reg. § 1.1362–2(a)(2)(i). The facts and circumstances rule applies regardless of how the indebtedness arises. The regulations provide examples of various fact patterns, such as loans directly from a shareholder to the S corporation, back-to-back loan arrangements where one S corporation makes a loan to a shareholder and the shareholder then loans money to a different S corporation, and a loan restructuring where a sole shareholder of two S corporations receives the loan of one corporation to the other in a distribution. See Reg. § 1.1362–2(a)(2)(iii) Examples 1–3.

3) Basis Credit for Shareholder Guarantee of S Corporation Debt

The regulations provide that a shareholder does not obtain basis credit in indebtedness of an S corporation merely by guaranteeing a loan or acting as a surety, accommodation party, or in some similar capacity relating to a loan. But if a shareholder is called upon to make a payment on the corporation's indebtedness as a result of a guaranty or similar arrangement, then the shareholder may increase the basis of that indebtedness to the extent of the amount of the payment. Reg. § 1.1362–2(a)(2)(ii); see also Reg. § 1.1362–2(a)(2)(iii) Example 4. Most courts that considered this issue took the same position as the regulations. The taxpayer's argument in these cases, accepted only by the Eleventh Circuit, was that since the lender is ultimately looking to the shareholder for repayment, the transaction should be treated as a loan to the shareholder followed by a capital contribution (or loan) to the corporation. *Selfe v. United States,* 778 F.2d 769 (11th Cir.1985). The issue is important because of the § 1366(d) limitation on pass through of losses.

4) No Basis Credit for Entity Debt

Unlike partners, who generally may include their share of the partnership's indebtedness in the basis of their partnership interest, S corporation shareholders may not include debts incurred by the corporation in their stock or debt basis.

5) **Use of Suspended Losses After Termination of S Corporation Status**

If a shareholder's losses or deductions are disallowed because of inadequate stock basis and the corporation's status as an S corporation terminates, the loss is treated as incurred at the end of the "post-termination transition period" (a period defined in § 1377(b) as extending at least one year after the last day of the corporation's last taxable year as an S corporation). § 1366(d)(3)(A). Thus, if the shareholder has adequate stock basis (debt basis is not considered) at that time by virtue of having made an additional contribution to the corporation, the suspended loss will pass through and reduce the shareholder's personal tax liability. § 1366(d)(3)(B). A corresponding reduction is required in the basis of the stock. § 1366(d)(3)(C).

6) **Other Loss Limitations**

Losses that pass through to the shareholders also may be disallowed by the at-risk rules in § 465, the passive activity limitations in § 469, and the limitations on excess business losses of noncorporate taxpayers in § 461(*l*). The at-risk rules are applied to an S corporation on an activity-by-activity basis, except that all activities constituting a trade or business are treated as one activity if the taxpayer actively participates in the management of the trade or business, or 65% or more of the losses are allocable to persons who actively participate in management of the trade or business. § 465(c)(3)(B). Under the passive loss limitations, if an S corporation shareholder does not materially participate in an activity, his losses from the activity will only be deductible against income from passive activities. § 469(a), (c)(1), (d)(1). Any disallowed passive activity loss may be carried forward to the next taxable year. § 469(b). Losses allowed under § 465 and § 469 may be limited by § 461(*l*), which disallows a current deduction for any "excess business loss" of a noncorporate taxpayer. § 461(*l*)(1)(B). An "excess business loss" is basically defined as a net loss from all of the taxpayer's trade or business activities in excess of $250,000, or $500,000 in the case of a joint return, determined without regard to this limitation. § 461(*l*)(3)(A). The $250,000 and $500,000 amounts are adjusted for inflation after 2018. § 461(*l*)(3)(B). Any loss disallowed under Section 461(*l*) carries over to the next year and is treated as a net operating loss under Section 172. § 461(*l*)(2).

d. Basis Adjustments

The basis of each shareholder's stock in an S corporation is first increased by the shareholder's share of both separately and nonseparately computed income items and decreased, but not below zero, by distributions to the shareholder and then decreased by the shareholder's share of separately and nonseparately computed losses, deductions, and nondeductible expenses which are not capital expenditures. § 1367(a). When an S corporation makes a charitable contribution of appreciated property, the shareholders reduce basis by their pro rata share of the adjusted basis (not fair market value) of the contributed property. § 1367(a)(2), flush language. For the rules providing that basis adjustments for distributions are made before applying the § 1366(d) loss limitation for the year, see §§ 1366(d)(1)(A); 1368(d), last sentence. If losses and deductions exceed the shareholder's stock basis, they may be applied against and reduce (but not below zero) the shareholder's basis in any S corporation debt. § 1367(b)(2)(A). If debt basis is reduced under this provision, later net increases are first applied to restore that basis before being applied to increase the basis of the shareholder's stock. § 1367(b)(2)(B). Basis adjustments are made at the end of the corporation's taxable year unless during the year the shareholder disposes of the stock or the debt is wholly or partially repaid in which case the adjustments are effective immediately before the disposition or repayment. Reg. § 1.1367–1(d)(1), –2(d)(1).

Example: C is a shareholder in an S corporation who paid $5,000 for her stock and loaned the corporation $1,000 in exchange for a corporate note. During the corporation's first taxable year (Year 1), C's share of the corporation's tax items is:

LTCG	$2,000
Operating Income	$4,000
STCL	$1,000

C will report and pay tax on these items in her taxable year in which the corporate taxable year ends. At the end of Year 1 her stock basis is adjusted as follows:

$ 5,000	Original Stock Basis
+ 2,000	§ 1367(a)(1)(A)
+ 4,000	§ 1367(a)(1)(B)
− 1,000	§ 1367(a)(2)(B)
$10,000	New Stock Basis

C's basis in the corporate note remains $1,000.

In Year 2, C's share of the corporation's tax items consists of $12,000 of operating loss. Under § 1366(d), C can only deduct $11,000 of the loss (the total of her stock and debt basis in the corporation). The remaining $1,000 of loss will be suspended and carry over to Year 3. C's basis in her stock and debt will be reduced to zero under § 1367(a)(2)(C) and § 1367(b)(2)(A).

In Year 3, the corporation's business improves and C's share of the corporation's tax items consists of $5,000 of operating income. C will include the $5,000 of income in her personal tax return and will be allowed to deduct the $1,000 loss from the prior year. For basis purposes, the $5,000 increase attributable to the income will be reduced by the $1,000 loss. The remaining $4,000 of basis will first be allocated to the debt to restore it to its original $1,000 basis. § 1367(b)(2)(B).

At the end of Year 3, C's stock basis is adjusted as follows:

$ 0	Beginning Basis
+5,000	Income
−1,000	Suspended Loss Deductible This Year
−1,000	Restoration of Debt Basis
$3,000	New Stock Basis

e. Deduction for Qualified Business Income

1) Introduction

Section 199A, enacted as part of the Tax Cuts and Jobs Act, generally allows noncorporate taxpayers to deduct the sum of 20% of their share of qualified business income ("QBI") from each of the taxpayer's qualified trades or businesses. § 199A(a)(1), (b)(1)(A), (b)(2)(A). The deduction effectively reduces the highest marginal rate on QBI from 37% to 29.6%. Section 199A applies to income generated by sole proprietorships, partnerships, limited liability companies, S corporations, trusts, and estates. The discussion in this outline is confined to a broad overview of the § 199A deduction and the special issues for S corporations and their shareholders. For more extensive coverage, see Schwarz, Lathrope & Hellwig, Black Letter on Partnership Taxation (9th ed.2019).

2) Allocation of § 199A Items to Shareholders

In the case of an S corporation, the § 199A deduction is taken at the shareholder level based on information provided by the corporation. § 199A(f)(1)(A)(i). Unlike partnerships, which have some flexibility in determining a partner's "allocable share" of § 199A items, an S corporation's allocation is pro rata, based on the shareholder's percentage stock ownership. §§ 199A(f)(1), flush language; 1377(a).

3) Qualified Business Income

QBI consists of the net amount of qualified income, gain, deduction and loss items that is effectively connected with the conduct of a trade or business within the United States and included or allowed in determining taxable income for the relevant year. § 199A(c)(3)(A). If the net amount of the taxpayer's combined QBI for the year is less than zero, that amount is treated as a loss from a qualified trade or business in the succeeding year. § 199A(c)(2). QBI excludes a broad range of items that generally are derived from investment activities. The excluded items include, among other things, capital gains and losses, dividends, and interest income (other than interest properly allocable to the trade or business). § 199(c)(3)(B).

4) QBI Does Not Include Reasonable Compensation

QBI does not include reasonable compensation for services. If an S corporation shareholder is also an employee of the S corporation, "reasonable compensation" paid by the corporation for the shareholder-employee's services or reclassified as such is not QBI. § 199A(c)(4)(A). However, a deduction allowable to the S corporation for reasonable compensation will reduce QBI if the deduction is attributable to the qualified trade or business. Reg. § 199A–3(b)(2)(ii)(H). Because an S corporation shareholder's pro rata share of net operating income may qualify for a § 199A deduction, but compensation for services rendered in an employee capacity is not QBI, majority owner-employees of S corporation may have an incentive to minimize the amount paid by the corporation as compensation for their services. If the compensation paid to the owner-employee is not "reasonable" based on the type of services provided, the IRS may reclassify the shareholder's share of net operating income that it determines to represent reasonable compensation. Id. The IRS applies a similar approach to prevent owner-employees of S corporation to minimize compensation in order to avoid employment taxes. See XV.G.3., at page 319, *infra*.

5) Taxable Income Limitation

The § 199A deduction is limited to 20% of the excess of the taxpayer's taxable income (determined without regard to the § 199A deduction) over the taxpayer's net capital gain (generally, net long-term capital gain plus qualified dividends). § 199A(a)(2). This limitation typically will apply only when the taxpayer's income consists largely of QBI.

6) Limitations Imposed on High-Income Taxpayers

a) In General

The calculation of the § 199A deduction becomes more complex once taxpayers reach certain taxable income thresholds: $157,000 for a single taxpayer, and $315,000 for married taxpayers filing jointly. § 199A(e)(2). These threshold amounts are determined without reference to the § 199A deduction, and they are adjusted for inflation after 2018. § 199A(e)(2)(B). For taxpayers with taxable income above the high-income thresholds, § 199A imposes two additional independent limitations, discussed below.

The limitations for high-income taxpayers begin when their taxable income reaches the threshold levels. They are fully phased in at $50,000 above the threshold level for single taxpayers and $100,000 above the threshold level for married taxpayers filing jointly. § 199A(b)(3)(B)(i)(I), (d)(3)(B). For 2019, the limitations apply in full to single taxpayers having taxable income of $210,725 and to married taxpayers having a combined taxable income of $421,400. Within the phase-in range, the limitations are each applied based on the ratio by which the excess of the taxable income of the taxpayer over the applicable threshold amount bears to $50,000 for single taxpayers, and $100,000 for married taxpayers filing jointly. § 199A(b)(3)(B)(i)(II), (d)(3)(B).

b) Exclusion for Specified Service Trade or Business

Under the first limitation for high-income taxpayers, a "specified service trade or business" ("SSTB") is excluded from the definition of a qualified trade or business. Generally, an SSTB includes any trade or business involving the performance of services in the fields of health, law, accounting, actuarial science, performing arts, consulting, athletics, financial services, and brokerage services. Any trade or business involving the performance of services in the fields of architecture or engineering is specifically excluded from the definition of an SSTB, while an SSTB specifically includes the performance of services that consist of investing and investment management, trading, or dealing in securities or other investments. § 199(d)(2).

To prevent high-income taxpayers from circumventing the limitations on service income by segregating SSTBs from related income-producing activities, the regulations include an anti-abuse rule. If a trade or business provides property or services to an SSTB and the two trades or businesses have 50% or more common ownership, directly or indirectly through attribution, that portion of the trade or business providing the property or service to the SSTB is treated as a separate SSTB with respect to the related parties. Reg. § 1.199A–5(c)(2)(i).

c) **Limitation on Amount of Deduction Measured by W-2 Wages and Unadjusted Basis in Qualified Property**

The second high-income taxpayer limitation is a cap on the amount of the § 199A deduction, determined by reference to the taxpayer's share of: (1) W-2 wages paid by the trade or business, and (2) the unadjusted basis immediately after acquisition of all qualified property held by the trade or business. That cap is the greater of (1) 50% of the W-2 wages (generally employee compensation, including certain deferred compensation) with respect to the trade or business, or (2) 25% of the W-2 wages with respect to the trade or business plus 2.5% of the unadjusted basis immediately after the acquisition of all qualified property of the trade or business. § 199A(b)(2)(B). Qualified property is depreciable tangible property, real or personal, which is held by and available for use in a qualified trade or business and used at any point during the taxable year in the production of QBI, but only if the "depreciable period" of the property did not end before the close of the taxable year. § 199A(b)(6)(A). The depreciable period for an item of qualified property begins when the property is placed in service and ends upon the later of ten years thereafter or the last day of the last full year of the recovery period of the property determined under § 168 (disregarding the alternative depreciation system under § 168(g)). § 199A(b)(6)(B).

7) **S Corporation Reporting Requirements**

An S corporation is required to determine and report to its shareholders on their Form K-1s all the necessary information attributable to any trades or businesses it is engaged in to enable the shareholders to determine their § 199A deductions. § 199A(f)(1)(A)(ii) & (iii); Reg. § 1.199A–6(b)(1). To do so, the S corporation must determine if it is engaged in one or more trades or businesses and whether any of them is a specified service trade or business. The S corporation then must determine the QBI, W-2 wages, and unadjusted basis immediately after acquisition of all qualified property for each trade or business in which it is directly engaged. Prop. Reg. § 1.199A–6(b)(2). If an S corporation fails to satisfy its reporting requirements, the shareholder's share of positive QBI, W-2 wages, and the unadjusted basis immediately after acquisition of qualified property attributable to trades or businesses engaged in by the S corporation is presumed to be zero. Reg. § 1.199A–6(b)(3)(iii).

8) Effect of § 199A Deduction

Because the § 199A deduction is basically a tax rate reduction, it has no effect on the adjusted basis of a shareholder's stock in an S corporation or on an S corporation's accumulated adjustments account. Reg. § 1.199A–1(e)(1).

f. Sale of S Corporation Stock

S corporation stock is a capital asset and historically was treated as such for purposes of characterizing gain or loss to a selling shareholder. More recently, the regulations apply a partial and fairly narrow "look-through" rule for sales and exchanges of S corporation stock. Reg. § 1.1(h)–1. Shareholders who sell S corporation stock held for more than one year may recognize either collectibles gain (taxable at a maximum rate of 28%) or residual capital gain (taxable at a maximum rate of 20%) or loss. A selling shareholder's share of collectibles gain is the amount of "net collectibles gain" (but not loss) that would be allocated to that shareholder if the S corporation sold all of its collectibles in a fully taxable transaction immediately before the sale of the stock. The "residual" capital gain (or loss) is the amount of long-term capital gain or loss that the shareholder would recognize on the sale of the stock ("pre-look-through capital gain or loss") less the shareholder's share of collectibles gain. Reg. § 1.1(h)–1(c). It is possible for a selling shareholder who has a pre-look-through gain to end up with a collectibles gain and a residual capital loss. These look-through rules do not extend to ordinary income assets or to the 25% "unrecaptured section 1250 gain" that may be realized on the sale of depreciable real estate.

Example: A, B and C are equal shareholders in S Corp., an S corporation that invests in antique collectibles. A, who has held her S Corp. stock for more than one year and has an adjusted basis of $1,000, sells her stock to P for $1,500, recognizing $500 of pre-look-through long-term capital gain. S Corp. owned antiques which, if sold for their fair market value, would result in $3,000 of collectibles gain, of which $1,000 would be allocable to A. Therefore, on the sale of her stock, A recognizes $1,000 of collectibles gain and $500 of residual long-term capital loss. Reg. § 1.1(h)–1(f) Example 4.

E. Distributions to Shareholders

Because the shareholders of an S corporation are taxed directly on their share of the corporation's income, whether actually received or not, distributions of that income should not be taxed again. Section 1368 accomplishes that result in straightforward fashion for corporations that do not have E & P. Distributions by S corporations with E & P (for example, from prior operation as a C corporation or acquisition of a C corporation) present some additional complications.

1. S Corporations Without E & P

Distributions by S corporations with no E & P are tax free to the extent of the shareholder's adjusted basis in stock of the corporation. § 1368(b)(1). If the distribution exceeds the shareholder's stock basis, the excess is treated as gain from the sale or exchange of the stock, normally capital gain if the stock is a capital asset. § 1368(b)(2). Finally, the shareholder's stock basis is reduced by the amount of any distribution which is not includible in income by reason of the distribution rules. § 1367(a)(2)(A).

Example: D is a shareholder in an S corporation and has a $5,000 basis in his stock. If the corporation distributes $8,000 of cash to D, $5,000 is treated as a tax-free return of capital and $3,000 is treated as gain from the sale or exchange of D's stock. D's stock basis will be reduced to zero as a result of the distribution.

2. S Corporations with E & P

a. In General

In order to determine the tax consequences of a distribution by an S corporation with E & P, a concept is needed to separate the results of the corporation's operations as an S corporation from its prior C corporation existence. The concept adopted for this purpose is the accumulated adjustments account (the "AAA"). To the extent of the AAA, distributions are treated in the same fashion as distributions by S corporations without E & P—first as a tax-free recovery of stock basis, then as gain from the sale or exchange of stock. If distributions during the year exceed the AAA, the AAA is proportionately allocated based on the amount of each distribution. Amounts distributed in excess of the AAA are first treated as a dividend to the extent of the corporation's E & P and then as a recovery of any remaining stock basis and gain from the sale or exchange of stock. § 1368(c). Alternatively, all shareholders receiving distributions during the year may jointly elect to have all distributions first treated as dividends to the extent of available E & P. § 1368(e)(3); Reg. § 1.1368–1(e)(2).

b. The Accumulated Adjustments Account

The AAA is an account of the corporation which is adjusted for the period since the corporation has been an S corporation (beginning in 1983) in the same general manner as adjustments are made to a shareholder's basis. § 1368(e)(1)(A). The AAA is a corporate account and is not apportioned among the shareholders. Reg. § 1.1368–2(a). The AAA is best understood as a running total of the undistributed earnings of the corporation which have been taxed to the shareholders during the time it has been an S corporation.

Example: On January 1, 2020, T Corporation elected to be an S corporation. Prior to 2020, T operated as a C corporation and at the time of its S election it had $6,000 of accumulated E & P. During 2020, T had $30,000 of operating income from its business and made no distributions to its shareholders. During 2021, T had a $10,000 LTCG, $20,000 of operating loss from its business and made no distributions. During 2022, T broke even in its business and distributed $20,000 to each of its two equal shareholders, A and B. Assume A's basis in her T stock at the beginning of 2022 is $12,000 and B's basis in his T stock is $8,000.

T's AAA is $20,000 for purposes of characterizing the distributions to A and B:

$ 30,000	2020 operating income
+ 10,000	2021 LTCG
− 20,000	2021 operating loss
$ 20,000	AAA

Thus, the first $10,000 of distributions will be treated as recovery of stock basis (to the extent thereof) and gain from the sale or exchange of stock. The next $3,000 of distributions will be a dividend as a result of T's accumulated E & P. The final $7,000 of distributions will be recovery of any remaining stock basis and gain. In summary, the results to A and B are:

A		B
$10,000	§ 1368(c)(1), (b)(1)	$8,000
	§ 1368(c)(1), (b)(2), (b)(1)	$2,000
$ 3,000	§ 1368(c)(2)	$3,000
$ 2,000	§ 1368(c)(3), (b)(1)	
$ 5,000	§ 1368(c)(3), (b)(2)	$7,000

As a result of the distributions, both A's and B's stock bases will be zero at the end of the year. § 1367(a)(2)(A). T's AAA will also be reduced to zero because it is allowed a $20,000 reduction for the amount of the distribution received by A and B tax free. §§ 1368(e)(1)(A); 1367(a)(2)(A). T's E & P will be zero at the end of the year. §§ 312(a)(1); 1371(c)(3). Since T no longer has E & P, it will be able to operate in the future without having to worry about its AAA unless it later obtains E & P—e.g., through an acquisition of a C corporation. Finally, it would not have mattered on these facts, but if the distributions had been smaller (e.g., $3,000 to each shareholder) A and B could have considered a joint election to treat the distribution as a dividend. The benefit of such an election would be to eliminate T's E & P and the need for the AAA. Elimination of E & P also would remove the threat of a termination or corporate-level tax as a result of passive investment income. See §§ 1362(d)(3) and 1375.

3. Distributions of Property

The rules in § 1368 do not distinguish between cash and property distributions at the shareholder level. The amount of a property distribution will be the fair market value of the property and a shareholder will take a fair market value basis in distributed property. § 301(b)(1), (d). The shareholder's stock basis also will be reduced by the fair market value of the distributed property. §§ 1367(a)(2)(A) and 1368.

At the corporate level, a distribution of appreciated property to a shareholder will require recognition of gain as if the property were sold. §§ 311(b)(1), 1368(a) and 1371(a)(1). The gain will be taxed directly to the shareholders like any other gain recognized by the corporation.

Example: Assume W Co. (an S corporation) has no E & P, breaks even in business during the year, and distributes appreciated land (a capital asset held long-term with a $50,000 fair market value and $20,000 adjusted basis) to C, one of its two equal shareholders. Also, assume C's basis in her W stock is $70,000 and W makes a simultaneous $50,000 cash distribution to D, its other shareholder. W will recognize $30,000 of LTCG, $15,000 of which will be taxed to each shareholder. C will receive a $50,000 tax-free distribution, and her stock basis beginning the next year will be:

$ 70,000	Stock Basis
+ 15,000	§§ 1366(a)(1)(A), 1367(a)(1)(A)
− 50,000	§§ 1368(b)(1), 1367(a)(2)(A)
$ 35,000	

4.   Ordering of Basis Adjustments

A shareholder's basis is first increased by his pro rata share of income and gain for the year and then decreased (but not below zero) by distributions before any further reduction for losses. § 1368(d), last sentence. Thus, downward basis adjustments for distributions are made before applying the § 1366(d) loss limitation for the year. § 1366(d)(1)(A). This is similar to the ordering rules used by partnerships. Reg. § 1.704–1(d)(2).

Example: A is the sole shareholder of X Corp., an S corporation with no accumulated E & P. On January 1 of the current year, A's adjusted basis in her X stock is $1,000, and A holds no X debt. During the year, X recognizes a $200 LTCG, sustains an operating loss of $900, and distributes $700 cash to A. A's adjusted basis in her X stock is first increased by $200, to $1,200, to reflect the $200 LTCG. A's basis is then reduced by the distribution to $500 ($1,200 less the $700 distribution) before applying the § 1366(d)(1) loss limitation. A may deduct $500 of X's operating loss and reduces her adjusted stock basis to zero. The remaining $400 of loss may be carried forward under § 1366(d)(2).

5.   Distributions Following Termination of S Corporation Status

Following termination of a corporation's S status, cash distributions during a "post-termination transition period" (a period defined in § 1377(b) as extending at least one year after the last day of the corporation's last taxable year as an S corporation) are applied against stock basis to the extent of the AAA. § 1371(e)(1). All shareholders receiving distributions during the post-termination transition period may elect to not have this rule apply. § 1371(e)(2).

F. Taxation of the S Corporation

The principal benefit of a corporation making an S election is relief from paying all corporate-level taxes. Thus, an S corporation is not subject to the § 11 tax on corporate taxable income, and various penalty taxes such as the § 531 accumulated earnings tax and the § 541 personal holding company tax. S corporations with a prior C corporation history, however, are subject to taxation in certain limited circumstances.

1.   § 1374 Tax on Built-in Gains

a.   Policy of Built-in Gains Tax

When Congress repealed the remaining remnants of the *General Utilities* doctrine, it was concerned that Subchapter S might be used to avoid tax on corporate-level gain. The fear was that a C corporation seeking to liquidate or distribute a highly appreciated asset to its shareholders could make an S election prior to the contemplated distribution. Although corporate-level gain would be recognized, it would pass through to the shareholders and no corporate-level tax would be paid. The shareholders possibly would be required to recognize gain on the liquidation but only after an upward adjustment in their stock basis as a result of taking the gain into income. If permitted, this technique would reduce or eliminate the full burden of the double tax.

To curtail this strategy, Congress enacted § 1374, which applies to S corporations making an election after 1986. In keeping with its narrow purpose, § 1374 does not apply to corporations that have always been S corporations. § 1374(c)(1).

b. Operation of § 1374

Section 1374 imposes a tax (generally at the highest § 11(b) rates, which is now the 21% flat rate) on an S corporation's net recognized built-in gain for any taxable year during a 5-year "recognition period" beginning with the first day it became an S corporation. § 1374(a), (b)(1), (d)(7). An S corporation's recognized built-in gain is any gain recognized during the relevant 5-year period unless the corporation establishes that it did not hold the asset when it made its S election or the gain recognized exceeded the gain inherent in the asset at the time of the S election. § 1374(d)(3). Built-in gains subject to § 1374 include not only gains from sales or exchanges of property but also other income items, such as cash basis accounts receivable, that were earned (but not collected) when the corporation was a C corporation. § 1374(c)(5)(A). The base for the tax, "net recognized built-in gain," is the lesser of the corporation's recognized built-in gains and losses for the year or the corporation's taxable income (computed with various modifications). § 1374(d)(2). The net recognized built-in gain, however, cannot exceed the excess of the total net unrealized gain in the corporation's assets at the time of its S election over the net recognized built-in gain for prior years in the 5-year period. § 1374(c)(2).

Example: Assume S Co. was formed as a C corporation in 2017 and made an S election effective as of the beginning of the current year, when it had no E & P and the following assets:

Asset	Adj. Basis	F. Mkt. Value
Asset # 1	$40,000	$20,000
Asset # 2	25,000	50,000
Asset # 3	5,000	15,000
Total	$70,000	$85,000

If S sells Asset #3 for $20,000 in the first year after its S election, it has a $15,000 gain ($20,000 amount realized less $5,000 adjusted basis). Its recognized built-in gain, however, is $10,000 ($15,000 FMV less $5,000 adjusted basis), assuming it can establish the $15,000 fair market value of the asset at the time of its S election. Assuming S's taxable income (computed with the relevant modifications) is greater than $10,000, its net recognized built-in gain will be $10,000 and its § 1374 tax is $2,100 (the § 11(b) rate of 21% times $10,000). If S's taxable income for the year were less than $10,000, the § 1374 tax would be 21% of the lesser amount. In that event, the difference between $10,000 and S's taxable income would be treated as a recognized built-in gain in S's next taxable year. § 1374(d)(2)(B).

If S sells Asset #2 for $50,000 in its next year as an S corporation, it will have a $25,000 gain ($50,000 amount realized less $25,000 adjusted basis). It also appears to have a $25,000 net recognized built-in gain. Section 1374(c)(2), however, limits the net recognized built-in gain for the year to the $15,000 of total gain potential in S's assets at the time of its election ($85,000 FMV less $70,000 adjusted basis) less the $10,000 of net recognized built-in gain in its first year. Thus, S's net recognized built-in gain for its second year is $5,000 and its § 1374(b) tax will be $1,050 (21% of $5,000), assuming its taxable income for the year is not less than $5,000.

If either of these sales had been made in the sixth or later year after the corporation's S election, they would be beyond the expiration of the recognition period and not be taxable under § 1374.

c. Treatment of Substituted Basis Properties

An S corporation may dispose of or acquire assets in a wide variety of nontaxable transactions. Section 1374(d)(6) and (8) describe the impact of these transactions under the § 1374 tax. Under § 1374(d)(6), if property held by an S corporation ("new property") has a basis determined by reference to the basis of property held by the corporation at the time of its S election ("old property"), the new property is treated as held by the corporation as of the time of the election, and if it is sold the recognized built-in gain or loss is determined with reference to the basis and value of the old property at the time of the election.

Example: If an S corporation exchanges property it held at the time of its S election ("old property") for property of like kind ("new property") in a nontaxable (or partially nontaxable) transaction under § 1031, any built-in gain in the old property will be recognized under § 1374 if the new property is disposed of in a taxable transaction during the recognition period.

Section 1374(d)(8) contains a similar rule for assets acquired by an S corporation from a C corporation in a tax-free reorganization. In that situation, the recognition period with respect to such property begins on the day the S corporation acquires the assets, not the day of its S election. § 1374(d)(8)(B)(i). The exclusion from § 1374 for corporations that have always been an S corporation does not apply if a corporation acquires assets from a C corporation in a tax-free reorganization. § 1374(d)(8)(B)(ii).

d. Installment Sales and § 1374

If an S corporation disposes of an asset with a built-in gain during the recognition period for deferred payments due after the recognition period, § 1374 continues to apply to the payments received after the recognition period. The gain in later years will be taxed to the extent it would have been taxed under

§ 1374 if the corporation had elected to recognize the gain in the year of sale under § 453(d). Reg. § 1.1374–4(g).

2.   § 1375 Tax on Excess Passive Investment Income

If an S corporation has E & P from Subchapter C operations and more than 25% of its gross receipts consist of "passive investment income," it is subject to a 21% tax (the current § 11(b) rate) on its "excess net passive income." An S corporation with no E & P is not subject to § 1375. "Passive investment income" generally consists of the classic forms of investment income (dividends, interest, rents, etc., but not gains from the disposition of property) and § 1375 borrows the definitions employed in § 1362(d)(3) relating to termination of an S election for excessive passive investment income. § 1375(b)(3); see XV.C.2.b.2, at page 298, *supra*.

The regulations define "rents" as amounts received for the use of, or right to use property. But if significant services are also provided, the amounts received are not considered rents. Reg. § 1.1362–2(c)(5)(ii)(B)(2). For example, payments made to a parking lot where an attendant parks the car are not rents. Rev. Rul. 65–91, 1965–1 C.B. 431. But rents received in a mobile home community are "rents" because the services provided (utilities, garbage collection, etc.) are of the type generally provided by a landlord and, hence, not "significant." *Stover v. Comm'r,* 781 F.2d 137 (8th Cir.1986).

"Excess net passive income," the base for the tax, is a portion of the corporation's net passive income, which is generally defined as passive income less directly connected deductions for the year. § 1375(b)(1). This amount is determined by a ratio. The numerator of the ratio is the amount by which the corporation's passive investment income exceeds 25% of its gross receipts for the year and the denominator is passive investment income. Excess net passive income, however, cannot exceed the corporation's taxable income (computed with certain changes). § 1375(b)(1)(B).

The Service may waive the § 1375 tax if the S corporation establishes that it determined in good faith that it had no E & P and within a reasonable time after discovering that it did have E & P it distributed the E & P to its shareholders. § 1375(d).

Example: S Corp. (which is an S corporation) has earnings and profits from its earlier time as a C corporation. During the current year, it has $150,000 of gross receipts, $50,000 of which are passive investment income. S also has $10,000 of expenses directly connected to the production of the passive investment income. S is subject to the § 1375 tax because it has E & P and its passive investment income is at least 25% of its gross receipts ($50,000 passive investment income/$150,000 gross receipts equals 33%). S's net passive income is $40,000 ($50,000 gross receipts less $10,000 of directly connected expenses). Its excess net passive income will be $40,000 (net passive income) multiplied by a ratio having $12,500 as its numerator ($50,000 of passive investment income less 25% of gross receipts) and $50,000 as the denominator (passive investment income). Thus, S's excess net passive income is $10,000 and its § 1375 tax will be $2,100 ($10,000 × 21%). This assumes that S's taxable income as computed under § 1375(b)(1)(B) is less than $10,000.

G. Coordination of Subchapter S with Subchapter C and Other Tax Provisions

1. Subchapter C

Even though it is not subject to the corporate income tax, an S corporation is still a corporation and can engage in a wide array of corporate-shareholder transactions. Thus, an S corporation may redeem its own stock or distribute its net assets to its shareholders in a liquidating distribution. An S corporation also may participate in potentially tax-free or taxable corporate acquisitions as the purchasing corporation or the target and it is free to rearrange its structure under § 355. If various other qualification requirements are met, a § 338(h)(10) or § 336(e) election may be made on the sale or other disposition of an 80% or more controlling interest in S corporation stock, with the result that transaction will be taxed as if it were a sale or disposition of the S corporation's assets. Subchapter S provides limited guidance on the tax treatment of an S corporation and its shareholders in these Subchapter C transactions. Section 1371(a) states that Subchapter C applies to an S corporation and its shareholders, except as otherwise provided or to the extent inconsistent with Subchapter S. Section 1368 also provides that its distribution rules apply to all distributions to which § 301(c) would otherwise apply. Thus, if an S corporation redeems some of its stock in a transaction that does not qualify for exchange treatment under § 302, the distribution will be taxed under § 1368.

2. Other Tax Provisions

Section 1363(b) provides that with certain exceptions an S corporation computes its taxable income in the same manner as an individual. Thus, the tax principles throughout the Code which apply to individual taxpayers generally apply to S corporations. For purposes of fringe benefit provisions in the Code, § 1372 provides that an S corporation is to be treated as a partnership and any 2% shareholder (direct or through attribution) shall be treated as a partner. This provision has the effect of denying the tax advantages of fringe benefits such as group-term life insurance and medical reimbursement plans to disqualified shareholders.

3. Employment Taxes

a. Background

Wages received by employees are subject to federal employment (Social Security and Medicare) taxes, which are paid equally by the employer and employee at a combined rate of 15.3% on wages up to an indexed threshold ($132,900 in 2019) and at 2.9% (the Medicare portion) on all wages above the threshold. Self-employed taxpayers (including general partners and member-managers of LLCs) are subject to self-employment tax, using the same rates and thresholds. An additional 0.9% Medicare tax is imposed on wages and self-employment earnings of high-income taxpayers. S corporations and their owner-employees must pay Social Security and Medicare taxes on wages paid for services rendered to the corporation but, unlike partners and LLC members who are active in the business, their pro rata shares of the entity's net business income, whether or not distributed, are not subject to self-employment tax. The pro rata shares of trade or business income of S corporation owners who are active in the business also are not subject to the 3.8% tax on net investment income imposed on high-income taxpayers.

b.   S Corporation Tax Avoidance Strategy

S corporation shareholders who are also service providers sometimes attempt to avoid paying federal employment taxes by disguising wages as tax-free distributions. The Service may reclassify these distributions as wages to the extent that the actual wages paid do not represent reasonable compensation for the services provided by the employee-shareholder. This strategy presents significant enforcement challenges. In extreme cases, where an S corporation paid little or no salary to its principal employee and shareholder, some courts have concluded that all or part of the corporation's distributions were, in substance, wages subject to federal employment taxes. *Joseph Radtke, S.C. v. United States*, 895 F.2d 1196 (7th Cir.1990); *David E. Watson P.C. v. United States*, 668 F.3d 1008 (8th Cir.2012).

> ***Example:***   Trial Lawyer ("TL") conducts his law practice as an S corporation (S Corp.) in which he is the sole shareholder. In the current year, the net income of the law practice was $5 million. S Corp. pays TL a salary of $500,000 for his services and distributes an additional $4.5 million to TL as a dividend. TL is seeking to avoid the Medicare portion of federal employment taxes on the amount he receives as a dividend (3.8% of $4.5 million, or $171,000). If it discovers this arrangement on an audit, the Service likely will attempt to reclassify all or part of the distribution as wages.

4.   Net Investment Income Tax

a.   Background

Section 1411, which applies to individuals, estate and trusts, imposes a 3.8% "net investment income tax" ("NIIT") on the lesser of a taxpayer's "net investment income" or adjusted gross income (with some specialized modifications) in excess of certain high-income thresholds ($250,000 for married filing jointly taxpayers and $200,000 for single and unmarried head of household taxpayers). "Net investment income" is generally interest, dividends, annuities, royalties, and income from a § 469 passive activity (i.e., a trade or business activity in which the taxpayer does not "materially participate").

b.   Application to S Corporation Shareholders

S corporations are not subject to the NIIT. Rather, they pass through net investment income items and related expenses to their shareholders. The net business income passing through to S corporation shareholders who materially participate in the business is not subject to the NIIT. As noted above, this same income is not subject to self-employment tax unless the shareholder performs services for the corporation and the IRS attempts to reclassify all or part of the business income as wages.

c.   Sale of S Corporation Stock

Under proposed regulations, gains and losses on sales of S corporation stock by a shareholder who does not materially participate in any activities of the business are included in net investment income for purposes of the NIIT. If the selling shareholder materially participates in one or more of the corporation's business activities, each separate activity is deemed to have been sold for its fair market value and the shareholder's pro rata share of gains and losses from hypothetical sales of material participation activities are excluded in determining net investment income. Prop. Reg. § 1.1411–7(a)(1). An optional simplified method is available for selling shareholders with very small shares of net investment income or if the gain or loss on the sale does not exceed $250,000. Prop. Reg. § 1.1411–7(c).

H. Review Questions

1. C Corp. has one 100% owned subsidiary which has been active for several years. In 2016, C decides to elect S corporation status. May it do so?

2. C Corp.'s 150 outstanding shares are owned as follows:

F and J (a married couple)	15 shs.
A and B (unrelated joint tenants)	15 shs.
98 individual unrelated shareholders	120 shs.

   Will C qualify as a "small business corporation"?

3. Assume that in question 2 the shares owned by A and B in joint tenancy are purchased by X Partnership. Will C now qualify as a "small business corporation"?

4. S Corp. (a small business corporation) has 95 individual shareholders. One of its shareholders, M, dies and pursuant to M's will the S stock is transferred to a trust. Does M's death affect S's ability to qualify as a small business corporation?

5. C Corp. has two classes of common stock authorized. Class A is issued and outstanding. Class B has been authorized but has not been issued. Does C qualify as a small business corporation?

6. Assume that S Corp. is an S Corporation with 20 shareholders and 100 shares outstanding and that A, who owns 10 shares, wants to revoke S's status as an S corporation. How many votes are necessary for A to achieve that result?

7. In question 6, assuming revocation is achieved, when will the revocation be effective?

8. Assume that a corporation's S status has been terminated because it violates the 100-shareholder limit. On what date is the termination of S status effective?

9. Does a corporation falling under the situation in question 8 have any recourse as to the termination of its S status?

10. Assume that B, a shareholder in S Corp., an S corporation, guarantees a loan made by a lender directly to S. Will B receive a basis increase for the amount of the loan guarantee?

11. In considering the pass through of losses from an S corporation to its shareholders, what limitations besides the shareholder's basis in S stock and debt are relevant?

12. A is a shareholder in an S corporation and at the beginning of the year has a $4,000 basis in her stock. The corporation does not have any E & P. The corporation distributes $10,000 to A on July 15. A's pro rata share of the corporation's income and loss for the year is:

Nonseparately Computed Income	$8,000
Long-Term Capital Loss	$6,000

   Determine the tax results to A for the year and the results of the July 15 distribution.

13.   What is the "AAA"?

14.   In what situations will an S corporation be concerned with the § 1374 tax on built-in gains?

Appendix A

Answers to Review Questions

II. CLASSIFICATION

1. No. A joint undertaking merely to share expenses is not a separate entity for federal tax purposes and X and Y will not be partners. Reg. § 301.7701–1(a)(2).

2. If A and B form a limited liability company or limited partnership to conduct their business venture, the entity will be classified as a partnership. If A alone forms a limited liability company to operate the business, the entity will be treated as a disregarded entity for tax purposes—i.e., a sole proprietorship if A is an individual or as part of A if A is a corporation. In both cases an election could be made to classify the entity as a corporation.

III. THE C CORPORATION AS A TAXABLE ENTITY

1. **(a)** X Corp.'s taxable income is determined as follows:

   Gross Income:

Income from Operations	$230,000
Dividends	25,000
§ 1231 Gain (LTCG)	30,000
Total	$285,000

   Deductions and Losses:

Operating Expenses	$ 85,000
LTCL (to extent of LTCG)	30,000
Bad Debt	10,000
Sub Dividend (100% Deduction)	20,000
IBM Dividend (50% Deduction)	2,500
Depreciation	45,000
Total	$192,500
Taxable Income	$ 92,500

   (b) X Corp.'s regular tax liability is $19,425 (21% of $92,500).

IV. FORMATION OF A CORPORATION

1. **(a)** Yes. A and B each exchanged property solely in exchange for Newco stock and, immediately after the exchange, A and B collectively own 100% of the total value of Newco's only class of stock.

    (b) A's § 358 basis in the Newco stock is: basis of property transferred ($15,000), less liabilities assumed by Newco ($8,000) = $7,000. A's holding period for the stock includes the period that A held the van. B takes a $7,000 cost basis and his holding period begins as of the date of the exchange. Newco's basis in the van is limited to its $11,000 fair market value under § 362(e)(2)(A) or, alternatively, the parties could elect under § 362(e)(2)(C) to reduce A's stock basis to $3,000 (fair market value), and Newco then could take a § 362 transferred basis of $15,000 in the van. Newco's holding period includes the period that A held the van.

    (c) Yes. A donative transfer after the incorporation will not cause the transaction to violate the "immediately after the exchange" requirement.

    (d) A must recognize $1,000 gain on the transfer under § 357(c) because liabilities assumed by Newco ($8,000) exceed the aggregate adjusted basis of the property transferred by A ($7,000). The gain is ordinary income under the depreciation recapture rule in § 1245.

    (e) A could have avoided gain by contributing $1,000 cash or property with up to a $1,000 basis, or if *Lessinger* or *Peracchi* is good law, by contributing a $1,000 promissory note to Newco.

2. Under § 362(e)(2)(A), Newco must reduce its basis in the land to its $100,000 fair market value. Shelterer's basis in the Newco Stock is $140,000 under § 358. Alternatively, Shelterer and Newco may elect under § 362(e)(2)(C) to not reduce the basis of the land but rather to reduce Shelterer's basis in the Newco stock to its $100,000 fair market value.

3. **(a)** Yes. Although B, as a service provider, is not considered a transferor of property, A has transferred property and, as an owner of 90% of Newco's only class of stock, A has "control" of Newco immediately after the exchange.

    (b) A recognizes $5,000 gain under § 351(b). A's basis in the Newco stock is: basis of land transferred ($30,000), less money received ($5,000), plus gain recognized ($5,000) = $30,000. A's holding period for the stock includes his holding period for the land.

    (c) If § 83(a) applies, B recognizes income to the extent that the shares received for services are not subject to a substantial risk of forfeiture. Since half the shares are not subject to such a risk, B recognizes $2,500 income when he receives the Newco stock. When the restrictions lapse on the other shares, B recognizes ordinary income in the amount of the fair market value of the stock at that time. If B makes the § 83(b) election, he recognizes $5,000 ordinary income in year 1.

    (d) B may not recognize any loss on the forfeiture. If B had paid an amount for the stock, he could deduct the amount paid on a forfeiture even if he made a § 83(b) election. Reg. § 1.83–2(a).

4. **(a)** The cash received by A is boot. The $10,000 boot is allocated to the two assets transferred by A in proportion to their relative fair market values—i.e., 80% ($8,000) to Gainacre, and 20% ($2,000) to Lossacre. Thus, A recognizes $8,000

gain, which is the boot allocated to Gainacre, but A may not recognize any of his loss on Lossacre.

(b) A's basis in the Newco stock is: basis in Gainacre ($8,000) plus basis in Lossacre ($15,000), less boot received ($10,000), plus gain recognized ($8,000) = $21,000. Newco's basis in Gainacre is: A's basis in Gainacre ($8,000), plus gain recognized by A ($8,000) = $16,000. Newco takes a $15,000 transferred basis from A in Lossacre. Newco is not required to reduce its basis in Lossacre under § 362(e)(2) because the aggregate adjusted basis in the two properties transferred to Newco in the § 351 transaction does not exceed the aggregate fair market value of those properties.

5. **(a)** A's realized gain is $45,000. A's recognized gain is $20,000 (the $5,000 cash and the $15,000 note) under § 351(b). Under Prop. Reg. § 1.453–1(f), A is treated as having exchanged $30,000 of Gainacre for $30,000 of Newco stock; A's entire $5,000 basis in Gainacre is allocated to this § 351(a) nonrecognition transaction. The remaining $20,000 of Gainacre (with a zero basis) is treated as having been exchanged for $5,000 cash and the $15,000 note in a § 453 installment sale. The "selling price," "total contract price" and "gross profit" are all $20,000, and the gross profit fraction is thus 100%. Payments in the year of sale are limited to the $5,000 cash. A thus recognizes $5,000 gain in the year of the incorporation and $3,000 gain per year over the next five years as principal payments are made on the note.

A's basis in the Newco stock is: basis in Gainacre ($5,000), less cash received ($5,000), less other boot received ($15,000), plus gain recognized ($20,000) = $5,000. § 358(a). The upward adjustment for the entire gain recognized is permitted even though some of the gain is deferred under § 453. Prop. Reg. § 1.453–1(f)(3)(ii).

(b) Newco's basis in Gainacre is: A's basis in Gainacre ($5,000), plus gain recognized by A in the year of incorporation ($5,000) = $10,000. Newco may increase its basis in Gainacre by $3,000 per year over the next five years as A recognizes gain on the installment method. See Prop. Reg. § 1.453–1(f)(3)(ii).

V. CAPITAL STRUCTURE

1. The five factors specified in § 385 that are taken into account in distinguishing debt from equity are:

   (1) The form of the obligation;

   (2) Subordination;

   (3) The debt/equity ratio;

   (4) Convertibility; and

   (5) Proportionality of the purported debt to the shareholders' equity interests in the corporation.

   The courts have considered many other factors, including the intent of the parties to create a debtor/creditor relationship, and whether a third-party lender would have made a loan on the same terms.

2. There are several approaches to determining a corporation's debt/equity ratio. Debt generally includes all long-term liabilities, including shareholder loans. In determining equity, the courts disagree as to whether to reflect assets at their

adjusted tax basis or at fair market value, and whether to include certain intangibles, such as goodwill. If the assets here are reflected at current value, the debt/equity ratio is $400,000/$600,000, which is very favorable. If assets are reflected at adjusted basis, the debt/equity ratio is $400,000/$100,000, which is higher but not excessive. Even if the shareholder loans are proportionate to stock holdings, the risk of reclassification is minimal when the debt/equity ratio is not excessive and there are no other negative factors.

3. A's $50,000 loss on the stock is a long-term capital loss under the worthless security rules in § 165(g). The promissory note is not a "security," as defined in § 165(g)(2), and thus A's $100,000 loss on the note is characterized by the bad debt rules in § 166. Since it is likely that A's dominant motivation in making the loan was to protect her investment interest in the corporation rather than her stake as an employee, the loss is a non-business bad debt under the *Generes* case and is treated as a short-term capital loss under § 166(d), not an ordinary loss under § 166(a).

VI. NONLIQUIDATING DISTRIBUTIONS

1. False. Although taxable income is typically the starting point, various additions, subtractions and adjustments are made to determine earnings and profits.

2. Yes. Able must amortize the § 179 expense ratably over five years for purposes of determining E & P. § 312(k)(3)(B). If Able deducts 100% of the cost of the property under § 168(k), it must use the alternative depreciation system under § 168(g) in determining its earnings and profits. § 312(k)(3)(A); Reg. § 1.168(k)–2(f)(7). Under the alternative depreciation system, the property would be depreciated using the straight-line method, the applicable convention, and the property's class life. § 168(g)(2).

3. Earnings and profits is a tax accounting concept that is used to measure the extent to which a distribution is made from a corporation's economic income. E & P are relevant even when a corporation makes no current distributions because the corporation also must keep track of its "accumulated" earnings and profits in order to determine if future distributions are dividends.

4. The entire distribution is a dividend out of current E & P, which are determined as of the end of the taxable year without reduction for distributions made during the year.

5. Calder recognizes $10,000 gain on the distribution under § 311(b). Calder must increase current E & P by that $10,000 gain, and, following the distribution, it may reduce accumulated earnings and profits by the $50,000 fair market value of the property. § 312(a)(3), (b). This treatment is equivalent to the result if the corporation had first sold the appreciated property and then distributed the net cash proceeds. The amount of the distribution is $50,000 (§ 301(b)), and A's basis in the distributed property is $50,000 (§ 301(d)).

6. Yes as to Calder but no as to A. Calder would not be permitted to recognize its $10,000 loss. § 311(a). It could have avoided this result by first selling the property and recognizing the loss, and then distributing the cash proceeds. Calder's accumulated E & P would be reduced by $60,000 under § 312(a)(3). The consequences to A are unchanged.

7. A corporation may be deemed to have made a constructive dividend in the following situations: payment of unreasonable compensation; low-interest loans; loans without

expectation of repayment; purported "interest" payments on debt that is reclassified as equity; bargain sales or leases with shareholders; excessive payments to shareholders for the purchase or rental of property; payment of shareholders' personal expenses; and certain transactions between commonly controlled corporations.

VII. STOCK REDEMPTIONS AND PARTIAL LIQUIDATIONS

1. H constructively owns 300 shares: 100 shares from his Wife under § 318(a)(1); 100 shares from the Trust through his Children (who are sole beneficiaries of the Trust) under § 318(a)(2)(B) and § 318(a)(1); and 100 shares from the HYZ Partnership under § 318(a)(2)(A). Although 100 shares are attributed from the HYZ Partnership to Y and then reattributed to his daughter, W, these shares may not be reattributed to H because of the rule in § 318(a)(5)(A) prohibiting double family attribution. Double family attribution also may not be used to attribute Y's 300 shares to H.

   H and W's children constructively own 500 shares: 200 shares from their father (H); 100 shares from their mother (W); 100 shares from the Trust for their benefit (§ 318(a)(2)(B)); and 100 shares from HYZ Partnership through their father (H). The shares actually owned and constructively owned from the Partnership by Y are not attributed to his grandchildren because § 318(a)(1) does not provide for grandparent to grandchild attribution.

   Z constructively owns 100 shares from the HYZ Partnership under § 318(a)(2)(A).

   Y constructively owns 300 shares: 100 shares from the HYZ Partnership; 100 shares from his daughter (W); and 100 shares from the Trust through his grandchildren.

2. Before the redemption, the Trust actually owns 100 shares and constructively owns an additional 400 shares (300 from H and W through the children, and 100 from the HYZ Partnership through H and the children), for a total of 500 out of the 1,000 outstanding shares of X Corp., or 50%. After the redemption, the Trust owns no shares actually but continues to own 400 shares constructively, for a total of 400 out of the 900 outstanding shares of X Corp., or 44.4%. This does not qualify as a substantially disproportionate redemption under § 302(b)(2) because the Trust does not own less than 40% of X Corp.—i.e., less than 80% of its 50% percentage ownership of X Corp. immediately before the redemption.

   The redemption may qualify as a complete termination under § 302(b)(3) if the Trust satisfies the waiver of family attribution by entity rules in § 302(c)(2)(C). To qualify, the Trust and all "related persons" (here, the children, to whom ownership of stock is attributable under family attribution and then is reattributable to the Trust) must satisfy the 10-year look back and forward rules in § 302(c), and the Trust and the children must agree to be jointly and severally liable for any tax deficiency that may result if a prohibited interest is acquired during the 10-year-look-forward period. If § 302(b)(3) applies, the redemption is treated as an exchange, and the Trust recognizes capital gain or loss equal to the difference between the amount distributed in the redemption and its adjusted basis in the stock.

   If § 302(b)(3) does not apply, the redemption may qualify under § 302(b)(1) as "not essentially equivalent to a dividend" because the Trust's interest fell from 50% (enough to cause a deadlock) to below 50%. This might be a meaningful reduction under the Service's rulings, but it would be safer to qualify the redemption under the § 302(b)(3) rules discussed above.

If the redemption is not treated as an exchange, the entire amount distributed will be a dividend because X has ample E & P. Since the Trust will not own any more shares, the regulations permit the Trust's basis in the redeemed stock to be added back to the basis of stock held by related shareholders under § 318. See Reg. § 1.302–2(c). Under proposed regulations, however, the Trust's basis could not be shifted. Instead, the Trust would recognize a deferred loss equal to the unutilized basis in the redeemed stock. That loss could not be taken into account until the first date when events occur that would have caused the redemption to be treated as an exchange under § 302 if they had occurred at the time of the redemption or perhaps earlier if the trust terminated. Prop. Reg. § 1.302–5(a)(3).

3. The distribution likely will be treated as a partial liquidation. X has undergone a significant contraction of its operations by selling the Depression division and may even qualify for partial liquidation treatment under the "termination of business" safe harbor in § 302(e)(2). Although the Depression division was opened only three years ago, it could be considered as an expansion of a trade or business that had been actively conducted throughout the five-year period ending on the date of the distribution. The fact that none of the shareholders surrendered any shares will not change this result because the sales proceeds were distributed pro rata. If the transaction qualifies as a partial liquidation, it will be treated as an exchange, and the shareholders will be entitled to capital gains treatment and recovery of a proportionate share of their stock basis.

If shareholder A were a corporation, it could not qualify for partial liquidation treatment. § 302(b)(4). In that event, the distribution to A would be a dividend. Although A Corp. would be entitled to a § 243 dividends received deduction, the distribution would be an "extraordinary dividend" under § 1059(e)(1) and A Corp. would be required to reduce its basis in its X Corp. stock by the untaxed portion of the dividend.

4. Section 304 applies because A has "control" (i.e., 50% ownership) of both X Corp. (the "issuing corporation") and Y Corp. (the "acquiring corporation") and has sold stock in X to Y in exchange for property. This is a "brother-sister" acquisition under § 304(a)(1). The $30,000 is treated as received by A as a distribution in redemption of Y Corp. stock. The redemption is tested by reference to A's stock ownership in X Corp. Before the constructive redemption, A owned 70% of X Corp. (700 out of 1,000 outstanding shares). After the redemption, A owns 55% of X Corp. (550 out of 1,000 shares—400 shares actually and 150 constructively through Y Corp.). The redemption thus will not qualify as an exchange (it is not "substantially disproportionate" because A owns more than 50% of X Corp.) but rather will be treated as a § 301 distribution. A is deemed to have transferred the X stock to Y in exchange for Y stock in a § 351(a) transaction, and then Y is treated as having distributed $30,000 to A in redemption of its stock. The distribution is a dividend to the extent of $25,000 (the combined E & P of both corporations). The remaining $5,000 is first treated as a reduction of A's $800 basis in his Y Corp. stock under § 301(c)(2) and the remaining $4,200 is a long-term capital gain under § 301(c)(3). (Note that A's $500 basis in his Y Corp. stock was increased by his $300 basis in the X stock that A transferred to Y.)

X and Y each reduce their E & P to zero. Y Corp. takes a $300 transferred basis in the 300 shares of X Corp. that it acquires from A.

VIII. STOCK DISTRIBUTIONS AND § 306 STOCK

1. These distributions are not taxable because they do not have the effect of increasing the shareholders' proportionate interests in the corporation. A tax-free "preferred on common" stock distribution, however, will be labelled as § 306 stock.

2. A receives 10 shares of nonconvertible preferred stock with a total value of $100. The distribution is not taxable to A under § 305(a). A must allocate her $1,000 basis in the common between the common and the new preferred based on the relative fair market values of the two classes of stock after the distribution—i.e., $1,900 (95%) and $100 (5%), respectively. § 307(a). A thus takes a $950 basis in the common stock and a $50 basis in the preferred, and she may tack her holding period in the common to the preferred. X Corp. does not recognize gain on the distribution, and its E & P are unaffected. §§ 311(a)(1); 312(d)(1)(B).

3. All shareholders, including A, who received preferred stock are treated as having received a § 301 distribution of $10 per share. The result is the same whether or not any shareholders elect to take cash in lieu of the preferred stock. This is an application of § 305(b)(1), which treats a stock distribution as taxable if, at any shareholder's election, it is payable either in stock of the distributing corporation or in cash or other property.

4. This falls within § 305(b)(3), which provides that a stock distribution (or series of distributions) is taxable if the effect is that some common shareholders receive preferred stock and others receive common stock. All shareholders, including A, will be treated as having received a § 301 distribution.

5. The preferred stock is § 306 stock because it was received as a tax-free stock distribution that was other than "common-on-common." A's amount realized on any sale of this § 306 stock must be treated as dividend income (which likely will qualify to be taxed as net capital gain under § 1(h)(11)) to the extent that the preferred stock distribution would have been a dividend at the time of the distribution if cash rather than stock had been distributed. § 306(a)(1). Since X has $100,000 of current E & P and distributed a total of $1,000 in preferred stock to its common shareholders, the entire distribution would have been a dividend to A if she had received $100 in cash instead of the preferred stock. On the sale, A thus must treat the first $100 of the $250 amount realized as ordinary income; the $150 balance is treated first as a reduction of her $50 basis (see Answer #2, above) in the preferred, and then as $100 long-term capital gain from a sale of the stock ($250 less $100 less $50).

6. A's entire $80 amount realized is treated as dividend income under § 306(a)(1). A may add her $50 basis in the preferred back to her basis in the common stock.

7. Although the preferred is still § 306 stock, § 306(a) does not apply on the sale because A has completely terminated her entire stock interest in the corporation. § 306(b)(1)(A). A thus recognizes a $200 long-term capital gain on the sale ($250 amount realized less $50 basis in the preferred).

IX. COMPLETE LIQUIDATIONS AND TAXABLE CORPORATE ACQUISITIONS

1. **(a)** X Corp. recognizes $400,000 gain on the distribution of Gainacre. § 336(a). X has distributed 80% ($400,000) of Lossacre, with a $640,000 basis, to A, and 20% ($100,000), with a $160,000 basis, to B. Under § 336(d)(1)(B), X may not recognize its $240,000 loss on the distribution of 80% of Lossacre because A, as

a more than 50% shareholder, is a § 267 "related person," and Lossacre, having been acquired by X in a § 351 transaction within the five-year period preceding the distribution, is "disqualified property." X may recognize its $60,000 loss on the distribution of 20% of Lossacre to B, however, because B is not a related person and thus § 336(d)(1)(B) does not apply.

Ignoring (for convenience) any adjustment resulting from the corporate-level tax imposed on X as a result of the distribution, A receives $800,000 in the liquidation and recognizes $500,000 long-term capital gain, and B receives $200,000 and recognizes $400,000 long-term capital loss. § 331(a). Each shareholder takes a fair market value basis for his or her respective interests in the distributed parcels. § 301(d).

(b) X recognizes $400,000 gain on the distribution of Gainacre. § 336(a). As discussed in the answer to (a), above, X may not recognize its $240,000 loss on the 80% of Lossacre distributed to A. § 336(d)(1)(B). Under § 336(d)(2), X must reduce its $160,000 adjusted basis in the 20% of Lossacre distributed to B by $20,000, which represents 20% of the $100,000 precontribution built-in loss at the time X acquired Lossacre in a § 351 transaction. As a result, X's adjusted basis is decreased to $140,000, and it may only recognize $40,000 of its $60,000 realized loss on the distribution to B. This assumes that Lossacre was acquired as part of a plan the principal purpose of which was to recognize loss by X in connection with its subsequent liquidation. Property acquired within the two-year period preceding the adoption of a liquidation plan is presumed to have been acquired as part of a plan to recognize loss if there is no clear and substantial relationship between the contributed property and the conduct of the corporation's current or future business. § 336(d)(2)(B)(ii). If no such avoidance plan is present, B may recognize its entire $60,000 loss on the distribution to B.

The results to A and B are the same as in (a), above.

Note that the problem stipulates that § 362(e)(2) did not require X Corp. to reduce the basis of Lossacre to its $700,000 fair market value at the time it was transferred to X in a § 351 transaction. If § 362(e)(2) did apply at the time of the incorporation, § 336(d)(2) would have no impact on these facts.

(c) X recognizes $400,000 gain on the distribution of Gainacre. § 336(a). If the § 351 transfer of Lossacre occurred six years prior to the liquidation, it is no longer "disqualified property." As a result, X may recognize its entire $300,000 loss on the distribution of Lossacre to A and B.

(d) This qualifies as a liquidation of a controlled subsidiary under §§ 332 and 337. X does not recognize gain or loss on the distribution of 80% of each parcel to A. X must recognize $80,000 gain on the distribution of 20% of Gainacre to B, who is a minority shareholder, but it may not recognize its $60,000 loss on the distribution of 20% of Lossacre to B. § 336(d)(3).

A Corp. does not recognize gain on the liquidation of X (§ 332) and takes a transferred basis in its 80% interest in Gainacre ($80,000) and Lossacre ($640,000), respectively. Ignoring the effect of any corporate-level tax imposed on X, B receives a $200,000 distribution and recognizes $400,000 long-term capital gain on the liquidation of X. B takes a fair market value basis in its 20% interest in the two parcels. § 334(a).

2. This qualifies as a liquidation of a controlled subsidiary under §§ 332 and 337. S distributes 90% of Gainacre ($90,000 value, $63,000 basis) to P Corp. and 10% of Gainacre ($10,000 value, $7,000 basis) to B. S does not recognize gain on the distribution to P (§ 337(a)) but recognizes $3,000 gain on the distribution to B (§ 336(a)).

    P does not recognize gain on the liquidation. § 332(a). P's $50,000 basis in its S stock disappears, and P takes a $63,000 transferred basis in its 90% interest in Gainacre. § 334(b). B recognizes $8,000 gain on the liquidation (§ 331(a)) and takes a $10,000 fair market value basis in its 10% interest in Gainacre (§ 334(a)). P succeeds to 90% of S's earnings and profits. § 381(a).

3. **(a)** Three methods for structuring the acquisition are: (1) P acquires T's assets from T, and T liquidates, distributing the cash (less any corporate-level tax imposed on the liquidating sales) to its shareholders; (2) T liquidates, distributes its assets to its shareholders, and the shareholders sell the assets directly to P; or (3) P purchases 100% of T's stock from S and I. As an alternative to method (1), T could stay in existence rather than liquidating after selling its assets to P. In connection with method (3), P must decide whether or not to make a § 338 election.

    (b) On an asset sale followed by a liquidation, T recognizes $250,000 gain, resulting in a corporate tax liability of $50,000 (using, for convenience, the 21% flat corporate rate assumed in the question). T then distributes $450,000 ($500,000 sale proceeds less $50,000 corporate-level tax) to its shareholders: $360,000 (80%) to S and $90,000 (20%) to I. S recognizes $260,000 long-term capital gain, and I recognizes $40,000 long-term capital gain on the liquidation. § 331(a). Note that the problem assigns a fair market value to each of the assets, including goodwill, and thus it avoids any asset allocation issues under § 1060.

    The results would be the same on a liquidation followed by an asset sale by the shareholders. T recognizes $250,000 gain on the distribution of its assets in complete liquidation. § 336(a). The amount realized by the shareholders is $450,000 (the $120,000 cash is reduced by the $50,000 corporate-level tax liability). The shareholders take a fair market value basis in the distributed assets and recognize no further gain when they sell the assets to P. P takes a fair market value (cost) basis in the assets.

    On a stock sale, each shareholder recognizes long-term capital gain in an amount equal to the difference between the amount realized on the sale and the shareholder's adjusted basis in his stock. If P does not make a § 338 election, T does not recognize gain on its assets, and its asset bases and other tax attributes are preserved. If P makes a § 338 election, T recognizes gain on the deemed sale of its assets to "new T," and "new T's" aggregate basis in its assets (on these simple facts) equals the price paid by P for the T stock, increased by the income tax liabilities of old T triggered by the deemed asset sale. P would bear the economic burden of any corporate-level tax imposed on the deemed sale of T's assets. Since P bears the economic burden of this corporate-level tax, it logically would pay less than $500,000 for the T stock. New T's aggregate basis in its assets would be the consideration paid by P for the T stock plus T's tax liability on the deemed sale. The basis would be allocated among T's assets using the residual method prescribed by the regulations.

(c) In general, the most favorable acquisition method on these facts is a stock purchase without a § 338 election. This method results in a deferral of corporate-level tax.

(d) Yes. In this situation, P would purchase T's stock, and P and S would make a joint election under §§ 338 and 338(h)(10). S's gain on its sale of T stock to P is ignored, and T is treated as having sold its assets for their $500,000 fair market value to "new T," which takes a fair market value basis in the noncash assets. The gain is includible on S and T's consolidated return, where it can be offset by S's net operating losses.

X. ANTI-AVOIDANCE RULES

1. False. Under § 533(a), if a corporation permits its earnings and profits to accumulate beyond the reasonable needs of its business, that fact establishes a tax avoidance purpose unless the corporation proves it does not have such a purpose by a preponderance of the evidence. It is generally difficult for a corporation to rebut the presumption of a tax avoidance purpose once one arises. The regulations provide a nonexclusive list of factors which indicate whether earnings and profits have been accumulated beyond the reasonable needs of the business. Reg. § 1.537–2(b), (c).

2. Under § 542(a), a "personal holding company" is a corporation which meets both an income and a stock ownership requirement. To meet the income requirement, at least 60% of the corporation's adjusted ordinary gross income for the taxable year must be personal holding company income. § 542(a)(1). To meet the stock ownership requirement, more than 50% in value of a corporation's stock must be owned, directly or indirectly, at any time during the last half of the taxable year by five or fewer individuals. § 542(a)(2). Special attribution rules are applied to determine stock ownership. § 544.

XI. TAX-FREE REORGANIZATIONS

1. **(a)** No. The use of nonvoting preferred stock disqualifies the transaction as a Type B reorganization.

   (b) Yes. If, as is likely, the liquidation of T was part of the overall reorganization plan, the transaction is tested as a Type C reorganization. Rev. Rul. 67–274, 1967–2 C.B. 141. The acquisition qualifies as a Type C reorganization under the boot relaxation rule in § 368(a)(2)(B) because at least 80% of T's assets were acquired in exchange for P voting stock.

   (c) This acquisition fails as a § 368(a)(2)(E) reverse triangular merger because P did not acquire "control" (i.e., 80%) of T in a single transaction in exchange for P voting stock. Under the regulations, however, the acquisition qualifies as a Type B reorganization if, as here, S is a transitory subsidiary formed solely to facilitate the merger. See Reg. § 1.368–2(j)(6) Example (4). This question illustrates that creeping acquisitions ordinarily will not qualify as reverse triangular mergers, but creeping Type B acquisitions are possible if P's earlier cash acquisitions are "old and cold."

   (d) No, under the Service's regulations and ruling guidelines. Although the transaction meets the continuity of proprietary interest test (75% of the consideration is stock), it fails the continuity of business enterprise requirement because P does not continue to conduct T's historic business or use a significant portion of T's historic business assets in a business. Reg. § 1.368–1(d).

(e) No. As a stock-for-assets acquisition, the transaction must meet the requirements for a Type C reorganization. It fails because P only acquired $150,000 out of T's $200,000 in assets (75%) for P voting stock, and thus the boot relaxation rule in § 368(a)(2)(B) has not been satisfied. For this purpose, the $25,000 of T liabilities taken over by P is treated as cash consideration.

2. (a) The transaction qualifies as a Type A reorganization. There is 100% continuity of interest even though T shareholders only receive nonvoting preferred stock. A and B do not recognize gain on the exchange of their T stock for P stock. § 354(a). A's and B's basis in the P stock received is the same as the basis of the T stock surrendered—$200,000 for A and $400,000 for B. It is unlikely that the P preferred stock received by A and B is § 306 stock because, under the *Clark* case, the receipt of cash rather than preferred stock would not have the effect of a dividend. Cf. § 356(a)(2). T does not recognize gain on the transfer of its assets to P or with respect to the assumption of its liabilities. §§ 361(a); 357(a). P takes a transferred basis in the T assets. § 362(b). P does not recognize any gain on the issuance of its stock in connection with the acquisition. § 1032(a). T's tax attributes (E & P, etc.) transfer to P. § 381(a).

(b) This transaction is not a statutory merger but rather a stock-for-assets acquisition. As such, it must meet the requirements for a Type C reorganization. It fails to do so because P has not used any of its voting stock. Because this is a failed reorganization, it is treated as a taxable asset acquisition followed by a taxable complete liquidation of T. T recognizes $500,000 gain on the sale of its assets to P. Assuming a 21% corporate tax rate, T's tax liability is $105,000. Since T has no cash to pay these taxes, A and B will be liable as transferees. P takes a cost (i.e., fair market value) basis in the T assets it acquires. Although § 336(a) applies, T has no gain when it distributes the P stock to its shareholders in complete liquidation because T took a $1,000,000 fair market value basis in that stock on the taxable asset exchange. The amount realized by each shareholder on the complete liquidation of T is $500,000 less the $52,500 corporate tax liability for which each is responsible, or $447,500. A thus recognizes $247,500 long-term capital gain, and B recognizes $47,500 long-term capital gain under § 331(a).

(c) The transaction qualifies as a Type A reorganization despite the use of P bonds because there is 60% continuity of interest. Although the P long-term bonds are "securities," they are treated as boot because A and B are receiving but not surrendering any securities. §§ 354(a)(2); 356(d). Each shareholder's realized gain must be recognized to the extent of the boot received. Thus, A recognizes $200,000 gain, but B only recognizes his $100,000 realized gain. The recognized gain is treated as a dividend to the extent that the exchange "has the effect of a distribution of a dividend." § 356(a)(2). Under the *Clark* case, the exchange is tested for dividend equivalency by treating A and B as having received only P stock, a portion of which is then redeemed by P for an amount equal to the bonds actually received. Without knowing the exact number of shares of P stock that A and B received, we are unable to determine whether the hypothetical redemption meets the tests for exchange treatment in § 302(b)(1) or § 302(b)(2). Since P is a publicly traded company with many shares outstanding, it is likely that one of those tests would be met. As a result, A and B would recognize long-term capital gain which they could report on the § 453 installment method. If the boot were characterized as a (qualified) dividend, the tax rate would be the same as for capital gain but § 453 deferral would not be available.

A's basis in the P stock received is $200,000 ($200,000 basis of T stock surrendered less $200,000 boot received plus $200,000 gain recognized). B's basis in the P stock received is $300,000 ($400,000 basis of T stock surrendered less $200,000 boot received plus $100,000 gain recognized).

T recognizes no gain, either on the transfer of its assets and liabilities to P (§ 361(a)), or on the distribution of the P stock and securities (both are "qualified property") to A and B. P does not recognize gain on the issuance of its stock or bonds, and it takes a transferred basis in the T assets.

(d) Since P acquires all of T's operating assets solely for P voting stock, the transaction should qualify as a Type C reorganization.

T does not recognize gain on the transfer of its operating assets for P voting stock. § 361(a). It also does not recognize gain on the transfer of $200,000 of the P voting stock to its creditors (a transfer of "qualified property" to creditors to satisfy T liabilities is treated as a distribution under § 361(b)(3)), or the distribution of the remaining voting stock to A and B. § 361(c). P recognizes no gain on the issuance of its voting stock (§ 1032(a)), and P takes a $600,000 transferred basis in the T assets. § 362(b).

The $200,000 of liquid assets distributed to A and B are treated as boot under §§ 354 and 356. Assuming the distribution is pro rata, A and B each recognize $100,000 gain. The remainder of A's realized gain is not recognized under § 354. The gain would be characterized under the principles of the *Clark* case. (See #2(c), above.) A's basis in the P voting stock received is $200,000 ($200,000 basis in T stock surrendered less $100,000 boot received plus $100,000 gain recognized). B's basis in the P voting stock received is $400,000 ($400,000 basis in T stock surrendered less $100,000 boot received plus $100,000 gain recognized).

(e) The first step is a taxable stock acquisition. A and B each recognize gain on the sale of their stock but, since no § 338 election was made, T has no gain and the bases of its assets are unchanged. The second step is a tax-free liquidation of T under §§ 332 and 337. P takes a transferred basis in T's assets. The step transaction doctrine is not applied here in deference to the policy of § 338. If it were applied, P would have been treated as having acquired T's assets for cash and would have taken a cost basis even though no § 338 election was made. Rev. Rul. 90–95, 1990–2 C.B. 67 would not permit application of the step transaction doctrine on these facts.

(f) Under Rev. Rul. 2001–46, the two steps will be integrated because the overall transaction qualifies as a Type A reorganization. A and B recognize their realized gain to the extent of the cash received. T does not recognize any gain and P takes a transferred basis in T's assets under § 362.

(g) Because the first step (P's acquisition of T stock from S in the reverse merger) is a § 338(d)(3) qualified stock purchase and the parties jointly made a § 338(h)(10) election, each step will be viewed independently for tax purposes. Thus, P's acquisition of T stock will not be treated as part of a reorganization. T recognizes gain or loss on the deemed sale of its assets, S does not recognize gain or loss on the sale of its T stock, and P will take a fair market value ("cost") basis in T's assets. Reg. § 1.338(h)(10)–1(c)(2), –1(e) Example 12.

XII. CORPORATE DIVISIONS

1. False. The distributing corporation may distribute stock of a preexisting controlled subsidiary. § 355(a)(2)(C). In that case, the division would not be pursuant to a Type D reorganization plan.

2. Probably not because there is no business purpose for the distribution. The business purpose requirement is not met if the distributing corporation's goals could have been achieved through a nontaxable transaction that would not have required the distribution of stock of the controlled corporation and was neither impractical nor unduly expensive. On these facts, P could have met its objectives simply by transferring the assets of one business to a new corporation in a § 351 transaction. Reg. § 1.355–2(b)(3).

3. **(a)** No, because S's ownership of investment securities is not an actively conducted trade or business. Reg. § 1.355–3(b)(2)(iv).

    (b) The answer depends on whether the hat business, which only has been conducted for two years, may be considered to be an expansion of the pants business that P has conducted for more than the requisite five-year period. If so, the active trade or business test is met. The regulations look to whether the new activity effects such a change in character that it constitutes a new or different business. Reg. § 1.355–3(b)(3)(ii). P will argue that it is merely expanding a diversified apparel business. The Service may contend that the hat business is different from the pants business and thus has not been actively conducted for five years.

    (c) Although P acquired control of the radio station corporation within the five years preceding the distribution, it did so in a transaction in which gain or loss was not recognized to the seller. As a result, the active business test is satisfied because the radio station business has been conducted for 15 years. § 355(b)(2)(D). It does not matter that P has owned the radio station for less than five years.

4. Under § 355(a)(1)(B), the "mere fact" that stock or securities of either the distributing or controlled corporations are sold subsequent to a distribution shall not be construed to mean that the distribution was used as a device unless the sale was negotiated or agreed upon prior to the distribution. Under the regulations, any sale or exchange of S stock after a spin-off is evidence of a device. The strength of the evidence increases as more stock is sold and decreases as more time passes between the distribution and subsequent sale. Prearranged sales are substantial evidence of a device, while other sales are only evidence. Reg. § 1.355–2(d)(2). The corporate business purpose for a distribution is evidence of a nondevice, the strength of which depends on all the facts and circumstances. Reg. § 1.355–3(d)(3)(i). The fact that federal law requires the divestiture may be helpful in weighing the device and nondevice factors, but the Service still might contend that the shareholders were not required to sell the S stock after the spin-off.

5. A does not recognize gain on the spin-off. § 355(a). A allocates his old basis in the P stock between the P and S stock in proportion to their relative fair market values as of the date of the distribution. The combined value of the P and S stock after the distribution is $800,000, of which 75% ($600,000) is attributable to the P stock and 25% ($200,000) is attributable to the S stock. A thus takes a $75,000 basis in the P stock and a $25,000 basis in the S stock. A's holding period in the S stock includes the period that she held the P stock.

P does not recognize gain on the distribution of the S stock to A. § 355(c). (Note that § 361(c) does not apply because the distribution was not preceded by a Type D reorganization, but § 355(c) provides essentially the same result.) S's basis in its assets remain unchanged after the distribution, but P's basis in its S stock disappears.

6. These are the facts of Rev. Rul. 93–62, 1993–2 C.B. 118. Under the ruling, the determination of whether a boot payment in a § 355 distribution is treated as a dividend under § 356(a)(2) is made prior to the exchange by applying § 302 principles. A's interest in P immediately before the exchange is compared to the interest A would have retained if A had surrendered only the P shares equal in value to the boot. On these facts, A owned 40% of the outstanding P stock before the distribution. If A had surrendered only the 200 shares for which he received boot, A still would hold 200 of the 800 remaining shares, or 25% of the P stock outstanding after the exchange. This represents less than 50% of P's voting stock, and 62.5% of A's pre-exchange stock interest in P. Thus, the hypothetical redemption would be treated as an exchange because it qualifies as substantially disproportionate under § 302(b)(2). The transaction does not have the effect of the distribution of a dividend. This issue is much less significant as long as dividends and long-term capital gains of noncorporate shareholders are taxed at the same rate.

XIII. CARRYOVERS OF CORPORATE TAX ATTRIBUTES

1. Section 382 limits the use of a loss corporation's net operating loss carryforwards if there is a substantial change in ownership of the corporation. After an ownership change, if the new corporation does not continue the business enterprise of the old loss corporation for at least two years, the preacquisition NOLs are disallowed. § 382(c)(1). If the continuity of business requirement is met, the taxable income permitted to be offset by preacquisition NOL's is limited to the value of the loss corporation multiplied by the long-term tax-exempt rate. § 382(b)(1).

2. **(a)** This is an ownership change. It is an owner shift involving a 5% shareholder in which a 5% shareholder's (P's) percentage ownership of the loss corporation (T) increased by more 50 percentage points. § 382(g)(1), (2).

    (b) This is not an ownership change because P's percentage ownership of T does not increase by *more than* 50 percentage points.

    (c) This is an equity structure shift and the less than 5% shareholders in each corporation are treated as one 5% shareholder. § 382(g)(4)(A), (B). P is the loss corporation for purposes of testing whether an ownership change has taken place. § 382(k)(1). An ownership change has taken place since the percentage of stock of the loss corporation (P) owned by one or more 5% shareholders (the T shareholders) has increased by more than 50 percentage points.

XIV. AFFILIATED CORPORATIONS

1.

	W Co.	X Co.	Y Co.	Z Co.	Identical Ownership
A	35%		25%		25% (W, Y)
B		50%		35%	
C	47%	25%	60%	10%	47% (W, Y)

W Co. and Y Co. are a brother-sister controlled group because A and C have aggregate identical ownership of more than 50% in the two corporations. X Co. and Y Co. are close to being a brother-sister controlled group but B's and C's identical ownership of those corporations totals only 45% (35% for B and 10% for C).

2.   The Service will most likely scrutinize intercompany transactions under § 482 when there is evidence that the transactions were not made at arm's length and when the potential for abuse is present. The Service, under these circumstances, may make adjustments to the books of the entities and allocate the appropriate tax effects of the transactions among the participants.

XV.   S CORPORATIONS

1.   Yes. Under current law, C corporation subsidiaries are permitted.

2.   No. C has 101 shareholders and therefore does not satisfy the 100-shareholder limit in § 1361(b)(1)(A). F and J are counted as one shareholder since they are husband and wife. A and B are unrelated joint tenants and therefore are considered to be two separate shareholders.

3.   No. Although C now satisfies the 100-shareholder limit, a small business corporation may not have a partnership as a shareholder. § 1361(b)(1)(B).

4.   A trust which has stock transferred to it pursuant to a will can be a shareholder in a small business corporation but only for a two-year period beginning on the day of transfer. § 1361(c)(2)(B)(iii).

5.   According to the regulations, the second class of authorized but unissued stock will not cause C to be in violation of the one class of stock requirement of § 1361(b)(1)(D). Therefore, assuming C meets all of the other requirements, it would qualify as a small business corporation.

6.   A majority of shares of stock must vote in favor of revocation. § 1362(d)(1)(B). Thus, A will need 41 additional votes to revoke the election.

7.   Any effective date on or after the date of revocation may be selected. If a date is not selected, then the revocation is effective on the first day of the taxable year if made before the sixteenth day of the third month of such year or on the first day of the next taxable year if it is made after the fifteenth day of the third month of the year. § 1362(d)(1)(C), (D). Thus, if S's taxable year ends on December 31, 2018 and the revocation is approved on March 10, 2018, if no prospective effective date is selected the revocation will be effective on January 1, 2018. Alternatively, if the revocation is approved on June 10, 2018, the revocation will be effective on January 1, 2019.

8.   The termination is effective on the date it acquired its 101st shareholder and terminated its S corporation status. § 1362(d)(2).

9.   Yes. The corporation may argue that the termination was inadvertent under § 1362(f). If the Treasury agrees that the termination was inadvertent, the corporation takes steps to correct the terminating event within a reasonable period, and the corporation agrees to make any adjustments required by the Treasury, the corporation will be treated as continuing to be an S corporation.

10.   Reg. § 1.1362–2 provides that loan guarantees do not result in basis credit to the shareholder until the shareholder makes an economic outlay pursuant to the guarantee. The vast majority of the cases decided before issuance of the regulation also took this position.

11. Even if a loss pass-through is allowed because it is less than the shareholder's adjusted basis in the corporation's stock and debt, the at-risk limitations in § 465 and the passive loss limitations in § 469 may limit the amount of loss that is currently deductible by the shareholder.

12. A will include her pro rata share of income and capital loss for the year and the basis of her S stock will be:

$$
\begin{array}{r}
\$\ 4{,}000 \\
+\ \underline{8{,}000} \quad \text{§ 1367(a)(1)(B)} \\
\$12{,}000
\end{array}
$$

Since S has no earnings and profits, the $10,000 distribution will be considered recovery of stock basis, and A's stock basis will be reduced to $2,000. A may deduct $2,000 of the long-term capital loss, and the remaining $4,000 of loss may be carried forward under § 1366(d)(2).

13. The accumulated adjustments account (otherwise known as the "AAA") is relevant to characterizing distributions by an S corporation with E & P. The AAA is a running total of the undistributed earnings of the corporation which have been taxed to its shareholders since it became an S corporation. Distributions are treated as recovery of stock basis and gain from the sale or exchange of the stock to the extent of the corporation's AAA. § 1368(c).

14. The § 1374 tax on built-in gains generally is relevant to an S corporation which was once a C corporation. Section 1374 imposes a corporate level tax on the appreciation in a corporation's assets which arose while it was a C corporation, but which is recognized within five years of its S election. The tax is designed to reduce the incentive for C corporations to elect S status to avoid corporate-level tax on pre-election gains. The tax does not apply to a corporation which has always been an S corporation except to the extent the corporation acquires assets from a C corporation with a transferred basis. § 1374(c)(1), (d)(8).

Appendix B

Practice Examination

QUESTION ONE

A, B and C, all individuals, wish to organize a "C" corporation to manufacture and sell computer software.

A will transfer the following assets to the new company:

Assets	Adj. Basis	F. Mkt. Value
Building	$ 30,000	$ 150,000
Land	$ 15,000	$ 50,000

The building is subject to a $50,000 nonrecourse mortgage, incurred by A many years ago for valid business reasons. The corporation will take the building subject to this mortgage.

B will transfer the following assets to the new company:

Assets	Adj. Basis	F. Mkt. Value
Cash	$ 50,000	$ 50,000
Accounts Receivable	$ 0	$ 200,000

In addition, the new corporation will assume $100,000 of accounts payable from B's cash basis sole proprietorship.

C will transfer a patent with a basis and appraised value of $60,000 and will be the "brains" behind the new enterprise.

A, B and C have agreed that each will own a one-third interest in the corporation in exchange for A and B's respective contributions of property and, in C's case, in exchange for his patent and future services.

Question:

Discuss and compare the tax consequences (gain realized and recognized, basis, etc.) to A, B, C *and* the corporation if they organize the corporation with A receiving $100,000 of unrestricted common stock and $50,000 of seven-year corporate notes bearing market rate interest, and B and C each receiving $150,000 of unrestricted common stock.

ANSWER TO QUESTION ONE

Qualification of the Exchanges Under § 351: A, B and C each transfer property to the newly formed corporation. The issue regarding qualification under § 351 is whether C will be considered part of the control group because C receives stock for both property and future services. If C is not part of the control group, all the exchanges fail under § 351 because A and B only own 62.5% of the corporation's common stock after the exchanges.

A person who receives stock in exchange for both property and services is considered a transferor of property and may count all of the stock received for the 80% control requirement unless the value of the property transferred is of relatively small value compared to the stock received for services and the primary purpose of the property transfer is to qualify the exchanges of other transferors for nonrecognition. Under the Service's ruling position, if the stock received by a transferor in exchange for property is at least 10% of the value of stock received for services, the transferor is treated as a member of the control group. Here, the stock received by C in exchange for property ($60,000) is equal to more than 10% of the value of stock received for services ($90,000). Thus, the transferors of property (A, B, and C) have "control" of the new corporation immediately after the exchange and the overall transaction qualifies under § 351. It is still necessary, however, to analyze the tax consequences to each shareholder.

Tax Consequences to A: A realizes $120,000 of gain on the building and $35,000 of gain on the land. Under § 357(c), A must first recognize the excess of the mortgage relief over the aggregate basis of the transferred assets. That $5,000 of gain ($50,000 mortgage less $45,000 of aggregate basis) is characterized by allocating it to the transferred assets in proportion to their fair market values. Thus, $3,750 of the gain is characterized as from the building and $1,250 is characterized as from the land.

The $50,000 seven-year notes are boot which also will require recognition of gain. Those notes are allocated to the building and land in proportion to their fair market values: $37,500 to the building and $12,500 to the land. The gain attributable to the notes will be recognized under the installment sale rules as payments on the notes are made. Under the § 453 proposed regulations, the basis of the transferred property is first allocated to the exchange of property for stock. Since the basis of the building and land is less than the value of the stock, no basis will be attributable to the exchange of property for the notes so the gross profit fraction is 100%, and thus A recognizes gain as principal payments are made on the notes.

A's basis in the stock under § 358(a)(1) is:

$45,000	Basis in Transferred Property
−50,000	Money Received (Debt Relief)
−50,000	Other Property (Notes)
+55,000	Gain Recognized
$ 0	

A is entitled to an upward basis adjustment for gain recognized even though part of his gain is deferred under § 453. Prop. Reg. § 1.453–1(f)(3)(ii). A's basis in the corporate notes is their face value ($50,000) less the income that will be taxable when they are satisfied in full ($50,000). § 453B(b). Thus, the notes take a zero basis. A's holding period in the stock will tack the holding period of the building and land assuming they are capital or § 1231 assets to A. If either the building or land has been held short-term by A, each share of stock will take a split holding period allocated in proportion to the fair market values of the transferred assets (75% building, 25% land). The seven-year notes will take a fresh holding period.

Tax Consequences to B: B's exchange is tax free. The assignment of income doctrine generally does not apply to a transfer of accounts receivable by a cash method taxpayer in a § 351 exchange. Under § 357(c)(3), the accounts payable are not considered a liability assumed or taken subject to by the corporation, so § 357(c) does not apply to B's exchange.

B's basis in the stock under § 358(a)(1) is $50,000, the basis of the exchanged property. The accounts payable are not treated as liabilities for purposes of calculating the stock's basis. § 358(d)(2). B will take a fresh holding period in the stock because the accounts receivable are not capital or § 1231 assets.

Tax Consequences to C: Even though C is considered a member of the control group, he must recognize ordinary income under § 61 on the value of the stock received for services. Since C's enjoyment of the stock is not subject to restrictions, he will have $90,000 of ordinary income in the year of the exchange. This result accepts the valuation placed on the common stock by the shareholders even though the net assets of the corporation may not support that valuation. Presumably, C's contribution of services adds to the value of the corporation.

C's basis in the stock is $150,000, which is the basis in the patent plus the amount included in income. C's holding period in the stock will tack the holding period of the patent, assuming it is a capital or § 1231 asset. Forty percent ($^{60}/_{150}$) of each share of stock will have the same holding period as the patent and 60% of each share will take a fresh holding period.

Tax Consequences to the Corporation: The corporation will not recognize gain or loss on the issuance of its stock and the seven-year notes. Under § 362, the corporation's basis in the building is $33,750 ($30,000 plus $3,750 of § 357(c) gain) and its basis in the land is $16,250 ($15,000 plus $1,250 of § 357(c) gain). In addition, the corporation will receive basis increases for those assets as A actually recognizes gain on the seven-year notes. Prop. Reg. § 1.453–1(f)(3)(ii). The corporation's basis in the accounts receivable is zero and its basis in the patent is $60,000. The corporation's holding period for each asset includes the transferor's holding period. The corporation will be allowed a deduction as it pays the accounts receivable. The corporation also may deduct $90,000 for C's services as they are performed, assuming the services are not capital in nature.

QUESTION TWO

Target Corporation ("T"), a manufacturer of children's apparel, is a closely held "C" corporation. T, an accrual method taxpayer with a fiscal year ending March 31, has 1,000 shares of common stock outstanding, owned as follows:

Shareholder	No. Shares	Adj. Basis	F. Mkt. Value
A	500	$ 30,000	$ 500,000
B	200	10,000	200,000
C Trust	200	100,000	200,000
D	100	200,000	100,000
Total	1,000	$ 340,000	$ 1,000,000

A and B, the founders of T, are in their mid-70's and have held their stock for over 20 years. The C Trust is a trust created for the benefit of A and B's two children and four grandchildren. The Trustee (a bank) has complete discretion to distribute or to accumulate income or principal of the trust to the beneficiaries. D is A's brother and has held his stock for two years.

T is a profitable company. It has $400,000 of accumulated earnings and profits and the following assets (all held long-term) and liabilities:

Asset	Adj. Basis	F. Mkt. Value
Inventory	$ 50,000	$ 300,000
Capital Asset	50,000	200,000
Equipment ($50,000 § 1245 recapture)	100,000	300,000
Land	100,000	200,000
Securities	500,000	300,000
Total	$800,000	$1,300,000

Liabilities	Amount
Accounts payable	$100,000
Bank loan	200,000
Total	$300,000

Assume it is November 15, 2018 and T and its shareholders are concerned about the future of their company. They have heard about converting to S corporation status and are intrigued by the possibility of avoiding the double tax. A friend has recommended that they conduct their apparel business as a partnership. They also are considering several offers to sell the Company. A and B are reaching retirement age and are inclined to sell. The Trustee of the C Trust is ambivalent. D, a chronic malcontent, is expected to oppose anything suggested by the others.

The details of the acquisition offers are as follows:

Fabric, Inc. ("F") has offered to buy the stock of T for $1,000 per share cash. Assume D is absolutely unwilling to sell his shares in 2018.

Genes, Inc. ("G"), a publicly held $50 million company with 1,000,000 common shares outstanding, would consider acquiring all T's assets *except* for the securities portfolio in exchange for up to $600,000 of G stock, with the remainder of the consideration consisting of short-term G notes. G would prefer not to assume T's liabilities. G does not wish to incur the expense of securing approval of its shareholders for the acquisition; such approval would be required on a straight merger of T into G.

Questions:

(a) Discuss the tax advantages, disadvantages, obstacles (if any) and timing considerations of the proposals for T to convert to "S" corporation status or to operate the business as a partnership.

(b) Discuss the tax consequences to all relevant parties of the acquisition offer from F.

(c) Discuss the tax consequences to all relevant parties of G's acquisition offer and suggest a method of structuring this transaction in a manner that is compatible with what you know about the tax and nontax objectives of the parties. (For this purpose, assume that shareholder D is unalterably opposed to receiving any G stock but the other shareholders would accept a combination of G stock and other consideration.)

ANSWER TO QUESTION TWO

(a) *Making an S Election:* The principal advantage of T making an S election and operating as an S corporation is avoidance of the double tax on future income. This advantage is limited somewhat by § 1374 (see below).

T could not presently make an S election unless the C Trust makes an election under § 1361(e) to be an Electing Small Business Trust. Otherwise, the trust is an impermissible shareholder. If such an election is made, the income attributable to the S corporation stock will be taxed to the trust at the highest applicable individual marginal rates, and each trust beneficiary will be counted as a shareholder for purposes of the 100-shareholder limit. Also, because of the relationships of the shareholders, they would be treated as members of a "family" and be counted as one shareholder.

A planning alternative would be to eliminate the C Trust as a shareholder. This could be accomplished by redeeming its shares or, alternatively, the trust could distribute the T stock to its beneficiaries and a voting trust, or qualified Subchapter S or grantor trusts could be established to hold the T shares. Another potential problem in T electing S status is shareholder D. All of the shareholders must consent to an S election, and D may not be cooperative. One option would be to redeem D's shares prior to filing the election. If a redemption of D or the C Trust is planned, it would be a good idea to sell an appropriate amount of the securities to raise the funds needed to repurchase the stock. A sale would produce a tax loss for T and reduce the amount of its passive investment income following the election which would reduce: (1) the chances of T's election terminating, and (2) T's exposure to the § 1375 tax. (See below). If T distributed the securities in redemption of T stock, no loss would be allowed. § 311(a)(2).

If T makes an S election, its taxable year under § 1378 will be a calendar year or a year for which it can establish a business purpose. T also would be able under § 444 to select a taxable year with up to three months of deferral if it makes the payments required by § 7519. An S election by the T shareholders could be made (1) during the year preceding its first taxable year as an S corporation, or (2) on or before the 15th day of the third month of its taxable year. § 1362(b)(1).

If T makes an S election, its potential future problems include the fact that under § 1362(d)(2) its election could terminate if more than 25% of its gross receipts in three consecutive years are passive investment income. If T's gross receipts are more than 25% passive investment income in any year, it also will be subject to the § 1375 tax. Both § 1362(d)(3) and § 1375 are potentially applicable because T has Subchapter C E & P.

T also will be subject to the § 1374 tax at a rate of 21% on the appreciation in its assets at the time of conversion to S status, up to the $500,000 net unrealized built-in gain (see § 1374(d)(1)) at that time. Thus, if an S election is made, it is important for T to obtain an appraisal of its assets on the effective date of the election. The tax applies to sales during the 5-year period following conversion to S status. One strategy for reducing the impact of § 1374 would be to time loss sales of the securities with sales of other assets which produce gains. That would be helpful because losses inherent in T's assets at the time of the S election may offset gains inherent in its assets at that time. § 1374(d)(2)(A)(i).

Conversion to a Partnership: Conversion of T to a partnership (or limited liability company) would not be advisable from a tax standpoint because it would require a liquidation of T which would cause T to immediately recognize all of its gains and losses and the shareholders to recognize their stock gains and losses. Since the T assets and shareholders (except D) have substantial appreciation, a liquidation would produce a large current tax liability.

(b) *Tax Consequences of the Acquisition Offer from F:* If F purchases the stock of the T shareholders for $1,000 per share, A will recognize a $470,000 gain, B will recognize a $190,000 gain, and the C Trust will recognize a $100,000 gain. Most likely, F will not want to make a § 338 election because such an election would trigger recognition of all of T's gains and losses in its assets. Note that T's potential tax liability makes the $1,000 per share price unrealistically high unless the business has an additional value as a going concern that is not reflected in the balance sheet.

(c) *Structure of the Acquisition by G:* The T shareholders would like to structure the acquisition as a reorganization so that all or part of their realized gains do not have to be recognized. A Type A merger likely is not feasible because G wants to avoid obtaining approval of the transaction from its shareholders.

The terms proposed by G also do not qualify as a Type C reorganization. G does propose to obtain substantially all of T's assets. Under its plan, G would acquire $1,000,000 of T's assets which is at least 90% of the fair market value of its net assets ($1,000,000 × .90 = $900,000) and at least 70% of the fair market value of its gross assets ($1,300,000 × .70 = $910,000). T would be left with the securities which it could use to pay the liabilities. The problem with the acquisition qualifying as a Type C reorganization is the mix of consideration proposed by G. If G uses $600,000 of its stock and $400,000 of short-term notes, the acquisition cannot qualify under the boot relaxation rule in § 368(a)(2)(B) as a Type C reorganization since only 60% of the total consideration is G stock.

Based on the objectives of the parties, the best alternative may be a forward triangular merger under § 368(a)(2)(D). G could form a new subsidiary, S, by transferring its stock and $400,000 of its short-term notes for S stock in a § 351 exchange. T would then merge into S with the T shareholders receiving the G stock and notes. G ordinarily does not have to secure the permission of its shareholders to accomplish this type of merger. The exchange would qualify under § 368(a)(2)(D) because:

(1)   S acquires substantially all of T's assets (see Type C reorganization discussion, above);

(2)   No S stock is used; and

(3)   The exchange would have qualified as a Type A merger if T had merged into G because the T shareholders as a group receive 60% G stock.

The remainder of the answer assumes that T and G undertake a forward triangular merger.

Consequences to the T Shareholders: The T shareholders, other than D, will receive a mixture of G stock and the short-term notes. The notes will be considered boot. Since D receives only boot, he will recognize his $100,000 loss. The other T shareholders (A, B and C Trust) will recognize their stock gains to the extent they receive G notes. The character of their gains will be determined under § 356(a)(2) by assuming that they received only G stock and then received the G notes in redemption of an appropriate portion of their G stock. These hypothetical redemptions will be tested for exchange or dividend treatment under § 302. Exchange treatment would entitle the shareholders to defer their recognized gain under § 453. See § 453(f)(6). Even though the shareholders would be taxed at the same 15% or 20% maximum rate if their gain is classified as a dividend or long-term capital gain, it is not likely that they could defer any "dividend" gain under § 453. The shareholders' bases in the G stock will be determined under § 358(a)(1). The stock will take a tacked holding period. The boot will take a fair market value basis and a fresh holding period.

Consequences to T: T recognizes no gain or loss on the exchange of its property for the P stock and short-term notes since the notes, which are § 361(c)(2)(B) "qualified property," are distributed to its shareholders. § 361(b)(1). Assuming T uses the retained securities to pay off the liabilities, it will recognize its $200,000 loss on that disposition.

Consequences to S: S recognizes no gain or loss on the exchange of the G stock and notes for the T assets. S will take a transferred basis in the T assets under § 362(b) and tack T's holding period for capital and § 1231 assets.

Appendix C

Glossary

This glossary is intended to provide the reader with brief definitions of some of the terms frequently encountered in a corporate tax course. More comprehensive definitions of many of these terms are included in the body of the outline.

A

Accumulated Adjustments Account (AAA): An account of the corporation which is adjusted for the period since the corporation has been an S corporation (beginning in 1983) in the same manner as adjustments are made to a shareholder's basis. The AAA is employed to characterize distributions by S corporations with E & P and, in general, represents the earnings of an S corporation previously taxed to the shareholders.

Accumulated Earnings Tax: An additional penalty tax which must be paid by any C corporation formed or availed of for the purpose of avoiding the individual income tax by accumulating rather than distributing E & P.

Active Trade or Business: A specific group of activities in which a corporation performs active and substantial management and operational functions for the purpose of earning income or profit. The concept is employed in connection with the qualification requirements for corporate divisions and partial liquidations.

Affiliated Group: One or more chains of corporations in which a parent corporation owns at least 80% of one corporation and at least 80% of each corporation is owned by other corporations in the group. An affiliated group may elect to file a consolidated tax return.

Aggregate Deemed Sales Price: The price for which a target corporation is treated as selling its assets if the target makes a § 338 election in connection with a taxable sale of 80% or more of its stock.

Association: An unincorporated entity with sufficient corporate attributes to be classified and taxed as a corporation.

Attribution Rules: Statutory rules that consider an individual or entity as owning stock owned by certain related family members or entities for purposes of various provisions of the Code where stock ownership is significant.

B

Bailout: A term used in tax parlance to describe a shareholder's attempt to withdraw profits accumulated by a C corporation in a transaction (e.g., a redemption, liquidation or sale) where the shareholder hopes to treat the amounts received first as a recovery of stock basis and then as a long-term capital gain instead of a fully taxable dividend.

Bond: A long-term corporate debt obligation that is secured by particular corporate property.

Boot: Tax jargon for "other property or money" received in a transaction that otherwise qualifies for nonrecognition of gain or loss. In such transactions, a taxpayer ordinarily must recognize gain to the extent of the boot received but may not recognize any loss.

Bootstrap Sale: An integrated transaction where part of a shareholder's stock is redeemed and the balance is sold to an unrelated buyer. The term also is used to refer to a leveraged transaction in which the assets of a target corporation are used to pay for its own acquisition.

Built-in Gain or Loss: The difference between the fair market value and the adjusted basis of an asset (or assets)—i.e., the unrealized appreciation or depreciation inherent in an asset at a given point in time. The concept is employed for purposes of the § 1374 tax on S corporations, the carryover of tax attributes following a corporate acquisition, and partnership allocations with respect to contributed property under § 704(c).

Business Purpose Doctrine: A judicial doctrine that may be applied to deny tax benefits when a transaction has no substance, purpose or utility apart from tax avoidance. The doctrine is most frequently applied as an independent requirement for tax-free corporate divisions.

C

C Corporation: A corporation fully subject to the provisions of Subchapter C (§§ 301–385) of the Internal Revenue Code that has not made an S election. See S Corporation.

Capital Structure: The mix of debt and equity that a corporation has used to finance its operations.

Consolidated Return: A corporate return that may be filed by an affiliated group of corporations in which the group pays tax on its consolidated taxable income.

Constructive Dividend: An economic benefit provided by a corporation to a shareholder that is not a formal dividend but which in substance is a distribution of corporate earnings.

Continuity of Business Enterprise: A judicial test for reorganizations that requires the acquiring corporation either to continue the target corporation's historic business or to use a significant portion of the target's historic business assets in a business. The requirement also limits the carryover of a target's net operating losses following a change of ownership.

Continuity of Interest: A judicial test for acquisitive reorganizations that requires the shareholders of a target corporation to retain a continuing proprietary interest (i.e., as shareholders) in the acquiring corporation. As applied to divisive reorganizations, the test requires the shareholders of the distributing corporation to retain a continuing proprietary interest in both the distributing and controlled corporations after the distribution.

Contribution to Capital: A transfer of cash or property to a corporation by a shareholder or nonshareholder when no stock or other consideration is received in exchange.

Control: Used generically, "control" may connote more than 50% of the voting power of a corporation. Several provisions in Subchapter C use the term in specialized contexts and with varying definitions. "Control" typically is defined as ownership of a specified percentage (80% and 50% are common thresholds) of the stock of a corporation. The percentage requirement may apply to voting power, nonvoting stock and/or the value of stock.

Controlled Group of Corporations: A group of corporations which satisfies specific common ownership requirements. The members of a controlled group are limited with respect to certain tax benefits, such as the lower graduated rates in § 11(b). Examples include a "parent-subsidiary" or "brother-sister" controlled group.

Convertible Preferred Stock: Preferred stock that is convertible into common stock at a specified price or ratio.

Creeping Acquisition: An acquisition of a target corporation in a series of steps. The tax consequences of an acquisition often depend on whether the separate steps are treated as an integrated transaction and the type of acquisitive reorganization that the taxpayer is seeking to qualify for tax-free status. Creeping acquisitions are sometimes referred to as multi-step acquisitions.

D

Debenture: A long-term corporate debt instrument that is unsecured. Debentures are nonetheless frequently referred to as "bonds" in some contexts—e.g., "junk bonds" are often really high-yield debentures.

Debt Security: A corporate instrument representing funds borrowed by the corporation from the holder of the debt obligation.

Debt-Equity Ratio: The ratio between a corporation's debt and equity capital. The debt-equity ratio is relevant to whether or not a corporation is thinly capitalized and whether instruments labelled as debt will be reclassified as equity.

Device Limitation: A limitation in § 355 that is intended to prevent the use of a tax-free corporate division to bail out corporate earnings at capital gains rates and avoid tax through a recovery of basis.

Distribution: Used broadly, a term that refers to any kind of payment (of cash, property, debt obligations) by a corporation to shareholders with respect to their stock, or a transfer of cash or property by a partnership to a partner.

Dividend: A distribution by a corporation to a shareholder out of the current or accumulated E & P of the corporation.

Dividends Received Deduction: A deduction of 50%, 65% or 100% of dividends received by corporate shareholders. The purpose of the deduction is to prevent multiple corporate-level taxation of income.

Double Tax: The result of the entity approach employed by Subchapter C, under which profits of C corporations are first taxed to the corporation when earned and taxed again to the shareholders when earnings are distributed as dividends.

E

Earnings and Profits (E & P): A corporate tax accounting concept that is used to measure the extent to which a distribution is made from a corporation's economic income. E & P generally are determined by making adjustments to a corporation's taxable income. The effects of various transactions on E & P are determined under § 312.

Electing Small Business Trust: A trust that may make an election in order to become a permissible shareholder of an S corporation. The current beneficiaries of such a trust must otherwise be eligible S corporation shareholders.

Entity Concept: An approach to taxing business organizations under which the organization is considered to be an entity that is separate and distinct from its owners.

Equity: A corporate ownership interest evidenced by shares of stock.

Extraordinary Dividend: A dividend which exceeds 5% of the shareholder's adjusted basis in preferred stock or 10% of the shareholder's basis in the case of other stock. In some circumstances, a corporate shareholder that receives an extraordinary dividend must reduce its stock basis by the portion of the dividend not taxed as a result of the dividends received deduction and recognize gain once basis has been reduced to zero.

F

Forward Triangular Merger: An acquisition in which a subsidiary merges into the target corporation with the target shareholders receiving stock of the subsidiary's parent corporation. A forward triangular merger may qualify as a reorganization if the requirements in § 368(a)(2)(D) are met.

G

***General Utilities* Doctrine:** A doctrine, named after an early Supreme Court case, under which a corporation did not recognize gain or loss on distributions of property to its shareholders and on certain sales of property pursuant to a plan of complete liquidation. The doctrine was repealed in the Tax Reform Act of 1986.

Grossed-up Basis: An amount calculated under a formula which is used to determine a target corporation's aggregate basis in its assets resulting from a deemed asset sale triggered by a § 338 election. Grossed-up basis generally is the basis of the corporation's recently purchased stock multiplied by a fraction which is designed to equate purchases of less than 100% of the target's stock with purchases of all the stock.

L

Limited Liability Company: A legal form of business entity that provides limited liability for each of its owners, who are usually known as "members." Limited liability companies with more than one member are usually classified as partnerships for federal tax purposes.

Limited Partnership: A partnership that has a general partner and at least one limited partner—i.e., one partner who is not liable for partnership debts beyond the partner's contributed capital.

Liquidation: A transaction in which a corporation ceases to be a going concern and its activities are merely for the purpose of winding up its affairs, paying its debts and distributing any remaining balance to its shareholders. A corporate liquidation may be preceded by sales of corporate assets. When used in connection with a partnership, a "liquidation" may connote a winding up of the entire partnership or simply a liquidation of the interest of a particular partner.

Liquidation-Reincorporation: A transaction designed to obtain a stepped-up fair market value basis for a corporation's assets, generally at the cost of a capital gain to the corporation's shareholders. The strategy is much less useful after repeal of the *General Utilities* doctrine.

N

Nonqualified Preferred Stock: Preferred stock with certain debt-like characteristics (such as a mandatory redemption feature). Nonqualified preferred stock is treated as boot rather than "nonrecognition property" for various corporate-shareholder transactions such as formations and reorganizations.

O

Old and Cold: A term used when analyzing the tax consequences of a series of transactions under the step transaction doctrine. Earlier steps that are not related to a later transaction for tax purposes are referred to as "old and cold."

Organizational Expenditures: Fees and expenses of organizing a corporation or partnership that normally would have to be capitalized but which may be deducted up to certain dollars limits and then amortized over 180 months if a corporation makes a § 248 election.

P

Partial Liquidation: A corporate distribution resulting from a genuine contraction of the corporation's business, including the termination of a trade or business that the corporation has actively conducted for the five-year period preceding the distribution.

Passive Activity: A term used to describe trade or business activities in which a taxpayer does not materially participate and most rental activities. In general, for taxpayers affected by the passive activity loss limitations, losses from passive activities are currently deductible only to the extent of income from such activities.

Personal Holding Company: In general, an investment company with a small number of shareholders that is subject to a penalty tax if it does not distribute its net investment income to its shareholders.

Personal Service Corporation: A term used in the Code to describe a corporation substantially all of the activities of which involve the performance of service—i.e., corporations that perform services in particular specified fields, such as law, accounting, architecture, etc., and which are substantially owned by the employees who perform such services.

Preferred Stock: Stock which, relative to other classes of corporate stock outstanding, enjoys certain limited rights and privileges (generally dividend and liquidation priorities) but does not participate in corporate growth.

Publicly Traded Partnership: A limited partnership whose interests are traded on an established securities market or are readily tradable on a secondary market. Publicly traded partnerships generally are classified as corporations for tax purposes unless 90% or more of the PTP's gross income is from certain qualified types of investment income.

Q

Qualified Business Income: Net operating income from a U.S. trade or business that qualifies for the 20% deduction provided by § 199A to noncorporate taxpayers who are sole proprietors, partners, members of LLCs, and S corporation shareholders. Qualified business income does not include investment income, wages, and other forms of compensation.

Qualified Dividend: A dividend received by a noncorporate shareholder from a domestic corporation and certain foreign corporations that meets certain holding period requirements. Qualified dividends are taxed as net capital gain under § 1(h)(11), but only until the end of 2012 unless Congress and the President agree to extend § 1(h).

Qualified Small Business Stock: Stock issued by certain C corporations that qualifies shareholders for a 100% or partial exclusion of gain on sale if various conditions are met.

Qualified Subchapter S Trust: A type of irrevocable trust that may elect to be a qualified shareholder of an S corporation.

R

Recapitalization: A readjustment of the capital structure of a single corporation which may qualify as a Type E reorganization for tax purposes.

Redemption: An acquisition of stock by the issuing corporation in exchange for property.

Reorganization: A term used in the Code to describe a variety of corporate combinations and adjustments falling into three broad categories: (1) acquisitive reorganizations, (2) nonacquisitive, nondivisive reorganizations (e.g., a recapitalization), and (3) divisive reorganizations.

Reverse Triangular Merger: An acquisition in which the target corporation merges into a subsidiary of the acquiring corporation. A reverse triangular merger may qualify as a reorganization if the target shareholders receive voting stock of the subsidiary's parent and certain other requirements in § 368(a)(2)(E) are met.

Rights: Short-term options, often distributed by a corporation to its shareholders with respect to their stock, to purchase a stock for a fixed price.

S

S Corporation: A corporation that qualifies to make an election to be treated as a pass-through entity subject to the provisions of Subchapter S (§§ 1361–1379) of the Code and which consequently avoids the double tax imposed on earnings of C corporations.

Section 306 Stock: In general, preferred stock received as a nontaxable stock dividend or in a reorganization that has bailout potential. All or part of the gain on a sale or redemption of § 306 stock may be characterized as dividend income rather than capital gain.

Section 336(e) Election: An election made jointly by the buyer (which need not be a corporation) and seller to treat a sale, exchange or distribution of 80% or more of the stock of the target corporation within a 12-month period as a sale of the target's assets.

Section 338 Election: An election that may be made by a purchasing corporation following a purchase of 80% or more of a target's stock within a 12-month period. The election triggers a deemed sale of all of the target's assets.

Section 338(h)(10) Election: An election made jointly by a corporate buyer and seller to treat a sale of 80% or more of the stock of the target corporation (which must be an 80% or more subsidiary of another corporation or an S corporation) within a 12-month period as a sale of the target's assets.

Section 1244 Stock: Stock (usually of a closely held corporation) that qualifies for ordinary loss treatment on sale or worthlessness if certain requirements in § 1244 are met.

Security: A term of art in the Code used to refer to corporate debt obligations that represent a degree of continuing participation in the corporation that falls short of an equity interest but is greater than an interest held by a short-term creditor. Long-term bonds (10 years or more) generally qualify as securities but short-term notes (5 years or less) do not.

Separate Affiliated Group ("SAG"): One or more chains of corporations in which a common parent owns at least 80% of the voting power and 80% of the total value of at least one other corporation and at least 80% (by vote and value) of each corporation is owned by another corporation in the chain. For purposes of the § 355 active trade or business rule, all members of a SAG are treated as one corporation.

Spin-off: A pro rata distribution of the stock of a controlled subsidiary corporation by a parent distributing corporation to its shareholders.

Split-off: A non pro rata distribution of the stock of a controlled subsidiary corporation by a parent distributing corporation to its shareholders in redemption of some or all of their parent stock.

Split-up: A distribution of the stock of more than one controlled subsidiary, either pro rata or non pro rata, by a parent corporation which owns no other assets to all of its shareholders in complete liquidation of the parent.

Stock Dividend: A distribution of stock which generally is not taxable when it does not increase the shareholders' proportionate interest in the company (e.g., common on common) but otherwise is treated as a distribution to which § 301 applies.

Subchapter C: Sections 301–385 of the Code. Subchapter C adopts an entity concept by treating corporations as separate taxpaying entities. When Subchapter S does not provide a specific rule, Subchapter C also may apply to S corporations and their shareholders.

Subchapter K: Sections 701–761 of the Code. Subchapter K is a pass-through taxing model under which partnerships are not treated as separate taxpaying entities, and partnership income and deductions pass through to the partners.

Subchapter S: Sections 1371–1379 of the Code. Subchapter S governs the tax treatment of S corporations and their shareholders.

Subordination: A status related to a debt or claim where the other creditors have a higher priority than the holders of the debt or claim. Subordination is a factor that may be considered in determining whether to reclassify nominal debt as equity.

T

Thin Capitalization: A term used to describe the capital structure of a corporation with a very high ratio of debt to equity.

W

Warrant: A contractual right (in the nature of a long-term option) to purchase a certain number of shares of stock at a set price. Warrants generally are not considered stock or securities of a corporation.

Table of Cases

Table of Internal Revenue Code Sections

Table of Regulations

Table of Revenue Rulings and Procedures

Index